Down from the 'Cross

A GAA Story
By Alan Rodgers

Published in October 2006 by Beragh Red Knights GAC
Main Street, Beragh, Co. Tyrone

A CIP record for this book is
available from the British Library

ISBN - 978-1-869919-12-2

Designed and produced by Capture Design, 047 38719

down from the 'cross

contents

foreword

Reamhra

Beragh Red Knights are celebrating one hundred years of Gaelic Football, hurling, Camogie, handball and Irish culture in Beragh Parish. From a humble beginning as Sixmilecross Wolfe Tones in 1906 to the official opening of the state of the art cross-community Pavilion by Uachtarain Cumann Luthchleas Gael, Nick Brennan, earlier this year, no effort is spared in according all the major events and people who shaped the club to what it is today. It is also fitting at this time to pay tribute to the great work of past members and players who have passed to their eternal reward.

As Cathaoirleach of Coiste Thir Eoghain it gives me great pleasure to extend my congratulations to the Beragh Red Knights committee and Alan Rodgers in particular on the publication of the club's history. It is a welcome and timely addition to your centenary celebrations as well as value added to the overall history of Cumann Luthchleas Gael in Tyrone.

Beragh Red Knights have a proud tradition within the GAA in Tyrone and this publication is testimony to the role played in providing social, cultural and sporting outlets for the people of the Beragh Parish. The contribution of past and present members to the overall administration of the GAA at National, Provincial and County level is also significant.

The basic element in any club involves three interrelated truths, namely the past, present and future. Our past history defines our present identity and shapes our future direction as gaels. This publication captures that essence.

Compilation of such a comprehensive book involved a significant amount of time and effort by the author. Alan Rodgers is to be commended on his professionalism and research in bringing to life the history of his club including numerous photographs which fill the pages with nostalgia and memories from bygone days.

I salute his efforts and urge you and your children to read this exciting memory evoking history of the Beragh Red Knights GAC.

Guim gach rath agus Blath Oraibh
Padraig O'Dorchai, Cathaoirleach, Coiste Thir Eoghain

A Chairde,

As Chairman of Beragh Red Knights GAA Club, it gives me the greatest of pleasure to welcome this long and eagerly awaited story of 100 years of the GAA in the parish of Beragh as related to us by the author, Alan Rodgers.

I congratulate Alan on the magnificent job he has done and I know that you, like me, will appreciate all the painstaking and diligent research done by him before putting pen to paper. It is a truly wonderful achievement on his part for which we will be forever grateful. And, I must say that as a native of The 'Cross, that I am particularly pleased to see that the formation of the first club there is highlighted in the title he has chosen for the book.

I know that he has had the co-operation of so many inside and outside the parish with his research that it is impossible for me to name them individually. So, on behalf of the Red Knights Club, I thank them all most sincerely for helping to make Alan's 'Down from The Cross' the publication that it is. I must also congratulate James Keenan of Capture Design Consultants whose layout and design speaks for itself in what is a superbly finish product.

Is Mise Le Meas
Michael McCann, *Cathaoirleach, Bearach an Chraobh Rua*

introduction

Sometimes it is easy to forget or take for granted just how important the GAA is in the lives of so many people. Everyone will have their own personal memories of games played, friendships made and their important role in the running of a team or club. The fact that it may be years or decades since they were last involved doesn't matter because every contribution counts.

It may be a weekend away, a title won or lost or even just one moment in a game which stands out from all the rest. In writing this history, I have attempted to go some way towards recognising the very many people who have had both small and big connections with the GAA in this area. Only a small fraction of the stories that could be told are related in the following pages. Hopefully, those that are included will provide some measure of acknowledgement for those who have felt part of gaelic games locally at one time or another.

I have been fortunate for a few reasons. The extensive coverage given to GAA and other affairs under the auspices of the Sixmilecross, Brackey and Beragh banners in the early years of the twentieth century have made compiling this story so much easier and more comprehensive. The arrival of Link in 1977 provided the perfect forum for the publication of old GAA-related pictures and stories from people involved in those formative years. The contribution of Link and those involved with its weekly completion cannot be emphasised strongly enough.

Interviews carried out by Frank Rodgers in the early 1980s aided the successful completion of this book. The stories of early players like Ned Rafferty, Felix Owens, Harry Owens and Lexie McLaren bring a contemporary human interest dimension to those first decades of involvement. Later, the personal memories of Sean Bennett, Frankie and Barney Owens, Bridget Keenan, Terry Kelly, Rose Peachman (nee Nugent) Vin and John Donaghy and Mick Kerr have given a first-hand account into various aspects of the GAA from the 1930s on.

Club and other archives have also been a big help. The documents of various types which were provided by Bernadette McGurn, Joe Martin and Frank Rodgers were invaluable and my thanks to them. One of the things that is most satisfying about the book is the quality and diversity of photographs. To this end, I would like to express my sincere thanks to all those who sourced precious family archives for images relating to the GAA and other affairs in the Beragh area since the beginning of the twentieth century. In particular, I would like to record my thanks to Pat McSorley and Michael Cullen, who went beyond the call of duty to help and whose images are quite simply top class. Also, the work of Red Knights PRO, Stephen Mullan, in scanning photographs eased the pressure considerably especially as the book neared completion.

Throughout this project a number of people have provided me with much encouragement which has added to my enjoyment in completing this book. The Centenary and Executive Committees of the Beragh Red Knights GAA Club deserve special mention for their general support. Most of all the assistance in a multitude of ways from my father, Frank Rodgers, has ensured that a long-term aim of both he and I has now been successfully realised.

Finally, it is my great pleasure to thank, James Keenan of Capture Design Consultants for his patience, effort and professionalism in bringing the various elements together in such a fine fashion.

Alan Rodgers, Beragh, October 5th, 2006

Chapter One
Pre 1900
Before the GAA

Chapter One
Before the GAA

WHILE there is no evidence of organised GAA activity in Beragh before 1906, evidence of life in the area goes back many centuries. The names of townlands as well as the numerous ancient monuments and legends give a glimpse of how the ancestors of today's population lived and died there.

Among such sites is Grainne's Grave, an ancient burial ground at Redergan which has been the subject of various archeological investigations. The Ordinance Survey refers to the tomb as a 'dolmen', indicating that it is probably around 4000 years old. The Gaelic people attributed many of these stone tombs to their folk heroes and it is from a legendary princess that Grainne's Grave takes its name.

A number of standing stones believed to date back to the Neolithic period have been identified in Cloughfin. Some of these were used as boundary markers, while others had ceremonial purposes where fires were lit for Festivities such as May Day or Midsummer and may have been gravestones or gigantic sundials to indicate the time of year.

Perhaps the best known and most prominent site of historical and indeed religious interest dating back sixteen hundred years is at Donaghanie, where St Patrick is reputed to have stopped during his journey. The story goes that the Church at Donaghanie was built to commemorate the killing of a giant serpent which was terrorising the people and the stone where St Patrick is said to have knelt can still be seen.

Perhaps the best known and most prominent site of historical and indeed religious interest dating back sixteen hundred years is Donaghanie, where St Patrick is reputed to have stopped during his journey

Conaodh, the Holy man, is said to have been left in charge by St Patrick and he is mentioned as a minister to the tribe which preceded the Cineal Eoghain. Their clan chief was killed at Donaghanie in 1518. The site was for many centuries a place of veneration for people making the annual 'pattern' on Lough Sundays. As a result, it is fair to assume that Donaghanie has been a place of prayer, interment and general importance for Christians for over 1400 years.

Further evidence of the area's ancient roots came to light with the widening of the main Beragh to Omagh road in the late 1950s. Workmen who were removing a ten feet high hedge and trees discovered a circular grave which a Senior Inspector from the Archaeological Survey of Ireland dated as being 'obviously pre-historic.'

Despite all the research, however, a definte link between the area and the original Red Branch Knights based at Cooley Co Louth has not been discovered. For the present then it must remain just a coincidence that Beragh's Red Knights GAA Club should have its base in a townland which is also called Cooley.

Towards the Plantation

Thriving communities in each of the townlands gradually evolved from those earliest stories of settlement. These are mentioned in church documents from the middle-ages. By the seventeenth century the Plantation of Ulster was taking place and the details of how it affected Beragh are worth noting.

In his Booklet, 'Ballintaken - Beragh in the 17th Century, ' PJ McCusker relates how the area covered by Ballintaken formed part of the land under the auspices of the Cineal Fearadhaigh, a branch of the Cineal Eoghain of which the O'Neills were part. At that time - and until 1777 - it formed part of the old parish of Termonmagurk and the lands of Ballintacken were subsequently assessed prior to the Plantation of Ulster in the early 1600s.

For the purposes of selling the land the area was divided into four separate sections or balliboes covering ground comprising most of the modern townlands. Planter tenants subsequently took control and the records kept by them and those charged with overseeing the success of the Plantation provide information on the native Irish in the 1600s.

These have provided a unique insight into the names of families residing in particular townlands, with many of them having survived down to the present 21st Century.

❙ Earl of Castlehaven ❙

For instance, Drumduff, which gets its name from the Irish word 'Driumdubh' or 'black ridge' was leased in 1616 by the Earl of Castlehaven to Neale Grome O'Donnelly, born at Ballytaken. Later, in the 1660s, various taxes were imposed on the locals, before the area was eventually sold to Robert Lowry in 1672.

The first appearance of Ramackin in state records was in 1610 when it was allocated to

> For the purposes of selling the land the area was divided into four separate sections or balliboes covering ground comprising most of the modern townlands

There was a stone cross about the same place and it is probable that it was this that gave the name to the modern village. Tradition states that this stone cross was ruthlessly destroyed by vandal hands not more than a century ago

the Earl of Castlehaven before again falling into the hands of O'Donnelly who is listed as becoming tenant on May 1 1615.

Nearer the end of the century some of the lands within the townland were sold by John Ussher to Lord Glenawley. At the same time Ussher also granted the townland of Roscavey to a Scotsman named John Galbraith. Land in the area had been leased to Neall and Patrick O'Donnelly in 1616.

Documents show that Sixmilecross was surveyed between 1596 and 1599 and patented to Lord Dudley, later created Lord Castlehaven in 1601. The ancestors of the Earl of Belmore purchased the manor of Sixmilecross in 1656-57.

According to the Sixmilecross Directory of 1898, the village was originally called Koragh or Carragh and also known as Tullyneil. It goes on to state that near the village is Cross Hill, where Mass was celebrated in the penal times and the stones which formed part of the altar were still to be seen at that time in Aughnaglea, in which the hill is situated.

"There was a stone cross about the same place and it is probable that it was this that gave the name to the modern village. Tradition states that this stone cross was ruthlessly destroyed by vandal hands not more than a century ago, but its actual site, measurements, or who demolished it, are mysteries which the present generation cannot solve."

The writer goes on to say that the demolition took place 'whilst Charles Colhoun was Captain of the Yeomen.' The Directory claims that Mr Colhoun's son, Edward, used a portion of the cross as a stone trough and subsequently Rafferty, of Drumlister got it and it was then, in 1898, located at Pat Rafferty's forge in the townland.

"It is said that there is another piece if it in some of those houses in the Cross Row, and that it was put in the floor of a public house there, for the express purpose of causing Catholics to trample upon a portion of the emblem of redemption," the Directory continues.

An important strategic site in the area was Bawntown, or Bantown. The bawn was erected close to the highway between Omagh and Dungannon overlooking the town and was the residence of Lord Audley (who was later to become the Earl of Castlehaven).

The Sixmilecross Directory of the late nineteenth century says that one of its walls was then part of Mr Owens' turfshed and that sometime in the 1830s its walls were levelled and cellars filled in.

The seventeenth century also saw the establishment of the first village in the district. Sixmilecross got its charter to hold a fair when the resident of Bawntown, Lord Glenawley, took over. A parish church for Termon was erected around the same time as the village continued to grow.

The Rebellion of 1798

Strong oral traditions surround the 1798 Rebellion in the Beragh and Sixmilecross districts. Much important information was compiled and, indeed, artefacts relating to the period were gathered by local MP and GAA official, HK McAleer, at the end of the nineteenth century.

Among his possessions were Volunteer and Yeoman buckles and he reported in a 1937 article that the Loyal Sixmilecross Infantry also had their own particular uniform and equipment. Both the villages of Sixmilecross and Beragh, as well as the surrounding rural hinterlands had developed as communities by the end of the eighteenth century and many played a part in the Rebellion.

HK McAleer recounted how he visited many of the people whose parents or grandparents took part in the Rebellion or were affected by it. Among the most famous was a man named Johnnie Kincaid of Cavanreagh, Sixmilecross, who was referred to in one report in the following terms:

I Theobald Wolfetone

"In the stirring days of 1798 he was a leading spirit in the United Irish movement and the authorities considered it necessary to put some restraint on the movements of this fearless young fellow."

The day of his trial arrived and 'Jack' was sentenced to transportation for life. At the conclusion of the case he was brought outside and ordered to mount a horse which was ready to convey him from home he struggled to get free. When jumping into the saddle he shouted "Here goes Kincaid, Who never was afraid."

It was related that Kincaid made good in Australia becoming 'immensely rich in land and cattle etc.' The McAleer notes go on to recall what are described as awful stories about Clogherney and Roscavey during the burning spree undertaken by Lord Blaney.

Among the houses reported to have been raised to the ground are Paddy McSorley's in Roscavey (just behind what was Mr James Maxwell's), Michael Heagney's (at Owens' of Deroar)) and a house in Killadroy on a site occupied a century ago by Pat Mullin.

Details are given about houses burned and how the United Irishmen recruited at the time by going around houses asking men to 'unite' and how the United Men of Brackey and the surrounding district 'were wont to meet in a field on the opposite side of the road from Mr McKelvey's.'

One of the first hand accounts given was that of John McFarland who remembered the Rebellion and told HK McAleer of how the United Men of Brackey and Drumnakilly had marched to Gortin for a conflict with the Yeomanry before being forced to retreat.

Tyrone Memoirs 1830s

More information about the locality prior to the establishment of local newspapers is contained in the Ordinance Survey Memoirs of the 1830s. These were compiled as a result of men travelling throughout the country and recording both their own observations and those of people with intimate knowledge of events, traditions and sites of interest within their areas.

> John McFarland who remembered the Rebellion and told HK McAleer of how the United Men of Brackey and Drumnakilly had marched to Gortin for a conflict with the Yeomanry before being forced to retreat

Beragh is described as being the property of Lord Belmore and consisting of one long street whose residents for the most part appear to be poor. Sixmilecross is said to have 65 meanly built houses and a recently established penny post between Omagh and Dungannon. Though small, Seskinore is said to contain some good houses.

It is interesting to note the biographical details of the people which are given in the Ordinance Survey 'Memoirs of Ireland' covering the period between 1825 and 1840. The author of the Memoirs, whose remit is the Church of Ireland Parish of Clogherney, says that the people of the district "are in generally good circumstances." He goes on to highlight their diet, health needs, education as well as their occupations.

Few are said to speak Irish, Potatoes, meal, milk and a little meat are their stable foods and, while the parish is very free from disease, those who are sick go to Omagh as there is no dispensary in Clogherney.

Schools are located in Clogherney Glebe Lower, Beragh under the Hibernian Society, a hedge school at Dervaghroy with twenty pupils, another in Ballyhallaghan with 40 to 70 children, one in Seskinore and another in Aughnagar under the Hibernian Society.

The roads were in good repair, there were seven principal bridges at Curr, on the mail road from Dublin to Derry, two in Seskinore, one in Letfern, one in Beagh, one in Beragh and one in Coolesker. Also located in the parish were eight mills and the rents varied from 15s to 30s an acre.

The Pattern

Among the big events for the people of the eighteenth and nineteenth centuries was the annual Pattern to Lough Patrick at Donaghanie. It took place on the first Sunday of August each year and attracted people of all denominations.

The first part of the penance was for the people to go around the Lough on their bare knees before adding a handful of earth to the hillocks of clay which surrounded it. Water from the the Lough was then added to the mix, those completing the ritual believing that it cleansed them from sin and cured their diseases.

Tents and booths were erected and after the ceremonies were completed, the usual amusement of dancing and drinking took place.

However, the 1834 Survey of Tyrone described the pattern as not being so well attended in recent years because of party riots.

"By the influence of the magistrates on the one hand and the priest on the other, it is not so publicly sought after now as eight years ago. People, however, come from all parts of Ireland to it.

"Tents and booths are erected and after the superstitutions are completed, the usual amusements of dancing, deeply mingled with whiskey, conclude this descration of the Lord's Holy Day. Whether those who do penance join in these festivals, it is not easy to say, as there are persons of all denominations present."

The references to education marked significant developments in the provision of schools and regular tutoring for young people. In the twenty year period between 1848 and 1868, the number of schools increased from thirteen to nineteen and included Beragh, Seskinore, Roscavey, Radargan Upper, Clogherney, Tullyrush, Killadroy, Sixmilecross, Drumlester, Benchran, Ramackin, Brackey and Drumnakilly.

The number had increased further by the end of the century and it was only in the later half of the twentieth century that centralisation brought the closure of so many of these closely knit rural schools.

The visit of Fr Matthew

It was to this backdrop that one of the most widely known Priests ever in Ireland visited the Drumduff neighbourhood during 1838. Fr Theobald Matthew, who is commemorated by a statue in O'Connell Street in Dublin, was the founder of the Pioneer movement and there is no doubt that his visit aroused much interest and enthusiasm among the people, and one thing for certain is that Fr Matthew was successful in encouraging many of them to take the pledge to abstain from alcohol. Among them was a Mr Michael McGlynn. An Ulster Herald Reporter who attended the scene of the fire at Drumduff Chapel in 1949, was told by Joe Maguire that he had served at the Requiem Mass for Mr McGlynn, in 1922, some sixty years after the visit.

The old graveyard at Donaghanie

This Michael McGlynn was said to have taken the pledge directly from Fr Matthew and observed it until his death. Mr Maguire said he had one of the original pioneer pins which were distributed at the time.

This visit took place around the time of the opening of Drumduff Chapel. Prior to that, Mass was celebrated at the local Mass Rock nearby and among the items destroyed in the fire was a wooden crucifix dated 1787.

Lowrystown to Beragh
A developing community

Tillage and pastoral lands occupied the site of
the present village of Beragh when work began
on the old chapel around 1800. The parish,
formerly known as Ballintacken, was formed in
1777 and within a generation efforts to provide
a permanent places of worship began.

Deeds were taken out for the new village of
Lowrystown with people from the surrounding district taking lots.
Thus the Clarkes came in from Curr, the Foxes from Drumduff, the
Johnstons and the Lynsdays from Tattykeeran, the Mullins from
Foremass, the Fultons and Gormleys from Osnagh, the Clements and
Cavanaghs from Killadroy, the Kyles from Benchran as well as
people named Fenton, Wilson, McCausland, Donnelly, Cochrane,
Thompson, Anderson, McSorley and McDowell.

Beragh Chapel as
it looked around
the turn of the
twentieth century

The new Church was opened by the then Archbishop of Armagh and
Primate of All-Ireland, Dr Curtis and in a 1937 article, HK McAleer
writes that 'the day was so stormy that the candles could not be kept
lighted." The piece also recounts that the panels of the altar were
painted by Pitchoni, an Italian artist and depicted the Nativity,
Cruicifixion and Resurrection.

Further extension work took place throughout the nineteenth century,
with major improvements being completed in 1842 and 1843. These
included the addition of the north and south galleries, windows,
confessionals and the seating on the walls of the ground floor. Names
mentioned in the accounts included Frank Rodgers, John Bergin
(painter, Omagh), John Evitt, John Donnelly, James McGuire, John
Johnston, Billy Fox and Phil McCusker.

It is interesting to speculate what impact the erection of the chapel
had on transforming the social and indeed political life of the parish
as it brought people from all areas together for the first time on a
regular basis. However, an insight into the type of activity
accompanying the religious services can be guaged from this snippet
of folklore from HK McAleer in 1937.

"Ninety years ago there was a very poor circulation of newspapers.
Matthew Rodgers of Sixmilecross used to bring the 'Nation' to

The piece also
recounts that the
panels of the altar
were painted by
Pitchoni, an Italian
artist and depicted
the Nativity,
Cruicifixion and
Resurrection

15

Beragh Chapel and before the priest would come he would read speeches by O'Connell and the leading patriots of the day.' The impact on the listeners must have been significant considering that the year was 1847 - right in the middle of the Famine.

Around the same time work was taking place on the second Church locally, St Patrick's at Drumduff, and it provided an example of the grievances felt by the Catholic population.

Prior to the beginning of building work on the chapel in 1846, Mass was said in a glen between the cross-roads and the river. But hopes of a speedy completion of the construction were delayed by around three years for reasons which were subject to much rumour. While the famine could have been a cause, it was claimed that an agent for the Belmore Estate remarked that the building would be used to stable his horses if it was ever roofed.

The man, renowned for his mistreatment of tenants, eventually emigrated with his family, the chapel was completed in 1850 and its first tiled floor and seats added at the beginning of the 1880s. By then, many of the cultural, sporting and political revivals of the late nineteenth and early twentieth century were taking place.

Sixmilecross was also growing steadily by the middle of the century. A Parliamentary Gazetteer of Ireland in 1846 described the town as having a meeting house, an Hibernian Society schoolhouse and a fair held on the nineteenth of every month. The population in 1831 was given as 275 and had risen to 355 by 1841.

> "
> Sixmilecross - A Parliamentary Gazetteer of Ireland in 1846 described the town as having a meeting house, an Hibernian Society schoolhouse and a fair held on the nineteenth of every month "

A Topographical Dictionary of Ireland gives an indication of what the village would have looked like to the visitor of that time. It states the number if residents as 355, living in 76 'meanly built houses,' many of which were thatched.

Of course, those descriptions came right in the middle of the Famine and amid what must have been extreme poverty. In January 1847 a Relief Meeting was held in Sixmilecross and attracted an attendance of 'all; the clergy, local gentry and respectable farmers of the district.'

It seems that many of the people at the time were, in the words of a report in the Tyrone Constitution, in 'destitution' and those at the meeting were attempting to 'send the most prompt and liberal aid to where ever severe distress existed.'

Among those attending was the Parish Priest, Rev B McAleer, The Rev Beresford CC was in the Chair and he explained the object of the meeting by saying that the only mode of meeting the present distress was by voluntary assessment and 'their intention in assembling was to ascertain whether the wealthy cess-payers were willing to unite with the gentry and the clergy in contributing towards the relief of the poor.'

The Land League and Home Rule campaigns - Parnell's visit

Ireland was beginning to experience stirring times by the 1860s and 1870s as a range of organisations came to the fore in a bid to secure a number of different objectives. Among them was Home Rule, a fixity of tenure and land ownership for tenants. On the sporting front, there was a growing desire to revive national games and to ensure greater participation in athletic events which at the time were patronised primarily by the ruling classes.

Charles Stewart Parnell, who visited Beragh in 1881

The absence in west Tyrone of a press sympathetic to the nationalist cause means that information as to the extent of the Land League and Home Rule campaigns in the Beragh area is fairly scant. However, a number of tantalising references to what did go on during that period are available.

A report in the Tyrone Constitution of a large Orange demonstration in Beragh in 1882 gives an indication of the prevailing mood. One speaker warned that those intending to establish a branch of the Land League locally would know the response that they would get.

However, his strong words seem to have been unheeded if an obituary for Matthew Rodgers in the Ulster Herald of December 26th 1903 is anything to go by. While failing to give particular details, the report states that it was from a platform on a field belonging to the deceased that 'JJ O'Kelly promulgated the principals of the Land League for the first time in this portion of the county.'

Further evidence that the Land League had a well organised group locally comes from the obituary of Patrick McAleer from

> The Land League candidate for the area was Mr Harold Rylett who gained the support of the leader of the Irish Party, Charles Stewart Parnell

Drumnakilly in 1922. He is said to have taken a leading part in the struggle on behalf of the tenantry during the Land League days.

Another man involved, died around the same time, in the early part of 1920. Thomas Clery, who was to become prominent in the Beragh Labourers Association at the start of the 20th Century, was described in his obituary as a 'leading spirit' in the Land League and the National League.

There is little doubt that there was a burgeoning national awareness in the locality at that time. This is particularly evident from the reports of the 1881 Tyrone Election at which the Home Rule and Land League issues were the burning topics of conversation. The Land League candidate for the area was Mr Harold Rylett who gained the support of the leader of the Irish Party, Charles Stewart Parnell.

A report in the Times of London on September 5 states that Parnell directed the Land League campaign from his base at the White Hart Hotel in Omagh. And, it was from there that one of Ireland's most famous politicians visited Beragh on market day, September 4th 1881.

Mr Rylett told those gathered that 'if the farmers stood together in the north as they had done in the south the happy day would arrive when landlords, bailiffs, agents and all their tribe would be cast bag and baggage out of the country.' In turn Parnell remarked that the 'Land League had taken the land question out of the hands of these tinkering, time-serving politicians.'

> Parnell said no matter what way the election went the landlords would have to go, the people would triumph and Ireland would gain legislative independence

The address took place, according to HK McAleer in a 1938 article, outside the premises of Mr Matthew Rodgers at Main Street, was chaired by Owen McSorley, an Irish-American from Roscavey, and attracted reporters from England, Ireland and Scotland. He goes on to talk of that night in early September 1881:

"There was great preparation to give a becoming torchlight procession to the 'uncrowned king'. Such enthusiasm! Parnell said no matter what way the election went the landlords would have to go, the people would triumph and Ireland would gain legislative independence. Father O'Boyle, who accompanied him, made a very impassioned speech."

Home Rule Bills were eventually passed in 1886 and 1912, although a change in Government and the outbreak of World War One meant that they were never enacted. Nevertheless, over the next twenty years various Land Acts finally realised the dreams of those who gathered in Beragh and elsewhere during those years. By the early 1900s the Belmore Estate was being sold off and new national organisations were occupying the attentions of the people.

Incidentally, it seems that the Owen McSorley mentioned in the report was involved in an earlier dispute connected with the land. In the summer of 1848, Mr McSorley, his wife and daughter were at the centre of a row regarding the possession of a farm at Beragh.

According to the Tyrone Constitution of June 2nd, 1848, it was another outrage resulting from the dispute between the Rev Fr Quinn, PP and the Clements family.

The report stated that Owen McSorley and his family claimed to be the real owners of the property and were occupying a small house on the farm contrary to the will of the priest.

"On Wednesday night last, a large party of men turned the family forcibly out of the house, the roof of which they tore off, and otherwise demolished the building so as to render it uninhabitable. We understand that informations have been sworn against the Rev Fr Quin and several other individuals as having been concerned in the outrage."

Rose Kavanagh

The cottage in Killadroy where Rose Kavanagh was born and lived

June 25th in 1859 marked the birth of perhaps one of Beragh's best known natives of the nineteenth or twentieth centuries. Born at Killadroy, Rose Kavanagh was to receive much of her schooling in her own townland before moving to Augher.

Following that she moved to the Loreto Convent in Omagh and then to Dublin to study drawing at the School of Art in Kildare Street. It was while there that she began writing, contributing a serial story for the magazine 'Young Ireland' and verse for the 'Irish Monthly.

she always looked far stronger than her state warranted - tall and handsome, with a dear fresh Irish beauty that delighted one

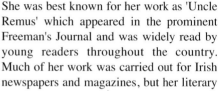

She was best known for her work as 'Uncle Remus' which appeared in the prominent Freeman's Journal and was widely read by young readers throughout the country. Much of her work was carried out for Irish newspapers and magazines, but her literary reputation had also extended to Australia where editors were anxious to publish her work.

Her serials such as 'The Cost of Her Coronet,' and 'Killavney' and her short tales and sketches were clearly illustrative of Irish country life.

She was said to have glorified in her literary work and no doubt much of what was described as her beautiful personality revealed itself from behind the Uncle Remus masquerade.

One article gave a glimpse of that personality when it stated that "she always looked far stronger than her state warranted - tall and handsome, with a dear fresh Irish beauty that delighted one."

"It was the most honest face in the world, with brave grey eyes, and a country brownness over the clear tints as if it loved sun and the breezes. I used to call her the wild rose and I remember that her fine forehead was white under the beautiful brown hair that rippled off it nobly. There was scarcely ever a face or form that expressed more truly the fair soul within."

However, that most dreaded of diseases - consumption - eventually took its terrible toll. Going home to see her mother one chilly Christmas, she took a cold on the journey from which she never recovered. She died on February 28th 1891, aged just 32.

Nineteenth Century Sporting Activity

Throughout the eighteenth and nineteenth centuries sporting activities and games were organised around holiday and religious festivals. Therefore, it is reasonable to speculate that some form of games would have accompanied the annual 'Lough Sunday' at Donaghanie and other important events in the lives of the people.

But it's not until the later part of the nineteenth century that clear evidence of sporting activity in the parish comes to light. And, it was to involve many of the names and people who would later become central to the formation of the GAA club in 1906.

Hurling and handball are the two oldest sports now covered by the Association and local folklore has it that both were played in the 1800s. When the Brackey Club was set-up in the late 1950s, details of the game being played a century earlier came to light.

While the alley used at that time had been in use since the 1920s, it replaced an earlier building dating back sixty years before that. It was stated that this made the building 'one of the oldest in Northern Ireland' and went on to recount the names of some of those who had participated.

Among the players known for their skill in the late nineteenth and early twentieth century were James and Frank Maguire, James Gibney, Arthur McGurk, Pat Martin, Frank Nugent and John McCrystall. It was no surprise that the game was popular in towns and villages so long ago considering the limited facilities that were needed. And, the ease at which a match could be staged led to localised differences in rules and the way handball was played.

For instance, players in Drumquin were not allowed to kick the ball up, in contrast to Pomeroy where kicking the ball was permitted. In Brackey the competitors served from the hand and in Beragh the players tossed the ball up before serving.

Handball wasn't one of the sports specifically cited when the GAA was originally set up for the 'preservation and cultivation' of national pastimes and culture. But it is easy to see the reasoning behind the efforts of Michael Cusack and others in the 1880s when the example of Beragh is considered.

For just over a year before the GAA was founded, a highly popular and well attended soccer match was staged on ground later used for gaelic games. A report in one of the first editions of Link includes a report from the Tyrone Free Press of 94 years previously on a soccer match on the Feast of the Annunciation.

"Beragh was taken completely by surprise on Wednesday when the Celtic club put on a masquerade as a winding up for the season. As it was the Feast of the Annunciation, and also a Roman Catholic Holiday, the town was thronged with country people, and the excitement was extraordinary when the boys marched from the corner as the people were leaving chapel after mid-day Mass.

They had their faces blackened, and were arrayed in fantastic

>
> It is also interesting to note that in 1884 much interest was aroused one Wednesday evening when members of the Omagh Cycling Club and two cyclists from Sixmilecross passed through Beragh and Sixmilecross

66

After a circuit of the town had been made, the processionists winded their way to a field kindly given for the occasion by Mr Frank Owens, Deroar, and a well contested match was played

99

costume and they created a terrible din with banjos, melodeons, whistles, harmonics, tambourines, etc and the funiosities and comicalities of the facetious clowns were beyond description.

Two youngsters led the process with the goalposts and the ball swinging thereon and close by was the inimitable 'Joe' mounted on a strangely caparisoned donkey, and the 'brothers' came next followed by a crowd which would be called a mass meeting in the days of the Repeal Movement."

"After a circuit of the town had been made, the processionists winded their way to a field kindly given for the occasion by Mr Frank Owens, Deroar, and a well contested match was played."

The Sixmilecross, or Sixmilecross and Beragh Races, which remained popular into the 1950s, also give an idea of how people spent their spare time in the second half of the nineteenth century. Taking place at various venues in Ballyhallaghan, the event seems to have had its origins in that nineteenth century and just a month after the founding of the GAA, December 26th 1884, it drew a huge crowd to Irwin's Holm.

It was estimated that an attendance of 10,000 had gathered in less than ideal conditions by the time of the first races. A severe frost totally blocked out the first and second races and the Tyrone Free Press reported that some people could 'only see in an imperfect way' due to the excess of the previous night.

It is also interesting to note that in 1884 much interest was aroused one Wednesday evening when members of the Omagh Cycling Club and two cyclists from Sixmilecross passed through Beragh and Sixmilecross. A report in the Tyrone Free Press stated that "A bugle sounded the advance of these Flying Men. These Philosopedes, as some old crones call them attracted a large crowd to the street, but they were almost out of sight before the people emerged from their houses."

An old-style bicycle of the type that would have been familiar to the people of Beragh and Sixmilecross around the late nineteenth and early twentieth century.

Further south, the fledgling Gaelic Athletic Association was, in the words of Michael Cusack, 'spreading like a prairie fire' by the end of 1884. Its first months saw athletic meetings being held on a regular basis, the first hurling and football matches under newly formulated rules and a massive athletics meeting took place in Clonmel with an estimated fifteen to twenty thousand people in attendance.

In his book, 'The GAA - A History' the noted GAA historian, Marcus deBurca describes the initial growth as causing something of a social revolution in rural Ireland. In Tyrone, though, and more specifically in Beragh, Sixmilecross and surrounding townlands, it is clear that the impact and awareness of this new organisation and of its aims was limited.

It was to be over two decades and into a new century before the GAA was to join other organisations locally as a new front in the revival of nationalist ideals that was taking root both county and country-wide.

Slow to make a mark in Ulster

The founder of the GAA, Michael Cusack

Soon after the GAA was founded Michael Cusack compared its spread to 'wildfire.' But apart from a number of notable exceptions, the organisation failed to take root in the northern part of the country. While Ballyconnell First Ulsters, Newtownbutler First Fermanaghs and Cookstown Brian Ogs were early starters, it wasn't until the early Twentieth Century that the anticipated growth eventually got underway in Ulster.

As a player, coach and administrator at all levels of the GAA with the Ballygawley and Beragh Clubs and with the Tyrone and Ulster Committees, PJ McClean has taken a lifelong interest in all aspects of the Association's development. He suggests that the delay in the establishment of GAA units in the north can be attributed to issues of nationality and land availability.

It has been seen that the GAA was part of the Irish Cultural revival of the late nineteenth and early twentieth centuries. Considering that the means of communication was good through the coming of the Railway in 1865 and the widespread availability of newspapers, this cannot be a reason for the delay. But he suggests that the first debates on Home Rule in 1884 may have sparked the flames for what is described as the 'Irish Renaissance.'

This may have created a threatening edge between the competing allegiances in the northern part of the country.

"In the Ireland of the 1880s and 1890s, space to play the new games presented problems which were not able to be addressed until the early years of the 20th Century. Until the passing through Parliament of the Land Acts of 1901, no tenant farmer owned his own land. Therefore, given the fear that the GAA might be see as the thin end of a divisive or even threatening wedge, is it logical to assume that there would be a reluctance to be seen to openly embrace the new games and the new dynamic driving them?

"Under the Land Acts, the then Liberal Government at Westminster bought out the landlords with lump sums and offered the tenants the right to purchase, by means of fifty year annuities collectible twice yearly, the holdings on which they lived."

"The era of the small farmer had begun. As long as he could pay his annuities, he could put his land to whatever use he pleased. The landlord had lost his grip. So, depending on crop rotation, certain fields were allowed to be used for the playing of GAA matches. Perhaps the acquisition of land by the farmers offers another reason as to why the GAA took so long to reach Northern Ireland."

Mr McClean goes on to say that the ban on 'foreign games' may also have been a contributory factor and quotes a letter from Archbishop Croke, a patron of the GAA, written to the Freeman's Journal in 1885, which stated:

"When I ventured to connect my name with the GAA I really felt pained and so had felt for many a long day previously at seeing all our fine national sports and pastimes dying out one by one and English and other non-native games introduced and almost universally patronised instead.

"Not that I am, or was, in the least opposed to foreign games as such, if manly and becoming, but only in so far as they were favoured by a certain class of people to the exclusion of those well known Irish exercises which were formerly so common and in which when young I was proud to take part myself.

"It did not, therefore, occur to me when becoming a patron of the GAA, that there was to be any substantial, much less a bitter persistent antagonism, except on the point just referred to, between it

Not that I am, or was, in the least opposed to foreign games as such, if manly and becoming, but only in so far as they were favoured by a certain class of people to the exclusion of those well known Irish exercises which were formerly so common and in which when young I was proud to take part myself

Archbishop Croke

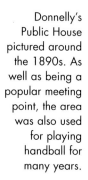

and any similar body already in existence or that may be called into existence afterwards.

Dr Croke continues: "Still less did I think that a society or association formed for the promotion of one class of game should boycott all similar bodies, to the extent, at all events, of not allowing a man who had competed for a prize or championship under one set of rules to contend for a prize or championship if offered by an athletic association whose rules were different."

However, whatever the reason for the slow northward progress of the GAA over the first thirty years he says that it has now matured almost to its full potential under its present administrative structures.

But it was all so different back at the dawn of the 1900s when the GAA had yet to make an impact in the Beragh and Sixmilecross areas despite the stirrings of the time on a number of different fronts.

Chapter Two
1900 - 1910
'Cross Start to GAA Journey

Chapter Two
1900 - 1910

EVENTS in the later half of the nineteenth century laid the foundations for the dramatic re-awakening of nationalist fervour which greeted the dawn of the twentieth century. The formation of the Gaelic Athletic Association, the Gaelic League, the Land League as well as the various campaigns for Home Rule focused attention on the desire for self-determination in Ireland.

This was to be replicated in Tyrone in general and in Beragh in particular from 1900 onwards with the formation of branches of the United Irish League, Ancient Order of Hibernians, the Beragh Labourers Association and, eventually the Gaelic Athletic Association. Combining with these was the availability of education and the increased involvement of the Catholic Church in social, cultural and political as well as spiritual affairs.

For the modern reader, the pages of the Ulster Herald provide a fascinating insight into community life at that time. Founded in August 1901, the newspaper immediately provided a platform for organisations to advertise and report their affairs on a weekly basis and they appear to have taken full advantage of this.

William O'Brien & Michael Davitt - Founders of the United Irish League

In addition to lengthy reports on the efforts of a number of organisations, the advertisements carried by the 'Herald' provide a snapshot of the people, subjects and areas of importance. Its coverage or lack of coverage of Tyrone GAA affairs reflect the Association's triumphs and tribulations during those formative years.

The United Irish League

By August 1901 the United Irish League contained in the region of 100,000 members in 1000 branches throughout Ireland and among the latest of them was the one known as 'Beragh Parochial.' While the precise sequence of events leading to the establishment of this and other organisations in the first decade of the twentieth century is unclear now, their influence reflected a growing trend.

The setting up of County Councils gave local people the opportunity to win election at a local Government level and influence the development of Irish ideals in the Beragh area.

"

as the people of those few townlands were tried to the core when asked to strike a blow for Ireland, it is anticipated that in the near future the National mantle will soon encircle these, including the outstanding townlands which are lagging behind in the forward march of our people in the other parts of the Parish

"

HK McAleer, a leading member of the GAA in both Sixmilecross and Tyrone during the early years of the twentieth century. He played a key role in the formation of the Sixmielcross Wolfe Tones in 1906 and maintained a keen interest in GAA affairs until his death

Brackey School in 1904 and venue for a concert organised by the Wolfe Tones in 1908. On the right is the late Packie McAleer (Sixmilecross) on his mother's knee and far left is Master Patrick McAleer, his Father.

It is fair to speculate that the impetus for the formation of the Beragh Parochial Branch came from a United Irish League Demonstration in Coalisland in September 1901. Trains were scheduled to leave Beragh and Sixmilecross shortly before 1pm, and just a month later local MP, HK McAleer, was listed as attending a meeting of the Tyrone UIL in Pomeroy on November 9th as a Sixmilecross representative.

Hardly surprising, then, that the first real sign of its activity locally comes just a week later. It is interesting to speculate just how Mr McAleer might have been encouraged to establish a branch in his own area and acted immediately by taking the steps required.

A report in the Ulster Herald of the following week states that a meeting of the new Beragh Parochial Branch was held in the League rooms, with HK McAleer presiding and a deputation from Seskinore explained where matters stood in their area.

"Everyone seemed anxious to do all they could to push for the sale of cards (membership cards) and the townlands seemed to vie with one another as to who shall have the smallest number of black sheep when the lists are read out before every meeting.

"As some routine work had been carried it was decided that a further meeting be held in Beragh on Sunday November 24th after second Mass when officers will be elected in the most democratic style as every member in the parish will have a vote and voice in the selection of the office-bearers. It is hoped that those elected should be nationalised and have proved themselves in the past to be capable, energetic and uncompromising."

Among the resolutions adopted at the meeting were ones in favour of legislative independence, that the only Bill acceptable that will please the farmers is a sweeping measure of Compulsory Purchase. The meeting also called for evicted tenants to be reinstated, it encouraged those professing nationalist views to become involved and resolved that any settlement of the Land Question would be incomplete and unsatisfactory unless agricultural labourers got suitable houses with portions of land attached.

At the subsequent meeting on November 24th, the following officers were elected: President - HK McAleer, Vice President - Patrick Toye, Seskinore, Treasurer - F Hepburn, Secretary - Owen Devlin, Assistant Secretary - Patrick Kerr, Beragh. Divisional Delegates - Patrick Rodgers, SMX, F Hepburn, John Maguire, Donaghanie, P Toye, HK McAleer, Francis Owens, RDC, Deroar.

One of their main concerns was that one portion of the Parish had so far remained uninvolved in the organisation - the area beyond Drumduff Chapel. Sounding an optimistic tone, though, the writer reported that "as the people of those few townlands were tried to the core when asked to strike a blow for Ireland, it is anticipated that in the near future the National mantle will soon encircle these, including the outstanding townlands which are lagging behind in the forward march of our people in the other parts of the Parish."

However, much stronger language was used when the matter of writing to the leading men in Drumduff was discussed. They were accused of 'showing by their apathy that they are content with misrule, landlordism, excessive taxation and the other ills which this country is a prey." Such concerns may have been compounded by the resignation of the Secretary, Owen Devlin, and poor attendance at meetings at the beginning of 1902.

The UIL struggled somewhat subsequently and had to be re-organised later in the year. This followed disagreements over the candidates which it had apparently chosen to represent the area in the Rural District Council elections.

It seems that members of the Labourers Association were among those angered by the move which resulted in a de-selection and a

Sixmilecross Hiring Fair held on Tuesday in rather unfavourable weather and attendance as a consequence not as large as usual. Ploughmen receiving £8 to £10 for the half year, Farm Labourers £7 to £8, Herds - £3 to £4, Women Servants £5 to £6 10 shillings

Michael Tierney, a member of the first Sixmilecross Wolfe Tones team, pictured in later years with his family.

special meeting being held in Beragh in the spring of 1902. On the suggestion of the then Parish Priest, Fr James Grimes, this meeting agreed to select two candidates for the forthcoming elections to the Rural District Council from a meeting comprising the three Parish Priests of the areas involved, six delegates from the UIL units and six from the Labourers Associations.

Beragh Labourers Association

An exact date for the formation of the local Labourers Association isn't clear either, but there is no doubt that, like the UIL, it was operating in 1901 and perhaps even earlier. What is clear is the determination of the organisation to stand up for the rights of agricultural labourers and the central part played by Thomas O'Clery, a Rural District Councillor.

Meetings were held fortnightly and on Saturday December 7th, 1901, Mr O'Clery, congratulated those present for the excellent attendance. He said that he was especially pleased to see so many of his Protestant brethern, stating that the Association 'being non-political, was formed on a platform on which Protestants and Roman Catholics could unite for the common good of the working classes.'

An insight into the determination of Mr O'Clery to protect the rights of Labourers can be guaged by a letter written by him in 1902 following a meeting of the RDC. It seems that he was rebuked concerning his own occupation while fighting what he described as the just claims of a labourer to a plot of ground.

"To be now told that your occupation is a barrier against you in local legislation would seem to have come down from the good old days of Ascendancy - 'No Catholic need apply.'

On March 5th 1904 that year Thomas O'Clery referred to the absence of farmers and business men from the meetings of the Labourers Association and proceeded to strongly condemn their inaction. He said their apathy contrasted strongly with the whole-hearted support given by the labourers to the tenants' movements in times gone by when he pointed out that the working men helped to swell the various league meetings.

The National Cause in Tyrone - 1902

Early progress by the United Irish League soon evaporated, leading at the end of 1902 to a meeting with the aim of re-organising the Branch locally as well and putting its future on a firmer footing.

The meeting took place after Second Mass and drew a large attendance, with the principal speakers being Father Grimes PP, George Murnaghan MP and Michael Lynch, MCC. Others present included Henry Owens, County Councillor and the District Councillors, Matthew Rodgers, Thomas O'Clery and D McGuirk.

Father Grimes told those present that the cause of the United Irish League had right on its side, adding that the people also wanted to have the Priests on their side in their struggle for justice and constitutional freedom.

Motions renewing a pledge to the national organisation, calling for the abolition of landlordism and the establishment of a Catholic University and a promise to subscribe to the Defence Fund recently started by the Irish Party were passed on the proposal of Henry Owens and seconded by Matthew Rodgers.

Some interesting population facts in support of the need for national organisation were quoted by George Murnaghan MP. He told the meeting that in the Sixmilecross Dispensary, the number of people had fallen from 6,173 in 1891 to 5,185 ten years later. The drop was even more dramatic when it was considered that the population twenty years earlier in 1881 was 7, 262. A further fall of 25% was reported for the townland of Beragh, while overall in the Omagh Rural District the number of people had fallen by an alarming 6000.

Mr Murnaghan went on to say that the changes sought by the UIL must be achieved to encourage people to stay at home and give them "the hope and prospect of making a living in their own land instead of going to other lands in search of their livelihood."

Father Grimes told those present that the cause of the United Irish League had right on its side

A meeting of the Agricultural Labourers Association in Beragh on March 5th that year heard in no uncertain terms about the failure of both farmers and business men to attend their gatherings and show their support.

The resolution passed by the meeting stated that "the want of work in the winter-season is the cause of untold poverty and distress to many labourers' families and a strong incentive to emigration and we hope some means will be devised - such as home industries - by which the enormous number of idle hands may be utilised to the advantage of the country and their own comfort, and we urge that the various Government and other public bodies should devote their attention to this matter."

Mat Gormley, a key member of early Sixmilecross Wolfe Tones teams

The report goes on to forecast that a 'brighter day is dawning when Irishmen can meet in broad daylight to discuss matters political, not like their forefathers who had to secretly meet in the 'old spot by the river, at the rising of the moon."

Recreation and Religion

It can be seen that the area was very politically aware in this period and that it was only a matter of time for the GAA to get a foothold. But perhaps some of the impetus for the eventual founding of the GAA in the Parish in 1906 came from the organisation of the Beragh Annual Sports, which took place from 1903 onwards and included a range of both familiar and novel events.

A field convenient to the village owned by a Mr McCausland was the venue for the first of these on Monday August 8th, 1903. They drew a large attendance and the hope was expressed that they would now become an annual fixture.

Thomas O'Clery, the Chairman of the Beragh Labourers Association and Rural Councillor, displayed his prowess in the step-dancing, one of the most keenly contested categories. His nimble and artistic performance was much admired in an event that drew competitors from the districts of Pomeroy, Carrickmore and Sixmilecross.

"It is gratifying to learn that there are still in the country a good number of people who admire and practice the old Irish jig and reel dancing," the Ulster Herald report of the sports said.

Other attractions included a Ladies Bicycle Race around a four mile radius of the village and all the old favourites like tug o'war between Beragh and the country district, high jump, half-mile flat race and a special greased pole climbing event which had a prize of 1lb of tobacco for the winner.

Both communities took part in the sports, for which the organising committee was: President - Dr Leitch, Vice-Presidents - M Rodgers, H Owens, JJ Kidd, Committee - Messrs David Cathers, F Hebron, A McFarland, ex-Sergeant Connolly, Alfred Clarke and R Browne.
  Judges of Athletic events - Presidents and Vice-Presidents, FJ Lynam, County Surveyor, Riding and Driving competition, Messrs R O. Clements, R J Kyle and FJ Lynam, Ladies Bicycle Parade - Mrs R.O Clements and Mrs RJ Kyle, Hon Secretaries - Messrs John Hutton BA and John McGrath.

Such community events inevitably depended very much upon the weather for their success. And, the conditions were described as fine for the blessing of the new Beragh Bell on March 29th, 1905. Cardinal Logue arrived in the village on the mid-day train and proceeded to the Church where the blessing of the bell, made in Dublin and weighing 18cwt, took place.

The report of the event stated that "During the ceremony his Eminence washed the bell with water he had specially blessed and then signed it with the oil of the sick on the outside and with chrism on the inside...The bell was then tolled, and there was no suppressing the joy and enthusiasm of the people as its sweet and musical tones were wafted away along the alternating vales and hills around the neat and quiet town of Beragh."

The GAA - A timely progression

The early years of the twentieth century saw the GAA in Tyrone begin to take shape. While evidence of hurling being played preceded the founding of the Association and Cookstown Pearse Ogs represented Tyrone in the 1890 Ulster Football Final, real and sustained growth didn't take place until from about 1903 onwards.

Call at the Cross L Bar, Sixmilecross - NB - I take my whiskies direct from the Bond Stres and I buy none under four years. Customers can rely on my supplying the very best drinks during the year 1903.

Hurling and gaelic football were enthusiastically embraced in many areas, and Strabane, Dungannon, Coalisland and Omagh were among the first districts to start GAA clubs. They were closely followed by a host of others, including Sixmilecross.

The first Tyrone County Board, established in January 1904, gave a focus to the emerging Association. All of this took place amid the burgeoning nationalist revival that had already taken root in the Beragh, Sixmilecross and other areas through organisations like the United Irish League, the Gaelic League and the Ancient Order of Hibernians.

This nurtured the growing sense locally that the native gaelic games needed to be promoted. People like HK McAleer, Thomas O'Clery and Henry Owens were among those representing the nationalist and Catholic populations at a time when a number of campaigns aimed at asserting civil and cultural objectives were gaining momentum.

The need to promote all things gaelic was accepted and it would have been a source of disappointment for those directly involved in such organisations to witness the popularity of soccer at the expense of Gaelic Games during those years.

Barney Rodgers and Tommy Gormley, two of the early Wolfe Tones players

Beragh's Scorchers and the Sixmilecross Stars

Exact dates for the formation of the Beragh Scorchers and Sixmilecross Stars Soccer teams are difficult to pinpoint. What is clear, though, is that their demise seems to have coincided with the establishment of the GAA locally.

The previous century had seen teams from the area take part in soccer games and this was again the case in the early 1900s. And, one of the most prominent examples came on St Patrick's Day 1904 when teams from Sixmilecross, Garvaghey and the Royal Inniskilling Fusiliers Depot in Omagh took part in a special competition in Sixmilecross.

Reporting that the National Festival would "long be remembered in the go ahead village of the Cross," the correspondent in the Ulster Herald claims that "it was certainly as enjoyable a day as has ever been spent about Sixmilecross."

"At two o clock a procession was formed near the Market Square, headed by the Carrickmore Brass Band. Then came the Sixmilecross team (in costume), marching two deep, followed by the military in the same order.

"It is unnecessary to say that the rear included all the available men and boys that gathered into the village. The procession was very imposing and on its descending the hill to the railway station, the spectacular effect was something grand. There was also a very large and respectable turnout of ladies."

It is worth noting that many of the players who lined out that day were within a matter of a year to represent the Sixmilecross Wolfe Tones GAA team. In March 1904, though, their sporting activity was soccer. The local players were - goal - B Rodgers, backs - Micky Tierney (Owen) and Mick Tierney (Hugh), half-backs - Hugh Owens, Owen Mullin and Patrick McCrystall, forwards - P Rodgers, John Devlin, John Owens (Joe) Hugh Donaghey and Willie Shields.

The Garvaghy Emmetts team lined out: goal - Turbitt, backs, Campbell and Kelly, halves, Montague, Quinn and Donnelly, forwards, McGirr, Conroy, Owens, Hetherington and Rodgers.

On the completion of the matches, which saw Sixmilecross and the Fusiliers draw and the Stars defeat Garvaghey twice, "the bands and players returned to the town and the vast crowds had cleared off by night-fall remarkably well pleased with the day's amusement."

Five days later a special meeting of the Sixmilecross Stars club expressed satisfaction with the success of the event, and "a good sum was made when all accounts were squared." Thanks were expressed to Patrick Rodgers for providing the field and to Master McGillion and Master McAleer for acting as collectors and to those whose useful work the good gate could be attributed to.

The Sixmilecross and Beragh teams took part regularly in competitive games which appear to have been well organised. For instance, a month prior to the St Patrick's Day games, the Beragh Scorchers played the strangely named, Ballygawley Pinks, in a return match that attracted 'about one hundred' spectators.'

Then, a month after the St Patrick's Day games, an attendance of some 1500 was at a game between Dungannon Rovers and the Beragh Scorchers which finished 2-1 for the Scorchers who led 1-0 at

On the completion of the matches, which saw Sixmilecross and the Fusiliers draw and the Stars defeat Garvaghey twice, "the bands and players returned to the town and the vast crowds had cleared off by night-fall remarkably well pleased with the day's amusement

half-time and lined out: Cleary, Mossey, Crawford, Conway, McQuade, McAllister, Kerr, W Healy, McCann, McLaren, Maguire.

Both clubs were on a fairly firm footing as indicated by a report of a Variety Entertainment at the Market House Hall in Sixmilecross in January 1905. It was held in aid of the local football club, with the dance music being by Joe McFarland, Mick McGrath, Patrick McGurgan, Frank Clery and Mr T Kelly.

Sixmilecross Main Street in 1905

The attractions included gramophone selections, songs by Miss Agnes Kerr, Beragh, James Clery and Frank Rafferty. Mr James McNamee sang 'Sweet County Clare' and 'The Brown Jug' and Mr Harry Owens, by special request sang 'I am dreaming of thee.'

Members of the club acted as stewarts and few seemed perturbed by the fact that the overtly garrison game of soccer was being promoted. Instead, it was believed that the most important feature of the night was the large number of reels and step-dances gone through. A report claimed that the performances showed that the Gaelic revival has given a strong impetus to 'our own national dances in this part of the country.'

The time was right

But the involvement in soccer would have been frowned upon by those associated with the GAA. They would have seen the fielding of soccer teams in Sixmilecross, Beragh and elsewhere as highlighting both the great need and the immense potential for the promotion of gaelic games locally.

And, it certainly did not go unnoticed elsewhere in the county either. One of the first meetings of the Tyrone County Committee in October 1904 signalled the intention to start a Gaelic Football league following the completion of the County Championships and targeted several areas, including Beragh, still not active.

"This is to be a busy season with the gaels. What are our Omagh friends doing and Cookstown and Beragh. Surely they are not going to allow the year to go without a share in honours. It is hoped that they will awaken soon and take their place in the revival of the national games," one report in the Ulster Herald stated.

At a time when just six clubs existed in Tyrone, the fact that Beragh should be singled out in a call for the gaelic games to be started there emphasises the importance of the area in nationalist activity. All the major organisations gained widespread support throughout the area and officials of the fledgling GAA in Tyrone were obviously anxious to tap into those reserves for the cultivation of the national pastimes.

That hope was to be fulfilled within a relatively short period, even though one writer to the Herald praised the fact that in Tyrone there were 'no vulgar Camans or Gaelic Football, but pure unadulterated hockey and rugby in visions of refinement and civilisation.'

It is possible now to imagine how the GAA came to be first formed in the Market Hall in Sixmilecross. Local men must indeed have taken heed of the Tyrone County Board call and become aware of the fact that their promotion of all things Irish must be extended to its games.

The formation of the Sixmilecross Wolfe Tones GAA Club

HK McAleer's central role as an active member of various organisation means that it was natural for him to be to the fore in the moves that led to the formation of the club. These began on Sunday January 21st when the appearance of the Killyclogher St Patrick's Hurling and Football teams caused a stir in Sixmilecross.

Their purpose was, as the Ulster Herald of the following week reported, to give impetus to the Irish game. Not withstanding the short notice, a large crowd watched as Sixmilecross marked their debut with a seven points to 1-2 victory described thus:

"The visitors played a manly game, but the locals, though not so well up in the rules, were somewhat faster and kept up the pressure for the greater part of the time, and their defence was sound."

On the following evening, Monday January 22nd 1906, the new Sixmilecross club was formed in the Market Hall situated at the top of the village which was then a popular venue for events. A report of the business carried out stated that; "On Monday evening a large and representative meeting of those interested in the introduction of our own old games was held in Sixmilecross, Mr HK McAleer presiding.

At a time when just six clubs existed in Tyrone, the fact that Beragh should be singled out in a call for the gaelic games to be started there emphasises the importance of the area in nationalist activity

"It was unanimously decided to establish a gaelic football club for the Beragh and Sixmilecross districts and the following officials were appointed - President - Mr J Corrigan, vice-president and treasurer, HK McAleer, captain, Mr Hugh Owens, vice-captain, Mr Mick McCann, secretary, Mr Patrick Rodgers, committee - Messrs Joseph Kerr, James Canavan, J McGillion, James Shields, Owen Mullin and Willie Mullan.

"Arrangements were made as to the future working of the club and members and sympathisers were requested to muster in full force in McElduff's Holm (temporary grounds) on next Sunday evening and show by their presence that they are willing to give either moral or material support to Irish Ireland pastimes."

The Mid-Tyrone League controversy

With the establishment of the Wolfe Tones, one of the first tasks was to provide a regular programme of games for those interested in playing. An initial decision seems to have been made to play in the East Tyrone League and on February 3rd they were listed to meet Coalisland Owen Roes.

While a meeting was held and subscriptions opened for the procurement of a Cup, the Wolfe Tones don't appear to have taken much involvement subsequently. However, some matches did take place and the newly formed Aughnacloy provided the opposition on February 18th, with the South Tyrone team travelling to Sixmilecross and returning home happy at a 1-6 to 0-8 victory.

It was a disappointing result for the Wolfe Tones, especially since they had gone 1-2 to no score ahead in the opening stages after losing the toss. With no record existing of

The Market House, the venue for that famous first meeting of the Sixmilecross Wolfe Tones in January 1906

Aughnacloy having competed in the Mid-Tyrone League that season, this game may either have been a friendly or taken place in the East Tyrone League.

Nevertheless, what is certain, is that the focus of the Wolfe Tones was fixed on the Mid-Tyrone League. It is not clear whether they played any games prior to a Mid-Division semi-final tie arranged for April 14th against Killyclogher.

From the throw-in in that match, Sixmilecross pressed hard and were boosted by a goal that saw them lead by 1-3 to 0-1 at half-time. The pace was maintained in the second half when the Wolfe Tones doubled their lead despite playing against the breeze. The Ulster Herald reported:

"The game was a very enjoyable one and would have been much more so if there had been less unnecessary shouting and arguing. That is a feature in our games which must disappear as there is nothing more calculated to injure their success and to bring discredit on the great national body under whose name those games are played."

That victory should have seen Sixmilecross through to the final of the competition, but instead their early enthusiasm was hit by an appeal from Killyclogher centred on the old chestnut of soccer.

The Killyclogher team won an initial protest against the Wolfe Tones for playing 'Association' players. A counter-appeal on the grounds that Killyclogher played an unregistered player resulted in a replay of

41

> the contingents arrived in Beragh from early morning on five special trains run by the Train Company from Strabane, Cookstown, Dungannon and Pomeroy and all the intermediate stations

the game taking place - a match that the previously defeated Killyclogher won by 2-5 to 1-7.

Then, for some reason, there was a second replay on May 1st, 1906, which Killyclogher won by four points to three. A goal chance near the end was saved by their goalkeeper - and they went on to defeat Letteree in the final.

A Cross reader writes

It is clear that the introduction of gaelic games to the area made an immediate impact. This was evidenced by the enthusiasm for those early games which finally afforded players and officials the opportunity to become directly involved in an Association enjoying rapid growth throughout Tyrone at the time.

Just weeks after the formation of the Wolfe Tones, a reader of the Ulster Herald from Ballintrain praised the efforts being made to promote gaelic games and condemned those in Beragh who continued their involvement in foreign games.

Signed 'A Neighbour's Child (Not a twin),' the letter published in the edition of February 3rd of 1906, the reader expresses their disgust at the holding of a Concert in Beragh on January 19 under the auspices of the Association Football Club.

"In the neighbouring village of Sixmilecross, the young men have cast the foreign games aside like old shoes - and ill fitting, corn provoking 'brogues' at that - and adopted the native and, if I may say so, indigenous games and pastimes of their own country.

"I hope soon to see it recorded that Beragh's youths have followed the manly, wholesome, Irish example set by their friends across the parish mearing."

20,000 at 1906 AOH Demonstration

Further evidence of the central role being played by Sixmilecross and Beragh in nationalist affairs of the time is provided by a report on the Annual August 15th Ancient Order of Hibernians Demonstration. The event in 1906 was hosted by Beragh and Sixmilecross, and drew an amazing crowd of 20,000 men, comprising a total of 75 Divisions who proceeded in line along the route between the two villages.

The report of the event states that "the contingents arrived in Beragh from early morning on five special trains run by the Train Company from Strabane, Cookstown, Dungannon and Pomeroy and all the intermediate stations."

Praise was heaped on the efficiency of the arrangements carried out by the Station Masters, Mr Rold, Mr Browne and Mr D Finnegan, with the procession forming in Beragh before making the journey to Sixmilecross.

Some idea of exactly how big the event was can be guaged from the fact that the authorities were described as taking the precaution of having an extra 21 police brought in under the command of Head Constable Sheehy of the Royal Irish Constabulary from Kildare.

Letters of apology were read, from among others, John Redmond, the then leader of the Irish Party, and the overwhelming desire of the meeting was that the country should be ruled by an 'Irish Parliament with an Executive Government responsible to Irish Public Opinion.'

A demand was made for Catholics to be placed on an equal educational footing and there was a call for an Act of Parliament to sort out the land issue.

The meeting also reiterated the whole-hearted support and sympathy of the AOH for the Gaelic League and the GAA, with a call for them to use every available means in their power to forward their ends and to support the industrial movement in a practical and thorough manner.

Some idea of the colour and spectacle of the occasion can be caught from the report which described the scene around the two villages on that Wednesday over 100 years ago.

"The procession, moving in serried ranks, was more than a mile in length, and took over an hour to pass a given point. The weather, though rather gloomy in the morning, turned out very fine and everything favoured the gathering.

> The procession, moving in serried ranks, was more than a mile in length, and took over an hour to pass a given point

"Beautiful arches bearing words of welcome spanned the streets in Beragh and Sixmilecross and the entire proceedings were of the most animating character. The meeting was held on a beautiful hillside above the village of Sixmilecross, which commanded a splendid view of the country stretching to the south and west."

Keeping the GAA going

GAA activity continued steadily after the initial enthusiasm of the early months receded to the normality of regular games. While the Association continued to face severe difficulties, the general trend was one of competitions running from autumn to spring with a lay-off in winter time.

On-field action often gave way to the greater priority of farm work during the summer months but there was no let-up in the enthusiasm of the Sixmilecross Wolfe Tones when the 1906-07 Mid-Tyrone League began in the autumn.

Things were becoming more organised. Teams wishing to enter the competitions were requested to affiliate with the County Board and register their players, and the Sixmilecross Wolfe Tones held a general meeting of members at the end of November.

At it, on Thursday November 22nd, the following officials were elected for the incoming season. President and Treasurer - Mr HK McAleer, Vice-President, Mr P Mullan, Secretary, Mr J McGillion, captain, Mr James Slane, vice-captain, Mr John Owens, committee Messrs Owen Mullan, Mick Tierney and the officials.

The gaelic season had opened with a high-scoring Tournament match against Omagh Sarsfields on October 27th. It finished 0-19 to 0-15 for the Wolfe Tones, who were thanked by the host club, St Patrick's Cappagh, for their help in organising the tournament.

On the competitive front, things were less successful as the Wolfe Tones lost both their opening games to the St Patrick's. The first at the beginning of December resulted in a 0-5 to 0-4 loss, while a week or so later the Killyclogher side again emerged winners.

Their fortunes did improve, though, when they defeated Young Irelands by 1-4 to 0-1 and their form continued to improve in the new year when they defeated Letteree by 1-6 to 0-4 and Sarsfields by 2-8 to 0-2 a month later. A 1-9 to 0-1 defeat was suffered at the hands of Dromore Young Irelands, but the team was said to have played well in defence during their 0-8 each draw with United Gaels in March.

The League programme concluded with a 'red-letter' day in gaelic football circles at the end of March at Castle Holm in Omagh. Games took place between Omagh Sarsfields and Sixmilecross and between St Patrick's of North Cappagh and Letteree's United Gaels and they were described as the most spirited of the season.

"Sarsfields and Wolfe Tones took the field first and the result was a very fast and exciting game, particularly during the opening twenty minutes when it would be a very difficult matter to say which would come out on top with the honours," the correspondent wrote.

Jamie Slane, Sixmilecross Wolfe Tones player and later official. He is pictured here with his daughter-in-law and wife of Ollie, Madeline.

"The Sarsfields were in tip-top form and never played a better game even though they had not a full team on the field. In the second half they completely outmanoeuvred the Sixmilecross men and kept them in their own territory during the greater part of the time."

Hardly much wonder, then, that the Wolfe Tones were defeated on a score of 0-12 to 0-4. Their disappointment was compounded by the fact that they had defeated the Sarsfields comfortably a few weeks earlier.

The impact of that defeat was undoubtedly negative and may explain why no record exists of them having played St Patrick's in the semi-final of the McAnespy Cup in May. Omagh and Killyclogher duly progressed to the final and efforts to stage the Mid-Tyrone League in the autumn floundered.

A hectic end to the decade

It would seem that League activity did not resume until the middle of 1908 , the stop-start nature of gaelic games at the time resulting in a considerable delay in getting things off the ground again. However, that didn't prevent the Sixmilecross Wolfe Tones from maintaining their efforts to promote all things gaelic.

On Friday January 31st, a Concert was held at Brackey in aid of Sixmilecross Gaelic Football Club with the purpose of clearing expenses incurred through participation in the McAnespie Cup.

This account of the event suggests that the 'Irish-Ireland movement' was taking root in the Beragh parish and particularly in the Sixmilecross area. "The Gaelic code has come to stay about Sixmilecross, and those who do not like it can only look on and grin and bear it."

Fr McArdle, the Parish Priest said that he 'was particularly anxious to associate himself and show sympathy with the Gaels of Sixmilecross in their efforts to put a new soul into the country.'

Duff's Holm outside Sixmilecross which was the venue for early Wolfe Tones matches and the County Finals of 1908 and 1914

Concerts were, of course, all the rage at the time and the year ended with one at a spacious granary lent by Thomas Montague RDC in Altmamuskin. Dance music was supplied by the Clery brothers and renditions included 'No Irish Wanted Here' and the 'Colleen Bawn' by James Clery, 'I Love Old Ireland still' and 'Robert Emmett' by Charles Donnelly, Beragh, and a beautiful rendition of 'Killarney' by the Misses Quinn of Carrickmore.

Listed as Secretary of the Club, HK McAleer represented the Wolfe Tones, one of twelve clubs in existence at the time which attended the Tyrone AGM. They might well have purchased a GAA football Rule Book at it, then on offer at the princely sum of 3d.

In August the Beragh GAA Sports were held, with an organising committee headed by joint secretaries, WH Healy, P Maguire and D Conway. The event took place at Cooley Park on Sunday August 20th when various athletic events were among the competitions.

However, in contrast to the early years of the century, patronage by both sides of the community, at least in the organisational structure, seems to have been missing. The changed outlook is clear from the report of the event carried in the Ulster Herald a week later.

"Never before did Tyrone take such a prominent place in the arena of sport as during the present year. Numerous have been the sports meetings promoted throughout the county during the past few months.

"The very same can, without hesitation, be said of the Beragh Gaelic Sports which were held on Sunday last. Indeed, the success of the meeting was far beyond the most sanguine expectations of the promoters. Notwithstanding various difficulties, the most prominent of which was the rather unfavourable weather conditions, the sports were all that could be desired."

Winners came from Carrickmore, Fintona, Omagh, Dungannon and Ballygawley, with P and D Maguire of Leap View coming out first and second respectively in the weight throwing competition.

Twelve months later the event was held at the end of July 1909 when the level of competition prompted the Ulster Herald correspondent to remark that GAA athletes and their supporters were well represented.

"It is to be hoped that Sunday's sports will be the forerunner of similar sports held under the same auspices and equally as successful and popular. GAA sports, for more reasons than one, deserve the whole-hearted public support.

"The Association stands for the encouragement and popularisation of our national games and pastimes. But it stands for more, for its grand central object is to re-win and maintain the Gael's dominance and superiority in the field of athletics. Its task is to bring in the sinew and brawn of the nation, for by the practice of and the recognition of our national games, only can we hope to effect the long desired, physical regeneration of our sons."

Appeal and counter-appeal leads to county decline

By the autumn of 1908 the Wolfe Tones were fulfilling at least one of the key aims of that particular writer. They opened their Mid-Tyrone League programme with a victory when they were 1-2 to 0-1 winners over Fintona at the end of November. The report of the game states that "F Cleary in goal for the homesters was safe, B Rodgers and H Donnelly played a splendid defence game. Slane was inclined to be rough at times and Cleary was the best of the forwards who were generally weak around goal. Tierney, Devlin, Donaghey and Mullin played a very good game."

Sixmilecross were now in second place in the Omagh District League behind Dromore Athletic and St Patrick's Killyclogher. However,

> " Never before did Tyrone take such a prominent place in the arena of sport as during the present year. Numerous have been the sports meetings promoted throughout the county during the past few months "

47

their fortunes were put in doubt when Fintona lodged a protest against the team which was to have some repercussions.

While the reason for the move was not mentioned, the matter was later heard and adjourned for six weeks at a meeting of the Board in December. A refixture was subsequently ordered, a move that prompted the Sixmilecross delegate, Bernard Rodgers, to say that they would be appealing the decision of the County Board.

An interesting aside to the competitive activities also came that autumn when Sixmilecross had the honour of playing against the new Pomeroy Emmetts Club. That game played on November 8 was Pomeroy's first ever. It took place at Sixmilecross and was described as "being a very interesting and exciting contest.

Wins either side of the new year over Rapparees maintained the form of the Wolfe Tones in the League as matters slowed down due to various appeals. Eventually, protests by Sixmilecross against both Davitts and Omagh Athletic were withdrawn.

At the meeting of the League in May, Bernard Rodgers remarked that the "withdrawal was being made to ensure that the competition could be finished and also to preserve what he said was "a true gaelic feeling between the clubs."

To applause for their decision, the Board Chairman, HK McAleer, said "the Wolfe Tones deserved the best of thanks for the very unselfish manner and the grand gaelic spirit which their actions displayed."

Some idea of the appeal of gaelic football at that time can be seen from the fact that a number of the players came from the Protestant community. The list of members registered at the 1909 Convention included Thomas James McLaren and Robert McAllister and Robert McQuade.

Thomas James McLaren, who was among those Wolfe Tones players who had previously taken part in soccer, lined out for the club in a number of games at the time and often recounted stories of his involvement to his son, Lexi.

"HK McAleer started the team in Sixmilecross and my father used to tell me about them going to Newtownstewart once. They were beaten and I think they resolved after that loss that they wouldn't be beaten again," he said.

> " An interesting aside to the competitive activities also came that autumn when Sixmilecross played against the newly formed Pomeroy Emmetts Club "

"Jimmy Slane was playing as well. It was a man called Peter McGinn, who worked at my father's who helped him to play. You see you weren't allowed to do anything on a Sunday, so they yoked a horse, met up at the top of the Cross Street and went to the match - at Pomeroy I think it was.

"Peter McGinn was told to stay at the horse and cart all the time and when the match was over my father went straight home. He changed his clothes on the way home. The soccer seemed to become more popular again then and I remember him telling me that they used to play it on the gaelic field. My father mentioned to me that himself and Jamie Slane used to be talking about this."

> The signs of decline in Tyrone generally were beginning to show and, although there was a hive of activity at the beginning of 1909, things fell away subsequently

The signs of decline in Tyrone generally were beginning to show and, although there was a hive of activity at the beginning of 1909, things fell away subsequently. The departure of a number of prominent officials like Michael V O'Nolan and Cathal O'Toole was undoubtedly a factor, although political events such as the 1910 Tyrone Elections and the re-emergence of soccer could also explain the lack of organised gaelic games for a number of years.

Soccer had been present in the area for much of that first decade of the 20th Century and in 1908 the 'soccerites' of Beragh were described as having spent the Christmas week engaged in a number of challenge games.

On Christmas Day Beragh Rangers had Dungannon Rovers as visitors, winning by 5-2 with Michael McCann acting as referee. Then, on the following day, junior club Belfast Fountainville visited the village by train to take on Beragh Scorchers.

"The day was extremely cold and stormy, but this did not prevent the local followers of the game from turning out as they did - en masse," a report of the game stated.

It goes on to relate how Beragh won by six goals to two and that afterwards the visitors were entertained by the committee of the Beragh club in the evening and a programme of music and dancing was enjoyed by all. This was the second visit of the Belfast club to Beragh and so well pleased were they with their trips that they decided to come again at some future date.

Other activities

For those whose interests did not include matters sporting, other activities included the regular productions staged by the Beragh Dramatic Club. Among them was the staging in January 1909 of an historical play said to have been the equal of those performed by first-class companies.

Their achievements in the past had earned the club a rather enviable reputation as clever dramatists and the high appreciation in which they stood was manifested by the large audiences that attended.

James Maxwell Remackin found drowned in the River Cooley, near Beragh. Estimated that the body must have been in the river for three or four days.

"Indeed, the Beragh artistes are beyond criticism and are deserving of every credit and encouragement, and it is only to be hoped that they will produce the play in some of the surrounding towns, thus giving the public an opportunity of appreciating the entertainment which is in every way worthy of their appreciation and support," one review said.

The artistes given such high praise included: Mr P Rodgers (Major Bleakley), Mr J Donnelly (Lieut Somers), F Rodgers (Sergeant Smith), J Healy (Corporal Diskey), C Donnelly (Edward O'Brien), J Conway (Mark Tape), J McKinney (Handel Squall), J Cleary (Miles O'Donnell), J Slane (P Kevin), H McElhinney (B Nolan), P Rodgers (P Murdock), R McGarrity (Lanty O'Flaherty), F Cleary (Norah O'Donnell), Miss Nellie Kerr (Kathleen, betrothed to Corporal Diskey), Miss E Donnelly.

Chapter Three
1910 - 1920
Through Troubled Times

Chapter Three
1910 - 1920

THE initial enthusiasm which sparked the early dramatic growth for the GAA in Tyrone from 1903 onwards had died away by the end of the decade. Organised activity effectively disappeared throughout the county apart from a few isolated pockets or instances of gaelic football.

The Cookstown and District Gaelic Football League took place between March and July 1911 between teams straddling the border between Tyrone and Derry. And, a number of cultural events like Summer Schools indicated that, while GAA and gaelic games were struggling, the interest in things Irish was being maintained.

Handball in Pomeroy appeared to be thriving and in September 1911 the handballers of the area issued an offer to play any team within a 30 mile radius. Their appeal had come after a challenge match against Moy on September 10th, but it seems that the call was not answered in the Drumduff, Brackey, Beragh or other localities where the game was practiced at the time.

However, gaelic games were still being played in the parish and two instances from the 1910s were recounted in the special Silver Jubilee Commemorative Magazine published by Roscavey Primary School in 1991.

Jimmy McCrory, then aged 93 and who would have attended the school during the first decade of the twentieth century, recalled how he had broken his arm while kicking football in the meadow opposite the school when Peter Mellon had fallen on top of him.

Others, too, recounted stories associated with the playing of football around that time, but perhaps the most interesting of all concerns the playing of hurling

Others, too, recounted stories associated with the playing of football around that time, but perhaps the most interesting of all concerns the playing of hurling.

Felix Owens, who died in 1998 at the age of 98 and who was a stalwart member of the first Red Knights team in the 1920s, attended Roscavey School. In an interview for the Roscavey Magazine, he told his grandson Sean McMahon, about the boys playing hurling.

"Sometimes we would get a stick with an end on it and we played 'Camman,' a dangerous game, because we played with stones and it was a bit like hurley. We also played football, we had no ball, so someone would take the pocket out of his jacket and stuff it with moss, then he'd sew it up. It was a hard ball to play with."

While those pupils of Roscavey Primary School laid the foundations for the future progress of the GAA through their impromptu games, the attentions of those who had previously been involved in gaelic games at adult level were perhaps drawn towards other matters. Towards the political scene, for example, where the 1911 Tyrone Elections were keenly contested, with the Sixmilecross ward sending representatives to Omagh Rural Council.

Polling was relatively close, with Patrick McCartan gained 149 votes to HK McAleer's 135 and the 109 for JH Anderson.

It is unclear now whether one particular nationalist in the area did in fact gain a vote. He was John McSorley of Clogherney who claimed one for the first time and went to court to prove his entitlement. Taking the book in his left hand, he claimed a vote and said that he was over 100 years of age.

On being questioned as to his age, he replied that he knew he was over 100, but did not know his exact age. Having repeated the words of the oath in Court he added "to the best of my knowledge." He said that he had been to Scotland and England.

The concerns of those elected included the introduction of the new Pension and the introduction of Home Rule which prompted renewed activity from the United Irish League at the time.

The re-organisation of the UIL in Tyrone resulted in a meeting of Nationalists of Beragh and the surrounding districts in March 1911 when the new Chairman, James O'Connor of Clogherney said that, although they were on the eve of Home Rule, it was their duty as nationalists to maintain the National Organisation in its full strength and attend to the important work of registration.

Aughnaglea School pictured soon after it was burned in July 1910.

Speaking at a meeting of the UIL in Sixmilecross around the same time, HK McAleer pointed out that he had nothing but loathing and contempt for the "miserable squad of factionists, self seekers and Catholic rotters who allied themselves with Unionists in what he termed the disruption of the National movement in Tyrone.

Despite the political atmosphere, though, many still lacked basic facilities, as highlighted by the debate on improving the provision of Sixmilecross Waterworks which raged during the summer of 1912.

A meeting of Omagh Rural Council in August of that year was told by HK McAleer that there had been a leakage from the reservoir since it was constructed 25 years before - in 1887. This resulted in a shortage and sometimes complete absence of water every dry season.

"Last year they had no water and were obliged to get it from a private supply and were also obliged to obtain water which had been condemned years ago," he said. "All the other towns and villages in the rural district had got improvements carried out to water and sewerage while the members of the Council from Sixmilecross district never interfered so it is only reasonable that Sixmilecross should get its water supply improved. As a matter of fact, there is as much water at present flowing away from the reservoir as could supply three or four villages."

The following autumn regret was expressed that the labourers and partisans in the area did not urge for better housing.

Sixmilecross GAA to the fore - 1912-1915

It is fair to conclude that many of those who had been to the fore in the organisation of GAA activities during the first decade of the century bemoaned the subsequent collapse of the Association.

By 1912 the Irish-Ireland movement was again springing to life in the Beragh and Sixmilecross areas and elsewhere. In January the AOH was receiving subscriptions for its Hall Building Fund and Easter Monday that year saw a concert at Eskerbouy at which the songs were said to "clearly indicate that the Irish-Ireland movement has taken root at the expense of the elimination of music hall ditties."

The first part of the programme was brought to a close with the singing of 'A Nation Once Again' and the greatest event of the night was said to be an exhibition of step-dancing by a Mr McCullagh. Owen Mullan was MC for the evening.

The GAA presence was still to the fore, however. The Sixmilecross Sports, licensed under GAA Rules and took place on Sunday August 11th on a field kindly provided by Bernard Rodgers.

The GAA committee included Patrick Rodgers, James Slane and HK McAleer, and attracted large numbers from as far away as Omagh, Cookstown, Dungannon and Irvinestown.

Music was provided by the Tir Eoghain Pipers and the events included the 100 Yards Flat Handicap, 330 Yards Boys Race, won by P Maguire, and the Three Mile Cycle Handicap which was described as the most exciting race of the day.

Rodgers' Holm was again the venue for the GAA Sports a year later when the admission was six pence. The event undoubtedly provided the opportunity to assess the prospects for the re-organisation of gaelic games which at that time were in the hands of Sixmilecross Wolfe Tones.

Their annual meeting was held in the autumn of 1913, with a concert and ball in aid of the club being held on Friday November 7th in the Market Hall, kindly granted for the occasion by Mr Simon Devlin.

It was also decided to purchase a set of jerseys, the colour selected being orange and green and a large attendance was expected on the following Sunday for practice to decide who would play against Dungannon.

The hope was expressed that all youths who had not already joined the club would do so and assist in making the Wolfe Tones a success in Sixmilecross.

HK McAleer at a meeting of the UIL in Sixmilecross said that he had nothing but loathing and contempt for the miserable squad of factionists, self seekers and Catholic rotters who allied themselves with Unionists in what could be termed the disruption of the Nationalist movement in Tyrone.

The club was also to the forefront on the county-wide scene and was one of only four which made attempts to reform the Tyrone County Board in July 1913 and at a subsequent meeting B Fitzimmons was appointed Vice-President. Two more meetings were held in Sixmilecross as the re-organised Wolfe Tones began to make their mark.

September saw a public meeting of those interested in gaelic games in Omagh, a further gathering was held two weeks later in Killyclogher and the third took place in Sixmilecross in mid-October.

Just four clubs were represented - Sixmilecross, Pomeroy, Killyclogher and Coalisland - with Sixmilecross making up the bulk of those attending in the presence of HK McAleer, Bernard Rodgers and Barney Fitzsimmons.

Permission was received for the club to hold their postponed match against Dungannon on October 26th, when the twelve clubs who had signalled their intention to affiliate would be asked to send representatives.

That month also saw the completion of the County Board reorganisation, with HK McAleer being elected President and Barney Fitzimmons Vice-President, a position he later withdrew from in order to make the Committee more representative.

The Sports Ground in Ballykeel was the venue for the match against Dungannon, with the visitors travelling to the venue by motor car. While heavy rain made the ground slippery, both teams displayed great enthusiasm from the start. Chances were missed by both, Dungannon led by three points to one at half-time and, while Sixmilecross put up a splendid fight on the resumption, they lost in the end by 0-6 to 0-3.

> " The club was also to the forefront on the county-wide scene and was one of only four which made attempts to reform the Tyrone County Board in July 1913 "

Action continued on November 9th when Sixmilecross lost to Fintona following an interesting game. December saw them down to play St Patrick's in the new Tyrone League.

With the County Board now operating again, the way was clear for the formation of a new League competition. Sixmilecross was represented by James Slane at a meeting in February 1914 to outline fixtures for the new Tyrone League.

On-field action

The opening game in 1914 for the Wolfe Tones was against the newly formed Ballygawley. It took place at Greenhill before a large attendance, with T Droogan in charge.

The Ulster Herald of March 7th reported that the Wolfe Tones started best, their forwards playing a good game and keeping up the pressure. They were rewarded with a goal within ten minutes and, while Ballygawley tried hard to equalise, the stonewall defence of Rodgers and Slane, assisted by Cleary in goals, stood firm.

Beragh Creamery pictured in 1913

However, McGorham did equalise soon after the restart and the scene was set for an exciting finish when Sixmilecross settled down again. In the end, though, Ballygawley scored a late point to win by 1-1 to 0-3.

By mid-March Sixmilecross trailed Errigal Kerrogue and Fintona on the League table, but they then defeated the Davitts by 0-4 to 0-2 with HK McAleer as referee. Subsequent results set up a decider against Errigal Ciaran on April 12th, with the winners to go through to meet the East Tyrone Champions.

Having a strong breeze behind them, Sixmilecross pressed hard in the first half and won three fifties. Jamie Slane was described as having made bad use of them. So, the sides were still scoreless at half-time. Although the Wolfe Tones defence stood firm on the restart, the St Kieran's still got a vital early goal.

They almost got another from the kick-out before Sixmilecross rallied, "the Wolfe Tones getting away and scored per Kane amid great enthusiasm." Nevertheless, it was all to no avail as Joe McKenna scored the winning point near the finish.

Evidence of the extent of GAA activity during the period can be guaged from the fact that Sixmilecross, along with Fintona and Ballygawley, played a total of eight games. The League was eventually won by the Fintona Davitts, who then went on to win their

School attendance officers tells Sixmilecross Petty Sessions that Aughnaglea school had the worst attendance in the district in the last six months.

first ever County title at the popular Sixmilecross venue in June, 1914.

It was the fourth and final County decider to be held at the Ballykeel venue, which was probably chosen for its easy access to the Railway line and central location for the clubs then involved in the GAA in Tyrone.

Another key factor was its suitability for spectators, the layout of the land being ideal to viewing major matches in those early years, with a higher piece of ground allowing spectators a fine chance to watch the action.

Ned Rafferty

A first-hand account of those early days of the Wolfe Tones was given by Ned Rafferty when he was interviewed by Frank Rodgers in 1980. Almost seventy years on from pre First World War, Ned recalled how their matches were usually tough and hard, especially when they travelled to the Loughshore.

"I remember some of the players who were around at that time. Jamie Slane was the captain, there was a man by the name of McCabe from Monaghan, Johnny Mullin of Foremass, Tom 'California' Mullan of Foremass and John McGarrity from Whitebridge, Fallaghern," he said.

"Barney Rodgers would let the nerves get to him. There was a man called Fitzimmons from Kerry and Jim Mallon who was originally from Dungannon.

"But going up to the Loughshore, well you could take your coffin with you. The men up there were over six foot tall and as hard as iron. Trillick had a good team, too, and we often played them at Rodgers' Holm.

"I remember the first league match that we played was against Dungannon, they beat us well that date. Rodgers scored the Cross goal and I think Fitzimmons scored three points for Dungannon. The team played nearly every Sunday and travelled on bikes. There was a time we went to the Loughshore and left after First Mass in Carrickmore to cycle there."

Ned Rafferty, who played in the Wolfe Tones teams in the period after 1910, goes on to provide a fascinating insight into the behind the scenes activity that even then surrounded the organisation of gaelic games locally.

"Jamie Slane was a great organiser and player, Jim Cleary of Beragh was another man who played. And we trained too on the Sundays that there wasn't a match. We'd put up the goals and play the backs against the forwards.

"At that time the matches were a big event and we had plenty of support. You made your own way to the game and always went to Mass first. The matches were very sporting and the travelling team to the Cross always got tea in Devlin's Eating House. The meetings were held there too in the Dining Room.

"Tom California was the best. He was like a steel bar. Everybody had football boots and shorts. The boots cost 5/- and we had ankle protectors which cost 7/-. The togs were made at home from flour bags."

> The boots cost 5/- and we had ankle protectors which cost 7/-. The togs were made at home from flour bags

A change in focus - The Irish National Volunteers

Sixmilecross' final match of that 1913-14 season took place against Errigal Ciaran in the County Championship on May 12th. But by then the attentions and energies of the young people of the area were switching to a different arena as the newly formed Irish National Volunteers became extremely active locally.

BERAGH FAIR.

Large crowds attend the Beragh Fair in 1911

Branches of the volunteers were established in Sixmilecross, Altamuskin, Dunmoyle and Lurganbuoy, Drumduff and Brackey, Clogherney, Beragh and Donaghanie in response to the earlier formation of the Ulster Volunteer Force, set up to oppose the introduction of Home Rule in Ireland.

With the support of the Ancient Order of Hibernians, the Volunteers immediately began drilling. On May 17th, five days after that game against Errigal Ciaran, a parade of the Volunteers took place to Beragh Chapel and it appears that the training was thorough.

An ex-army man conducted twice weekly drills at Maguire's of the Leap Bridge, Hugh Rodgers, a non-commissioned officer in the United States Army who went through 'the fiery ordeal of the Philippine war, instructed those at Sixmilecross and Mr Joseph Gallagher, an ex-army sergeant with Boer War experience, carried out the duty for the Drumduff and Brackey branch.

Roger Casement, who visited Beragh in May 1914

"The movement has been taken up very warmly in the Sixmilecross district, as evident by the large roll of membership and also by the blessing and encouragement given by the mothers and fathers to their sons to drill and get into the most effective state of military mobilisation if required," the Ulster Herald reported.

"It would seem that the dream of the poet has been realised as in this National Volunteer organisation,' we have the young men with their sinewy hands and the old men with their prayers."

The Visit of Roger Casement

The enthusiasm of the new Volunteers was rewarded by a morale-boosting visit by Roger Casement to Beragh and Sixmilecross at the end of May, 1914, just weeks after the passing of the Home Rule Bill and only a month prior to the beginning of World War One.

> 27/11/1915 - Passing of Barney Martin, born in 1818 and one of seven brothers born at Cooley Sweep and remembered the dreadful cholera of 1833 and the famine.

A turnout of men to meet Casement, who was accompanied by Dr Patrick McCartan and Professor Eoin McNeill, was described as thrilling and amazing.

"Company after company of drilled men swung along the dusty road and saluted the distinguished visitors. By walk and evolution they showed how assiduously they had trained and how efficient it is possible for a citizen force to become if they have put their hearts in the glorious work of drilling for the defence of their country's liberty."

The Volunteers then marched to the parade ground for inspection before speeches were given by HK McAleer, Dr McCartan, Roger Casement, Professor McNeill and FJ O'Connor. Sir Roger told the gathering that the fewer speeches and the more rifles they had in future the better it would be for their country.

Special May devotions were conducted by Fr McArdle in Beragh Chapel to coincide with the visit of Roger Casement, special seats being reserved for the Volunteers in what was described as the largest muster of Irish Volunteers ever held in Tyrone.

HK McAleer led the men to the chapel, where they were congratulated for their efficiency by Fr McArdle. A feature of the parade on that Sunday May 31st, 1914, was the attendance of a corp of Red Cross nurses 'composed of the young ladies of the district, who marched in procession wearing white armlets with a red cross.'

A cycle corp also took part in the procession, which included the Clogherney, Eskra, Beragh, Dunmoyle, Altamuskin, Sixmilecross, Donaghanie, Drumduff, Tremogue, Carrickmore and Errigal Kieran companies.

World War One and the 1916 Rising

Civil War over the Home Rule issue did not materialise as many anticipated in 1914. Instead, the outbreak of the First World War resulted in the Bill being temporarily shelved as the resources of the British Government turned to the battlefields of France and Belgium.

Preparations for World War One included a recruitment drive in Sixmilecross

The members of the Ulster Volunteer Force were quick to join the recruitment drive famously summed up by the 'Your Country Needs You' banners. The war was seen by many, including those in Ireland, as a fight for the small nations, and the pages of the Ulster Herald - which published an evening edition for a period - were filled with reports of battles and news of local men at the front.

Private John McKenna, Benchran, thanked the people of Beragh for their gift to him at the front in January 1915 and in June the casualty list included Edward Mulholland, Donaghanie, killed in action on May 16th.

The Irish National Volunteers, who were closely connected to the Irish Party of John Redmond, saw their participation in the war as a chance to prove their worthiness to have the Home Rule Bill brought into effect when hostilities ended.

Accordingly, the Volunteers were urged to join the Irish Regiments, including the Irish Division. To this end a series of recruitment rallies were held during the later part of 1915.

In late August, the Sixmilecross Volunteers were commissioned to procure rifles and ammunition without further delay. Captain Eckersdeley was to visit on August 29th, when it was hoped that the local companies would turn out in full force to be drilled.

Full page advertisements were taken out in the Ulster Herald in the autumn calling on Irishmen "not to permit their regiments to be kept up to strength by other than Ireland's son." The campaign reached Sixmilecross to coincide with the half-yearly fair on Friday November 19th.

Fourteen young girls paraded the street with the inscription 'Irish Volunteers - We won't have Conscription' emblazoned on their clothes in bold gold letters.

Among the speakers at a meeting in the afternoon was Rev S Stuart, who said: "It has been said by some people in Ireland, especially the Roman Catholic section, that if the Germans came to Ireland, they (the Catholics) would be all right.

"These people had never made a bigger mistake in their lives than this because what had the Germans done with Poland, which was almost entirely Roman Catholic."

Another speaker opined that those who sought Home Rule should not fight for the British Empire, this would show that they had really been in earnest and that they were capable of ruling Ireland, he said

Exact figures on how many eventually joined up are difficult to get and later the events of Easter 1916 ensured that the nationalists of the north were reluctant to publicise their involvement in the First World War. By then, attitudes were hardening and the continuing involvement of the British in the War was seen as Ireland's opportunity in more ways than one.

The 1916 Rising

Attempts to ensure that self-Government for Ireland was achieved continued into 1916 when the United Irish League locally got a new impetus. The reorganisation of the Sixmilecross Branch took place at the end of January when calls for it to be kept in existence until Home Rule was in operation were made.

HK McAleer said no changes should be made to the Home Rule act and that their efforts shouldn't be eased until an independent Parliament working for the common good of the people, irrespective of either creed or class, and for the people of the North as well as the South and West of Ireland was established.

"They should show to the people of England and every other part of the Empire that they were determined to carry on the fight and that they would not surrender so long as a single county in Ireland was left outside the operations of the Parliament," he added.

That fight was taken into a new sphere on Easter Monday 1916 with the reading of the Proclamation of the Irish Republic on the steps of the GPO in Sackville Street in Dublin. And, the momentous events of that day echoed throughout the country, including northward to the Beragh area.

During the years prior to the Rising, the Irish National Volunteers were, of course, active locally. Many of its members subsequently became involved in the Irish Republican Brotherhood and prepared to participate in the Rebellion planned for Easter 1916.

Eamon DeValera being led away by armed guards in 1916

The circumstances of those days are well recorded and locally a group of people from the Beragh, Sixmilecross and Carrickmore areas were summoned to congregate at the home of Dr Patrick McCartan in Lurganbouy. However, they were in contact with Dublin and it was through two Beragh women that news of the apparent abandonment of the Rising came through.

Katherine Owens, later wife of GAA official FH Rodgers, and her sister Josephine arrived back from Dublin with the information. The assembled gathering was dispersed on that Easter weekend as the Rebellion did in fact go ahead as anticipated.

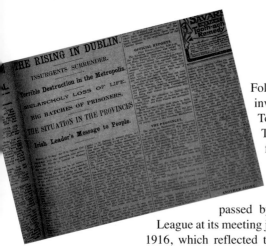

Folklore recounts some of the names of those involved and they included Sixmilecross Wolfe Tones players such as the Mullin brothers, Tom 'Californian' and David, the Rodgers from Sixmilecross and others from the Altamuskin and Dunmoyle localities.

An interesting aside was a resolution passed by the Beragh Branch of the United Irish League at its meeting just days after the Rising on Sunday May 7th, 1916, which reflected the general feeling at the time prior to the executions.

The Ulster Herald reports the events of Easter 1916 in Dublin

Having completed the business of the meeting, a resolution was unanimously passed deploring what was described as "the recent disturbances in Dublin and elsewhere in Ireland."

The resolution went on to state that the UIL was "strongly convinced that the dupers who started the insurrection were led on by the enemies of our country, and now see that it would have been a wiser course if they had followed the advice of the Irish Party, led by Mr John Redmond; and we also endorse the action of Mr Redmond in appealing to the Government to extend clemency to the offenders."

A County Final place lost in the Boardroom

After a year's absence, the struggling GAA in Tyrone reconvened in September 1916 with a meeting in the Town Hall, Pomeroy. Once again the gaels of Sixmilecross were to the fore in the revival which was to last well into the following year and in the summer of that year played Fintona in a challenge matched organised as part of the annual sports.

It was to this backdrop that Hugh Rodgers represented the club at the second meeting of the Board on October 3rd which prompted a sustained spurt of growth during the months that followed. And, at a time of increasing political tension, the Secretary of the Ulster Council, Owen O'Duffy, reminded delegates by letter that politics needed to be kept out of GAA activities.

The Wolfe Tones played Fintona at the beginning of September and, after playing against the breeze in the first half and trailing at half-time by 0-5 to 0-1, came back strongly to draw seven points each.

The team lined out: Goal - J Connor, Backs - B Rodgers, J Mullan, Half-Backs - F Devlin, E Rafferty, J McNamee; Quarter Backs - P McNamee, C McClenaghan; forwards - H Rafferty, J Rodgers, P Farrell, J Farrell, H Hughes.

The team also displayed good form in the Tyrone County Championship competition, scoring a win and draw in the opening two games and going on to enjoy a busy schedule of matches throughout the later part of 1916 and first half of 1917.

As well as competing at the Carrickmore Sports, that autumn saw the Wolfe Tones play Augher, Carrickmore, Kilskeery and Fintona Davitts. The last day of 1916 saw Kilskeery easily defeat the visiting Wolfe Tones, while frost on the Sixmilecross pitch caused the postponement of the match against Carrickmore in the new year.

Devlin Entertainment Centre, a venue for meetings of the Sixmilecross Wolfe Tones in the 1910-1920 period

Later they took on Fintona Davitts and Ballygawley in April and finished joint top of the West Tyrone section of the League with seventeen points along with Kilskeery.

But the competition ended in some controversy when Kilskeery were awarded the title after an appeal to the County Board. It seems that the issue centred on Carrickmore losing the points from a drawn game, the points instead being awarded to Kilskeery in a decision that placed them one ahead of Sixmilecross at the top.

The unhappy Wolfe Tones were not content to let the matter sit, understandably so considering that a County Final place was at stake. Obviously anxious to prove their worth, the club issued a challenge to Kilskeery to play them at the Gaelic Park in Fintona. It is unclear whether or not the game took place, although the extensive coverage given to GAA affairs at the time suggests not, and Kilskeery went on to represent the West in the County Final at Omagh where they lost to Cookstown Brian Og by 3-6 to 2-1.

Patrick Rafferty of Sixmilecross died of heart failure brought on by excitement. Aged 55, he had been attending wedding celebrations for PJ Maguire, Merchant.

Gaelic Sunday in Sixmilecross

The after-shocks of the 1916 Rising dramatically changed the political landscape in Ireland in the following months and year. Sinn Fein, which had been formed in 1905, saw a sustained rise in its influence which culminated in its widespread success at the 1918 Elections.

Its growth was reflected in the Beragh area where a Sinn Fein Club had recently been established. Under the Chairmanship of FH Rodgers, the body held regular meetings and in September 1917 its Chair called on Richard McGhee to resign as MP as it was felt by the group that he did not represent the views of the electorate of Mid-Tyrone.

The social awareness displayed by the club was in evidence during the early part of 1918 when another famine was a real threat. At a meeting on March 16 it was resolved that, because of the scarcity of food and the fear that potatoes might be bought up before the people were supplied, the club should buy in potatoes and stock them so as to make provision for the poor of the district.

The heightening of political tensions also impacted on the GAA as the British Government introduced an order prohibiting the holding of games, athletic events and other activities without a permit. Unsurprisingly, the requirement was almost totally ignored, including in the Beragh and Sixmilecross areas where a number of events in the summer of 1918 were held and were the subject of raids by the Royal Irish Constabulary.

While it is unclear whether Gaelic Sunday, which involved GAA organised matches and athletic meetings throughout the country on the first Sunday in August, was observed in the district, but the previous two weekends saw major sports events and Aeridheacht held locally.

"

The after-shocks of the 1916 Rising dramatically changed the political landscape in Ireland in the following months and year

"

On July 20th the Gaelic League, described as having one of the best organised branches in the country in Beragh, held a 'splendid gaelic festival' on the grounds kindly given by Mr Patrick Owens at Deroar.

Among the attractions was music by the Omagh Sinn Fein Flute Band, the Omagh War Pipers Band and the Aldrummond band. There were also half-hour concerts, athletic sports, whist drives and various sideshows. Another popular event on the day was a match between Fintona Pearses and Omagh Colemans.

Vocal contributions came from the Beragh Gaelic League Choir, under the conductorship of Miss J Owens and including Misses C Kerr, F Kerr, Lizzie Donnelly, A Casey, K Casey, W Donnelly, K Owens and Messrs Francis O'Cleary, Joe Donnelly, Felix Cassidy and Frank Owens.

Speaking towards the close of the proceedings the Omagh-based solicitor, George Murnaghan, reflected the mood of the time when he said that, by helping to promote a knowledge of the Irish Language, national music, singing, dancing and pastimes, they were helping to build up a nation.

A week later the aeridheacht advertised to take place at Ballykeel, was disrupted when a 'large party of military from Omagh' proceeded to take possession of the field. The Ulster Herald account stated:

"Later, a number of police under District Inspector Conlin motored from Omagh. From two o clock onward large numbers approached the field, and some congregated on the road, but they were dispersed by police, who were fully armed, and police scouts were posted all over the district.

"After some time, one of these scouts intimated that the aeridheacht was being held at Deroar, near Beragh, and immediately a party of military, accompanied by police, proceeded to the place and dispersed some people who were congregated on the road. The incident passed off quietly, except that some of those present protested that they had a right to use the public thoroughfare."

The event eventually went ahead at Foremass with an estimated attendance of 2000 who undoubtedly enjoyed the varied programme of singing, story-telling (in Irish), recitation, conversation (in Irish) and athletic and cycling events.

A unidentified schoolgroup from the Beragh parish in the early 1900s

But while those attempts to instill a greater desire for and love of gaelic pastimes didn't always yield the desired success, the Beragh, Sixmilecross and Drumduff localities remained to the forefront in attempting to promote them.

While the state of gaelic games was once again precarious and the cultural events and aeridheachts seem to have diminished in comparison to earlier years, there is clear evidence that there was still a very strong desire for all things Irish including football.

According to Ned Rafferty in that 1980 interview a team was formed in Brackey round about the end of the first World War in 1918. While they did not take part in official competitions, which were virtually non-existent at the time anyway, they did play regular challenge matches.

It is no wonder, then, that in June 1919 it was hoped that GAA clubs would be formed in Sixmilecross and Carrickmore and the Beragh Aeridheacht on July 20th of that year once again promised to be one of the most attractive Irish Ireland events in the country for some time. In addition to vocal and musical competitions, an athletic sports programme and a football match were arranged.

Perhaps the expectation of a large attendance from throughout the country prompted the County Board to hold its meeting in the village on that particular day. However, there was no representation from Sixmilecross, but sports under the auspices of the GAA continued to take place in the parish.

The potential for progress was definitely growing and in the summer of that year the team from Brackey played against Cloughfin, Arvalee and Mullaslin at the Cloughfin Sports on July 19th.

> While they did not take part in official competitions, which were virtually non-existent at the time anyway, they did play regular challenge matches

From our vantage point in the 21st Century it can be stated that by the close of the second decade of the 1900s the people involved in fostering gaelic games and culture in the Sixmilecross and Beragh areas could be reasonably pleased with their progress to date. In that ten years the localities had been among the precious few that had worked hard to sustain the GAA and Irish ideals against all the odds and their work had borne some fruit.

Officials of the Wolfe Tones had been to the forefront of the GAA in Tyrone throughout the 1910-1919 period. Now the mantle would be carried forward just as enthusiastically by new groups as the Twenties dawned.

Chapter Four
1920 - 1930
The First Red Knights

Chapter Four
1920 - 1930

EVENTS that were organised under the auspices of the GAA continued to play a prominent part in the lives of the people of the Beragh parish in the early twenties despite the almost total absence of organised activities on a district or county wide basis.

What was described as the Irish Ireland movement had taken root in the Beragh, Sixmilecross and Brackey areas during the previous two decades. But few could have envisaged, then, how the GAA would go on to become one of the strongest organisations of all after a decade of sustained growth.

The Beragh Shamrocks team of 1925. Back row (left to right) - FH Rodgers, Frank Rafferty, Packie McAleer, Jack Donnelly, Francis Cleary, Cecil Meehan, Joe Donnelly, James Hagan. Middle Row - Micksie Boyle, Harry Owens, Paddy Donaghy, Felix Owens. Front Row - Jim McCann, Hughie Owens, Felix Hughes, Peter McGarrity, Joe Colton

There is plenty of evidence to support the view that the promotion of gaelic games and culture was being enthusiastically embraced locally. In the 1920s the determination of the people to see their ideals fulfilled set them apart from many other areas of Tyrone where those same objectives were being neglected or totally ignored. Just as in the period from 1912 on, the roaring twenties would often see the rest of the county follow the lead of their GAA colleagues in Beragh.

There was positive proof of this as early as 1920 when the local GAA club continued to organise its Aeridheacht Mhor at Sixmilecross. One of the Chief organisers was the Secretary, Michael Donnelly, and the billing for the event included a football match at the end of proceedings.

Admission was one shilling and the other attractions were staples of popular promotions of that time. Athletics disciplines were complimented by a three-legged race, the egg and spoon race, the sack race and one and three mile cycle races.

It is also interesting to note that a similar Aeridheacht Mhor was scheduled for Beragh on the same date. Bands from several parts of Tyrone were due to play, no alcoholic drinks were allowed and in that hot summer organisers would have been confident about the success of their Ceilidh Mhor in the Open Air.

The Troubles

But the enjoyment generated by those GAA events that summer belied the Troubled times of the period. And, while the happenings in Dublin, Belfast and other places are well documented, the Beragh, Sixmilecross and Drumduff areas were not entirely unscathed.

Raids on homes in the district were a regular feature in the tense atmosphere. The premises of Mrs Owens and Joseph Kerr at Beragh were raided on a number of occasions. In July 1921 police entered the homes of the cattle dealer, Joe Donnelly, and Creamery Manager, Patrick Kerr at 6am and proceeded to carry out exhaustive searches. However, nothing was taken away.

That same month the 'A' and 'B' Specials in Beragh were said to have been involved in erecting Orange flags prior to the annual Twelfth commemorations. The 'A' or regular officers were reported to have re-entered the barracks afterwards by the back entrance.

> There is no doubt that the burning of the vehicles would have caused much debate locally, although probably nowhere near as intense as the famed case involving Sixmilecross man, Hugh Rodgers of Sixmilecross and Frank Boyle of Beragh

Another incident, although apparently unrelated to the Troubles, involved the burning of two vans belonging to Inglis and Company of Belfast in August 1920. The vehicles, which were regularly driven by James McKeagney and Peter Shields were taken from Armstrong's yard and set alight using petrol cans which were subsequently found nearby.

Sean Bennett pictured standing beside the Inglis Bread Van. His father and Beragh official, Peter, was employed with the firm from the 1920s.

When found, the points of the shafts and ironwork were practically all that remained of the vehicles, which had been bought in 1918 and valued at around £95. There is no doubt that the burning of the vehicles would have caused much debate locally, although probably nowhere near as intense as the famed case involving Sixmilecross man, Hugh Rodgers of Sixmilecross and Frank Boyle of Beragh.

In the autumn of 1920 the two stood trial for the murder of William McDowell during a robbery in Gilford and the repercussions of the event lasted long after the initial developments which led to their arrest and trial.

It seems that a petition was gathered locally calling for their release and among the signatories were two Protestant clergymen who later in May 1921 were the victims of a number of attacks.

The Ulster Herald reported that: "At the residence of Rev Dr Hunter, Clogherney, the attack made on the house was of a most alarming nature, a bomb being exploded at the front of the building with the result that a glass portico was completely smashed. Fortunately none of the occupants were injured. Offensive epithets were painted on the walls of the house.

Matthew Rodgers, a player of the early 1920s and a witness at the 1926 Court Case.

"The house of the Rev Mr Stutt, Methodist Minister in Beragh, was also attacked, and the following inscription, amongst a number of others painted on the walls. To ___ with Stutt, who allied himself with the Sinn Fein murderers." The correspondent states that the outrages were the cause of great indignation and that several of the Protest signatories had in the meantime received threatening letters.

Subsequent to the events a decree for £50 was awarded to Dr Hunter who at a hearing held in Omagh Quarter Sessions said he had understood the petition to be a memorial to the men and not one calling for a reprieve.

66

They refused to recognise the authority of the so-called Belfast Parliament and affirmed their "unalterable determination to resist its operation by every available means

Paddy Daly, who was later to become well-known for his taxi business, recounted later in life making dummy guns, while Paddy Hackett remembered marching from Clogherney and Roscavey around the same time.

Affairs were, of course, coming to a head on a number of different fronts, not least on the political scene where negotiations culminated in the signing of the Anglo Irish Treaty on December 6th, 1921.

One of its main consequences was the partition of Ireland into the 26 Counties of the Free State and the Six of the new Northern Ireland state. Suffice it's to say that the move generated much debate and concern long before being established in law.

September of 1921 saw the holding of a large and representative meeting in Beragh on the issue and after which a resolution was passed by the parishioners present. They refused to recognise the authority of the so-called Belfast Parliament and affirmed their

FH Rodgers, front left and James McMahon, back left, are pictured in this group from the 1920s.

Peter Bennett and his wife, pictured with their son Sean shortly after his birth in 1920

"unalterable determination to resist its operation by every available means." Speakers included Rev J Devlin and the County Councillors, Matthew Rodgers and John O'Hanrahan.

In 1923, three men from the area, Dan Woods and Peter Mullan of Sixmilecross Joe Donnelly of Beragh were internees on the ship, Argenta.

Triumph and tragedy - the formation of Beragh Red Knights

It is to the backdrop of these dramatic events that the original Beragh Red Knights Club was formed in the autumn of 1921. A matter of weeks after the meeting of parishioners called for Partition and the

Belfast Parliament to be resisted, another group met to re-ignite GAA affairs not only in Beragh but also elsewhere.

Their efforts came at a time when the GAA in Tyrone was virtually non-existent. While 1920 had seen the county compete in the Ulster Championship, the following months were marked by a complete collapse of the organisational and other structures so necessary for the growth of the Association and promotion of gaelic games.

In his book, 'The GAA in Tyrone' Joseph Martin relates how the disruption of normal life arising from the Troubles had serious effects on the operations of the GAA in Tyrone and throughout Ulster. Few seemed interested in taking part in gaelic football and the county wasn't even represented at a meeting to reform the Ulster Council on October 21st, 1921.

Ulster Herald announces a dance at Market Hall, proceeds in aid of the unemployment and deserving poor of Sixmilecross and District.

Perhaps they should have come to Beragh where the desire to promote gaelic games was still very evident. Indeed, that Ulster Council reformation meeting took place a week after a similar event in the village.

A large number of interested people attended the formation meeting which was held on Saturday night, October 15th, to organise a gaelic football meeting. The report the following week, one of only a few GAA items in the Ulster Herald that year, went on to state that "the officers elected for the coming season were Mr John Owens, captain, Mr Harry Owens, Treasurer, and Mr Jamie Hagan, Secretary."

"A selection committee for the team was then elected. It is desired by the members of the team that the other districts in Tyrone will fall into line and learn the national game, so that in the near future a League could be formed."

Regular games did take place in the new year, but not before the new club was hit by a tragedy of immense proportions only a month after the enthusiasm and sense of purpose generated by that initial meeting.

In November its new captain, John Owens, a brother of Felix and the Treasurer, Harry, died in Omagh Hospital following a short illness. He had contracted a chill which then developed into pneumonia, causing death in spite of the tender care of his relatives and the medical skill of the doctors and nurses.

Aged just eighteen, he was described as gentle and unassuming, with a disposition which made him beloved by all his companions. The report goes on:

"He was a devoted member of the Gaelic Club, and was one of its indefatigable workers. In spite of his youth, being only a lad of eighteen, he joined the local company of the Volunteers, of which he was a proud member. As a true gael, he was very devoted to his religious duties and was a staunch Knight of the Blessed Sacrament.

"The funeral, which was very edifying, took place on Thursday last, to Beragh Catholic Church. The coffin, wrapped in the Tricolour, was borne by companion Volunteers. The remains were escorted by the

Packie McAleer, a player with the Red Knights in the 1920s, is among this group carrying out essential mechanical repairs.

IRA company of which he was a member. On the last sod being placed on the grave, three volleys were fired - thus giving the last living respect to a dead Volunteer."

Steady Progress 1921-1923

Further evidence of exactly how strong the interest in gaelic football and Irish culture in the area was, can be guaged by the opening games following the formation of the Red Knights in 1921. For the first time three teams from the parish lined out on a regular basis, namely Beragh, Brackey and Sixmilecross.

On March 22nd, 1922, Jamie Slane refereed a challenge which

resulted in a 0-6 to 0-5 win for Brackey over Beragh, they met again in April while later the Red Knights forwards were said to have been strong in a 1-0 to 0-0 victory over Sixmilecross.

The team lined out was: Jim Hagan, M Rodgers, McGirr, Doyle, Harry Owens, P Owens, McGrath, Woods, M Owens, Donnelly, Conway, McGillion, Colton.

There is also no doubt that the dreams of the new club back in October to see others fall into line was realised to some extent. A meeting to form the Omagh District League was held and Beragh's prominent role was clear as they encouraged the progress of other teams by staging friendly matches against Ballygawley and Pomeroy in the early summer.

The Ulster Herald report of Bloody Sunday in Croke Park in November 1920

Competing in the Pomeroy and District League, the Red Knights mostly played teams from the east, including Dungannon Clarkes, who provided the opposition for their opening League game in 1922.

With no parish rule, players from outside the area were included and the team that lined out against the Clarkes was: Pat Owens, Harry Owens, Hughie Owens, Felix Owens, Paddy Donaghy, Johnny Donaghy, Hugh Colton, Higgins (Ballygawley), McWilliams (a vet from Augher), Ned McGee, Keenan (Clogher), Willie O'Hanlon, the goalkeeper, from Ballygawley) and Tom Kelly (originally from Dungannon but teaching in Garvaghey).

> We were the only west team in the Pomeroy District League and after we won it there was a fair bit of training done for the semi-final

Donaghmore also travelled to what was described as "the splendid grounds at Deroar Park," where the abilities of the Beragh team were emphasised in a 0-6 to 0-1 win, with Barney Farrell notching each of the scores in the first half. Pomeroy, Dungannon and Edendork competed alongside Beragh and Donaghmore in the competition.

First County Semi-Final - Winners of the Pomeroy District League

By 1923 things were very definitely on an upward curve, as evidenced by victories over Arvalee Emmetts in June and then their successful participation in the Dungannon League later in the summer.

Good form was also displayed in games against Donaghmore at the end of September, Pomeroy on October 14th and again on December 2nd and then Donaghmore again on December 9th. They lost to Cookstown by 0-10 to 0-9 in what was described as a very tough match and went on to meet Dungannon at Deroar Park on December 16th and Rock on December 23rd.

The end result of this was that the Red Knights won the Pomeroy District League and progressed to the later stages of the County Championship along with Omagh Colemans, winners of the Omagh District League and Stewartstown Harps, winners of the Stewartstown District League.

Now the stage was set for the County Semi-Final against Stewartstown in McLarnon Park, Donaghmore on April 6th, 1924. Preparations for the match were understandably taken extremely seriously and included a high profile challenge match against Dungannon, another of the top teams of the time.

Interviewed in 1980, Harry Owens, who played in that 1924 team, recalled the excitement of the period leading up to and during that semi-final against Stewartstown.

"We were the only west team in the Pomeroy District League and after we won it there was a fair bit of training done for the semi-final. The team was picked from Beragh, the Cross and the Altamuskin area," he said.

"On the day of the match nobody was left in Beragh at all. The spectators travelled on bikes and the team went in cars. I remember there was a very big crowd at the match. There was very little between the teams and one of the main players for Stewartstown was a man by the name of Tohill.

1920s players, Felix Owens, Micksie Boyle and Hughie Owens, pictured no doubt reminiscing on old times.

"He said he would get Ned Magee in the second half, but it was him who came off the worst. The team wasn't much changed for the game from other matches, apart from Francie Cleary in goals, O'Hanlon at full-back and Harry moved to half-back. Francie Cleary did ok, punched one ball over the bar. But we didn't play as well as earlier in the league."

Referee for the game was Dan McElhohm from Trillick and the Beragh team in their red jerseys, lined out: Francie Cleary, Harry Owens, Jamie Slane, Jim McMahon, Ned McGee, Packie Farrell, Jimmy Donaghy, P Mulgrew, Pat Owens, Pat Shields, Mick O'Hanlon, G Williams, Felix Hughes.

With play starting at a brisk pace, Beragh enjoyed the best of the early exchanges and were quickly two points in front. The report of the match continued:

"After this the play remained in midfield, but shortly before half-time, Beragh got away and scored a further point. Their good form continued and by the half-time break they were 0-3 to 0-2 ahead."

Hopes of a first County Final place were further boosted on the resumption when the Red Knights scored a goal. However, Stewartstown fought back and midway through the second half went in front by 1-4 to 1-3. Swapped goals made it 2-4 to 2-3 before the Harps sealed the win with another score just before the finish.

The 2-5 to 2-3 defeat was bitterly disappointing for the Red Knights, who were best served by Jamie Slane, Jim McMahon, Williams and Ned McGee, whose magnificent kicking and catching was described as a particular highlight.

Various reasons were offered for the narrow defeat, including one far-fetched (or is it) rumour that the team's interval lead had prompted some of the players to take drink during the break and were therefore somewhat "under the weather" in the second half!

Stewartstown duly went on to defeat Omagh St Enda's in the County Final by a massive 0-18 to 0-4. That final, incidentally, was refereed by Beragh official, FH Rodgers.

Other Developments

Many positive benefits, of course, led on from that appearance by the Red Knights in the County Semi-Final. They included the first tentative steps towards fielding a team comprised of young players from the area.

In March, the Beragh Junior Knights defeated Carrickmore Juniors by 4-3 to 1-0 in a challenge match at Deroar Park, with the teams due to meet again in mid-April.

> Hopes of a first County Final place were further boosted on the resumption when the Red Knights scored a goal

And, the progress to the semi-final no doubt also contributed to several of the Red Knights players being selected to play for Tyrone, among them Mick O'Hanlon and Packie Farrell. The county side which met Cavan in that year's Ulster Championship included Ned McGee.

A year later Henry Owens became the first from the club to represent Tyrone in the Ulster Championship when he played at full-back against a Cavan team that went on to reach the All-Ireland Final for the very first time.

FH Rodgers was part of the selection team for the game, with special trains costing 2-6 from Beragh and 2/- from Sixmilecross being organised to take spectators to Dungannon.

A group of Sixmilecross Hibernians from the 1920s

Behind the Scenes

Organising GAA clubs was never just a case of fielding teams or playing games, not even back in those early days when much behind the scenes work went into ensuring that the young people of the area were given the opportunity to participate.

From the very earliest days there was an active social side attached to the GAA in keeping with the twin aims of promoting the games and Irish culture generally. Back in 1912, Ned Rafferty remembered a man playing a medoleon travelling with the Coalisland team which came to Sixmilecross and Felix Owens also recalled many of the events which accompanied the organisation of the newly formed Red Knights in the early to mid-twenties.

He told Frank Rodgers in 1980 how the team travelled to matches with Robert Clarke, Paddy Daly and John Rutherford and that the officials included FH Rodgers, Joe McCann, Matt Rodgers and Jamie Hagan.

"We togged out in our barn and I remember that at the time the Shamrocks team played in blue jerseys with white shamrocks. The Shamrocks were sown onto the jerseys by Jamie Hagan," he said.

"Some of the players then were Mickey Conway, Jamie Hagan,

From the very earliest days there was an active social side attached to the GAA in keeping with the twin aims of promoting the games and Irish culture generally

> The name Red Knights came from the famous Irish mythical saga of Cuchulainn and his Red Branch Knights

Johnny Donaghy, a lovely footballer and Paddy Donaghy. Brackey had started in 1918 and I remember us playing each other week about.

"The name was changed to Beragh Sons of the Gael on the suggestion of Henry McKernan. He lived where Peter McNamee lives now and he wasn't happy with the name Shamrocks. Some of the young boys were playing soccer at Rosie McGlynn's and Fr Taggart came past and saw them and started them at the gaelic.

"There was a game against Ballygawley at Glencull which Joe Donnelly was refereeing. But Ballygawley wouldn't give him the 5/- for taking charge of the match. Master McMahon got up with the Beragh ones that day, but wouldn't come back with them."

The name Red Knights came from the famous Irish mythical saga of Cuchulainn and his Red Branch Knights. The connections with the Brown Bull of Cooley and Cooley in Beragh was included among the reasons why the Red Knights name was chosen.

The Beragh Havanna Dance Band of the 1920s

Felix's brother, Harry, who moved to Limavady in the early thirties and went on to play a central role in the formation and establishment of GAA affairs in Derry, told how difficult it was at times to keep things going.

"Some of the players in the Beragh Shamrocks were Jim Doherty, a postman from Strabane, Joe Carr, Frankie Rafferty. Mrs Kay Owens was a great supporter and I remember the jerseys being changed in colour to yellow or tangerine around that time," he said.

"The Shamrocks players were all local because the Parish Rule was then in operation. The early matches were played in Conway's Holm and then moved to Owens field. Lack of finance put the team out of business because it was costly to bring players from Augher, Ballygawley and so on and the gates wouldn't meet the costs. It was 6d into a match."

He also recalled playing for Tyrone against a Kildare team including the famous midfielder of the time, Larry Stanley.

Beragh Football Club's debts

It is tempting from the vantage point of the vibrant Tyrone GAA of the 21st Century to think that things were all very different during the early days of the Association in the county. And, while there is no doubt that affairs are now very much advanced compared to the twenties, the people involved during those early decades were no less committed.

This is certainly very evident in Beragh where a high profile Court case in 1926 highlighted the deep-rooted feelings surrounding gaelic games at the time. But the circumstances also give a valuable insight into the running of the club.

At Omagh Quarter Sessions in November of that year Felix Hughes from Sixmilecross sued FH Rodgers to recover £15 seven shillings alleged to be due for motor hire on behalf of the club. The plaintiff, Mr Hughes, said he had been asked by the defendant to attend at certain places and pick up players for the GAA club. The report of the hearing continues.

"Cross examined by Mr Murnaghan, witness (Mr Hughes) said he was a player in the club and the defendant seemed to be at the head of affairs. The 'gate' money was collected by the defendant and he paid for motor cars, teas etc. The club was called Beragh Red Knights.

Mr Murnaghan - I would suggest you only put in Rodgers' name when the team went down, so as to stick him for the money.

Witness - That is wrong

Defendant said he went as a supporter of the Beragh team and sometimes refereed Gaelic matches. He always paid for his seat in the cars and he denied that he hired the plaintiff's car. Dances were organised to defray the expenses of the club, but on the first occasion the night was wet and only a few people attended and the dance was not a success. Dances were also organised in Sixmilecross hall in aid of the club funds, but nobody knew what became of this money. Witness had nothing do with it. Witness was a member of the County Board and he endeavoured to get the Board to pay the plaintiff.

Cross-examined by Mr Donnelly, the witness said there was no committee in connection with the club. Witness denied that he lifted the gate money or paid for cars or teas."

> This is certainly very evident in Beragh where a high profile Court case in 1926 highlighted the deep-rooted feelings surrounding gaelic games at the time

FH Rodgers, club
official, referee
for the 1924
County Final and
defendant in the
1926 Court Case

Among those appearing for the defendant were his brother, Matthew, who said that from conversations he had with the plaintiff, the plaintiff was of the opinion that the County Board should pay him.

Henry Owens, a member of the Beragh team, said the defendant took no leading part in the affairs of the club. He added that the plaintiff had no authority to bring players from outside districts.

Joseph Kerr said he carried the players on several occasions and the defendant paid for his seat in the car.

However, James Slane, called by Mr Donnelly, said that on one occasion in 1922 he got instructions from the defendant to order a car for the plaintiff.

Dismissing the case, the presiding Judge said the plaintiff had been unable to point to any definite evidence showing a contract on the part of the defendant to pay for these cars. He said they were all members of the one same football club and apparently there was nobody who could be made responsible. The Judge said it was not possible for the plaintiff to pick out one of the players and make him pay for the transport.

Red Knights in First O'Neill Cup

While the Court hearing undoubtedly created a stir among those involved in the club, the team continued to participate enthusiastically in the various competitions organised during a decade that saw sustained growth in the GAA in Tyrone.

Earlier in 1926 a West Tyrone Committee was formed as part of the re-organisation of the Association. With the boost of Harry Owens and Patrick Shields being selected on the Tyrone Senior and Junior teams respectively, the reputation of Beragh Red Knights as strong contenders was soon being enhanced.

In May they travelled to and defeated Beltony by 4-4 to 3-3 after leading by 3-2 to 0-1 at half-time. They defeated Carrickmore in a 'robust' friendly game by 0-11 to 0-10 and by the end of the month were top of the West Tyrone League.

A resounding 0-17 to 0-5 win over Fintona was certainly pleasing, and the happy mood that must surely have prevailed was enhanced by an amusing incident reported during the game.

"A young hare entered the playing pitch and some of the players joined in the chase. The play was forgotten for the moment, but the hare made good its escape," said the Ulster Herald report of the match.

However, occasional spurts of activity were rarely sustained. A game against Ballygawley had to be postponed because both clubs had players involved in a county match at Armagh and, while Omagh were comprehensively defeated in June, it wasn't until September that a decision had to be taken to revive matters.

But the Court case involving Felix Hughes and FH Rodgers wasn't the only disruption. Ballygawley lodged a protest against Beragh on the grounds that the official referee was not in attendance for their match in November and the League was still unfinished entering 1927.

Beragh topped the League on twelve points, although Ballygawley forced a play-off subsequently by defeating Fintona. No record exists of the game having taken place and the St Ciaran's went on to become West Tyrone Champions - and take the 1926 County title with a win over Ardboe.

Sixmilecross Red Knights 1928

One of the features of the late twenties was the number of names under which the players of the parish represented themselves. While they played under the title of Beragh Red Knights for most of the time, a team called Sixmilecross Red Knights made an appearance during 1928 when Beragh Shamrocks withdrew despite having being affiliated at the start.

During that year they were one of only ten registered clubs and took part in the senior league along with Coalisland Fianna, Dungannon Clarkes, Donaghmore Eire Ogs and Moortown St Malachy's.

In the O'Neill Cup they were drawn against Dungannon Clarkes, a team with whom they enjoyed a number of interesting and, at times, controversial meetings that season.

At the end of April the Clarkes travelled to the Red Knights at Sixmilecross where the teams proceeded to produce what was described as a splendid exhibition of football in front of a large attendance.

The report of the match certainly bears the point out, as Sixmilecross started well and led by the 2-6 to 1-2 at half-time. Three goals in quick succession brought Dungannon right back into the contest on the resumption, before the 'Cross regained their composure and emerged winners by two points on a scoreline of 3-7 to 4-2.

However, at a subsequent County Board meeting, at which Sixmilecross were represented by Jamie Slane and Felix Hughes, an objection was raised against the accuracy of the referee's report on the time that both teams had taken to the pitch. It is unclear whether the objection was upheld.

Controversy, though, seemed to go hand in hand with Sixmilecross throughout that season. In September a second meeting against Dungannon at O'Neill Park had to be abandoned over a disputed point.

Dungannon led the game at half-time before Sixmilecross fought back well on the resumption. Points from JJ Kelly and Ned Magee helped them take the lead as D McGirr in the Red Knights goals was praised for the way in which he punched away some well directed and fast shots.

The final score was 0-5 to 0-4 in favour of Sixmilecross, but there was much annoyance when Dungannon subsequently claimed that they should have been allowed a point which had initially been flagged wide.

The report of the match states how this action 'aroused the indignation' of the Red Knights and that matters were assuming a 'very ugly appearance' when Sixmilecross reluctantly left the field in protest. And, there was a strong message from the reporter to the Clarkes when he wrote:

"If from selfishness or any other cause whatever, any

team participating in a GAA match, which fails to take defeat in a sportsmanlike manner, tends in no small way to the complete destruction sooner or later of the grand old principals for which the Gaelic Association stands.

"Certainly the termination of the game left a bad impression, particularly on the spectators, as to the future of the pastimes in Tyrone." The teams were subsequently awarded a point each from the match.

For the record the Sixmilecross team was: D McGirr, William O'Hanlon, Barney Farrell, James Mulgrew, Ned McGee, Felix Hughes, JJ Kelly, T McCann, J Donnelly, J McCaul, G McWilliams, F Farrell, Packie Farrell.

Sixmilecross had earlier defeated Coalisland by 2-3 to 1-2 in the County Championship at McGirr's Holm, where the admission price was 6p. However, their form for much of 1928 makes it all the more surprising to hear of the difficulties which they subsequently faced.

In July of that year they were one of the teams entered in the O'Neill Cup competition and were due to play Dungannon on January 27th, 1929. But by then they appeared to have ceased competing. Instead, Dungannon were awarded a victory over them and Ned Magee, one of the stars of the time, was the subsequent subject of an appeal over his transfer from Sixmilecross to Donaghmore. The protest by Pomeroy was thrown out by the Tyrone County Board on the grounds that no transfer was necessary because Sixmilecross no longer existed as a club.

> *The protest by Pomeroy was thrown out by the Tyrone County Board on the grounds that no transfer was necessary because Sixmilecross no longer existed as a club*

Back in Beragh -
Junior League Champions 1929

Among the initiatives carried out at the beginning of 1929 was one to encourage teams from different areas to participate in competitions. Fr Sheridan of Beragh was asked to contact people in his area to revive the team there, although it is fair to assume that they didn't need much prompting.

Exactly why it was felt that such a step on behalf of the County Board was necessary is hard to understand. Afterall, Beragh had been entered in the 1928 Junior League and played a number of games and gaelic games were still very much to the forefront of activities locally.

By October the title
appears to have been
secured and one of
the top matches for
the club that season
came against
Fintona at Eskra
in November

Frank Kerr was among those involved, but they withdrew in the summer of that year.

While Sixmilecross was the only affiliated GAA club in the west in 1928, there was a revival of affairs the following season. A Junior League was organised on the prompting of Beragh, who were represented by James McMahon, and Beltony Clubs, with its participants including Omagh, Beltony, Fintona Pearses and Beragh Red Knights, whose registered colours were dark blue.

Beragh were scheduled to play Fintona as part of Lacca Sports at the end of July, while in September their good form continued with a 3-5 to 3-2 victory over Omagh. Refereed by Jamie Hagan, the home side were reported to have had to fight hard for the win against vastly improved opponents.

The failure of the town team to take a number of good scoring chances was cited as a major factor in their defeat. The victory saw Beragh take an important step towards eventually winning the competition.

By October the title appears to have been secured and one of the top matches for the club that season came against Fintona at Eskra in November. After an evenly contested opening, Beragh scored 4-2 in quick succession, and led 4-2 to no score at half-time.

Fintona did make some inroads in the second half, although not near enough to make a difference as Beragh emerged comfortable winners. The team was: Patrick Donaghy, Patrick Shields, James Mulgrew, Patrick McGirr, Jas McCann, Felix Owens, Frank McMahon, Frank Kerr, Peter McGarrity, P Kelly, Mickie Boyle, Joseph Colton.

Youth team revived - Other Developments

One of the most enlightened attempts in the twenties was the efforts made to provide gaelic football for the youth of the area. We have seen how these began in 1923 and the efforts were renewed later in the decade as well. In the summer of 1928 the Beragh Juniors defeated Omagh CBS by 0-12 to 0-10 in a second meeting between the teams.

Teams from Beragh and Sixmilecross took part in a Junior Tournament at Drumduff Sports and in 1929 the work continued with a challenge match against Pomeroy Juveniles on May 4th of that year. The Ulster Herald report of the game gives a taster of the day.

"The teams were accompanied by the St Mary's Temperance Flute Band and a large crowd of supporters. The parade elicited favourable comment as it went through Sixmilecross en-route to the field at Beragh.

"Beragh fielded a much stronger team and they got the best of the matters in the first half, leading by 0-5 to 0-0 at half-time. Pomeroy played a much better type of football and on the final whistle Beragh were winners by 0-7 to 0-5. Jamie Slane was the referee and the game was noticeable for the great promise showed by both teams which illustrates that the game is alive in Pomeroy and the village of Beragh."

Gaelic games and community events generally seemed to carry a bit more razzmatazz during those years than might be the case today. Drumduff Sports in 1929 included greyhound racing among its attractions and the Beragh Greyhound Racing Club promoted a meeting on July 31st at FH Rodgers Holm, with one shilling admission.

Sixmilecross Dramatic Club presented the 'Middle Man' in the AOH Hall, a play telling of the Land League times in Ireland and with music accompaniment by the Beragh Havanna Dance Band.

Over 250 people attended a Dance in Beragh AOH Hall at the beginning of 1928. Billed as an annual function, patrons were advised that the doors would open at 7.30pm, tea at 12 midnight, music by the Beragh Band and admission of 1/6 for Ladies and 2/- for Gents.

And, it wasn't just on the football field or on the dancefloor that the Beragh players were showing their prowess during the decade. In the summer of 1926 Harry Owens won the High Jump and the Pulling the Weight at Carrickmore Sports, the Beragh team won the Tug of War, Hugh Owens was first in the half mile race and Hugh Owens and M Boyle were second in the Siamese Race.

County competitions

Tyrone won the Ulster Senior League for the McKenna Cup in 1926 in what was the highlight of a decade at county level. Those years were also marked by the progress of a number of players from the Beragh and Sixmilecross ranks to Tyrone teams.

In 1924 W O'Hanlon, Ned McGee and Pat Farrell were listed on Tyrone Possibles and Probables teams, FH Rodgers was a selector a year later and Harry Owens featured on that victorious 1926 Tyrone team.

The Beragh Havanna Dance Band during a big night out in the 1920s

Ned McGee, a native of Augher, but then playing for Sixmilecross, was rated as the star of that era and in 1928 was one of four players from the area listed on a Tyrone team to play Derry. The others were Jim McMahon, B Farrell, W O'Hanlon and P Shiels.

It was a decade that saw Tyrone begin to make progress on the inter-county scene. The introduction of the National Leagues in 1926 aided this process and generally raised the profile of inter-county games.

Clear proof of this came in 1927 when 700 people, including many from Beragh and Sixmilecross, travelled on a GAA excursion to Bundoran for a trip to the seaside and match between Tyrone and Donegal.

A motion passed at the 1928 Tyrone Convention saw Beragh being fixed as the travelling centre for inter-county matches. It was decided that the Railway fares of players to venues would be paid by the Ulster Council in addition to motoring expenses to the nearest Railway Station.

Harry Owens, of course, was a regular on the Tyrone team around this time. But his move to Limavady sometime around the end of 1927 caused problems. He had asked for travelling expenses from there, but the County Board decided to write back telling him that 'owing to financial difficulty we are unable to continue his services.'

In December 1929 a West Tyrone selection, including Jim McMahon, Pat Shields and T Farrell from Beragh, took on a Derry County team and the list of players from the area who represented Tyrone in the Ulster Championship in the decade provides further evidence of its central involvement.

Achievements of the Decade

Few clubs could have reflected on progress at the end of the Twenties with more satisfaction than Beragh. Their involvement in GAA affairs had been successfully maintained and enhanced at a time when the Association in Tyrone continued to struggle.

The signs of growth included the regular fielding of teams, the providing of an outlet for the youth of the area and the organising of functions to showcase Irish music as well entertain and raise funds.

While Beragh might not have managed to capture a County title despite being strong contenders, their example must have been the envy of many others striving to establish clubs and field teams.

This was achieved against the backdrop of periodic internal and external turmoil. The Troubles of the early twenties, the death of their team captain, John Owens, at such a young age, the Courtroom drama of 1926 and the various boardroom controversies must have tested the resolve of those involved. Their ability to continue with the promotion of gaelic games and culture despite these setbacks says much at a time when so many clubs so regularly fell by the wayside.

This ensured that the GAA in Beragh consolidated the growth of the 1906-1920 period and laid solid foundations for further progress in the following decade.

The Pomeroy District League medal awarded to the Beragh team. Their success in the competition earned them a place in the 1924 County Semi-Final

Chapter Five
1930 - 1940
A Period of Progress

Chapter Five
1930 - 1940

Fresh challenges

Each year of GAA activity in the Beragh parish brought fresh challenges for those involved. But as well as promoting gaelic games and culture locally they also had a significant influence on its development in Tyrone.

From the earliest years of the Association in the county, officials from Beragh played a key role. Their efforts are evident and not least in a decade that was to prove decisive in sealing the survival of the GAA in West Tyrone.

While Beragh, Sixmilecross and Brackey teams had consistently taken part in gaelic games and actively promoted other activities from 1906 onwards, other areas struggled to maintain their involvement. However, all that changed in 1931 with the setting up of the West Tyrone Board which over the next forty years provided a focus for the sustained growth of clubs and competitions.

Its establishment at a meeting at the end of October 1931 heralded the start of a golden era of activity for clubs within its catchment area. And, the central role played by officials from Beragh was evident right from the start. The new board was immediately faced with a number of important decisions.

Beragh, Fintona, Augher, Altamuskin, Dregish and Eskra were the clubs present at that important inaugural gathering and men from the newly named Sons of the Gael assumed central parts. Jim McGurn was elected Secretary and Frank Kerr, Treasurer, as the task of reviving matters in the west began.

66

From the earliest years of the Association in the county, officials from Beragh played a key role

99

On August 23rd 1931 Eskra had met Beragh and caused a surprise with a ten point win and a month later a team from Clougherney met Altamuskin in a return match which was won by a 'safe' margin. A re-organised Fintona team provided the opposition in October when Fr Hurson threw in the ball and the Pearses won by 2-2 to 1-1.

Central to the decisions facing the new West Tyrone Board was the introduction of the Parish Rule which designated that players could only line out for their native parish club. At a meeting in November, Beragh delegate, James Hagan enquired about the position of a number of players from the parish that were on the Ballygawley team then challenging for a second O'Neill Cup title.

It was decided that they would be allowed to complete their involvement in the championship before returning to their native club. This meant that James and Frank McMahon won senior championship medals with Ballygawley in 1931 and were back in Beragh ranks for 1932.

One of the new competitions introduced to coincide with the formation of the West Tyrone Board was the McAleer Cup. Named after the former Sixmilecross Wolfe Tones official, HK McAleer, the competition was keenly contested throughout the 1930s before being re-named the St Enda Cup after being won for a third time by Omagh in 1939.

Fair Day in Sixmilecross, 1930

HK McAleer presented the Cup bearing his name to the Killyclogher captain after they won the competition in December 1932. Among those who spoke after the final was James McMahon, who gave an insight into the prevailing mood of the time.

He remarked how he had many recollections of Cup Finals, but that many who had seen the McAleer decider would be sure that it was one which that they could look back on with pleasant recollections. He added that the gaelic spirit had been handed down to them and it was their duty to see it was passed to the next generation unsullied.

West Tyrone League - Early Thirties

Beragh's involvement in League competitions got off to the usual start in 1930 when they were listed to play a number of games. However, in a subsequent letter to the Tyrone County Board in June 1930, Frank Kerr, stated that the team was withdrawing and asked that they not be included in any further fixtures.

But they were back on track within the year following the formation of the West Tyrone Board. The opening round of the new West Tyrone

League took place in December 1931 when Beragh lost by seven points to Fintona. They also went down to Augher on a score of 1-5 to 1-0 and had only recorded one win from four games by the turn of the year. It was a 2-4 to 2-2 win over Eskra, with one of the goals coming from James McMahon following a goalmouth tussle.

Augher went on to win the League while for Beragh, it was a case of making further improvements and arrangements for the next season.

Wins were recorded at the start of the 1932 League, among them a victory over Altamuskin which apparently was particularly pleasing. The report of the game stated that "since the start of the League no team had taken their departure so jubilantly as the visiting Beragh side."

Jim McGurn on the bike and Peter Bennett getting ready for a trip. Both were influential members of the GAA in Beragh during the decade

The improvements continued with a 0-11 to 0-4 win over Eskra which put them third on the League table. But the re-match against Altamuskin resulted in defeat and the mixed fortunes continued with wins over Omagh and Fintona and defeats by Newtownstewart and Eskra.

By June they were in mid-table. Their position hadn't changed by October, but by the end of November they had moved into joint third with 32 points from 21 games. That improved placing was due to wins over Newtownstewart, Aughafad, Killyclogher and Eskra.

The team that played against Killyclogher in the 3-1 to 0-2 win at the end of February was: McDermott, Michael McCaffrey, Frank Rafferty, Harry Kerr, Mackle Grimes, McCann, Boyle, Johnny Ward, Jim McMahon, McCarron, Peter Daly, Francis Maguire, Peter McMahon, Owens, Owenie McMahon.

The League competition of 1932 continued into 1933 when Beragh eventually finished in fourth place behind Fintona on 37 points and Eskra and Altamuskin on 36 points each.

Little time was wasted in beginning the 1933 activities once the affairs of the previous season had been sorted out. Beragh started well and they were unbeaten ahead of their game against Omagh at the start of April. From then on, though, their efforts lacked real consistency. Games against Eskra and Carrickmore were lost, although the one against Eskra was later awarded to Beragh following a protest over an ineligible player.

They produced a better display against Omagh despite losing by 1-3 to 1-2, Trillick were defeated at the end of the month and by the middle of May they were mid-table with six points. But then defeats followed at the hands of Dromore and Trillick to leave them well adrift of the leaders.

Omagh were to go on and win the competition, in the process of defeating Beragh by 0-7 to 0-1 in the process and the club was further hit later in the year when one of its most influential players, Felix Owens, transferred to Carrickmore.

Nevertheless, there was some joy for Beragh when they were declared winners of the new Mid-Week League, a competition organised during the summer of 1933. They went through that League unbeaten which was said to be a great achievement for them and they were presented with the Cup at a subsequent meeting of the West Tyrone Board.

O'Neill Cup competition 1933

Although their League form in the early thirties was a litany of less than impressive results along with some noteworthy victories, evidence of Beragh's growing prominence on the field did come in the West Tyrone Championship for the O'Neill Cup. The wins over Fintona, Trillick and Dromore saw them progress to the District Final and defy the odds.

Fintona were dispatched by 0-10 to 0-0 at the end of March, Trillick were then defeated to set up an interesting tie against Dromore in the semi-final on April 30. Described in the Ulster Herald as being "eagerly looked forward to by spectators, brilliant football was the exception rather than the rule as dogged determination dominated proceedings."

Nevertheless, goals from Peter and James McMahon got them going and, while Dromore responded with a goal and pressed hard with the wind in the second half, Beragh were holding out in some style.

The performance of Micksey Boyle pleased the Beragh supporters but the game was to end in controversy. A 'violent charge' by 'Mr McMahon' led to him being sent to the sideline and an angry rush to the field by spectators. Calm was eventually restored and Beragh won by 2-1 to 1-3.

> *1932 Christmas Night ceile under the auspices of the Beragh GFC to be held in the AOH Hall. Prices of admission are moderate and expected that there will be a large attendance*

Beragh player, Packie McAleer, in relaxed mood in this shot from the 1930s

95

These young players were among the first to represent the Beragh club at underage level. Included in the picture are at front, Sean Bennett and Jack McCann

There was no shortage of excitement, either, ahead of the West Tyrone final against Omagh in Killyclogher on June 18, admission 6d. With a place in the County Final against Dungannon at stake, interest in the tie was said to be spreading right across Tyrone and even into Fermanagh, with both teams expected to field their strongest selections.

For the Beragh men this meant, according to a preview of the game, that they would have the assistance of the McMahon brothers, "who have served the county team on many occasions. Harry Owens, also a well-known county player, will pull his weight for the club of his boyhood. Owenie McMahon, too, will be hard to get past. Jim McCann, Frank Rafferty, Kerr brothers, Michael McCaffrey and Rodgers are all players of ability and promise and will no doubt give of their best." The preview forecast that Beragh would win by a point.

It was estimated that the game drew an attendance of some 2000. And, they weren't disappointed as "a splendid final, a brilliant display of gaelic football and a game worthy of the best traditions of the association" was served up.

Most laudable of all was the sportsmanship despite many hard tackles. In the game itself, the St Enda's started well, with Frank Rafferty having to be on his toes to deny Omagh's McCanny. McCaffrey and Harry Owens were also strong in defence as chances fell to Mackle Grimes and Dan McSorley in the forwards.

However, the task facing Beragh became tougher when Omagh led by 0-4 to 0-0 at half-time. Expectations were high that they would get back on track on the resumption and there were certainly plenty of chances for them to do so.

Paddy Turbitt saved from Paddy McMahon and James McMahon while Grimes and Ward also did well. But the game was slipping away and, although Harry Owens scored the point of the day following a contest close to the Omagh goals, Beragh lost by 0-6 to 0-1.

The team was: Micksey Boyle, Michael McCaffrey, Harry Owens, Frank Rafferty, Jack Kerr, Jim McCann, Owenie McMahon, James McMahon, Frank McMahon, Jas Rodgers, Dan McSorley, Paddy McMahon, Mackle Grimes, Francie Maguire, Johnny Ward.

In the County Final on October 29th, Omagh lost to Dungannon by a single point on a score of 2-2 to 2-1.

Junior League

Interest in the GAA enjoyed sustained growth during the 1930s. For a time this was highlighted by a West Tyrone Junior League, which showed that there was no shortage of playing resources in any of the areas then participating.

This competition was a sort of modern day 'Reserve' League, complete with a share of underage players, and was aimed at providing additional competition. The Beragh parish was represented by a team carrying the Sixmilecross name. In one game at the beginning of April 1933, they played out a scoreless draw against Greencastle at Beragh and it's interesting to note the names of those who lined out on that occasion.

> " It was estimated that the game drew an attendance of some 2000. And, they weren't disappointed as "a splendid final, a brilliant display of gaelic football and a game worthy of the best traditions of the association" was served up "

Club Treasurer and Secretary from the 1930s, WJ Conway, flanked by Alphonsus and Packie McAleer

Sixmilecross - B Gormley, F Rafferty, J Coyle, F Rafferty, T Mullin, R Nixon, J Rodgers, Frank Hagan, Leo Kelly, J Ramsey, J Kelly, P McGuire, P McAleer, J Rafferty, J Colton.

Among the other teams were Fivemiletown, Tattysallagh, St Enda's Seconds, Tattyreagh, Augher, Fintona Seconds, Dromore Seconds and Killyclogher Seconds, Mountfield and Greencastle. Sixmilecross showed good form by moving into second place on the table behind Fivemiletown.

But Omagh defeated them in the Junior Championship, the League momentum wasn't maintained and as the year progressed they slipped down the table until they eventually withdrew from the competition when it resumed in the early part of 1934.

At a meeting of the West Tyrone Board a letter was received from the club stating that the team was in 'bad straits'owing to the shortage of players and they were afraid that they wouldn't be able to fulfil their remaining matches. This led to a harsh retort from the Chairman, Fr Collins, who expressed the belief that it was harmful for teams to enter competitions when they had no intention of completing them.

Camogie

One of the most important developments of the 1930s was the attempts made throughout West Tyrone to secure the establishment of both camogie and hurling and the Beragh and Sixmilecross areas certainly adopted the games enthusiastically.

A Beragh Camogie team gets ready for action

Jim McGurn, who played a key role in the West Tyrone Board, was the organiser of camogie in the district and then of hurling. And, the oral and contemporary evidence from those areas shows that the efforts by him and others made definite progress.

The Tyrone Camogie Board had been formed in the early part of 1933 with Sixmilecross among the very first clubs to become active. In May the first step towards the inauguration of a team came with a meeting of the local girls in Sixmilecross when the following committee was formed.

Chairman - Miss Donaghy, Vice-Chairman - Miss B Owens, Secretary - Miss McCrudden, PET, Treasurer - Mrs Rafferty PE. Committee - Misses M Farley, M Owens, Peggy Nugent and ME Shields.

Training sessions and games were organised and arrangements made for the provision of uniforms and camans. Clubs were also formed in Altamuskin, Omagh and Dregish among others and within months a West Tyrone League was being played.

But the team seems to have changed its name to Beragh St Brigid's fairly quickly and one of their first games was away to Dregish in July which finished five goals to three for the home team. A few weeks later they travelled to Newtownstewart where this time they lost by five goals to one.

The team was: Mollie Hagan, Kathleen McCann, Mary Nugent, Peggie Nugent, Josie Owens, Maggie Owens, Bernadette Owens, Katie Ward, Rosie McDermott, Mary E Shields, Lalla

There was no let-up in camogie activity towards the end of the year either. At the Tyrone Convention the influence of the club was emphasised when Annie McCrudden was elected County Chairperson and Mrs Rafferty Treasurer. On the field a return match against Altamuskin in December saw Beragh win by four goals to one.

A West Tyrone League started at the beginning of 1934 when Beragh opened their campaign with another victory against Altamuskin, this time by 1-0 to 0-0. The team lined out: Mollie Hagan, Kathleen McCann, Alice Hughes, Minnie McNamee, Kitty Ward, Mary Nugent, Peggy Nugent, Brigid Rafferty, Maggie Donnelly, Maggie Owens, Josephine Owens, Bernadette Owens.

Ballygawley were defeated by 5-0 to 1-0, the goals coming from Alice Hughes, Bernadette Owens, Minnie McNamee and Maggie Nugent, although the backs were said to have been faulty in placing the ball and erratic in meeting attacks.

All of this activity prompted the establishment of a West Tyrone Camogie Board and the first meeting heard Jim McGurn explain how the destiny of the game locally would now be entrusted to its members.

"About four years ago there was only one camogie team in the county, but with good organisation the game progressed by leaps and bounds. I see no reason why camogie should not make great progress in Tyrone," he said.

At the Tyrone Convention the influence of the club was emphasised when Annie McCrudden was elected County Chairperson and Mrs Rafferty Treasurer

1936 - Owen Carroll (publican and grocer) appealed against valuation increase from £10 to £20 for his premises

"The county has sufficient history and tradition behind it to bring them well to the forefront in the national life of the country and I hope that Tyrone, which is one of the old counties that always stood out for the old Irish civilisation, will also be to the forefront in the revival of camogie."

Beragh did well in the West Tyrone League at the start and were second with three points from two games. They struggled from then on, though, and by the middle of 1934 had slipped to bottom of the table.

Nevertheless the games continued to come regularly and Moybridge defeated them in September to consolidate their place at the top of the table. But Beragh were improving and sat in fourth place with five points.

The club wasn't just concerned with playing games, though, and was granted the use of the AOH Hall for a concert in aid of the Band. And, when the league was completed, they rounded off a busy 1934 with a challenge game at Pomeroy, which they won by 3-0 to 1-0.

The growth in the number of clubs also had a corresponding benefit for Tyrone's inter-county camogie fortunes. That year saw them participate in the Ulster Championship for the first time and they marked their first year by going all the way to the final. Among their number was Beragh's Nora Devine, but the Tyrone hopes of taking the title were dashed when they failed to reach the heights of previous matches and lost by 2-1 to 0-0.

The three Nugent sisters who played important parts on the Beragh Camogie teams of the time

In the Beragh parish, camogie continued to flourish into 1935 under the banner of Beragh and then Remackin. A challenge involving Beragh took place in January against Fivemiletown but by April the name of the club had changed to Remackin.

They lost to Killyclogher, defeated Omagh by 0-6 to 0-3 and were then boosted by the transfer to them from Altamuskin of Annie and Bridget Mullin. The team then reverted back to the Beragh name for the subsequent West Tyrone League but they didn't enjoy the same success as in the previous season.

By August they were bottom of the table with only one game played and there is no further mention of the club having taken part in competitions. The revival in camogie throughout Tyrone lasted for several more years, although the progress of the period 1933-1935 wasn't matched in 1936.

In Beragh, another possible reason for the decline may have been the loss of one of its most dedicated officials and promoters. It is probably no

'A number of the Beragh Camogie players of the period pictured at a re-union in the 1980s

coincidence that the absence of the game locally after 1935 came following the death at the beginning of 1936 of Mrs Rafferty.

She had come to the area thirty years previously from Maghera and on her death was described as a staunch advocate of Irish games and dancing in Beragh. She was credited with giving voluntary lessons in dancing and her involvement in the Camoguidheacht Association was also highlighted in her obituary report.

Remembering a special time for the girls of Beragh

What was undoubtedly a special time for the girls of Beragh is remembered fondly, with a twinkle in her eye, by the goalkeeper in some of those camogie games of the thirties. Now, over seventy years on, Mrs Rose Peachman (nee Nugent) recounts the excitement of taking part at a time when sporting opportunities were few for the girls.

"We used to play on the farm every evening with sticks that we made from sally bushes. There was a bend in them which made them look like the ash camogie sticks but they broke very easily," she said.

"All three of us sisters played for the Beragh team and I was the goalie and Peggy and Mary played out the field. It was great for the girls to be playing and we always used to enjoy visiting other teams.

"Two teams that I remember playing against were Moy and Dungannon. The thing I remember is that we seemed to be beaten more often and not and perhaps that's why the camogie never lasted at that time.

"Some of those who played were Louis McNamee's mother, Minnie, her sister, Annie Ward, Bernadette Owens and her sister from outside Sixmilecross. There were a lot of girls in the Beragh parish then, but despite this it was often hard to find a team.

"Jim McGurn was in charge and organised the whole camogie. When he married my sister, Peggy, and moved to Fintona the camogie died away. Players moved out of the area, some got married and I went to England."

Rose received her early education at Aughnaglea school and recalls that another person involved was Mrs Rafferty, the teacher there. Her husband delivered tea and other goods in a horse and cart, they lived in Beragh and her son was, of course, also involved in the GAA.

"We played in maroon coloured skirts that were made for us, but I don't remember the team training or anything like that. We just turned up for the matches. These things can fade away naturally, we had an Irish Dancing class and sewing that also stopped after being successful for a while."

Another former camog who remembers well the enjoyment of playing camogie with the various teams in the Beragh parish during the 1930s is Brigid Keenan. Wife of the late, Mick, she was still just a teenager when the promotion of camogie was taken up with great enthusiasm during that time.

"We wore sliver, grey and black uniforms which the players bought themselves. The team practiced any time that we got the chance, and mostly on Sunday evenings and during the long summer nights," she recalled.

"Minnie McNamee was a great player and I remember going to Newtownstewart to play. The pitch was out of the town on the way to Strabane. Jim McGurn was the man that started the team and others who played were the McCann's, Jack's sisters, and Josie Owens.

"Ellen Donnelly was another player, Alice Montgomery was from out in the direction of Brackey, and Sarah Grimes was from Clogherney. Maggie Hackett was a good player and I remember Jim McGurn teaching us all how to lift the ball.

"Peggy McCrory was Nugent before she was married and Jim McGurn married another sister. The one thing I remember was that there would always be a good crowd out to watch us.

"We trained in a field in Deroar behind Grimes's house and McNamee's had a good field out in Remackin which was very level. But I don't remember where we got our sticks from. Kitty Ward used to walk over to our house to collect me and we'd then go together to the training and matches," she added.

The McGurn Archives

Jim McGurn was a Fermanagh native who resided in Beragh for a time in the 1930s. He was Secretary of the Beragh Shamrocks Club in 1931 and was elected as the first Secretary of the West Tyrone Board on its founding in 1931. He remained in that post until 1934 and played a major part in establishing and strengthening clubs throughout the area.

Mickey Donnelly togged out and ready for action

He was also to the fore in establishing and promoting camogie throughout the county in the thirties and the success of the St Brigid's team in the Beragh parish was in no small way due to his know-how, enthusiasm and love of the game. He married one of the stars of the Beragh Camogie team – Mary Ellen Nugent from Ballintrain, Sixmilecross – and took up residence in Fintona where his interest in the GAA remained lifelong.

Contemporary evidence from his personal archives, now in the possession of his daughter, Bernadette, provide a fascinating insight into the running of the GAA in Beragh and Tyrone at this important time.

His future wife, Peggy, asks him to bring his hurley and camogie stick in a letter dated May 10th, 1935, while in another letter she asks him to remember to 'take my camogie shoes which are in your house over to Sixmilecross on Sunday.'

And, another letter gives details of the difficulties being faced by the Camogie club in the mid-thirties as they struggled to make ends meet in terms of finance. It's written by Mary Nugent to her future husband and details some of the outstanding accounts.

The Camogie Club are in £8.4 of debt, £5 to Charleton, £2 to Mrs Owens, £2 to the 'Herald,' £1 to Robert Clarke and 4/- or 5/- to the Cross AOH Hall

"First I'll tell you about the camogie meeting which was held in Owens' Sixmilecross on last Thursday night. The Camogie Club are in about £10 of debt, £5 to Charleton, £2 to Mrs Owens, £2 to the 'Herald,' £1 to Robert Clarke and 4/- or 5/- to the Cross AOH Hall.

"I don't know how it will ever be got paid. I never thought they had near so much debt. We are not travelling to Fivemiletown on 10th March unless they get some money before that day. There is no way of making any now Lent is so near. McGirr didn't give Maggie and Josie the Barn. It is full of straw. I know things a barn of straw would be useful for. But not a camogie ceilidhe."

A group of schoolboys pictured outside Aughnaglea

Jim McGurn was in big demand at the time for his organisational abilities, as evidenced by a a letter from Altamuskin written in September 1933 asks for support in helping to form a camogie team there. It was written after Lizzie McCann had requested him in July that year to attend practice on a Sunday evening in July that year as "we cannot get along very well without knowing the rules."

Hurling

needed fillip to the native games locally

⊙⊙⊙

HURLING

BERAGH v. GLASSMULLAGH.

The above teams met on Sunday evening at Deroar Park, Beragh, in a return match, when a fine exhibition of the game was witnessed. The teams lined up at 7 p.m., and for sixty minutes latent memories of past glories were awakened by the clash of camans in the green fields of Deroar. Generations have faded into oblivion since last the resounding ash made the welkin ring in the Beragh district, and the display given by the local combination on Sunday against seasoned players is well worthy of the traditions of the district and merits a greater measure of support and encouragement than that afforded by the attendance at Sunday's fixture.

The match started off in a vigorous style, and for twenty minutes Glassmullagh had the best of the exchanges, during which J. M'Elholm scored two goals. After this Beragh opened their first determined raid on Glassmullagh territory and scored one goal and one point during the fastest bout of play in he match.

The second half was vigorously contested throughout, during which some brilliant passages of play were witnessed. Glassmullagh scored two goals and two points and Beragh scored one point in lay and three points per Rafferty from

It goes without saying that hurling in Tyrone has always played a very poor second fiddle to football. But such a statement fails to account for the periodic and at times sustained attempts to secure a better future for Ireland's oldest field game.

Evidence exists of caman having played in and around Roscavey school during the 1900s and the knowledge of this was undoubtedly still fresh when the game made a brief but memorable re-appearance in the parish during the summer of 1934.

Looking back now, the reasons for its promotion can be clearly guaged considering how Camogie had taken root in the area a year earlier. Jim McGurn was again among those to the fore in promoting and coaching the sport and the skills of the girls probably raised awareness and interest among the young men of the district at the time.

So, the decision was taken to purchase sticks and establish a team. And, the efforts led the Ulster Herald to raise the topic in July of that year when it urged other clubs to revive hurling by following the example of the

Beragh Gaels who it said had 'for some time past been making strenuous efforts to revive hurling' and 'to their credit it must be said that they have been successful to a certain extent.'

Among the first games was a match against Glasmullagh at Deroar Park in August when the reporter wrote about hurling having been played in the district many years earlier.

"The teams lined up at 7pm and for sixty minutes the latent memories of past glories were awakened by the clash of camans in the green fields of Deroar. Generations have faded into oblivion since last the resounding ash made the welkin ring in the Beragh district and the display given by the local combination on Sunday against seasoned players is well worthy of the traditions of the district and merits a greater measure of support and encouragement than that afforded by the attendance at Sunday's fixture."

The scorers for Beragh were Frank McMahon, Jack McCann and Frank Rafferty and a week later they made a return visit to Killyclogher where the only score of the game was a goal for the home side.

Fortunately, from an historical perspective, the Beragh team list is provided and is: J Doherty, Frank Rafferty, Michael McCaffrey, Jim McGurn, Frank McMahon, Leo Kelly, J McCartan, J Collins, Frank Kerr, Jack McCann, M McDermott, Frank Hagan.

Sean Bennett Looks Back

One of those who remembers well many of the developments of the 1930s was former Secretary and club official, Sean Bennett. He was born in Belfast in June 1920, and the family moved to Tyrone two years later when his father, Peter, got a job with Inglis's Bread Cart in Beragh. They initially lived in Cooley for three years when they moved to the village to the house in Main Street where Paddy Joe Keenan later lived.

"My mother ran a shop where McDowell the chemist lived. The Kerr sisters were next door and the chemist as well. I went to school in Beragh where the teachers were Master and Mrs McGrath. Master Fyffe was in the higher class," he said.

"In later years we moved down the street to what's

Pictured on the old pitch behind Owens of Deroar in the mid-30s are at back, Frank Donnelly, Eugene McCann, John Donnelly and Joe Colton. At front are Mickey Donnelly, John Boyle and Kieran McCann

Sean Bennett
pictured in 1933

now Gibson's. Inglis's had a depot there, the bread came in on the train every morning. My father had a heart attack and I was kept on to give him a hand on the horse cart. I started work in March 1938.

"Nearly all of my own family were born in Beragh and then we moved to Omagh in about the middle eighties. A few years before that my father had moved to Beech Valley in Dungannon.

"My father and Master Conway were among the people who kept the football going in Beragh in the earlier thirties. I remember them buying eighteen pairs of football boots to get the young fellows started off because they had nothing to do.

"I suppose my father wanted to get them started. He and my uncle were involved in Dungannon before that. But the boots eventually all disappeared, they went here, there and everywhere. Master Conway got them and I suppose they didn't cost much. He was very thorough in whatever he did.

"Dan Conway would have got a special order for the boots and I remember the big box coming into our house. If there was a match they would play it, but they didn't practice and there wasn't a league. We might have played Brackey, but there wasn't any games far away.

"I didn't play very much myself because I had a bad knee. The team was made up of young boys. They came after the Red Knights. This was the time of Johnny Ward, Jim McCann and Michael McCaffrey and they used to play out at the 'Big House' as Owens was called, and they went on to play up at 'Big Frankie's' where Mick Grimes is now.

"Beragh would have depended on players from Brackey and Sixmilecross. If Beragh started, Brackey would have to go out and eventually they came to compromise and both sets of players came together. There was nothing else for people to do in the summer time," he added.

Sean mentions Frankie Owens and Harry Kerr, whom he describes as a 'nice footballer.' A brother of Mickey, he played for a number of teams, including Cranagh at one time before they were drawn to meet Beragh and Kerr chose his native club team.

"The people involved were GAA minded but there was also soccer on the go. The club would have been kept going to counter-act that because, while boys went to go to see soccer matches, it wasn't liked," he continued.

"There was a hurling team as well, Jim McGurn came from Fermanagh and started it up. He used to stop in our house. He was a hurling man and one of the teams that they played was Glasmullagh, who came from around Dregish. More fellows got cracks in the head with the ball and it didn't really get off the ground."

West Tyrone Finalists - County semi-finalists

Defeat by Trillick on a score of 0-7 to 0-1 failed to seriously affect the fortunes of the Beragh footballers in a 1934 season that was to provide the prelude to them reaching the heights first scaled in the mid-twenties.

The return of Felix Owens from Carrickmore was a welcome tonic and notable results included a 4-5 to 0-5 win over Dromore, a 0-10 to 0-3 defeat by Carrickmore and 0-9 to 0-8 win over Fintona following a 'ding-dong' battle.

In the summer they were in joint third place in the West Tyrone Senior League with six points before things took a turn for the worse. A mis-understanding led to some players not turning up for a match against Ballygawley in September and the struggles of the club were highlighted in the Ulster Herald a month later.

Saying that some of the members seemed to be suffering from 'acute inertia,' it goes on to state how only about half of the team travelled to Fintona for a Senior League game which as a result could not be played. "This is a bad breach on the part of Beragh because hitherto it was one of the strongest and most active teams in the district. Perhaps indifference is responsible for it, but at any rate it is hoped that they will pull themselves together and get into their former stride again."

> On July 21 1934, there was havoc in Beragh due to a rainstorm. Storm lasted for little more than six hours, but the Main Street flowed with water to the depth of six inches, while water coursed like a river through houses. Large quantities of hay in ricks were caught and swept away, as was poultry belonging to M McMackin, The storm also swept away potatoes, oats blown down, trees taken up by the roots

That advice was apparently accepted in the right spirit by the club as they entered the new year 1935 with renewed vigour. Their rivalry with Omagh was a key feature of a busy season.

Main Street Beragh in 1933. To the left is where the club developed its first clubrooms

The sides met in the League twice in January, the first game finishing 0-2 each and the second going in

> Presentation to Jim
> McCann, a popular
> member of the club,
> on the occasion of
> his marriage. At an
> interval Mr
> McCaffrey, who was
> MC, presented a
> valuable clock
> suitably inscribed to
> Mr McCann on
> behalf of the club

favour of the St Enda's by 3-3 to 2-2. A 0-5 each draw was the result in the McAleer Cup, although Beragh later protested on the grounds that Omagh had fielded illegal players.

A 0-6 to 0-3 win over them was recorded in May as they defeated Trillick by 0-6 to 0-3 and Killyclogher by 2-4 to 2-1. Although holidays caused the cancellation of the game against Fintona in September, Beragh were subsequently victorious over them by 3-2 to 0-3 and in November were second in the SFL with twelve points from six games.

Deep satisfaction must have permeated the ranks of the players and officials as they prepared for the West Tyrone Final against Omagh. And, the Ulster Herald of December 21st emphasised what was at stake as arrangements for the County Final stated that the game would be at Omagh if between Beragh and Dungannon or Coalisland and at Sixmilecross if between Omagh and the East Tyrone Champions.

Further excitement was added to the fixture when Beragh failed to turn up for the game when it was originally scheduled. The matter was discussed at a meeting of the Tyrone County Board when the club informed that they were unable to play the semi-final due to 'unforeseen circumstances.'

A further twist in the tale came with the fact that Beragh's James McMahon chaired the meeting at which the matter was discussed. And, rather than declaring an interest and withdrawing as would probably be the case now, he remained firmly in the hot seat to defend the position of his club.

He said this had been the first match that Beragh had to put off and there was a good deal of talk about it. "If all clubs played their fixtures as well as Beragh and if they had the same loyalty amongst their members as the Beragh club, it would be a better West Tyrone League," he told the meeting.

The Beragh team
of 1933 pose for
the camera

When questions were asked about the possible reasons for the postponement, Jim Slane, representing Beragh, said the amount asked by the Transport Board for travelling a bus from Beragh to Dromore was exorbitant. He pointed out that the bus would not leave Beragh without being paid first.

Mr Doody, Secretary of the Omagh club, did not accept official notification of the postponement, claimed that the superintendent of the buses in Omagh had not even been contacted by the

Beragh club and requested that the letter received by the Beragh club from the Transport Board be produced at the next meeting.

A few weeks later, the letter from the local Transport Official was duly produced showing that the charge was £3 8s 6d, although even this did not satisfy the St Enda's officials present. After unsuccessfully objecting to the transfer of Barney Farrell from Ballygawley to Beragh earlier in the meeting, Mr G O'Neill said that he had been led to believe that the quotation had been obtained from Belfast.

He went on to state how he had received a different quotation from the Transport Authority, at which point Master McMahon, the Chairman, intervened. Saying that the Board was bound to accept the official letter, he angrily added that there had been a lot of comments about this bus outside, one of which was that the Beragh club had failed to look for a bus.

He asked Mr Doody to withdraw the statement that he made at the last meeting, having said that he evidently doubted the word of Jim Slane on the matter. This was accepted and the way was clear for a match that was capturing the imagination despite the delay.

Perhaps understandably considering the earlier postponement and the boardroom quarrels, the West Tyrone League Final for 1935 on February 2nd the following year, turned out to be an ill-tempered affair. It resulted in a 0-2 to 0-1 win for Omagh and the attitude of the teams was summed up by the Ulster Herald reporter who remarked that "the ambition to win resulted in the two teams ignoring the essentials that go into a clean and hard-fought game."

Statistics for the game were offered to support the point. There were eleven frees to Beragh and eight to Omagh in the first half, six frees to Beragh and seven to Omagh in the second half. A total of nine wides to Beragh and six to the St Enda's and that final score of 0-2 to 0-1 told its own story.

Time and again pressure from both teams failed to yield scores but Beragh took the lead coming up to half-time when Frank Rafferty sent the ball upfield where Lawrence Kelly from the wing registered their first and only point.

Dan McSorley and Frank McMahon came close to scoring in the second half, but Omagh equalised and gained what turned out to be the winner after fifteen minutes from McCrumlish.

So, defeat in a second County semi-final had left Beragh disappointed,

TINS 3d. & 6d.

POLISHES, PRESERVE
and **PROTECTS SHOE**

MADE IN DUBLIN
SINCE 1922

A few weeks later, the letter from the local Transport Official was duly produced showing that the charge was £3 8s 6d, although even this did not satisfy the St Enda's officials present

Paddy McCrumlish who was centrally involved with the Beragh and Brackey clubs from the 1930s and also took a keen interest in handball affairs

especially considering their strong bid and the number of chances created. Nevertheless, the efforts displayed had proved their ability even though the experience was never consolidated in the coming seasons.

The team in a 0-2 to 0-1 loss was: Barney Gormley, Mackle McCaffrey, Barney Farrell, Frank Rafferty, Jim McCann, James McMahon, Jack Mullan, Paddy McMahon, Frank McMahon, Dan McSorley, Lawrence Kelly, Felix Owens, Johnny Ward, Frank Farrell, Peter Montague.

Omagh lost to Dungannon by 2-5 to 2-1 in the 1935 final played at Atlamuskin.

Senior League Champions 1935

As well as their excellent championship form, Beragh were also showing plenty of resolve in the Senior League. The two went hand in hand and at January 31st Beragh and Omagh were locked at the top with eighteen points each.

No sooner had the dust settled on their West Tyrone Championship Final meeting than the completion of the West Tyrone League took precedence. Ironically, the fixture list pitted Beragh against Omagh yet again which was seen as another mouthwatering clash considering all that had gone on during the previous months.

Yet again the pairing aroused controversy. Beragh led by 1-2 to 0-2 at half-time, Omagh equalised soon after the restart and F Farrell and Paddy McMahon combined for a good point that put them back into the lead again. Good defence kept Omagh at bay, although all to no avail as they still managed to get important scores for a 1-6 to 1-4 win.

However, it seems that one of the Beragh points should have been accredited to them as a goal. And, at a subsequent meeting the referee, Fr McGilligan, stated in his report that the game had actually been a 1-6 to 2-3 draw.

The respected Carrickmore Priest, a native of Swatragh who died suddenly in 1940, said that he was absolutely positive the score was a goal and his report of the match was accepted by the Chairman, James McMahon. Arising out of the same report, Jim McCann was suspended for a month for striking an opponent.

However, Beragh still remained to the forefront in the League and got a few late scores to defeat Dromore by 0-8 to 0-3. This set up another meeting against Omagh when Beragh would need only a point to win the title.

But as things turned out, the title was to be secured even before that match. Double wins over Carrickmore by 0-7 to 0-3 on Sunday March 8 and then by 0-11 to 1-3 a week later clinched the points needed.

This was indeed fortunate because things didn't go according to plan in the final match when Omagh scored a 2-5 to 0-3 win. The Ulster Herald reported that Beragh had started off briskly with the confidence that they were League winners no matter what the result.

And, congratulations were certainly forthcoming for the new champions. The Ulster Herald offered hearty praise for the Sons of the Gael and added. "Throughout the league they were remarkable for their consistently excellent displays. This high attainment was due in no small measure to their energetic and enterprising captain, James McMahon who is also vice-chairman of the West Tyrone Board and member of the County Tyrone Committee. He has long associations with the GAA. Great merit is also due to the other members of the team."

> The momentum generated by the 1935 Senior League win was maintained into the summer of 1936

1936 Senior Championship - A time of decline

The momentum generated by the 1935 Senior League win was maintained into the summer of 1936. A close and hard fought game resulted in Beragh defeating Omagh in the Senior Championship by 3-3 to 2-4, Johnny Ward, Frank Owens and Paddy McCrumlish getting the goals.

Sixmilecross Main Street in the 30's

There was further evidence of their good form when they proved their worth in the McAleer Cup, going on to reach the final against Killyclogher at the end of July. While starting promisingly, they faded subsequently and only a goal from H McCrory kept them in contention.

The 1934 Beragh team which went on to reach the County Semi-Final. Included are Jim McGurn, Jim Doherty, Dan McSorley, Jim McCann, Felix Owens, Frank Parsons, Jim McMahon, Jack Kerr, Frank Kerr, Frankie Rafferty, Packie McMackin, Johnny Ward, John Kelly, Peter McGarrity, Pete McMahon, Paddy Casey, Michael McCaffrey. Members not in snap are Micksey Boyle, Vincent McCann, Joe Colton, Michael Grimes, Frank McMahon, Jim Rodgers.

In October 1939 a boy named Mick McCartan aged 6 years when playing with his brother, fell and sustained a fracture of his arm and injury to his shoulder. He was medically treated by Dr H Watson

Their improvement continued after half-time but they pressured the Killyclogher goal to no effect. As a result, the game stretched beyond them and, while Johnny Ward and Peter Montague got scores, they ended up losing by 4-4 to 1-5.

The Beragh Sons of the Gael team in that match was- Francis Maguire, Michael McCaffrey, Jim McMahon, Dan McSorley, Peter Montague, Frank Hagan, Hugh McCrystal, J Mullen, J Ward, Felix Owens, H McCrory, F McSorley, P Owens, F Mallon, Frank Owens.

Progress to the McAleer Cup Final, however, only slightly camouflaged their declining fortunes and their growing struggles in the West Tyrone League. By May 1936 they had still not made their debut in the League, although there was still hope held out as they were expected to 'make things hum' when they did. This didn't materialise, though. They offered poor resistance in a heavy defeat at the hands of Dromore, when they lost by 4-9 to 4-3 in July and that same month weren't included at all on the published League table.

No fixtures were given for them subsequently and the concerns were highlighted at a meeting of the West Tyrone Board in the autumn when they failed to give any explanation for their failure to fulfil a championship fixture against Fintona who were awarded the match.

Brackey to the fore

The second half of the thirties saw a new name from the parish make its mark on the Tyrone GAA scene with the arrival of Brackey in competitions. While teams from the area had existed prior to the 1920s, it wasn't until almost twenty years later that they really made an impact.

Paddy McCrumlish was central to the efforts to get them going, being elected Chairman of the Brackey Wolfe Tones for 1936. Other officials were Vice-Chairman – Michael Gallagher, Treasurer – Felix Owens and Secretary – Frank Maguire, Patrick Owens and Jas McGinn were the committee members and the team played in green and yellow with black knicks.

(2)

Brackey G.F. C. (Players)

William Barr,
John Daly,
Michael Daly,
Patk. Garety,
Patk. Kelly,
John Kelly,
Harry Kerr,
Jos. Mc Gale, Jas. Eagle,
Eugene Mc Cann,
Patk. Mc Crumlish,
Frank Mullan, Frank Rafferty
John Maguire,
Jas. Mc Ginn,
Felix Owens,
Patk. Owens,
Fras. Owens,
Frank Maguire.

Brackey's registration for 1936

Competing in the Junior League from 1936 on, the attention of players from the parish gradually turned to them as the Beragh team went into decline.

One of their first matches was a challenge in April 1936 when they showed great promise for the coming season. That promise, though, wasn't immediately apparent, when they lost to Cranagh by 0-5 to 0-2. They suffered defeat at home to Castlederg and were still without a win by October.

"Brackey is a new club with many of its members having little or no experience of gaelic football hitherto," reported the Ulster Herald. "They are improving, however, at every outing and are not disheartened by the succession of defeats. Victory will be all the sweeter when it does come and, though they may not distinguish themselves this season, they should give a good account of themselves next league."

Among the players said to have played well in a game at the end of the year were Frank Maguire, Harry Kerr, Begley, Johnny Ward and Frank Owens. By then Brackey were bottom of the table with two points.

However, those words in late 1936 failed to prove accurate in 1937 when

> *Because it was the only competition completed in 1938, that victory in the Herald Cup put Brackey through to the Junior Final against the East Tyrone Champions, Edendork, at the CBS Park in Omagh on March 12, 1939*

the poor fortunes of the Brackey men continued to prove frustrating. Cranagh defeated them in the West Tyrone Championship and then they lost by 1-8 to 1-1 to Tummery in the league.

But their first win did indeed come during that season when they reversed the result at home against Tummery. For the first ten minutes the visitors looked like winners, putting up the first scores. The home team's first goal was the climax of a hand-passing movement, Peter McCrory on the left scoring a goal in the first half when the ball rebounded off the crossbar behind the goalline. The final score was 1-18 to 1-13.

And the new year of 1938 brought them encouragement in the Herald Cup. At Sixmilecross in May they defeated Cranagh on the scoreline of 5-6 to 1-3. Their cleverer play was crucial, and after leading by a 2-1 to 1-3 at half-time they scored 3-5 without reply in the second half as their defence also held firm.

The Herald Cup Final was played on May 15th at Killyclogher when the determination of both teams in maintaining a high standard of football throughout the match was praised. The report of the game continues that "the Brackey team was soon performing like a freely working machine which gradually forged its way to victory."

Farrell, Dan McSorley, Harry Kerr and Gormley played well in defence and the game took a decisive turn when Laurence Kelly pointed nearing half-time. Frank Hagan scored a goal after being set up by Kelly, McQuaid's shot was deflected into the net to leave them well ahead at half-time before Peter Daly got their third goal on the resumption. The 4-3 to 0-3 win was clinched near the end when Peter Daly and Laurence Kelly scored a goal and a point respectively.

Life moves on for the players of the 1930s

Because it was the only competition completed in 1938, that victory in the Herald Cup put Brackey through to the Junior Final against the East Tyrone Champions, Edendork, at the CBS Park in Omagh on March 12th, 1939. St Eugene's Brass and Reed Band headed a parade of the teams around the field and on to the centre of the grounds where the National Anthem was played.

Ideal weather conditions aided the quality of play as Brackey dominated the first half exchanges. Their control came after a shaky enough beginning, but they were back on track when points from Peter Daly and Laurence Kelly settled them. Then 1-1 from Frank Mullan boosted them further before a second goal from Peter Daly helped them into a 2-5 to no score interval lead.

But they failed to maintain the momentum in the second half. Packie Owens in the goals was called upon to make a number of important saves and the task facing them was made all the tougher by the dismissal of an unnamed player for striking.

The game ended at a rousing pace with the visitors making a desperate but forlorn effort to reduce their deficit and Brackey holding on tenaciously to their hard-earned lead to win by 2-6 to 0-3.

The team was: Packie Owens, John Kelly, Harry Kerr, Johnny Ward, Laurence Kelly, Peter Daly, Dan McSorley, Felix Owens, Peter Daly, Johnny McAleer, Frank Hagan, Mick Keenan, Jas Rodgers, Frank Mullan, Michael Daly.

Members listed for the GAA in Beragh during the early 1930s

But Brackey's joy at winning the title was to prove shortlived. The next meeting of the West Tyrone Board in June 1939 raised the thorny question of them having fielded two players registered with Carrickmore in the win over Edendork.

The two were Mick Keenan and Peter McCrory who were, of course, resident in the Beragh parish but affiliated with the nearby St Colmcille's. Brackey were represented at the meeting by Paddy McCrumlish who said that it was through ignorance that they had transgressed the rules.

He pointed out that they had not been aware of the extent of the operations of the parish rule and were under the opinion that when a player from an adjoining parish was not being played regularly that he could be played by that parish. Adding that he had experienced great difficulty in keeping the game alive in the Beragh parish, McCrumlish hinted at many obstacles being placed in his way. He was prepared to apologise on behalf of the club and gave the assurance that nothing of the kind would happen again.

Fr McGilligan, Chairman, hoped that none of the people responsible for committing the breach were on the new committee. He spoke of his

A CEILIDHE MÓR
IN AID OF
ST. BRIGID'S CAMOGUIDE A.C. & CLUB
AT DEROAR PARK
SUNDAY 16th JULY, 1...
7 P.M. T....

Ticket for a
Beragh St Brigid's
Camogie Ceile in
the middle part of
the decade

awareness of Mr McCrumlish's interest in the game in Beragh parish and knew that he was largely responsible for its continuance there.

With this the matter was dropped by the West Tyrone Board, but it was then revisited at County Board level with the result that Edendork were duly awarded the title.

However, that did little to dampen the enthusiasm of the Brackey club. They lost to Ballygawley by 6-6 to 2-2 in June and games took place in the Junior League against Drumragh in May and June both of which were on by large margins. The team also took part in a seven a side tournament against Pomeroy at the Loughmacrory Sports in July.

Then came their second consecutive Herald Cup Final. It was against Drumquin on Sunday October 8th and resulted in a resounding 2-6 to 0-1 victory for a team described as being the more finished footballers. According to the Ulster Herald, the foundation for their victory lay in the strength of their forwards who easily outclassed the Drumquin attacking forces while both defences gave a good display.

Harry Kerr, Owens and Kelly were on top in defence as points from Ollie Slane, Frank Hagan, and two from Ward eased them in front. Owens at centre half back, Mullin and McCanny were also prominent and goals from McGarrity and Ollie Slane effectively sealed the issue.

The team was: Barney Gormley, Harry Kerr, John Kelly, Peter Daly, Packie Owens, Johnny Ward, John Mullin, Ollie Slane, Felix Owens, Frank Hagan, Francie Gallagher, Patrick McGarrity, Peter Montague, Dan McSorley.

In an interesting aside to the Herald Cup campaign, the club's appeal against Ballygawley was upheld and resulted in the Ballygawley club having to pay the Brackey expenses for the match.

A hectic decade of 1930s activity for the parish's footballers ended when Brackey failed to turn up for a match against Clogher in the St Enda Cup on December 3 that year. Clogher claimed victory, although Brackey had the power of appeal and were still included in the semi-final draw.

However, the West Tyrone Board was informed at the start of 1940 that Brackey were being replaced by a team representing the area under the Beragh banner.

Rare documents and new clubrooms

The month of October 1931 mark a watershed in the history of the GAA in Tyrone with the formation of the West Tyrone Board. But that month also marked the setting up of the Beragh Shamrocks Club at a meeting in the Chapel School on October 11th as evidenced in rare snippets of minutes obtained in 2006 from the Jim McGurn archive.

The club colours were selected as red and the committee elected was as follows: President – Father Hurson, Chairman – Francis Rafferty, Vice-Chairman, M Canavan, Secretary – Jim McGurn, Treasurer – Frankie Kerr, Committee – James Hagan, Jim Doherty, Mick Conway.

A selection committee was directed to meet on the following Wednesday, October 14th, to pick a team to play Augher on the following Sunday, Frank Kerr was directed to obtain a set of jerseys and the Secretary was asked to arrange for a Stop-Watch competition card to be got and 'assist in organising a sale of such cards.'

But a subsequent meeting on November 10th decided on Amber as the club colours and on that same date an arrangement was made to share pitch facilities on alternative Sundays with Altamuskin. It is interesting to note that among the points to be discussed at one meeting was the requirement for 'any person or member that has anything to say to now speak.'

The decision was taken to rent Kerr's House and do it up for clubrooms for the Beragh club by white-washing the room. These were situated at Main Street, to the rear of the house adjoining the 'Corner Bar' and the Minutes clearly state the requirements.

"Clubrooms manager to be appointed. Duties to include opening and closing of rooms, collecting 1/- per head from each and every person who enters for the purpose of pastime. To arrange card tables so that everyone in the room gets equal benefit from the light and fire arrangements. To arrange Tournaments etc among club members and to see that no gambling is carried out."

> The decision was taken to take Kerr's House and do it up for clubrooms for the Beragh club by white-washing the room

Michael Conway was appointed as manager, the activities started on a Thursday night and no doubt provided many hours of entertainment and talk of football and other matters for those attending.

Duties relating to the running of the club were always taken seriously,

The Minutes of the first meeting of the reformed Beragh club in 1931

players and officials were registered each year. Among those listed for 1933 were Henry Owens, David Christie and Bertie Browne and on April 16th, 1934, the Secretary, Master Conway, provided the following names to the West Tyrone Board.

They were: Felix Owens, John Kelly, Joseph Colton, James Hagan, Francis H Rodgers, Matthew Rodgers, William J Conway, Peter Bennett, Patrick McAleer, James Doherty, James McGurn, Francis McDermott, Michael McDermott, John Ward, Francis Owens, Pat Collins, John McCrory, Jim McCrory, Pat McCrory, Francis Mullin, Tom Slane, Leo Gordon, John Mulgrew, James Slane, Pat Shields, Terry McCann, Hughie McCrory, James Coyle.

Other activities

Increased action on the field required better organisation off it with more people becoming involved in GAA activities. The controversy surrounding the 1935 County Semi-Final and the debate over bus expenses showed that running a club involved more than the fielding of teams.

It was hardly surprising, then, that a range of events were held in the thirties to help defray costs as well as promoting what could best be described as a 'GAA spirit' among members and others with the interests of Irish culture and gaelic games at heart.

This was highlighted in December 1933 when Fr Hurson spoke at a function in the hall following football and camogie challenge matches between Beragh and the visiting Newtownstewart.

He said foreign dances could not be compared with the beauty and grace of their own National Dances. It was most encouraging, he remarked, to see that the proper Gaelic spirit was developing rapidly all over the north and he spoke of his delight at seeing that the games and dances were prospering.

However, he warned the youth that "they could not be called Irishmen until they had a knowledge of their own language" and encouraged the establishment of Gaelic League branches throughout the north. He congratulated the teams for their efforts earlier in the day, especially the girls who were making an effort to popularise the national game and referred to how "the good lessons learned on the football field helped to cultivate a true spirit of sportsmanship."

January 1932 saw the Annual General Meeting which attracted a large attendance of members and made arrangements for the future working of the club. Their awareness of fundraising issues was highlighted by the announcement of results for the Stop Watch competition and satisfaction was expressed at the good returns. A vote of thanks was passed to all who assisted in the competition and it was proposed that those who sent subscriptions to the club be entered in the list of patrons.

> However, he warned the youth that they could not be called Irishmen until they had a knowledge of their own language and encouraged the establishment of Gaelic League branches throughout the north

A Christmas Ceili was organised under the auspices of the club on December 31st 1932, with music being provided by Mr Joseph Nugent's Orchestra from Omagh. "Throughout the evening the large gathering thoroughly enjoyed themselves as they danced with enthusiasm to the strains of appropriate Irish music rendered in first class style," reported the Ulster Herald.

Barney Gormley, a prominent player of the 1930s, pictured with Jim Boyle

Of course, the GAA weren't the only organisation promoting dances and a report of the Hibernian's entertainment in September 1934 gives an indication of the other attractions. The music was 'high class', Miss Norah McAleer presided at the piano kindly lent by Miss Loughran and Mr Alphonus McAleer played the violin while Mr Murphy excelled himself on the accordion.

The members in regalia opened to the singing of 'God Save Ireland', 'A Nation Once Again' was also sung and the night closed with a rendition of 'O Donnell Abu' with great spirit. The comic element of the night was well sustained by B McAleer and Francis Rafferty and a most popular item was the traditional reel danced by Paddy Nugent of Carrickmore and Francis Rafferty, Cloughfin.

Of course, the GAA weren't the only organisation promoting dances and a report of the Hibernian's entertainment in September 1934 gives an indication of the other attractions

If none of these attractions tickled the fancy of club members, then they could also avail of a number of excursions. Extra tickets were sent to Beragh and Sixmilecross for the annual GAA trip to Bundoran. And in 1935 trek to the Cavan v Kildare All-Ireland Final proved very popular.

Three men from Omagh were said to have cycled the 100 miles to the match, but for the rest the train was the preferred mode of transport. Day Excursion tickets were available at a price of 7s 6d from Beragh and Sixmilecross, leaving at 8.40am and 8.45am respectively.

It all seemed so relaxed but maybe the spirit of relaxation was just too much since one game against Fintona at the time had to be postponed because several players were away on holiday.

In 1937, the club recognised the contribution of one of its popular members and regular players, Jim McCann, when they presented him with a valuable clock suitably inscribed to mark his forthcoming marriage. Music for the event was supplied by the Melody Makers and hornpipes were danced by Miss Ita McGarrity and songs contributed by Gerard Rafferty.

Youth football

It was inevitable that efforts to field teams at adult level would eventually involve the younger people in the parish who also wanted to begin participating. In the 1920s Beragh became one of the very first areas of Tyrone where youth football was promoted and that process continued into the 1930s.

A meeting of the Beragh Minor Football Club was held in January 1932 when the following officers were elected: Chairman - James Hagan, Secretary - Jack McCann, Treasurer - Leo Kelly. It was decided by them to enter a team in the West Tyrone League and also to ask Fintona for a friendly game on February 21st.

Those efforts proved successful and by April the two clubs had met on three separate occasions. The third on March 27th was refereed by James Hagan and a point from McGarrity saw Beragh lead 0-1 to 0-0 at half-time. The final score isn't given, but the team lined out - Breen, McMackin, Hagan, Owens, McCann, Mullan, White, McCann, McGarrity, Rafferty, Kelly, McGarrity and Campbell.

On Ascension Thursday 1933 Beragh schoolboys met their Killyclogher counterparts in what was billed as "the first inter-school game in a number of years and an event worthy of support." The Herald stated that "it was gratifying to note that at least some support was being devoted to give them the chance to learn the native games."

Periodic activity on the youth scene continued and in March 1936 Beragh played Pomeroy in a match that attracted a large gathering of spectators to the Pomeroy venue. Among the players to the fore for Beragh were Leo Kelly, Harry Owens, McGarrity, Ollie Slane and Fyffe and they emerged worthy winners by 2-7 to 1-6.

Other events

A major event of the 1930s was the opening of Drumduff Primary School in July 1936 by Fr Hurson. After Benediction in the nearby chapel, "the

On Ascension Thursday 1933 Beragh schoolboys met their Killyclogher counterparts in what was billed as the first inter-school game in a number of years and an event worthy of support

A Camogie teamsheet lists the Beragh players for a match against Altamuskin

congregation proceeded in procession led by the acolytes, bearing crucifix, thurible and lighted candles and followed by schoolchildren and adults to the school. "

Fr Hurson consecrated the building after which those present inspected the building which "is constructed on modern lines with the latest appointments and provided with an extensive playground."

After the ceremony a very entertaining outdoor programme of Irish dances, recitation and singing was presented by the pupils of the school under the direction of Mr and Mrs McCullagh, teachers and Mrs Michael Kerr. Mr John Daly also contributed songs and the music for the dancing was supplied by Mr Joe McMenamin. In conclusion, Fr Hurson, wished Mr and Mrs McCullagh many long and happy days in the school.

Another organisation to the fore at the time was the Sixmilecross Co-Operative Society, which showed profits of £215 for one year during the mid-thirties. Sales amounted to £12, 929 as compared with £8,300 the previous year and exactly four times what they had been four years previously. The committee and the manager, Mr Tommy McGarvey and the staff were congratulated on the excellent results for the year's work.

The political scene of those years was heated to say the least as opposition to partition continued to command the attention of nationalist politicians and the community at large. This was emphasised when the annual AOH Demonstration on St Patrick's Day drew a crowd of 10,000 to Sixmilecross.

HK McAleer and Joseph Stewart, MP addressed the event, with McAleer saying that "the majority of Unionist thinking men were thoroughly disgusted by the so-called Government of Northern Ireland." He added that "it was a pity that those most sincere and successful businessmen were not more articulate." He also talked about "Unionist domination" while Mr Stewart highlighted "gerrymandering."

These matters were particularly topical at the time since just months earlier, control of Omagh Urban Council had been won by the Unionists through gerrymandering despite the fact that Nationalists were the majority population by over two thirds.

A report in the Ulster Herald stated that 'when nationalist spokesmen accused Unionist leaders with perpetrating a gross wrong in Omagh Rural District, where the Nationalist majority is 8000 strong, they were met with the retort that they themselves allowed the Unionist scheme in that area to proceed without submitting a counter-scheme."

The later thirties also resulted in the tragic deaths of two prominent members of the Beragh club. In March 1937 Francis Rafferty, a former official, died in the County Hospital of injuries suffered while on deliveries for his employer, Mrs Kathleen Rodgers. While delivering the goods he fed the horse. Afterwards, as he was removing the nosebag, the horse moved off and he was knocked down and the wheel of the van passed over his body.

Frank McMahon, a player of the 1920s and 1930s, also died prematurely in September 1938. A brother of James and Pete, he had transferred to Sean McDermott's in Dublin, where he had built up a thriving business as a cabinet maker. However, he contracted an illness which lasted a number of months and was to result in his death. He was buried in the family burial ground at Carrickatee, Castleblayney.

Inter-County GAA matters

Greater organisation at club level in Tyrone with the introduction of the East and West Divisional Board was further enhanced as the thirties progressed with some notable achievements at inter-county level.

White jerseys with a red hand were first used in 1931 when Tyrone gained their first ever success by winning the Four-County League. The Minors won their first Ulster title that same year and the visit of Kerry to Coalisland in 1932 provided a further boost.

This progress culminated in the first provincial final appearance by Tyrone at Senior level in 1933. That was to prove a particularly memorable occasion for Beragh's James McMahon who lined out at midfield. However, his efforts and those of his teammates came to nought as the Cavan team on its way to a first ever All-Ireland title won by 6-13 to 1-2.

The political scene of those years was heated to say the least as opposition to partition continued to command the attention of nationalist politicians and the community at large

123

The establishment of the West Tyrone Board gave a new impetus to the GAA in Tyrone and prompted sustained growth in the Beragh area

Apart from Jim McMahon on the Seniors in 1933, other Beragh players occasionally made their mark for Tyrone teams at various levels. Leo Kelly represented the club during the early thirties, but is listed with Ballygawley in the Minor team which won the 1934 Ulster title.

Kelly was one of three from the club who took part in the Probables v Possibles Trial match at the start of 1933. The others were H McKiernan and Frank Hagan, who did goals to little effect if a report of the trial is anything to go by. He was described as "not being of the desired standard for the position, though he was keen enough, but seemed nervous and was noticeably lacking in dash."

Conclusion

The establishment of the West Tyrone Board gave a new impetus to the GAA in Tyrone and prompted sustained growth in the Beragh area. This was highlighted by a number of successes throughout the thirties, in particular the 1935 Senior League win and the Championship semi-final appearance by Beragh and the progress of Brackey to the Junior Finals of 1938 and 1939.

Each of these events called for greater organisation on the part of officials and the area was fortunate to have a number of able people who worked at both local and county level. Promotion of hurling, camogie, underage football and fairly regular social events shows that there was also an increased awareness of the wider responsibilities of a GAA club at the time. They were soundly placed to move forward when the beginning of World War Two made a serious impact on gaelic games in Beragh specifically and West Tyrone generally.

Chapter Six
1940 - 1950
Mixed Fortunes in the Forties

Chapter Six
1940 - 1950

CONFIDENCE must have been high entering the new decade as the gaels of the Beragh parish reflected with pride on the exciting momentum which was built up on the GAA scene during the 1930s. The general outlook was positive even though there had been occasional problems and setbacks.

The exploits at the end of the thirties of the team based in Brackey gave a new impetus. Their successes in Junior Football included winning the Herald Cup and reaching the Championship Final and these augured well for the future at a time when the difficulties of subsequent years weren't yet apparent.

All of this came at a time when the GAA in Tyrone as a whole was enjoying sustained growth. The formation of the East and West Tyrone Boards, regular

Sixmilecross from outside Armstrong's shop in the early 1940s

annual League and knock-out competitions and better administrative organisation was reflected in the rise in the number of competing teams.

It is easy to understand why there was a determination to keep things going as the new decade opened with the potential problems brought about by World War Two looming large on the horizon. While the impact of the War was not immediately apparent, severe fuel restrictions, curbs on travel and the introduction of police permits, identity cards and so on would soon bite. Soon after the war was declared on All-Ireland Hurling Final Day in 1939, police visited each household in Beragh and Sixmilecross to ensure that the blackout was being observed.

But the prevailing circumstances didn't prevent GAA activities from continuing. Brackey were represented at the 1940 West Tyrone Convention in January and were soon preparing for the start of the decade on the football field as well.

January 1942 – Report of police objection to the renewal of Sixmilecross AOH Entertainments License on the grounds that in the past there had been rowdy and noisy conduct. Recommendation that the annual License be refused was granted

> Last big dance of
> the season on
> February 28th,
> 1943 in the Beragh
> Parochial Hall.
> Music by Nugent's
> Dance Band,
> Omagh. Dancing
> from 9pm
> until 3am.
> Ladies 1/- Gents 2/-

Junior Final 1939

Delays in the completion of competitions were a regular feature of gaelic football activity over sixty years ago. By the beginning of 1940, there still had not been any games played in the 1939 Junior Championship.

But Brackey certainly entered it expecting to do well. After all, their triumphs in the Herald Cup, the fact that they had won and been stripped of the Junior title in 1938 suggested that they were well capable of defeating the best in Tyrone at their level.

This was highlighted when they progressed to the Final for the second year running. Details of their run are scant in the newspapers of the time, but what is known is that the game took place in Coalisland on Sunday April 6th 1940.

Standing in their way was a recently established Mountjoy team which made its mark on the day with a resounding victory. Their winning margin of 4-2 to 0-2 indicates their control in the game as they took the last title of the 1930s.

But by then a Beragh team was back in the West Tyrone Senior League. Fixtures for the month of the Junior Final pitted them against Carrickmore, Eskra and Dromore and the team included some veterans of the heady days of the middle thirties.

Senior League struggles 1940-1943

One match that receives particular prominence in the Ulster Herald of that year was the tie against Dromore at the beginning of May. The St Dympna's were the undisputed League leaders with full points from five games, well ahead of their nearest challengers, the prospective County Champions, Carrickmore, and Clogher.

In contrast, Beragh were struggling alongside Killyclogher at the bottom of the table. Still, that didn't prevent them from making a strong bid to upset the odds even though it took them most of the game to get going.

"Beragh were in arrears to the extent of seven points about ten minutes from the finish," recounts the Ulster Herald report of the match.

"But they refused to accept defeat without putting forth a tremendous effort. They notched two fine goals by Pat McKernan and Kieran

McCann, but despite a hectic finish they failed to secure the equaliser."
Dromore won by 0-7 to 2-0 and the Beragh team lined out: Packie Owens,
Dan McSorley, Mick McCaffrey, Peter Daly, Harry Kerr, Peter Montague,
Frank Owens, Frank Hagan, Ollie Slane, Johnny Ward, Mick Daly, Kieran
McCann and Pat McKernan.

Whatever about the low number of games completed by the team, there
was no shortage of competitive action. As well as the matches in the
Senior League, they also took part in the Dromore Sports against Ederney,
Irvinestown, Trillick, Fintona, Clogher, Carrickmore and Omagh.

And, they were also aware of the need for the development of gaelic
games in the county. Paddy McCrumlish, Jack McCann and Frank Hagan,
were regulars at West Tyrone Board meetings and were not afraid to air
their views on different subjects on a monthly basis.

For instance, in a debate on the state of the GAA in Omagh and
Killyclogher, Paddy McCrumlish told delegates that their absence would
be a big blow to the Association. He also expressed concern about a
proposed change to the Parish Rule, saying that it would be detrimental to
club football if clubs were allowed to select players from another parish
where there was no team.

This group of
young players
and officials were
to the fore in
the 1940s

This was obviously a matter of some importance at the time considering how
both Beragh and Brackey were finding the going tougher than previously.
The defection of a number of players to Carrickmore and elsewhere, most
notably Ollie Slane, was a talking
point of the time.

Of course, those early years of
the 1940s did witness some good
performances by Beragh teams.
In June 1940 they competed
with pride at a Nine-a-Side
tournament in Pomeroy, beating
Dunamore by 3-3 to 0-0 and
Donaghmore before losing out at
the semi-final stage to
Carrickmore.

Two months later they played a
real thriller against old rivals,
Ballygawley. Good tackling by
McCann and Kerr helped them

CO. CHAMPIONSHIP

BERAGH v. DUNGANNON.

In one of the best games of their career Beragh came near to creating a first-rate sensation when they ran Dungannon Clarkes to a goal in the Co. Championship at Beragh on Sunday. Their display was all the more remarkable and praiseworthy in view of the great reputation of the opposition, which consisted of eight county players. Up to about ten minutes from the finish, the homesters looked certain winners, but a rather lucky goal to the Clarkes altered the trend of the game. All the Beragh players rose to the big occasion, Kerr, Owens, M'Sorley and Hagan being very outstanding.

The final score was—Beragh, 1gl. 2pts. ; Dungannon, 2gls. 2pts.

A good attendance enjoyed a really high-class game.

The teams :—

Beragh—J. M'Aleer, J. Kelly, H. Kerr, P. Teague, J. Donaghey, F. Hagan, P. Daly, D. M'Sorley, S. Owens, J. Mullan, J. Ward, F. Gallagher, P. M'Kernan, M. Grimes, K. M'Cann.

Dungannon—J. Skeffington, S. Herron, L. M'Grath, A. Hamill, J. Logan, P. Barker, P. Rice, J. Hamill, F. Comac, J. Connolly, J. Rafferty, Skeffington, F. M'Neill, T. Corrigan, O. Barker.

Mr. M. M'Elduff, P.E.T., was referee. Play was of an even character in the opening minutes, and after some tentative efforts on both sides Dungannon succeeded in scoring per Rafferty (pt.). Beragh fought back in spirited style and had the equaliser per Grimes. The home team continued to show to fine advantage, their display surprising even their most enthusiastic admirers, and before long they went into the lead with a point from a free per Gallagher. Later, Dun-

The report of the Beragh v Dungannon Senior Championship tie in 1940

into a 3-3 to 1-1 half-time lead. However, things fell apart on the resumption, with superior catching by the Ballygawley defence helping them to an eventual 3-8 to 3-5 win. Two teams were brought to the Eskra Sports later in the month where they lost to Castlecaulfield and Carrickmore.

Things seem to have been on a downward spiral in the Senior League, however. Regular fixtures appeared against teams such as Eskra, Killyclogher, Trillick and Carrickmore throughout the summer and early autumn of 1940. But it seems few of these were actually fulfilled, as Beragh weren't listed on the published league table soon after.

The true picture is hard to guage as in December the team was described as "having presented stiff opposition since its entry into Senior ranks." A challenge game against Carrickmore at Deroar brought an end to the 1940 activities and provided a focus for the start of the new season. There was obviously an anxiety to improve on the previous year and in February a large attendance witnessed what was described as a fine exhibition of football in arctic conditions against Pomeroy.

It was a game that set them up nicely for a clash against Dromore in the Senior Championship the following month. However, while they played well, Dromore repeated their League success of the previous year.

Defeat in that game left the way clear to concentrate on the Senior League, but Beragh were once again struggling to make an impact. Games against Eskra, Carrickmore, Ballygawley, Trillick and Omagh were fixed, but by mid-summer they were on just one point.

There was further controversy when they were expelled from the St Enda Cup after failing to fulfil a fixture against Trillick in September. At the subsequent meeting of the West Tyrone Board, which was not attended by a Beragh delegate, the Chairman said that no more fixtures would be granted to them.

However, at the November meeting, Jack McCann asked why Beragh were disqualified as four members of the team had a bereavement the day before the match. But the Chairman told him that this explanation should have been given at the previous meeting and it was now too late to raise the question.

Six games had been played by the end of 1941 and the increasing difficulties brought about by travel and other restrictions resulted in a proposal at the beginning of 1942 to separate West Tyrone into two separate divisions.

Perhaps this restructuring gave things a new lease of life. As the GAA President, Padraig McNamee, called for gaels in the north to lead a revival in national spirit, Beragh travelled to Clogher in the opening round of the West Tyrone League. The home team ran out winners by 4-6 to 2-6, but there was better luck on the last Sunday in April against the County Champions, Carrickmore.

In a clean and spiritedly contested match, Beragh defeated them by 2-2 to 1-1. Owens, Mullan, Rafferty, McCann and Hagan were best and scores from Gallagher (1-2) and Owens (1-1) secured two points.

Affairs continued to struggle along as the year progressed. There was controversy in the St Enda Cup in May when the match against Omagh at St Patrick's Park had to be finished abruptly with about ten minutes remaining following the awarding of a 14 yard free to Omagh. At the time the teams were level at 1-2 each, Owens (1-1) and Gallagher (0-1) being the Beragh scorers.

The referee, in his report to the subsequent meeting of the West Tyrone Board, stated that the match was terminated because the Beragh players had objected to the awarding of the free. He said he was unable to restart the game owing to the 'attitude taken' by some Beragh players.

Speaking at the meeting, the Chairman, Rev T Kirke, said that he had no hesitation in awarding the match to Omagh and, if the names of the Beragh players responsible for the interruption had been given, he would have dealt with them in an exemplary manner.

"It was not to the credit of the Beragh club that such an occurrence should take place. In reprimanding the Beragh club, he gave a general warning to all clubs that such conduct would not be tolerated," the Ulster Herald report of the meeting stated.

The problems of organising games were reaching a critical stage and were raised at a meeting of the West Tyrone Board in August. The difficulties of providing transport for travelling teams were discussed at length and it was proposed to revert to the old system of playing the County Championship as two Divisions. The winners of each were then due to

1945 – Diptheriua Immunisation – November 6th in Beragh PES, November 8th in Aughnaglea PES, November 14th in Drumduff, November 15th in Cloughfin and November 16th in Roscavey

meet, with the victors in that game progressing to meet their counterparts from the East.

However, it seems that these arrangements came too late to ensure Beragh's participation. While the club continued to function and Jack McCann and Robert Collins represented them at the May 1942 meeting of the West Tyrone a fine of £2 was imposed when they failed to field in the West Tyrone League in August of 1942. It was to be two years before they competed at a West Tyrone level again.

"Teams couldn't travel very far because of the shortage of petrol. Games could only take place within a thirty mile radius and that's why things sort of died for a while in Beragh," remarked Sean Bennett, who was, of course, involved in the revival from the mid forties on.

"We used to travel by bus for a few years afterwards. Jimmy Callan used to drive us. There was a sort of a team which got together every so often, but there was nothing permanent until the St Mary's Club was started."

Championship clash with the Clarkes

While Beragh had mixed fortunes in the League during the early years of the 1940s, the County Championship appeared to take the best out of the players and they progressed to the Quarter Final in 1940. Drawn against Eskra in the first round at the end of August, they went on to meet Killyclogher at the next stage.

Neither team played impressively in the game at Deroar, with the action being interrupted by a number of free kicks. The shooting was also described as being weak, although Beragh fared best and emerged winners by 2-0 to 0-2.

This set up an attractive clash against one of the top teams of the time, Dungannon Clarkes, on Sunday December 1st. With home advantage, the Beragh players were confident of making their mark and duly did so with a performance rated by the Ulster Herald as 'one of the best of their careers.'

In fact, the home team came close to causing the sensation of the championship and the reporter continued his praise by saying that their display was "all the more remarkable and praiseworthy in view of the great reputation of the opposition, which included eight county players.

Roads in Clogherney and Redergan in deplorable state during 1947. Farmers and others complain bitterly and in some cases it is impossible to take a horse and cart over them

"Up to about ten minutes from the finish, the homesters looked certain winners, but a rather lucky goal to the Clarkes altered the trend of the game. All the Beragh players rose to the big occasion, Kerr, Owens, McSorley and Hagan being very outstanding."

A goal and point from Francie Gallagher and a point from M Grimes highlighted Beragh's form, much to the delight of their enthusiastic support. They led at half-time and were also the better team on the resumption as their defence 'seemed prepared for all emergencies.'

The early part of the decade saw Nancy Hagan arrive in the area and become one of the club's most regular supporters

However, disaster struck near the finish when a high ball into the goalmouth from Leo McGrath was accidentally punched into his own goal by a Beragh defender. A point from Hamill and a second goal from P Barker gave the Clarkes control, although the home team never gave up.

They took up the running again in the closing stages and made determined efforts to regain lost ground, but to no avail as Dungannon held on to their winning lead.

The final score of 2-2 to 1-2 highlights just how close Beragh came to causing a shock and reaching the County Semi-Final again. Dungannon went on to defeat Moortown in the semi-final, before losing to Carrickmore in the final.

Beragh lined out: Johnny McAleer, John Kelly, Harry Kerr, Peter Teague, John Donaghy, Frank Hagan, Packie Daly, Dan McSorley, Sonny Owens, Johnny Mullan, Johnny Ward, Francie Gallagher, Packie McKernan, Mackle Grimes, K McCann.

Incidentally, that Carrickmore win in the 1940 Final earned them their first O'Neill Cup success.

Frankie Owens looks back

A playing career stretching from the late thirties to early fifties helped make Frankie Owens a 'mentioned footballer' as a member of the Brackey team of the late thirties and then the Beragh team from the mid-forties onwards. He remembers many of the names and games of that time.

133

"There were a lot of players around in the late thirties when Brackey won the Junior Cup. Packie (Owens) was on the team at that time, there was John Kelly, Johnny Ward, Peter McAleer and Johnny McAleer. Packie Daly would have been playing as well, Paddy Gillen was a good footballer and Bill Davy," he said.

"Lawrence McGale would have been good, but he took a sort of a fever and died young. Mickey Owens of Remackin was a 'rough and tumble' type, we had Francie McCrystal, Willie Barr was a forward and Francie Maguire did goals.

"I think the jerseys were green, they were a good new set and the field that we played on at one time was beside McGlinn's. We then had games in the field behind our house. Pa Casey was a man who was around the team getting the good players out for matches.

Francie Gallagher, Secretary in 1941 and 1942 and keeper of the football and jerseys during this period

"But McCrumlish (Paddy) was a damn bad player. He hit a fifty one time and hardly moved it at all. Before that he was kicking the ball the length of the field in training.

"Francie Farrell, Barney Farrell, Dan McSorley and Peter Montague all played for Brackey as well because there was no team in Beragh. Mickey Donaghy came out before he went to Cookstown later on."

Others of note recalled by Frankie were Mick and John McCollum, Pat Doherty and Barney McAleer. He recalls Barney Gormley doing goals and being a 'good scrapper' a useful enough quality at a time when football could be a lot rougher than now!

Sports Meetings - 1941-1945

What makes a GAA Club is a question that has often been posed throughout the 120 years that the Association has been in existence. Activity in athletic events, the promotion of all gaelic games and culture were obvious requirements especially during the early years.

But as the first half of the twentieth century progressed, the role of the GAA club became increasingly blurred. While the organisation of cultural activities and the

---

2

BERAGH PAROCHIAL FUND.

Football Tournament and Athletic Sports
(Under N.A. and C.A.I. Rules, Official Handicapper), will be held in
COOLEY PARK, BERAGH
On SUNDAY, 1st AUGUST, 1943
Commencing 2 p.m. (E.S.T.).
TRAINS FROM BELFAST AND DERRY ARRIVE BERAGH 12 NOON.

PROGRAMME:

1. 100 Yards Flat	7. Two Mile Cycle Championship of Ulster	
2. 220 Yards Flat		
3. 440 Yards Flat	8. "Devil Take Hindmost" Cycle Race.	
4. 880 Yards Flat		
5. 100 Yards (confined to Sixmile- cross Club).	9. Three Mile Cycle Race.	
6. One Mile Cycle Race.	10. High Jump	
	11. Pole Vault.	

The following well-known Ulster and Irish Champions will compete:—
T. WALL, J. VALLELY, J. McCANN, P. McQUADE,

SEVEN-A-SIDE FOOTBALL TOURNAMENT—Value £3 10s.
ST. EUGENE'S SILVER BAND WILL ATTEND.
REFRESHMENTS SUPPLIED ON FIELD.
ENTERTAINMENT AND BALLOT DRAW will be held in Parochial Hall after Sports. Music by Nugent's Band.

ADMISSION TO FIELD—1/-.   CHILDREN 6d.

promotion of hurling, football, handball and camogie were the central aims, the reality was that most clubs really only fielded a team at senior level, held occasional meetings and competed in whatever Leagues and Championships were organised by their governing bodies.

This however doesn't diminish the central reasons behind why the GAA was established in the first place back in 1884. In the 1940s, though, the tasks of fulfilling these was very difficult in the restrictive climate of World War Two.

One problem was the scarcity of money which resulted in teams finding it hard to travel to away games. This was acknowledged by the West Tyrone Board who allowed clubs a certain amount of freedom in arranging matches as the fixtures lists grew longer.

In Beragh, GAA officials organised their first ever Tournament in 1940 as a fundraiser not for themselves but for the local St Malachy's Branch of the St Vincent De Paul and it grew into a very substantial annual event as the decade progressed.

The Tournament in 1942 was held on Sunday August 11th that year and those who came to help were amply rewarded by witnessing some stirring games. There was no luck, though, for the hosts who went out to Fintona in the first round by 2-3 to 1-4. Fintona went all the way to the final where they were beaten by Trillick and afterwards Patrick Donnelly, President of the SVP Branch paid tribute to Frank Hagan and Jack McCann for organising the Tournament and Robert Logue and Tom Fyffe who acted as gate stewards.

By the following year the event had grown to include athletic events as well as the football tournament. A high jump and Pole Vault - which aroused great interest - were added to the schedule which was said to have been greatly enhanced by the attendance of St Eugene's Brass and Reed Band from Omagh.

Two cycling events proved very popular, with fast times being recorded, and the catering arrangements were in the hands of the Ladies committee. Field arrangements were described as being a tribute to the ability and initiative of the organisers.

The thirteen a side football tournament drew seven teams, namely the hosts, Beragh, Dromore, Eskra, Irvinestown, Carrickmore, Omagh and Fintona. Beragh lost to Irvinestown in the opening round, the semi-finals

Although it was reported in 1948 that a caretaker would be appointed to look after the Beragh dump, nobody knows who the man is. Situated near the Railway Station, the dump continues to be an eyesore and there is no supervision on it

Sean Bennett and Frank Hagan are pictured with this group of young players from the mid-1940s when the St Mary's club was getting off the ground

resulted in wins for Dromore over Carrickmore and Omagh over Irvinestown, with Dromore beating Omagh in the final by 1-2 to 0-2.

The GAA grounds were once again the venue in 1942 when a big attraction was the appearance of the Irish Pole-Vaulting Champion, J Vallely. He cleared 5ft 7 inches in the High Jump, but was thwarted in his attempt to take the Pole-Vault title when the breaking of the pole in the competition brought it to a premature finish. Big achievements were being anticipated, after three of those taking part cleared 10ft 2 inches. The pole broke during a vault by the last competitor, John MacAmbrose from Dromore.

Another competition was the Seven-a-Side Football Tournament, which included teams from Brackey, Beragh, Sixmilecross, Carrickmore and Dromore. Carrickmore were the eventual winners by 4-3 to 1-2 over Dromore in the final.

And, the Ulster Herald report of the event was in no doubt about its success and the quality of competition on offer. "The outstanding achievement of the evening was that of the young Omagh cyclist, Joe McCann, when he annexed the Ulster Senior Two Miles Cycling Championship in brilliant fashion.

"Athletic prowess of a high order was the keynote in all cases, the results in many of the events being well in keeping with championship standard."

The GAA involvement was again central to the running of the event in 1943. Master Conway, Jack McCann, Sean Bennett and Frank Hagan were the main organisers of an event which included the unusually named 'Devil Take Hindmost' Cycle Race. Its length depended on the number of competitors and it was eventually won by Joe McQuaide from Dungannon by half a wheel length from Omagh's Joe McCann.

Organised that year for Parochial purposes, the football tournament was won by Ballygawley. Once again there were teams from Beragh and Sixmilecross, with Ballygawley and Carrickmore reaching the final.

The seeds of revival

Perhaps it is more than a coincidence that the revival in various sports events, Aeriocht, language classes and other cultural activities came at a time when the GAA in West Tyrone was appealing to its clubs to become the focal point of their communities.

Realising the difficulties being faced, the Chairman, Rev Father Kirke, urged clubs to run concerts, Irish dancing classes and generally to become focused on the aims of the GAA and the preservation of Irish culture.

The mid forties resulted in his calls being wholeheartedly adopted in Beragh. After the success of the sports events held earlier in the decade, there was an even broader embracing of Gaelic ideals.

By 1944 the Sports event had become the Beragh Annual Sports and Aeridheact Mhor. They were held that year on a field lent by Fadie McCusker and, as well as the usual extensive athletics programme, there were a number of Irish cultural activities.

These included Language, Story-telling and Dialogue, with two poems of the competitor's own choice in Irish or with an Irish sentiment. There were also categories for instrumental music, violin, melodeon and Ceilidhe Bands. Proceeds at the event were in aid of Parochial Funds, and it was to be followed by a Ceilidhe Mhor in the hall. The Sixmilecross Pipe Band was on hand to provide music.

Large contingents came to the event from as far as Derry, Belfast and Omagh and an indication of its success was the fact that entries totalled some 500. Indeed, the Ulster Herald of the following week reported that the renewed resurgence of the Irish spirit augured well for the continued success of the important work which was being so wholeheartedly undertaken.

For the record the Ladies and Mens committee who looked after the arrangements included: Miss F Kerr PET, Miss A White, Miss A McCusker PET, Miss J McGarrity, Mrs J McCann, Miss L Collins, Miss V Devine, Miss Mary Campbell, Miss L Corrigan, Miss A Conway, Miss M and A McCartan, Miss M Grimes, Miss Margaret McCarney, Miss A Donaghy, Mrs Gallagher, Miss Rodgers, Miss V Donnelly, Miss B Devlin, Miss K McCann.

The Mens committee consisted of Rev James McKeever CC, Chairman, James McMahon PET, P McCusker PET, WJ Conway PET, John

Patrick Owens died at his residence in Deroar. Belongs to an old Catholic family thought to have been in the district for four centuries. Interment in the old cemetery

McCullagh PET, J McCann, P Collins, Sean Bennett, Sonny Hagan, RJ Logue, P Donnelly, J Colton (sen), Jack McCann (Secretary) and P Collins (Sports Secretary).

The following year the event commenced with a parade through the village, a loud-speaking system was in operation and the competitions took place at Deroar Park with three separate platforms in operation.

During the afternoon a raffle was organised in aid of the Gaelic League and an interesting feature was the fact that the Beragh Gaelic League Choir and its counterpart from Sixmilecross recorded 88% and 86% respectively in the Choir's section.

An insight into the thinking of the time can be guaged from comments made by the Chairman of the South Tyrone Gaelic League at a Ceilidhe in Sixmilecross in March 1945. Rev C McDonald made an impassioned plea for the promotion of Irish culture and games.

"The attitude of a certain section with regard to Irish dancing, music and games is sometimes described as narrow-minded and bigoted, but that policy is not based on bigotry and hatred," he said.

"We have no fault to find with good manly sport and amusement fostered by any nation, but we feel that the games our fathers played, the songs they sang and the dances which formed part of their evenings' recreation can hold their own with any of them, and it behoves us to foster and cherish them until they are safe for ourselves and future generations."

Another concert, which took place in Beragh at Halloween 1944 included in it, songs such as 'Peggy O'Dea from Mullinalee,' 'The Bold Fenian Men,' and 'Sitting on the Bridge Below the Town.'

Brackey Club's Application

All this activity certainly prompted some in the parish to bemoan the absence of a gaelic football team and the call for action to remedy the situation. And, at the April 1945 meeting of the West Tyrone Board, a letter was received from Paddy McCrumlish highlighting the anxiety of people in the area to form a Junior team.

He wanted to know if they could claim the Beragh parish players who were at the time with Altamuskin and Carrickmore. In response, the Rev Chairman said that there were no players with Carrickmore now and that

> We have no fault to find with good manly sport and amusement fostered by any nation, but we feel that the games our fathers played, the songs they sang and the dances which formed part of their evenings' recreation can hold their own with any of them, and it behoves us to foster and cherish them until they are safe for ourselves and future generations

there were five players transferred to Altamuskin at the March meeting and that if these players were taken back there might be no team left in that area.

The minutes continue: "Mr McElduff then raised the position of Ollie Slane who was refused permission to play for them (Carrickmore) at the last meeting stating that he was granted permission to play for Altamuskin, a club which never applied for nor which he never applied to get playing for.

"He said he though the Board's action was highly irregular. Mr Coleman said that Ollie Slane could not play for Brackey and the Rev Chairman pointed out that if the Brackey club start up, another club will go out of existence."

After further discussion it was suggested that Brackey should wait and enter a team in the Junior Championship and this was agreed by the Brackey delegate. Carrickmore, meanwhile, intimated their intention to continue fielding Ollie Slane.

However, the Brackey club never did get around to fielding in that year's Junior Championship and it was to be some months before GAA activity in the parish was finally re-established.

Sean Bennett, a key mover in the re-establishment of the Beragh St Mary's, pictured on his wedding day.

A New Lease of Life

West Tyrone League competitions had been without a team from the Beragh Parish for some two years by the time the decision was taken to once again affiliate. Things were put in motion when a new group of enthusiasts, helped by some more experienced members, formed the St Mary's Club sometime towards the end of 1944 or early the following year.

Exact details of this latest reformation meeting are scare, but it is possible to give a fairly accurate rundown on who could have been present. The years around that time had seen the Sports and Aeridheact held annually and many of those involved in their organisation became deeply involved when GAA affairs and specifically the gaelic football team was re-established.

One of them was Sean Bennett. He had been born in Dungannon, but moved to Beragh with his family in the early twenties and was part of the youth team that took part in a number of games in the 1930s.

Two prominent members from the 1940s, Peter McNamee and Mickey Gallagher, hard at work and recalling recent footballing events

The absence of minute books means that a full register of those who attended is unknown, but we do know the make-up of the committee. The Chairman was Terry McCann from Altamuskin.

Sean Bennett became Secretary and WJ Conway, a teacher in Beragh school, took on the role of Treasurer that he had previously held in the 1930s. Others in attendance were Frank Hagan, Jack McCann, Patrick Collins, Fr Murtagh and, of course, many of the players who would go on to represent the new St Mary's in the coming seasons.

"It was great for the team to get back into Junior football and in fact win the Junior Cup a few years later. Big Terry McCann was Chairman and I saw him walk from where he lived in Altamuskin, to Beragh school for a meeting," added Sean Bennett.

"He took an interest in the club even though he was from outside the parish. I was Secretary from the very start to the club and on flitting and shifting from one place to the other I lost the minute books. Master Conway was still Treasurer during those years.

"The name St Mary's was chosen because it was the name of the parish. To be honest, I can't remember the first meeting. But things just carried on from one Sunday to the next and kept going on from there.

"Then when things got going a bit better the meetings were called. The players would have been doing a bit of playing, Master Conway looked after the finances and I looked after the travelling.

"Half-time there were only ourselves at the meetings, myself, Master Conway, John Donaghy and Terry McCann. We got jerseys out of Dublin through Fr Donnelly and I looked after getting and paying for the buses. You had to put the money down when the bus was ordered.

Terry McCann, Chairman from 1946-1951 and again in 1953

A feature of that first year's activities included a double-bill featuring Altamuskin against Seskilgree and Sixmilecross against Seskinore at Duff's Holm on June 29th. The referees were Dan McSorley and Packie Owens. Admission was one shilling and patrons were assured of two well contested games.

Then a South Tyrone Junior League was established and the increasing popularity of it was evident when a team from Cloughfin applied for affiliation. Patrick Collins and Jack McCann presented a set of medals for competition which the Board decided to offer to the winners of a championship.

The Beragh Sports Football Tournament in July added to the new sense of optimism. Carrickmore defeated Sixmilecross in the first round and went on to defeat Eskra in the final.

Events like that brought the talents of the Beragh players to a wider audience and several from the club were selected on a South Tyrone team picked to play in September 1946. They included Vincent Laverty, Peter Montague, Peter Daly and Dan McSorley.

All of this set things up perfectly for the new year. When the South Tyrone League resumed Brackey were among the competing teams and a real sign of progress appeared in August.

At the West Tyrone Board meeting, a letter was submitted by Sean Bennett asking permission to start a Parochial League in Beragh. Permission was granted on the understanding that it should not interfere with county matters or take players away from senior, junior or minor teams affiliated to the Board.

Miss Ima Weight, World's Fattest Girl, quarter of a tone, will visit Omagh on Tuesday December 20, 1949, for two days. On view daily

While all this was going on, Brackey's good form continued in the South Tyrone Junior League and they eventually went on to contest the final of the competition. The decider against Ballygawley was fixed for September 28th. Although the match received some pre-publicity, it is difficult to ascertain whether it actually took place.

1947 Junior Champions

Older members of the current Red Knights recall with a sense of pride and a twinkle in their eyes the events of 1948 when the then St Mary's captured the Tyrone Junior title following an eventful campaign.

Although set up towards the end of 1944, the St Mary's Club had taken time to establish firm roots. But things began to get on track in 1946 and 1947 to such an extent that an all-parish team was ready for action in the 1947 Junior Championship. The seeds of success in the competition had been sown by the successful participation of Sixmilecross and Brackey in the South Tyrone Junior League during the previous two years.

The campaign began in November of 1947 when Beragh were drawn to play and subsequently defeated Aughabrack. This earned them a place in the Semi-Final of the Western Section against Tattysallagh on February 1.

The match took place at the CBS Park in Omagh and resulted in a 1-2 to 1-1 victory for Beragh after a game played in high winds and showers. The important fact, however, was that the St Mary's were now through to meet Cranagh, winners of the other section after defeating Leckpatrick.

Played at Omagh on Sunday February 15th, there was no doubting Beragh's control as they won by 2-7 to 0-5. An outstanding feature was the display at centre half forward of Harry Kerr. He was said to have been "easily the best player on the field, his accurate passes and clever solo runs making a big contribution to the win. "

Beragh had led by 0-4 to 0-2 at half-time and the scorers were Harry Kerr (1-4), V McCaughey (0-2), Francie Gallagher (1-0) and Jim McAleer (0-1).

This set them up for the County Final against Washingbay which was scheduled for Pomeroy on Sunday April 11th. Mickey Toal from Carrickmore was in charge, but it was the nature of the play which was the main memory for some.

The Ulster Herald described it as a 'disgusting display of bad temper and

> This set them up for the County Final against Washingbay which was scheduled for Pomeroy on Sunday April 11. Mickey Toal from Carrickmore was in charge, but it was the nature of the play which was the main memory for some

unsportsmanship,' and went on to lambaste the poor standard of play. Little detail is given about the course of the game, except to say that Beragh won by 0-4 to 0-3 after Washingbay had drawn level at 0-2 each in the closing stages.

Two late points clinched the title and sparked a row which is still talked about sixty years later. It seems that the referee was struck by a Washingbay player and that a Beragh player was seen running down the field pursued by a 'throng of spectators.'

Many of the spectators who attended the game then became involved in a melee involving them and players around the centre of the field which lasted about ten minutes. The crowd eventually dispersed, leaving several players the 'worse for wear.'

Arising out of the incidents, Beragh's Tommy Owens was suspended for three months for striking the Washingbay player who had struck the referee. The members of the Board who were present at the meeting in June of that year voiced strong opinions on the conduct of the Washingbay club. Indeed, according to the Ulster Herald report of the meeting, one member said that he had tried to prevent a number of Washingbay players and spectators from engaging in the disturbances, but that he 'might as well have been trying to stop a crowd of lunatics."

Newspaper cuttings relating to the 1947 Junior Final

Perhaps the 'good behaviour' of the Beragh players and supporters on the occasion of the Junior Final was due to them having been cautioned on discipline just the week previously at a West Tyrone Board meeting.

The conduct of the supporters on two occasions was commented on by the referees, much to the annoyance of the Beragh delegate who protested at comments that "the fans were not a credit to the club."

Reacting to the Chairman, Peter Coleman, when he said that the grounds would have to be closed if the bad behaviour continued, the delegate remarked that 'it would be no harm.' He went on to say that the referee had ruined three matches for Beragh.

The Chairman said he did not like the Beragh delegate's attitude, saying that he was

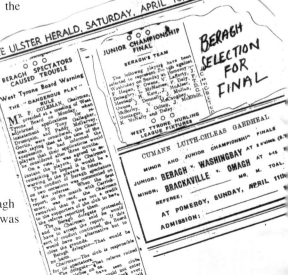

'condoning the spectators' conduct and added that the grounds would be closed if there was any further trouble.

For the record the team in the Junior Final lined out: Frank Hagan, Frank Owens, Vincent Laverty, John Donaghy, Louis McNamee, Peter Daly (captain), Peter Meenagh, Harry Kerr and Johnny McAleer, Tommy Owens, John Donnelly, Jack Attie Mullan, Vincent McCaughey, Charlie Montague, Dan McSorley. Subs – James Colton, Jack McEnhill, Kevin McNally.

After returning from the game in the cars that they had travelled in, the team were marched down Beragh street to the field and enjoyed a good night's celebration with a little help from local publicans as Louis McNamee explains.

"All the team gathered up after the match and the publicans set up a tray of drink for the players. You could have what you liked," he said.

"I remember that match well because Washingbay had a player in the forwards who scored a couple of points. Frankie Owens came over, caught me by the jersey and told me to make sure that he didn't come through again. The next time we challenged for a high ball, he fell accidentally and had to be taken to hospital. There wasn't a player left Pomeroy that day without a black eye."

At the May Board Meeting, the Chairman of the West Tyrone Board congratulated Beragh on their Junior win and expressed the hope that they would go on to win further successes at Senior level. A month later the victorious captain, Peter Daly, accompanied by the Beragh and Pomeroy Senior teams and Beragh and Clogher Minors teams were paraded from the school to Deroar Park. The captain led the parade with the Junior Cup, recently won by the St Mary's.

Other activities

Confidence was high, following the Junior title win, for Beragh's return to the Senior League in 1948. Prior to the final, the team was helped by games against Carrickmore, Clogher and Ballygawley in March and, while they lost to Aughabrack in the Davis Cup by 2-3 to 1-3, there was no doubting the anxiety of the players to do well. Just a few weeks after their belated 1947 Junior Final played on April 11th, 1948, they met Gortin in the 1948 Senior Championship.

They lost that game, but, not for the first time, it had a sequel in the boardroom. The Beragh delegate at the next West Tyrone Board meeting complained that the pitch was not in order and that the referee did not pass a copy of the Gortin players' list to the Beragh club. Their complaint was noted but no action was taken

Overall the form of the team in the 1948 Senior League was mixed to say the least. They lost to Greencastle by 3-3 to 1-3 on August 15th before defeating Fintona by 1-3 to 0-5 in September. Scores for Beragh in that one were registered by James Colton, Kevin McNally and John Donaghy and the goal was scored by Tommy Owens.

However, while they failed to really make an impact and finished second from the bottom, the experience of 1948 left them well placed to make a better impact in the final year of the decade.

In that 1949 season, Beragh were in Section B along with Dungannon, Pomeroy, Ballygawley, Carrickmore and Clogher and in March they got their season off to a fine start with a 3-8 to 0-3 win over Carrickmore. Carrickmore avenged that defeat by 3-3 to 1-1 in the second round, but

The winning Beragh Junior team of 1947 pictured at the 1988 annual dinner at which the surviving members of the team were special guests there was no stopping Beragh when they secured another two points by beating Ballygawley on a score of 1-10 to 1-0.

Gusty McMackin scored a goal and Frank Owens 1-1 in the game against Clogher in May and even the efforts of Sean Canavan failed to stop Beragh from beating Ballygawley again in June, this time by 2-4 to 1-3.

By now the performances pf the team were gaining them support and so a bus was run to the game against Dungannon. Tickets were available from Frank Owens of Drumduff, James Colton of Beragh or Felix McCann of Sixmilecross.

However, they were brought back to reality with a bang when Iggy Jones of Dungannon ran riot against them. He scored 2-3 as the Clarkes were runaway winners by 4-10 to 0-2. P Montague and P McGovern got the Beragh points.

So, Beragh didn't finish the forties on a high by winning the Senior League, but they certainly served notice of their abilities. A League table for September shows that with the competition almost completed, they lay in joint second place on twelve points with Dungannon. Clogher were top on fourteen points, with Pomeroy, Carrickmore and Ballygawley back on six, four and no points respectively.

Youth affairs

A number of high profile Inter-County successes emphasised the growing strength of the GAA in Tyrone at the end of the forties. All-Ireland Minor triumphs in 1947 and 1948 and the inclusion of several players from the eastern end of the county in the St Patrick's Armagh team which won the Hogan Cup in Colleges Football indicated that quality footballers were being produced.

There is no doubt that this was due to the setting up of youth teams and leagues in various parts during the later part of the decade. Beragh, of course, had always been to the fore in promoting youth football throughout the 1920s and 1930s and enthusiastically embraced these latest attempts to get young players off to the right start.

Permission was granted to the club to hold a Schoolboys League in 1948, by which time the efforts of Fr Murtagh towards promoting Minor football were beginning to yield dividends.

Sean Bennett pictured with the Junior Cup won for 1947

"STILL RUNNING"
A COMEDY, by J. J. McKEOWN
WILL BE PRESENTED BY
BERAGH PLAYERS
IN
BERAGH PAROCHIAL HALL
ON
SUNDAY, 9th & SUNDAY, 16th APRIL
AT 9 P.M., SHARP (E.S.T.). DOORS OPEN 8 P.M.
ADMISSION: - - - 2/6 and 2/-.
NO STANDING.
Tickets from: W. J. CONWAY, Beragh.
P. COLLINS, Seskinecross.
J. McCULLOGH, Drumduff.
P. McCUSKER, Seskinore.
LIMITED NUMBER OBTAINABLE AT DOOR.

For the first time ever teams were fielded at both Minor and Juvenile level and that year a derby double-bill of matches against Ballygawley at Glencull raised a lot of interest. Ballygawley won the Minor game by 5-9 to 3-4, but there was a turnaround for the Juveniles who won by a comfortable margin.

Beragh, of course, had always been to the fore in promoting youth football throughout the 1920s and 1930s and enthusiastically embraced these latest attempts to get young players off to the right start

Things then really took off in 1949 when Beragh reached the West Tyrone Minor Semi-Final and also the South Tyrone Juvenile Final. The players on the Minor team that year included G McNamee, J McAleer, John McCann, J Boyle, M McNamee, P Doherty, Vincent Donaghy, Joe McCann, M McGarrity, F McCaughey, S Gillen, Mick Kerr, P Campbell, T Kelly, H McCann, FH Owens, Basil Neville, P McAleer, JJ Colton.

They produced some good early season performances and met Dromore in the semi-finals of the Championship at Omagh in May of 1949. But their hopes of going to the final were dashed when they lost by 1-8 to 0-4. It was 0-4 to 0-2 at half-time and the Beragh scorers were Joe McCann and J Donnelly.

The team was selected from Gus McNamee, John Boyle, Gusty McMackin, John McCann, Vincent Donaghy, Pat Doherty, Terry Kelly, John Donnelly, Jim McAleer, Morris McGarrity, Joe McCann, John O'Connor, Francis McCaughey, Francis Gormley, Mick Kerr, Frank McNamee.

For the Juveniles, T McCann, J Kelly, K McNamee and M McNamee were among the scorers in a win over Aughnacloy in Beragh in May. The other teams involved in the competition were Carrickmore, Killeeshil, Clogher and the eventual double-winners were Ballygawley. Beragh came second to Ballygawley in the League with fourteen points from ten games.

The two met in the championship final which took place at the end of August at Omagh. But there was no luck for the St Mary's who lost by 6-2 to 2-4, having really only offered resistance in the closing stages. Nevertheless, the efforts of both teams were praiseworthy, prompting the hope that some of them would progress to Tyrone Minor teams in the All-Ireland during the subsequent years.

That desire didn't materialise, but the forties had ended as it had started on a high note for Beragh.

Club events of the decade

Regular meetings, the attendance of delegates at West Tyrone Board meetings and the organisation of buses to matches were among the responsibilities of those involved in the GAA in the Beragh Parish throughout the 1940s.

As early as January 1940, Ollie Slane represented Brackey at the West Tyrone Convention while Paddy McCrumlish often aired his views on a range of subjects at subsequent meetings. The organisation of the first Tournament in 1940 also highlighted the growing awareness that gaelic games weren't just about the completion of competitions organised by the relevant West Tyrone or County Board.

Club events were also held often and the big Junior Final win was probably a topic of conversation when members gathered in the Hall on May 9th 1948 for a Ceili. The Fear a Toige was Felix McCann, the event was well patronised and visitors were present from neighbouring towns.

Responsibilities also expanded to meet the demands of Tyrone teams. In 1948 a collection was taken up locally to help train the county Minors who won the All-Ireland for the second time that year.

There were three £1 donations on the list that included J McNally, Sixmilecross, Sean Bennett, Master Conway, Rev Fr Murtagh, Jim McCann, Jack McCann, T Connolly, V McCann, P Donnelly, P Daly, Hughie Boyle, Matthew Rodgers, Peter McCusker, T Fyffe, Dan Conway, Frank Kerr, J Callan, P Meenagh, T Devlin, F Reid, J Colton, Dan McSorley, A Ogle, P Mallan, P Casey, M McDermott, J McCusker, P Devlin and a Mr Deighan. Total contributions came to £9 2 shillings.

Of course, the securing of a pitch for the action was an important annual priority. There must have been some problem with the regular park at Deroar at the beginning of 1949 The end result was that at a meeting of the club in the Hall, it was revealed that Miss Sarah McCusker, Cooley, had granted them the use of a field in Cooley

Trips to big matches at Clones and Croke Park had become very popular and in 1941, tickets for the Railway Cup Final were available from Jack McCann and Ollie Slane. Those wishing to travel to the 1949 All-Ireland

Responsibilities also expanded to meet the demands of Tyrone teams. In 1948 a collection was taken up locally to help train the county Minors who had won the All-Ireland for the second time that year

Final when Meath won their first title could have left Beragh at 7.05am, Sixmilecross five minutes later and arrived in Dublin at 10.40am.

Tickets costing 18p for that particular train journey were available from Peter Bennett in Beragh and Packie McAleer in Sixmilecross and after the excitement of the final the return train departed Dublin at 7pm.

The death of HK McAleer

It could have been that those involved in the GAA in the parish in the 1940s did not have any real idea of the origins of the Association locally. But that would probably have changed in the spring of 1941 when one of the founders died at the age of 75.

HK McAleer, who was so closely involved with the Sixmilecross Wolfe Tones prior to 1920, died on Monday May 12th after a short illness. His passing marked the end of an era not only for the GAA locally, but also local politics and the Ancient Order of Hibernians in which he was deeply involved as President of the Sixmilecross Branch for over forty years.

The detailed Ulster Herald Obituary said he was the last surviving member of the old Omagh Poor Law Board. The extensive list of organisations that he was involved in included Tyrone County Council, Tyrone County Hospital Committee, Omagh Board of Guardians, the Rural District Council and the Omagh Regional Education Committee.

A local auctioneer and publican, he had been a Nationalist Parliamentary Representative at Stormont since 1929. However, it was his role in the AOH and GAA which were most noteworthy and the report stated:

"From early life, he was a pioneer of the Ancient Order of Hibernians and for many years past was President of the organisation in Tyrone as well as being a member of the National Board.

"He took a live interest in the spread of this organisation and spoke at many of the big demonstrations held under its auspices in different parts of the north.

"In his early years the deceased was a valued exponent of gaelic games in Tyrone and a prominent player on the football field and throughout his life he gave every possible assistance in the promotion of the national pastimes. In recent years was the donor of a Cup for competition amongst the GAA teams."

The Drumduff Chapel Fire

A big event that caused plenty of debate in the life of the parish occurred at the end of June 1949 when a fire at Drumduff Chapel destroyed the sacristy and vestments and caused a total of around £200-£300 damage.

A mission was being conducted in the chapel at the time and the fire was discovered early on the Tuesday morning when Mrs Owens, the Sacristan, arrived to open the church for 8am Mass. She saw smoke and, through a broken window of the sacristy, the flames which at that time had got a grip of the interior woodwork.

Paddy McCrumlish was also on the scene almost immediately and, while Omagh Fire Brigade were quickly called, a shortage of water hampered the effort to combat the blaze.

"Among the valuable sacerdotal articles destroyed in the fire were a Monstrance, a Chalice and vestments. An interesting relic of the Penal days was also lost. This was a carved wooden crucifix dated 1787 which had been preserved in the sacristy. It had been used in the Mass Rock nearby and had been taken to the Church when the later had been erected in 1829," a report of the fire stated.

> A big event that caused plenty of debate in the life of the parish occurred at the end of June 1949 when a fire at Drumduff Chapel destroyed the sacristy and vestments and caused a total of around £200-£300 damage

Earlier in the decade much concern was also caused in the Brackey, Drumduff and wider area in 1942 when the creamery at Brackey was one of seven earmarked for closure in Tyrone in 1942. It eventually closed down when opposition to the opening of the Nestle Milk Factory at Coneywarren collapsed.

The end of the creamery came despite protests from local farmers. In June they had undertaken to continue sending their milk to the Co-Op Creamery. But the move prompted the Stormont Government to issue an order requiring them to send it to the new factory.

A month later there was an attempt to starve the farmers out as the dispute continued. The problems then escalated when in October it was revealed that the Beragh Co-Operative and Diary Society and its auxiliaries at Ranelly and Moylagh would also close.

All this came at a cost. That month a meeting of the Omagh Rural Council heard concerns from Dr Hugh Watson of Beragh about the difficulties in obtaining fresh milk. This was because the usual suppliers were refusing to give milk to the public, especially under the 'Sent Milk' Scheme.

In March 1944, Brackey was further hit when a fire at the Flax Mill resulted in one ton of flax and two tons of tows being destroyed. Firemen attended to the blaze from 10.30pm to 5.30am, pumping water from the nearby Drumduff River.

Times were difficult for all including the local farmers and were compounded by everyday difficulties. Coal shortages were regular and in 1945 there were queues for coal at Omagh Station. There were pleas for increases in produce prices for farmers a year later and September 1946 saw little progress in saving the harvest and prospects were poor in many parts of Tyrone.

The Big Snow of 1947 didn't do much to help either. That March there were heavy snow storms and the road between Sixmilecross and Omagh had to be cleared by a snow plough. Farmers were said to have been working from dawn to dusk to keep up to date with the tillage activities

The Parish Priest in 1940, Fr James Macken, wrote to Omagh Council calling for "a change to the present public drain used to dispose of surface water along the south side of Main Street, Beragh, into a drain with bathroom connections."

He said that in dry or frosty weather, any ordinary trap would not prevent sewer gas from escaping from these gratings, thus causing serious risk to the health of those living in the vicinity.

Prayer played an extremely important part in the life of the area at the time and Confirmation 1949 heard Archbishop Dalton urge the importance of the family Rosary. On his arrival in Beragh, he was met outside the village by a large crowd of people and led by Sixmilecross Pipe Band. He drove in state through the village, escorted by the children who were to receive Confirmation.

Sixty children from the Parish were Confirmed and the Archbishop also presented prizes to children who had been the winners in a recent religious examination. They were: AUGHNAGLEA - James Campbell, Patricia Cleary and

> Times were difficult for all including the local farmers and were compounded by everyday difficulties. Coal shortages were regular and in 1945 there were queues for coal at Omagh Station. There were pleas for increases in produce prices for farmers a year later and September 1946 saw little progress in saving the harvest and prospects were poor in many parts of Tyrone

SEVEN TYRONE CREAMERIES CLOSED

Opposition to Factory Collapses

FARMERS' DISSATISFACTION EXPRESSED AT OMAGH MEETINGS

THE MINISTRY CRITICISED

Joseph Maloney; BERAGH - Anthony Hagan, Sean McCartan and Patrick McCrystal, DRUMDUFF - Michael McCullagh, Arthur McCrystal and Maureen McKeown; SESKINORE - Maureen McGurn and Annie McCool; ROSCAVEY - Seamus McMahon and John McCrystal.

Anti-Partition League

One of the big events in 1949 was the establishment of an Anti-Partition League Branch in Beragh. It was formed following a meeting in Beragh at the end of April which was addressed by the local MP, EV McCullagh of Greencastle

The Sports Day Fancy Dress proved a big attraction for these children and parents in 1940s Beragh

Since its formation in 1946, the organisation had been aiming, according to Mr McCullagh, to publicise the existence of the border which it said could only exist 'through ignorance of its existence.'

The meeting was also told that equal rights did not exist in the Six Counties at the time and the main speaker lambasted the then Northern Ireland Prime Minister, Sir Basil Brooke, for claiming that freedom of speech and action was allowed.

Responding to incidents at Carrickmore on Easter Sunday, Mr McCullagh said they had denied the nationalist people of Tyrone the right to honour their dead by banning the parade and baton-charging' those attending.

"It is becoming more apparent every day that there can be no justice in these Six Counties as long as the Tory Unionists who live on bigotry are in power," he said.

The committee elected was: Chairman - Fr McKernan, Vice-Chairmen - Mr James McMahon, Mr Patrick Donnelly, Secretary - Mr Michael Donnelly, Treasurer - Mr Patrick Collins, Committee - Messrs James Slane, Jack McCann, Patrick Kelly, WJ Shields, Joseph Donnelly, Patrick McSorley, James Mullan, Frank Kearney, Francis Maguire, John Farrelly, Seamus Rafferty.

"Recent experiences at the past election have shown who causes the damage to property in these Six Counties and it is absolutely ridiculous to insinuate that the people who went to Carrickmore on Easter Sunday were likely to cause damage to any property in that village which is 100% Nationalist."

Sixmilecross and Beragh Races

The Sixmilecross and Beragh Races were a feature of the nineteenth century which were successful revived during the decade from the mid-forties. Usually held on Easter Monday, the Races for 1944 had a prize fund of over £150, including £30 for the 1.5 mile flat.

Among the main races in 1945 were the Bencran Plate, the Sixmilecross Plate, the Beragh and Sixmilecross Derby, the Beragh Plate and the Ballyhallaghan Plate and that year saw the event being staged over a new course convenient to Sixmilecross.

There was good weather and a large attendance, Mr J McCullagh PET and Mr J Barton were the Secretaries and the names of some the horses provide interesting reading. They included 'Anxious Moments', 'Geraldine's Pet', 'Don't Ask Me', 'Little Wonder', and 'Golden Princess'.

The first race in 1946 was timed for 2pm summertime, the stakes were £160 and the event was to be followed by a dance on the same night in the AOH Hall with admission 2/6. In 1947 the event continued to go from strength to strength and that year saw the introduction of a £25 Publican's Plate.

A report of the meeting stated that, "although punters had a lean day, there were a number of upsets and most of the races were thrilling affairs." The day was a triumph for TJ McCann's son from Aughnacloy who scored a treble victory on 'The Devil's Bit, 'Fred's Charger'and 'No More.'

Inter-County activities

It was perhaps inevitable that the growth in participation in gaelic football during the 1930s would bring new rewards at inter-county level. However, few could have envisaged just how much Tyrone's fortunes would improve courtesy of a number of major achievements which enlivened the 1940s.

The decade began well when Tyrone reached the 1940 McKenna Cup Final only to lose to their old adversaries and the kingpins of the time,

One of the big events in 1949 was the establishment of an Anti-Partition League Branch for Beragh

The Tyrone All-Ireland
Minor Champions,
1948. Included is
JJ Donnelly of Beragh

Cavan. But this didn't halt the progress being made and it was no real surprise when the county reached the 1941 Ulster Final courtesy of good wins over Armagh and Down.

A special training fund was among the initiatives set up for the final, with collective training taking place prior to the game. However, Cavan once again proved an obstacle too far and emerged comfortable winners by 3-9 to 0-5.

One of the members of that Tyrone team of 1941 was Mick Keenan, then playing with Carrickmore, but of course closely associated with the Beragh parish. Unfortunately, though, he wasn't involved when the team of 1942 finally made the breakthrough by capturing the Lagan Cup.

Antrim, Armagh, Derry and Tyrone were the teams taking part and, despite losing to Antrim in the first round, Tyrone recovered well to set up a repeat clash against them in the final in November at Armagh. This time there was to be no mistake as Tyrone led by 3-5 to 1-3 at half-time and ended up winning by 4-7 to 2-8.

Ollie Slane represented the county in 1945. The later part of the decade was dominated by the unheralded success of the Minors who captured the Ulster title in 1946 and went on to win the All-Ireland for the next two years.

There were great celebrations in 1947 at Croke Park when Tyrone edged out Mayo by the narrowest of margins, 4-5 to 4-4, in the All-Ireland Final. The win was all the more impressive considering that Tyrone had trailed by 4-4 to 0-2 at half-time and came back strongly to take the title on the resumption.

"I remember that match well because Washingbay had a player in the forwards who scored a couple of points. Frankie Owens came over, caught me by the jersey and told me to make sure that he didn't come through again. The next time we challenged for a high ball, he fell accidentally and had to be taken to hospital. There wasn't a player left Pomeroy that day without a black eye.

> While things didn't turn out as they had hoped, the sports and aeridheact of the middle part of the decade kept the flame burning before the resurgence under the St Mary's banner culminated in the 1948 Junior Championship win

A year later the Ulster title was retained thanks to wins over Fermanagh, Donegal and Derry before Galway were defeated in the All-Ireland Semi-Final. This set-up an All-Ireland Final against Dublin which again provided plenty of excitement for the sizeable support which followed the team's fortunes.

The panel on that occasion included Beragh's John Donnelly, who had come through the ranks of the youth promotion taking place at the time. He experienced the matches on the way to the final, the training and, of course, the excitement of lining out at Croke Park on All-Ireland Final Day.

Tyrone won the match by 0-11 to 1-5, having enjoyed a six point advantage at one stage during the second half before enduring some anxious moments as Dublin fought their way back. The win climaxed a fine decade on the inter-county scene and the promise of more to come in the fifties.

Looking ahead with confidence

Confidence surely permeated the ranks of the Beragh St Mary's as they also looked ahead to the new decade. For them, the 1940s was a decade of consolidation, decline and they renewed growth as the impact of restrictions caused by World War Two were left behind..

Throughout that time, though, the officials involved in the promotion of gaelic games and culture had remained strong in their determination to see both flourish. The early part of the decade had seen the team briefly threaten to maintain the progress made during the forties.

While things didn't turn out as they had hoped, the sports and aeridheact of the middle part of the decade kept the flame burning before the resurgence under the St Mary's banner culminated in the 1948 Junior Championship win, the growth in youth football and a generally optimistic outlook that was to bring further progress on and off the field during the fifties.

IN GAELIC FIELDS.

TYRONE FOOTBALL CHAMPIONSHIP.

CRAOBH RUADH (DUNGANNON) v. DAVITTS (FINTONA).

The above teams met at Sixmilecross on Sunday in the final of Tyrone Football Championship, and in presence of a large gathering of spectators. The match was well contested and in a very friendly spirit. Mr. M'Gillian acted as referee.

Teams :—Craobh Ruadh — J. Kelly, J. M'Caughey, E. Jones, W. Cunningham, J. Cunningham, P. Mallon, P. M'Naney, M. M'Dermott, T. O'Neill, P. Carey, J. Toner, P. Toner, T. C. O'Neill.

Davitts—J. Donnelly, P. M'Elhatton, W. M'Auley, J. Cole, P. Bradley, J. Bradley, M. Hanna, J. Hanna, F. Campbell, D. Flanagan, Irvine, Mullan, M'Bride.

Craobh Ruadh, winning the toss, played with the sun in their favour. Davitts, opening the score, kept play well up in the first few minutes, but after some fine forward play their opponents scored a point. The game was well contested in this half, Craobh Ruadh adding four points to their score, while Davitts were unable to increase their score, which at half-time stood—

Craobh Ruadh—5 points.

Davitts—1 point.

In the second half Dungannon came away at first, and scored a point, soon followed by another. Fintona then pulled up well, scoring a point. The game was keenly contested from this to the end, Fintona adding three more points, while Dungannon towards the finish made the game secure by adding two goals, the score at full time being—

Craobh Ruadh—2 goals 9 points.

For Fintona, M'Kelvey ?? ?? played well. M'Elhatton in goal gave a splendid display. For Dungannon it would be difficult to ?? any ?? ?? ?? each on-

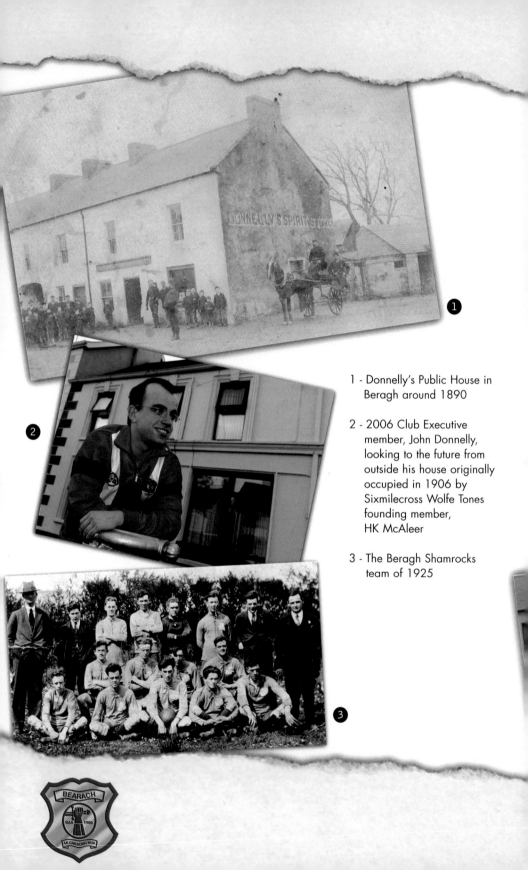

1 - Donnelly's Public House in Beragh around 1890

2 - 2006 Club Executive member, John Donnelly, looking to the future from outside his house originally occupied in 1906 by Sixmilecross Wolfe Tones founding member, HK McAleer

3 - The Beragh Shamrocks team of 1925

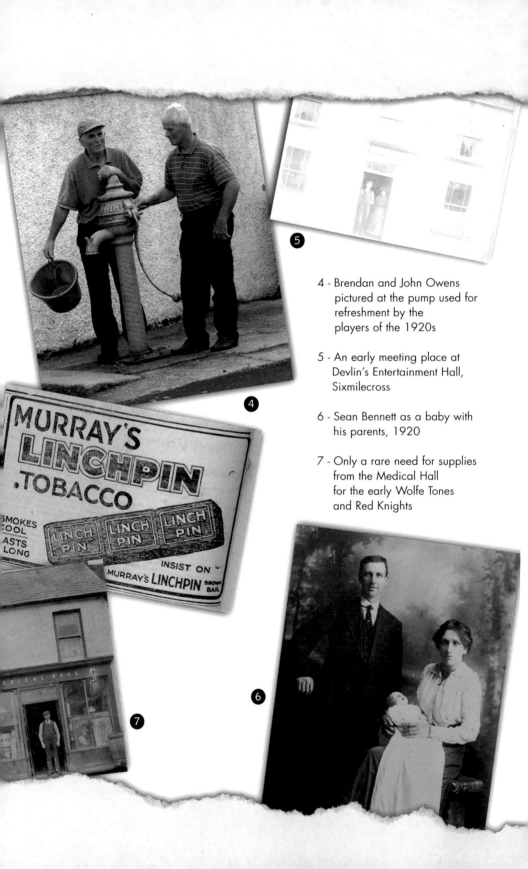

4 - Brendan and John Owens
    pictured at the pump used for
    refreshment by the
    players of the 1920s

5 - An early meeting place at
    Devlin's Entertainment Hall,
    Sixmilecross

6 - Sean Bennett as a baby with
    his parents, 1920

7 - Only a rare need for supplies
    from the Medical Hall
    for the early Wolfe Tones
    and Red Knights

1- Sixmilecross Main Street in the early 1900s

2 - Beragh Creamery in 1913

3 - The first field used by the Wolfe Tones in 1906 at Duff's Holm outside Sixmilecross

4 - Thomas Kelly, who lived to be 107 years old and Henry Owens, Rural Councillor and prominent resident of the Beragh area who died in 1909.

5 - Action from the 1950 Davis Cup against Castlederg

6 - Donaghanie Graveyard

7 - Packie McAleer ready to carry out mechanical repairs

LATE MR. THOMAS KELLY.

THE LATE MR. HENRY OWENS, J.P.

1 - The Sixmilecross Band was tops
in the Ireland of the 1950s

2 - The Beragh players of the mid-1930s.

3 - Beragh schoolgroup from the 1950s including
many members of the GAA

4 - Beragh in highfielding action
in the early 1950

5 - Getting ready for an early outing
with the St Mary's

Mick Kerr and Jim McAleer pictured prior to playing their part in Tyrone's historic Ulster title breakthrough in 1956

team, which has met *_____*
date.

The legion of faithful supporters who will make the journey to Dublin *_____*
certain of one thing. The team has been as well prepared for this match as *_____*
most exacting of them would wish. Every player has done his part to fit hims*_____*
for the big hour. The carefully thought-out training schedule at Pomeroy has *_____*
only ensured that the players will last the pace on the wide sward of Croke Pa*_____*
but has been designed to meet almost every forseeable playing eventuality. Pla*_____*
_____

Cavan Outcaught, Outmanoeuvred

sin*_____*
day's *_____*
completel*_____*
tion.

In the Ulst*_____*
they caused the *_____*
all when they *_____*
mighty Cavan. Y*_____*
the word, for there *_____*
about their victory *_____*
second-half superior*_____*

Not a defen*_____*
country could *_____*
Tyrone on that *_____*
Clones pitch. *_____*
was that for a *_____*
the Tyrone fifte*_____*
the rain (rem*_____*
against Derry*_____*
gannon). Pr*_____*
O'Neill county *_____*
dry-day football*_____*
thought the *_____*
the rain would*_____*
Cavan.

But can T*_____*
that second-half*_____*
Galway. That *_____*
big questions for *_____*
Galway's road to Dublin

Galways road to Dublin has *_____*
__ included some good victories.
gave title-holders Mayo *_____*
_____ defeat in years—*__*

The current Galway team
shows little change from the side
which fell *__* Kerry two years

___ for the first time in so important a game, and it is no help
at all to learn that Galway, their
opponents, are already being *_____*
as All-Ireland champions. However, it seems to be an advantage
to start as outsiders in a game this
season. Tyrone did not suffer on *__*
_____ Cavan, and *__*
____

opportunities *_____*
gained a tremendous *__*
by easily defeating Ma*__*
bar in the first round *__*
nacht Championship *__*
since then over Ros*__*
Sligo have been equal *__*
have not carried so *__*
since there was a fa*__*
the qu*_____*

BRIAN McSORLEY (right full-back), a 24-year-old farmer from Eskra, plays club football with Clogher. He is a most consistent player this year and gives of his best when under greatest pressure.

IGGY JONES (right half-forward), a 28-year-old Dungannon school-teacher, is the second member of the Clarkes Club on the side. Iggy will always be remembered for his

d Outplayed in Senior Football Final

centre-field is the youngest county captain in Ireland and still a schoolboy (Dungannon Academy). Long a star for the Coalisland Club (incidentally there are three Coalisland men on the team), Jodi has played starring games with

is a 23-year-old grocer from Carrickmore and the only member of the team born outside the O'Neill County (Keady, County Armagh, another footballing stronghold). His is a marksman of renown.

Tyrone's hopes repose in this team for Sunday. Reading from the top right, the first seven players are—L. Devlin, D. Donnelly, B. McSorley, J. O'Neill, Teggart, and E. Devlin.

1 - The wedding day party of Packie and Gabrielle Owens

2 - Tommy and Veronica Owens pictured on their wedding day

1 - Striking a deal at Sixmilecross Fair

2 - Remembering the halycon days of the 1950s at McGirr's Holm are Hughie McCann and Terry Kelly

3- Three generations of players, Louis McNamee, his son Hugh and daughter, Rose, with 2006 youth players, Niall McNamee and Catriona and Pauric Grimes

4 - John and Brendan Owens
on the field previously used
as a football pitch

Ready to party to the Beragh Havanna Dance Band during the 1920s

Chapter Seven
1950 - 1960
A Base Bought in Beragh

Chapter Seven

1950 - 1960

THE growth of experience in officials and players was to play a vital role as the GAA in the Beragh parish continued to grow in the early fifties. A look through the lists of people involved at that time indicates how well the Association was equipped to make significant progress.

In contrast to some other areas in the county, gaelic games locally was actively promoted under the banner of Beragh St Mary's. Teams were being fielded at Juvenile, Minor and Senior level and decisions at the regular committee meetings ensured that things were properly structured at all levels.

It is perhaps fair to say that those who played the central roles were not too bothered about what went before. However, there is no doubt that the advice of some of the people who had played a part as far back as the 1920s provided a support that was often missing in other areas where the GAA was only entering its first or second decade of sustained activity.

All of these factors contributed to a quite remarkable decade. Minor Final appearances in 1950 and 1952, the reaching of the first Senior Semi-Final for twenty years in 1955, Davis and St Enda Cup successes, and the participation of Mick Kerr and Jim McAleer and on the first Tyrone team to win the Ulster title in 1956, were among the playing highlights. Then, there was the purchase of St Mary's Park in a move that set the club years ahead of others in development terms.

Action from the meeting of Beragh and Castlederg in the 1950 Davis Cup. Frankie Owens is pictured rising for the ball

Davis Cup success 1950

Many of the players who had been part of the team which won the Junior title in 1947 remained on board as the new decade dawned in 1950. They were joined by others who had cut their footballing teeth in the South Tyrone Juvenile and Minor Leagues of the late forties to form a team that would become increasingly formidable opponents in the forthcoming seasons.

The first evidence came in the opening months of the new year. The greater experience and better combination of the St Mary's was referred to following a League win over Galbally as the St Enda Cup provided good match practice ahead of the start of the Senior League in the spring.

But it was in the Davis Cup that the team really came into its own. While the competition was to take months to complete, further signs of Beragh's resolve was seen against Castlederg on Sunday April 16th. They won by 3-5 to 2-6 after trailing by 2-5 to 0-0 at half-time. Two quick goals got them going on the resumption and they scored 1-5 in the final quarter to win by two points.

Second half control was again the key when they defeated Newtownstewart in the semi-final in August. While they led by 2-3 to 1-4 at the break, it was on the resumption that they really forged ahead with S Owens getting 2-1 and Frankie Owens, Doherty and Mullan registering points in what turned out to be a 4-7 to 1-7 victory. Others to impress included Joe McCann and Jim McAleer.

The final took place in Eskra on Sunday October 8th when the teams were paraded around the pitch by the All-Ireland winning, Sixmilecross Pipe Band. Weather conditions were against good football as a gale blowing across the pitch made scoring difficult.

Once again, the St Mary's were slow-starters and trailed by 1-1 to 0-1 at half-time. However, not for the first time in that Davis Cup campaign, things came together in the second half. Points from Doherty and McCann reduced the deficit to a point as the Beragh goalkeeper distinguished himself by diving full length to save one particular shot.

And, the winning point came late in the game when M Mullan cleared to Joe McCann who went on a thirty yard solo run before driving over the clinching score in the 0-6 to 1-2 victory. The report of the game in the Ulster Herald lists the McCanns, D Mullan, B Mullan, Donaghy, McAleer, Doherty, Owens, Laverty and McNally as being best for the St Mary's.

A few weeks later the members of the team and their friends attended a dinner in the School in honour of the team's achievement in getting the season off to such a fine start. An impromptu concert followed the meal with several members contributing items.

The celebrations continued with a Ceili in the Hall, at which the Club

> Parents fined for not sending their children to school because they were at home gathering potatoes. Penalties of 5 shillings to 34 shillings were imposed and sometimes there were more than one child per family involved

Chairman, Terry McCann, presented the Davis Cup to team captain, John Donaghy. Mr McCann paid tribute to the manner in which the team had played throughout the competition.

West Tyrone League 1950-1954

While that Davis Cup success generated great enthusiasm in the ranks of the St Mary's, the fortunes of the team in the West Tyrone Senior League and Senior Championship during the first half of the decade left a lot to be desired.

Although some results were very noteworthy and included morale-boosting wins. The momentum wasn't maintained and the team never made the breakthrough to emerge winners of the title.

Their mixed form might have been due to the general state of the League which often saw the majority of games being unplayed especially in the second half of the year. Protests, counter-appeals and other problems also afflicted the organisation of games in West Tyrone.

One of these arose in the early part of 1950 when Beragh were due to play Pomeroy in the St Enda Cup. At a meeting of the West Tyrone Board, the Pomeroy delegate, J Grimes, said that they would only play the game if the Beragh pitch was the regulation size. He was assured by the St Mary's delegate, Kevin McNally, that everything was in order.

A game against Carrickmore later that year was called off when the referee failed to turn up. Regular fixtures continued to be made, but the competition was still not finished in January 1951.

By the start of April that year, the St Mary's had still to make their opening appearance in that year's SFL. However, a busy schedule lay ahead with matches scheduled against Ballygawley, Dromore and Pomeroy in the League and Urney in the St Enda Cup.

Results during that period included a 6-7 to 2-3 defeat at the hands of Dromore, they lost to Clogher by 0-9 to 0-3 in May but reversed that result with a 3-5 to 2-2 win on August 12th when Terry Kelly, B Mullan and B McCann got goals and Joe McCann 0-2 and John Donaghy 0-3 were the other scorers.

By the autumn of 1951 the mixed form was illustrated on the table where Beragh lay third from the bottom with eight points just ahead of Pomeroy

In October 1954 the Division Sanitary Officer reported that of 88 houses in Beragh village, 26 required major repairs. Number of houses with WCs was 30, 57 had dry closests and one had a chemical closet. 33 houses had no internal water supply and all houses possessed dustbins. Mr Murray proposed sending notices on the owners to provide WCs as soon as possible

Some of the Fifties players with Sixties counterparts at a club function.
Back: Basil Neville, Michael Kelly, Anthony Donaghy, Kevin Nixon, Benny Donaghy, Mick McCarten
Front: Felix McCann, Frank H. Owens, Tommy Owens, Vin Donaghy, Brian Grimes, Peter Grimes.

and Fintona. Their position didn't change before the end of the campaign which came down to a title play-off between Dromore and Clogher at Beragh.

Things did improve slightly at the beginning of 1952. Beragh were drawn to play Dromore at the end of March, they lost to Fintona by 3-3 to 0-6 in April and the team to play Tattysallagh on Sunday June 8th was selected from a list of players made up: Peter Daly, Donal Mullan, Kevin McNally, Jack Kavanagh, John Donaghy, Ollie Slane, Vin Donaghy, Mick Kerr, Joe McCann, Hughie McCann, Tommy Owens, Frank Owens, Terry Kelly, Jim McAleer, Terry McCann, Gerry Kavanagh and Phil Campbell.

An idea of the mix of youth and experience can be gauged from the fact that around eight of the players who lined out against Gortin in the autumn of 1952 were Minors. The game was won by 4-6 to 1-0 before a good crowd who saw Owens and McAleer gain a foothold at midfield in the second half.

During the game, the Beragh defence of Mullan, the Donaghy brothers, the McCann brothers and Kelly were in great form catching and kicking with confidence. In the forward line veteran Paddy Daly was a tower of strength and ably supported by Kerr, Kavanagh, McAleer and McCann.

However, the frustrations caused by unfulfilled fixtures were coming to a head and the Beragh club submitted a motion to the 1952 West Tyrone

James Colton, Vin Donaghy, Gussy McKeever and John John Donaghy pictured with the Davis Cup won by Beragh in 1950

Convention calling for clubs who did not fulfill fixtures to be banned from playing until the outstanding games took place.

Pomeroy, Beragh, Carrickmore, Trillick, Fintona, Clogher and Ballygawley formed a new eastern division of the West Tyrone League in 1953. But the usual problems persisted, results and league tables were few and far between and at the end of the year the St Mary's again sought to bring about improvements when they forwarded the same motion on postponed games originally proposed the previous year.

Amid all this, two very notable results stand out to give an indication of Beragh's worth. They were against Omagh St Enda's, then in the middle of their most successful period of three O'Neill Cup wins in a row.

The first game took place in January 1953 and, although Omagh were missing Donal Donnelly, Dr Pat O'Neill and Harry Scully, there was no doubting their disappointment at a 2-6 to 2-4 defeat according to the Ulster Herald report of the game.

A youthful Beragh team lined out and it was prompted by Ollie Slane, who captained the team and produced one of his best games to date. The St Mary's were boosted when Owens scored a first half goal that helped them into a 1-3 to 1-1 interval lead.

While Ollie Slane missed a penalty at the start of the second half and Omagh levelled, further scores from Slane and Jim McAleer put Beragh back in front before a goal from Mick Kerr really set them up. They held out to win with those two points to spare.

Just two weeks later the teams met again in the West Tyrone League, with Omagh fielding all of their big names with the exception of goalkeeper, Thady Turbett. And, the Ulster Herald report of the match had once again no doubts that Beragh deserved their 2-6 to 1-8 victory.

The midfield partnership of Mick Kerr and Joe McCann was seen as crucial, while Campbell, McAleer and Owens were among the others who produced notable performance in a match summed up as follows:

"Let there be no doubt about it, this young Beragh side deserved their victory. They played as a team, were perfect in the air and found their men with accurate passes. But it was their stamina which won the day. They played at a cracking pace which it seemed they would be unable to maintain.

"With only minutes left to play, victory was within their grasp when they led by one point. Then Donnelly gave Omagh the lead with a goal. It was all over. Or was it? Back came courageous Beragh and with only seconds left, Slane moved up from the full-back position to score a great goal from twenty five yards. Beragh had won."

Pat Grimes who died in 1955 pictured with Francis Hugh Owens. Both made the breakthrough onto the Beragh team in the early 1950s

The results also benefited them on the West Tyrone Table, where the two wins brought them into joint third place with Omagh behind unbeaten Carrickmore and Fintona. Unfortunately, the momentum of the wins was halted by delays, unfulfilled fixtures and poor form. A few weeks later Carrickmore duly clinched the title when they scored a 3-5 to 1-1 over the youthful St Mary's at Sixmilecross.

Other competitions

Tournament games provided a varied fixture list for the St Mary's while the West Tyrone League struggled to really come to life. Matches in competitions like the St Enda and McElduff Cups as well as the visits to other club provided an opportunity to meet teams from outside the immediate West Tyrone locality.

Every game, of course, was treated seriously, as evidenced by the successful protest lodged against Clogher in the 1950 McElduff Cup. That same year the Carrickmore Sports promoted a match billed as a Grand Challenge between the prospective County Champions, Beragh, and Carrickmore.

Complaint about litter louts in Beragh and SMX. One member of Omagh Rural Council blamed the people of SMX, saying that they had litter bins, but did not use them and had no pride in their own village

179

Teams from Beragh and Sixmilecross took part in the Mountfield Sports football tournament in 1952 and a year later Beragh's prowess outside the confines of the West Tyrone League and Championship was highlighted when they won the Feis Cup.

Wins over Dromore and Newtownstewart clinched them the title and the praise of one correspondent who described them as being the 'soundest team in the Tournament.'

> In August 1958 a small oak cross depicting the crucifixion was found by Master Brian Dillon, son of Mr and Mrs Tom Dillon, Deroar Beragh. About six inches in length, is in good condition and clearly carved. Inscribed on the back is the year 1790 and it was found adjacent to the Dillon home on a patch of bog. Since the cross is 168 years old, there should be an interesting historical background to it

Similar progress was harder to achieve in the McElduff and St Enda Cup around that time. Early round defeats were the norm, although in 1953 Beragh reached the semi-finals of both competitions only to lose to Fintona and Carrickmore respectively.

Their progress to the McElduff semi-final was especially significant as the competition in 1953 was used as a replacement for the West Tyrone League. The main competition was abandoned at a West Tyrone Board meeting in October as interest in the League was waning and it was hoped that the Cup would revive interest.

Their success in the 1953 Feis Cup saw them being hotly tipped for the Omagh Carnival, one of the big events of the time and aimed at raising money for school-building and other works in the town. They were tipped to give a good account of themselves and this certainly proved to be the case as they progressed to the semi-final.

In it they gave Desertmartin, the famed Derry team of the time, a fright losing by just 0-10 to 0-7. The captain, Ollie Slane, who had returned from Carrickmore the previous year, gave a great display alongside Joe McCann, Jim McAleer and McClean. The two teams met again at the same stage of the competition two years later in 1956 when the Derry team again emerged winners despite the best efforts of Mick Kerr and FH Owens.

The Ballygawley controversy

While Tyrone were winning their way through to the Ulster Final and eventual provincial glory, Beragh were at Newtownstewart set up a second round meeting between them and arch rivals Ballygawley. But nobody could have forecast how bitter the exchanges over this would become in the course of the subsequent weeks.

Scheduled for Sunday July 6th, Ballygawley wrote to the West Tyrone Board indicating their refusal to play the game in what they said was 'in

the interests of the GAA as we feel that another meeting of Beragh and Ballygawley would lead to a possible riot."

Beragh were represented at the meeting by Ollie Slane, who said that it would be bad for football in West Tyrone if one team could say who they would or would not play. The stand-in Chairman, Paddy McCaffrey, remarked that the situation 'spoke very bad' of Beragh, but then added:

"I think it is bad sportsmanship on the part of Ballygawley to come here and say there would be a riot if they played Beragh. I would like Fr McEvoy's reason for not fulfilling the match.

Fr McEvoy - "There is no question of sportsmanship at all. There is the question, first of all, of the good name of our club and second of our own park. I would like to point out that we have absolutely nothing against the Beragh team. But we do think that some of the Beragh supporters are not under the proper control of the Beragh club and events this year would prove that."

Remarks like that, of course, incensed the Beragh delegate and Ollie Slane retorted that "if the Board was going to permit clubs to send letters stating who they would or would not play, and run things like that, then Beragh would withdraw from football."

The Beragh team of the early 1950s which competed in the West Tyrone Senior League and Championship

Taking a break from the rigours of the day in the early 1950s is this group which includes Beragh player, Tommy Owens and former Sixmilecross Wolfe Tones player, Hugh Tierney

The Official Guide was checked, and no reason was found making preventing Ballygawley from taking such a move, and Ollie Slane responded by asking the Board's permission to withdraw from all competitions.

The Board Secretary, Sean Bennett, also resigned his position and said that the Beragh club would only reconsider its position if Ballygawley agreed to fulfill the fixture. In 2004, he recalled the events of that time and how Sean Canavan, father of Peter, and his brother Ciaran came to be playing for Beragh.

"The two Canavans were supposed to be staying at John McGirr's of Ballykeel, who was a friend of the Canavans. The Canavans and Ballygawley weren't getting on well at that time. They came because they were staying at McGirr's," he said.

"I suppose in total they would have played for a bit under a year before things got settled again. That was where the rivalry between Beragh and Ballygawley started out.

> ❝
> The row started because somebody was supposed to have hit Tommy Owens and everyone started to fight. Anybody that met a Ballygawley man floored him
> ❞

"The row started because somebody was supposed to have hit Tommy Owens and everyone started to fight. Anybody that met a Ballygawley man floored him. The match was played at the waterside in Glencull, a very small pitch.

"Later a protest came in from Ballygawley against Beragh. It came to me as West Tyrone Secretary. The first thing I noticed that it wasn't signed by the Secretary. That night about a quarter to twelve they came and withdrew it and lodged another one. Brian Hamill was their Secretary then."

It was a volatile decade at times for the St Mary's, a view highlighted by a second incident which led to the suspension of Vin Donaghy and eventually to a 'clear the air' meeting in Beragh school.

Matters came to a head when Vin Donaghy and FH Owens left the dressing room prior to a Tournament game against Omagh in Pomeroy, apparently while awaiting the arrival of the contingent of players from Brackey and Drumduff.

"A few days later my brother John came with a letter from the Beragh club telling me that I had to apologise. I asked Frank Owens and he said he wasn't apologising, so I followed that line," he said.

"The club suspended me and to this day I still haven't apologised. But it was tough because you would be going into Mass getting stick and I even hit one other player on the stairs coming down from the gallery in the old chapel for something that was said.

"Eventually, Paddy Cullen and Paddy O'Neill of the County Board came to a meeting in the school. Brackey were trying to start a Junior team and there was a fear that this could spilt the Beragh team. But anyhow, Frank Owens said that he was the instigator of the move to leave the dressing-room and the matter ended there."

Vin subsequently returned to play for Beragh before transferring for a number of years to Omagh St Enda's.

Senior Championship

Success in the O'Neill Cup was the main target of teams back in the forties and fifties as well as today. All sides that competed in the West Tyrone Senior League were eligible to take part.

Beragh enjoyed mixed fortunes in it in the initial part of the decade. Their first outing on July 19th, 1950, resulted in a win for Clogher over them at Pomeroy. They also went out at the first a year later at the Holm, Sixmilecross when they lost to Carrickmore.

While the opening exchanges in that 1951 game were tight, Beragh were soon on top thanks to scores from Donal Mullin, Jim McAleer and 1-1 from Terry Kelly. They led by 1-3 to 0-4 at half-time and were expected to make a strong challenge in the second half as well.

However, that didn't prove to be the case. An injury to James Grimes restricted them badly and while Brian and Hughie McCann both hit the crossbar, Carrickmore pulled away to win by 1-10 to 1-3.

They defeated Trillick in the first round of the 1952 Championship on May 11th by 1-7 to 1-6 but lost in the next round.

In 1953 Newtownstewart provided the opposition, with the original fixture having to be abandoned due to a constant downpour and the absence of an official referee. A week later the refixed match saw Beragh emerge winners by 0-8 to 1-3 and they progressed to play Fintona who beat them in the next round.

Hopes of defeating Omagh must have been high entering the 1954 Championship, considering their double league successes over them the previous year. But Beragh found the County Champions too hot to handle and lost by 1-7 to 0-4.

However, they were still capable of claiming the odd high profile victim. In the Quarter Final of the 1956 Omagh Carnival competition they defeated Dungannon by 0-8 to 1-3. The match was notable for the display of Iggy Jones, while Mickey McCann, Mick Kerr, John McGlinn and Joe McCann were among the stars for the St Mary's. Within weeks, of course, Iggy Jones and Mick Kerr were to shine in Tyrone's first ever Ulster title win.

1955 Senior Semi-Finalists

Indications of Beragh's growing potential were clearly evident at the start of the fifties. An increasingly experienced team had made its mark on a number of occasions before finally getting the mix just right in the 1955 Championship.

There was no doubt that the St Mary's officials and players realised that they were capable of much better than had been displayed in the previous couple of years. At the 1955 West Tyrone Convention in February, the Secretary, Sean Bennett told delegates that the players would benefit from being more actively engaged and expressed the hope that all competitions would be completed on time in the coming year.

Crowds gather in Sixmilecross for the Sports which were a big attraction in the 1950s

Further evidence of the growing number of players in the club was highlighted when a Parish League was started to provide regular football for those from the various townlands. The competition took place from April and involved Clogherney St Mary's, Sixmilecross Plunkett's, Brackey St Patrick's and Beragh Wolfe Tones.

This went in tandem with the West Tyrone League which in 1955 saw Beragh St Mary's begin in March against Ballygawley and continued over subsequent weeks with matches against Pomeroy and Carrickmore.

Old rivals Ballygawley provided the opposition in the opening round of

An early picture of a youth match involving a Beragh team. Many of the players who progressed from underage in the early 1950s lined out in the 1955 Senior Semi-Final

the championship at Pomeroy on June 19th. They were duly defeated and Beragh's good form continued when they ousted Moortown in the Quarter Final, again at Pomeroy, on June 24th.

Victory over the St Malachy's, who had won the County title in 1950, earned Beragh the distinction of being the only team from the West in the semi-finals of that year's championship. It was also their first appearance at that stage since 1935. Standing in their way was a Coalisland team which had surprised many by also progressing to the last four.

The Fianna's challenge was spearheaded by an eighteen year old, Jody O'Neill, who according to the Ulster Herald, gave a "footballing lesson to his county colleague and opposite number, Jim McAleer."

Described as a dull and drab affair, it was Coalisland who were off the mark quickest. They led by 1-3 to 0-3 nearing the half-time break when suddenly Beragh sprang to life.

"With veteran, Ollie Slane, oozing out all his football tricks, and full-back FH Owens playing his heart out, Beragh still looked like having a chance when they were only a solitary goal - one kick of the ball- behind at the thirty minute signal," the report stated.

"But it was a slim chance. The Coalisland boys tanned the hide of last year's champions, Omagh St Enda's in the previous round, came out in the second half and, although they never got moving in their best style, kicked the St Mary's out of the championship by knocking up a further five points."

A 1-8 to 0-3 defeat proved extremely disappointing for Beragh who had high hopes of reaching the County Final for the first time. All they could do was watch as Coalisland went on to defeat Dungannon in the decider.

Vin Donaghy remembers that the dropping of Frankie Owens for that

The Beragh team which reached the Senior Championship Semi-Final in 1955

game concerned him and that many of the same mistakes which had dogged their performance in the Minor Finals against the Fianna surfaced again.

"I remember Ollie Slane getting us into Sixmilecross Hall and drawing a pitch on the blackboard before that semi-final. We travelled to the match in the bus, but the early goal for Coalisland was the difference, it was a very soft score to give away and Jim Devlin, who I was marking said that to me at the time," he recalled.

"I could have cried coming off the field that day because I believe that if Beragh had won then we would have gone on to beat Dungannon in the County Final. After that the team broke up, players like Matt McNamee left and we lost a few more as well.

"That team had come through the football revival that Fr Murtagh was involved in at the end of the forties. We reached the Minor Finals in 1950 and 1952 and progressed onto the Seniors then. There were some great players for Beragh around that time.

Hopes were still high of further progress in the 1956 Championship when Beragh lined out against Fintona in the opening round at the Brothers Park in Omagh. Persistent rain made the conditions difficult, but Beragh's first half control was to prove crucial.

Points from Mick Kerr and Joe McCann helped them into a 0-5 to 0-2 lead despite an injury to defender, John Donaghy. Basil Neville and Mickey

Surviving members of the 1955 team pictured as guests of honour at the 1989 Annual Dinner

committee level, and that the Secretary should write to the Secretary of the Ulster Council protesting against the increase.

BERAGH V TRILLICK. CHAMPIONSHIP GAME

On the motion of F. Droogan, seconded by P. Bradley the referee's report was adopted for discussion. On being asked for his remarks on the report, Mr. J. McMahon, the Beragh delegate, stated that he was the prime mover in ordering the Beragh players to leave the field. He stated that in his opinion if the game had continued players, who were sitting an examination during the following week, could have been injured. It was his opinion that injury could have serious effect on the the futures of these boys, and consequently he took action. He admitted that Trillick were leading and would have won the match. Mr. M. McGaughey, Trillick, stated that the tackle by the Trillick player may have been over-keen but was not dangerous. He said that Trillick were leading, and that his club had taken heavy defeats but had never rushed the field, and had always played the game.

Mr. J. McCann denied allegations in the Ref's report re the statement concerning Beragh officials.

On being asked his opinion, P. Coleman stated that there was only one player giving trouble, but he thought that the Beragh team was not able to stand up to the heavier charging of the Trillick Team & that Trillick officials should have kept more control of their team.

Mr. P. Kelly, Trillick, said the tackle referred to in the ref's report was accidental & due to a fall.

On the motion of M. McGaughey seconded by Mr. Chisman

> The report of the Referee into the game was adopted and the Beragh delegate, James McMahon, was asked for his views. He replied that he was the prime mover in ordering the Beragh players to leave the field

McCann added to the total on the resumption when goals from Jim McAleer and Basil Neville helped them to a resounding 2-8 to 0-2 victory.

The win left them favourites to once again progress to the semi-final at the expense of Clonoe, who provided the Quarter Final opposition. However, at Coalisland on August 26th, the O'Rahilly's proved far superior with a clear 5-4 to 2-2 win.

Only a point separated the teams at half-time, but the attacking role of Tyrone star, John Joe O'Hagan, really made the difference for Clonoe in the second half. Terry McCann, Mick Kerr, Vin Donaghy, Francis Hugh Owens and P Grimes all shone to no avail as Clonoe went through to the semi-final.

Problems beset Beragh's championship bid in 1957 when their first round clash against Trillick had to be abandoned. The repeated intrusions by spectators led to the match being called off, and perhaps all the better for Beragh who were trailing by 3-2 to 0-2 at the time.

However, another version of the story emerges from the Minutes of the West Tyrone Board following the game. The report of the Referee into the game was adopted and the Beragh delegate, James McMahon, was asked for his views. He replied that he was the prime mover in ordering the Beragh players to leave the field.

According to the Minutes, he went on to state that "in his opinion if the game had continued players, who were sitting an examination during the following week, could have been injured."

It was his opinion that injury could have serious effect on the futures of the boys and, consequently, he took action. He admitted that Trillick were winning at the time and would have won the match.

Jack McCann denied allegations in the Referee's report concerning Beragh officials, while Peter Coleman stated that there was only one player giving trouble, but he thought that the Beragh team was not able to stand up to the heavier charging of the Trillick team and that the Trillick officials should have had more control of their team. And remarkably the game was refixed by the board.

Circumstances were much better on and off the field in the replay on June 23 when Beragh emerged comfortable winners by 3-4 to 1-4. They led by 2-2 to 0-1 at half-time and were complimented for their expert positional play. The scorers were J McCann (1-3), Anthony McGrath (1-1) and Basil Neville (1-0).

Victory over Trillick set up a Quarter Final meeting against Derrylaughan, who were confidently expected to overcome what was considered a lighter and relatively more inexperienced Beragh team. Mick Cushnahan and Mick McIlkenny formed the Kevin Barry's strong midfield partnership and they were to the fore in guiding their team to a big win.

Just as in 1956, Clonoe ended Beragh's hopes in 1958 when they scored a comprehensive 3-8 to 2-2 win. The East Tyrone side led by 1-4 to 1-0 at half-time and it was all one-way traffic in the second half despite the Beragh efforts to turn the tide.

Then in 1959 there was another Quarter Final defeat by Dungannon to end the decade on a very disappointing note.

The West Tyrone Senior League 1955-1959

For the reader more accustomed to modern GAA ways, it would be easy to assume that the momentum gathered by the County Semi-Final appearance would be maintained for the rest of the season.

But the world of gaelic football in West Tyrone was very different half a century ago. Instead of perhaps challenging for Senior League honours, games were few and far between for the St Mary's from then on.

There is little indication of activity either in Beragh or throughout West Tyrone following the completion of the championship, except for a defeat by Carrickmore in the Quarter Final of the St Enda Cup in November.

Action began anew at the beginning of 1956 when Beragh were drawn with Clogher, Carrickmore and Pomeroy in Section C of the West Tyrone League and produced some good form. Clogher were defeated by 3-6 to 1-3 before they lost narrowly to Carrickmore on a score of 1-7 to 1-6.

While intermittent action continued in the Senior League, Beragh's form appears to have remained reasonably positive. By the autumn they were scheduled to play

Taking a break from the excitement of playing football for Beragh are these teenagers of the mid 1950s

A fun day out on
the bicycle
in the 1950s

Carrickmore in a Section C play-off with the winners meeting Urney or Tattysallagh in the League decider.

That game was lost, but they came back strongly in the 1957 League. A 4-5 to 1-2 win was recorded over Ballygawley when Basil Neville scored 3-2 and Jack Heaney 1-0. Games continued on an irregular basis but by the end of the year Beragh had won their section of the League to progress to the semi-final.

In it, the St Mary's took on and lost to Clogher at Dunmoyle on November 17th. In 1958 they were placed in the mid-West Section of the West Tyrone League along with Carrickmore, Ballygawley and Pomeroy.

They started with a 2-6 to 0-2 loss to the St Colmcille's, the points from Dessie McMahon and Frank Rodgers, didn't help matters, although their form did improve. That game took place in August and in October Beragh were second on the table with four points, Carrickmore being on top with six and Ballygawley and Pomeroy each having two.

Carrickmore duly progressed to the West Tyrone Final against Clogher at Beragh in February 1959 and the re-organisation of the competition at that year's Annual Meeting led to an earlier start and more games.

Beragh had four points at the beginning of March 1959 and a 1-10 to 1-6 defeat by Dromore contributed to a poor run subsequently. Their positioning remained the same in the middle of May but the momentum of the competition seems to have been largely maintained.

By the early summer they had more games played than any of the other teams, a schedule which saw them improve upon the precarious position of earlier in the year. Victory over Newtownstewart left them in good form for the championship and a month later they travelled full of confidence to Clogher.

In October the new Secretary of the West Tyrone Board, Jack Woods, doubted whether it would be completed at all.

However, things did proceed even though the St Mary's failed to add to their points total. While Omagh, Urney and Dromore were the leading teams, Beragh were just above the relegation zone ahead of Pomeroy, Newtownstewart and Carrickmore.

The Omagh CBS McRory Cup team of 1958 included Beragh players, Frank Rodgers, Paddy Bogan and Seamus Coyle

St Enda Cup Champions 1956

Among the most important competitions of the 1950s was the St Enda Cup. It had originally been the McAleer Cup presented by HK McAleer in 1932 and always attracted considerable interest as it complimented the West Tyrone League and provided regular footballing action for local teams.

While the mid-fifties saw Beragh progress to the Senior Championship Semi-Final 1956 was marked by substantial progress in the St Enda Cup. They won that year's Cup competition, although the final wasn't played until almost two years later.

Perhaps the delay was due to the fact that the competition didn't start until the end of what was an historic year for Tyrone. Beragh were drawn against Tattysallagh in the first round, but the game doesn't appear to have taken place until the start of 1957.

On that occasion, a young team was fielded that proved its worth with a 3-8 to 0-4 victory. Brian Grimes top scored with 2-2, Michael McCann notched 1-3 and the other scorers were Mick Kerr 0-2 and Joe McCann 0-1.

They were then scheduled to play Urney in the next round with the team to be selected from the following: Hugh McCann, Frank Rodgers, Pat Grimes, Nickle Grimes, Seamus McMahon, Terry McCann, Terry Kelly, Anthony McGrath, Michael McCann, Joe McCann, Jack Heaney, Mick Kerr, Brian Grimes, Basil Neville, Hughie Owens, John McGlinn, Barney Owens, Patsy Farley, John Breen, Dessie McMahon and Barney Horisk.

Urney didn't field in that game, Beragh were awarded the points and a semi-final win over Omagh put them through to the final against

While the mid-fifties saw Beragh progress to the Senior Semi-Final and 1956 was also marked by substantial progress in the St Enda Cup

191

Carrickmore. This game on May 4th 1958 resulted in Beragh taking the title thanks mainly to an outstanding display of scoretaking from Mickey Kerr.

Described by the Ulster Herald as a 'sparkling game of football played under ideal conditions' on a well prepared Dunmoyle pitch. The defences were on top in the first half, the highlight of which was a goal from Oliver Kerr after a pass from Mickey Quinn. But Beragh's challenge was transformed when Mickey Kerr safely dispatched a penalty to the net in the second half.

This helped Beragh to win by 1-8 to 1-7 and it's hardly surprising that Mickey Kerr was mentioned as being the star man on view. He scored 1-6 of the Beragh total, with Jim McAleer, Dessie McMahon, Michael McCann and FH Owens mentioned in the report.

It was at a subsequent West Tyrone Board meeting on the Monday night following the match that the Cup was presented to Pat McCartan on behalf of the club. He said the match had been cleanly contested, went on to thank Carrickmore for making this possible and added that it was an enjoyable affair.

The Board Chairman said that "The Association would benefit if more of these games were witnessed," he said, before paying tribute with thanks to the Beragh team.

By the time that final was played, Beragh had gone out of the 1958 competition following a heavy defeat at the hands of an Omagh team spearheaded by the goalscoring abilities of Jackie Taggart.

"If Beragh are team building, they should know just exactly what their boys are made of when they saw them step up against the toughest opposition in Tyrone at the moment. The Omagh team was very much below strength, but they were still tough meat for Beragh. Too tough perhaps," said the Ulster Herald report.

> " Urney didn't field in that game, Beragh were awarded the points and a semi-final win over Omagh put them through to the final against Carrickmore "

Beragh's fortunes didn't improve the following year either when they defeated Trillick by 2-4 to 1-4 but then lost to Pomeroy at the semi-final stage in November on a score of 1-6 to 2-0. Faulty finishing from the forwards was given as a reason for the loss, which came despite the good distribution work of Mickey Kerr and Frank Rodgers.

A goal from Brian Grimes brought them back into it near the end, but they couldn't overturn the Pomeroy lead even though FH Owens, Anthony and Liam McGrath, Brian Grimes and Terry Kelly all tried hard.

Minor Finalists 1950 and 1952 - (Youth Football)

The arrival of Fr Murtagh in the area was combined with the introduction of the South Tyrone Juvenile League to transform youth football at the end of the forties in a process that continued apace in the new decade.

Beragh was to the forefront of these efforts by taking part enthusiastically in the competitions organised. These factors contributed to an exciting time for the young players of the area as they progressed to the County Minor Final on two separate occasions.

In April 1950 they accounted for Ballygawley by 0-7 to 0-4 despite trailing at half-time. The abilities of the players were highlighted that year, too, when Jim McAleer, Joe McCann and Terry Kelly lined out on a West Tyrone Minor select.

Regular matches continued to be held and their place in the County Final was secured when they defeated Omagh in the West Tyrone Final in January. Despite the bad weather conditions, a 3-0 to 1-4 victory was recorded, with a goal by Mick McCartan putting them ahead after a poor start. He added two more goals to leave Beragh ahead by 3-0 to 1-1 at half-time and they held firm in the second half.

This win put Beragh into the County Final against Coalisland which took place on April 8th 1951. But there was to be no joy as the Fianna proved far superior on a score of 5-1 to 1-5.

The players were presented with their West Tyrone medals at a Ceile

Early action as the Beragh Minors progress to the County Final where they lost to Coalisland

in the INF Hall in Omagh and there was no let-up in the amount of activity which captured the attention of the players into the new year, 1952.

A place in the West Tyrone Final was again secured in 1951 and saw a repeat pairing against Omagh in mid-May. On this occasion the match finished in a 1-4 each draw, Beragh equalising after trailing. Basil Neville got the goal and there were also good displays from Mickey Kerr and Terry Kelly.

However, there was no luck in the replay when Omagh turned the tables by winning 3-5 to 1-4 after enjoying a 2-4 to 0-1 interval advantage. Mick McCartan, Mickey Kerr and Terry Kelly were among the Beragh scorers, while another player mentioned was Jerry Kavanagh. Omagh later lost to Ardboe in the Tyrone Final.

By the end of the year Beragh were back in the West Tyrone Final for the third year running against Dromore on November 23, 1952. "Both teams served up some brilliant flashes of positional play," according to the Ulster Herald, and it was midfield superiority which proved decisive.

Terry Kelly was said to have played "the game of his life, catching and

The Beragh Minor team which reached the County Final in 1952. Pictured at back are John Boyle, FH Owens, Sean Kelly, Mick McAleer, Terry Kelly, Matt McNamee, Maurice McGarrity, Mickey McNamee, Jim McA;leer and Jack Kavanagh. At front are Mick Kerr, Phil Campbell, Tommy McCann, Vin Donaghy, Joe McCann, and Jerry Kavanagh. Missing from the picture is Gus McNamee.

> "
>
> The whole team would have done the bit of running and I remember some smart fella saying to us that we were overtrained
>
> "

kicking with great accuracy" and the Beragh half-back line of Sean Kelly,

Terry McCann and Seamus Colton were also on form.

Beragh led by 2-3 to 0-1 at half-time, the goals coming from Mick McCartan and John McSorley. Terry Kelly also scored in the win by 2-3 to 0-4. Mick Kerr was

Raring to go for a Minor game against Castlederg in the early 1950s

described as being "the brains of the forward line" and the team was: Leo Kavanagh, McGale, Jerry Kavanagh, Pat Grimes, Sean Kelly, Terry McCann, Seamus Colton, Terry Kelly, P McAleer, Kieran McCann, Mick Kerr, Seamus Heagney, Ian McCool, Mick McCartan and John McSorley.

It took some time for the County Final to be played and it actually didn't take place until April 19th, 1953, at Dungannon prior to an inter-county game. However, the Coalisland boys once again proved to be too strong, led as they were by Jody O'Neill and Eddie Devlin.

The Ulster Herald reported that Beragh were perhaps not as inferior as the 3-11 to 0-4 final scoreline suggested. "For while their defence was fairly sound, their forwards methods were not direct enough and their midfield pair Terry Kelly and Sean Kelly, while always trying valiantly, were no equal to the Coalisland section." Seamus Colton, Gerry Kavanagh and Pat Grimes stood out in defence with Mickey Kerr again being one of the main players up front.

Mickey Kerr recalls how the team had trained for the game under the watchful eye of John Brannigan who followed them on his bicycle for road runs around Sixmilecross and Ballyhallaghan.

Relaxation in the countryside for the Beragh youth players of the 1950s

"The whole team would have done the bit of running and I remember some 'smart fella' saying to us that we were overtrained. I was marking Jody O'Neill in that match, but Coalisland had a very good team and won easily enough," he added.

While the South Tyrone Juvenile League seems to have faltered a little in the middle of the decade, Beragh continued to actively promote the playing of gaelic football at youth level. In 1958 they lost to Ballygawley by 2-3 to 2-1 in the Juvenile Final.

The panel of players listed for that 1958 Final was: Ward, B Cunningham, Dan Montgomery, Noel Maguire, L McAleer, T Baxter, M Kelly, K Caldwell, B Grimes, P McCusker, D Caldwell, P McQuaid, Liam McGrath, S McCann, Connie McMahon, Pete McQuaid, N Kelly, M McGarvey, Cahir Woods, Kieran McCann, FH Ward.

Most of the players advanced to Minor level for 1959 when the list was: J Ward, B Cunningham, Paddy Bogan, Peter McQuaid, Liam McGrath, Noel Maguire, Dan Montgomery, Seamus Coyle, S McCann, Vincent McCullagh, Hugh Ward, T Baxter, Seamus Rodgers, B Grimes, Anthony Heagney, P McCusker, D Caldwell, M Kelly, K Kelly, M Donnelly, Connie McMahon.

Other activities

Innovative proposals to various West Tyrone and County Conventions indicated that the officials of Beragh St Mary's club had their finger on the pulse of GAA activity in the 1950s.

In 1951 the club suggested an increase of £1 in referee's fees, the following year it proposed that all teams consist of fifteen players and in 1954 it called for each club to be required to submit the names of two referees. The club also called for players to be sent to the line for a "period of time," a move that is still under discussion.

The annual Convention and the monthly committee meetings provided time for reflection among the club officials and supporters and at one in 1953, John Brannigan, J McNamee, J McCartan and P Mullan were appointed gatemen while a vote of congratulations was passed to Cardinal D'Alton on his elevation to the Sacred College of Cardinals.

That year also, members were exhorted to attend all meetings when possible. The importance of promoting the Irish language and Irish dances was stressed and a decision was taken to start a Gaelic League branch.

Similar sentiments were echoed by the West Tyrone Chairman, Paddy McCaffrey, when he told clubs that "to play football for an hour on a Sunday does not given someone the right to call themselves a Gael."

The wedding day party for Jack McCann, Chairman of the Beragh club from 1939-1942 and 1956-1957

Language and dance classes were indeed held in Beragh at that time and fifty members attended the 1954 Convention when Rev A McKernan was appointed President and Rev Fr Cooney and Rev Fr Sheridan as Vice-Presidents.

In 1955 the AGM was held in Sixmilecross where the Chairman, Tommy McGarvey, urged to all members "the importance of discipline both among players and spectators." He felt that the support of all would lead to a successful year.

Throughout the decade the long-serving Treasurer, WJ Conway, invariably reported on a sound financial position and his work was undoubtedly appreciated.

Conventions then as now gave members the opportunity to voice their opinion on a variety of matters. And at the 1959 Convention Paddy McCrumlish wanted to see a Juvenile League started while Mickey Kerr, the team captain, suggested that a Parish Adult League would also be beneficial.

Before standing down from the post of Secretary that year, Pat McCartan, commented on what he said was "the lack of gaelic spirit in the district and the decline of interest in the welfare of the club." Those complaints may have prompted action and in July, an all-Irish night was held as part of the annual GAA Ceile as the decade drew to a close.

Pitch purchase and the Beragh Tournament

Top class facilities are now normal throughout the country. Millions have been spent in the provision of dressing-rooms, clubhouses, training pitches and spectator accommodation of the highest possible standard.

Hardly surprising, then, that some might find it difficult to visualise how different things once were. Up until the 1970s most clubs struggled with inadequate or no changing facilities and poor pitches and depended mostly on sympathetic local farmers for whatever ground they could get.

A Beragh schoolgroup from the 1950s pictured outside the chapel

From the earliest years of the Association in Tyrone, the various teams in the Beragh parish were fortunate. Pitches at Sixmilecross, Deroar and Drumduff meant that many of the problems experienced elsewhere were less acute.

Nevertheless, the officials of the early fifties were a forward-thinking group whose decision to carry out probably the most significant move of the first half-century of GAA activity in the parish had far-reaching benefits.

The simple fact is that the decision to purchase the ground at the eastern end of the village beside the Great Northern Railway Station set the standard that other clubs are still following.

The story of how this came to pass is told in the minutes of the 'Beragh Field Committee' which was set up to carry out the business of purchasing a ground for the St Mary's Club. A series of meetings took place, with two in particular during January proving especially important.

Getting togged out in the sun of a summer's afternoon out for a 1950s match

In attendance at the first were FH Rodgers, PW Donnelly, Sean Bennett, James McMahon, WJ Conway, Peter McNamee, Jamie Slane, Mick Kelly, Packie Mullin, Felix McCann, John Donaghy, James Colton, Tommy McGarvey and Jamie Donnelly.

The minutes, taken by the Secretary, WJ Conway, recount how various sites were considered but deemed to be unsuitable because of surface, position, car parking, accommodation and other reasons.

Peter McNamee then proposed that FH Rodgers would sell fields at the Railway. Mr Rodgers said that he would have to think over the matter and would let the members know of his decision in a few days.

At the subsequent meeting on January 21st, 1954, FH Rodgers intimated his willingness to sell the field at a price of £200 per acre. The price was considered too much and Paddy Donnelly, WJ Conway and Peter McNamee were deputised to visit him and find out at what lower price he would be willing to sell.

The minutes state that; "they reported back that he would sell the ten acres for £1500 which was considered very reasonable. And so the ground was bought and a number of Trustees were proposed. These were - Thomas McGarvey,

One of the races at the Sports which were a popular fixture on the calendar in the 1950s

Paddy Donnelly, James Slane, Michael Kelly, WJ Conway, Packie Mullin, Joe Donnelly, Peter McNamee and James McMahon."

It was decided that the Trustees would carry out the work of having the land transferred, the securing of a loan from the Northern Bank and the appointment of a solicitor to act for the Club.

In February ways and means of getting the money needed were discussed and a house to house collection was one of the ways decided upon. A total of £443 was raised by this means, while at a meeting in April a Whist Drive, Card Drive in November or December, sports, a collection in Omagh and Carrickmore and the Football Tournament were also suggested.

Each of these brought in much-needed finance - the Tournament profit was £26, the Whist Generated £18 and the collections in Omagh and Carrickmore raised £95 and £24 respectively. However, just £6 was raised from the Sports due to a wet day.

ANY REPLY TO THIS LETTER SHOULD BE ADDRESSED TO "THE AGENT"

BANK OF IRELAND,

OMAGH,21st September, 1954.
CO. TYRONE.

Thomas McGarvey Esq.,
Manager,
Sixmilecorss Co-Operative Society Ltd.,
Omagh.

Dear Mr. McGarvey,

Sports & Football Field.

Referring to your recent visit, my Directors have agreed to give a donation of £5 towards the cost of Sports and Football Field for the Beragh and Sixmilecross district. I enclose a cheque for that amount. Would you kindly let me have a receipt.

Yours truly,

Agent.

Joe Hardy
Ballygawly

> "Clear evidence of just how significant the purchase was came at that year's Tyrone Convention when the Secretary, Paddy O'Neill congratulated the club on its efforts. The meeting heard that the Beragh ground was only the fourth in Tyrone to be vested in the GAA, following in the footsteps of the recognised county venues at Dungannon, Coalisland and Pomeroy"

Clear evidence of just how significant the purchase was came at that year's Tyrone Convention when the County Secretary, Paddy O'Neill congratulated the club on its efforts. The meeting heard that the Beragh ground was only the fourth in Tyrone to be vested in the GAA, following in the footsteps of the recognised county venues at Dungannon, Coalisland and Pomeroy.

With its easy access to the Railway Station and close proximity to the village, the ground soon became a popular and much-used venue for matches at all levels. One of the first games was between Beragh and Carrickmore in March and many West Tyrone League play-offs and County Championship matches were held at the new ground over subsequent seasons.

The Tournament attracted many of the top teams from within Tyrone and neighbouring counties. The host club were highly fancied in it in1956 following a win over Desertmartin, but the final saw Clogher overcome Urney.

Now billed as the Beragh GAA Week, Clogher lost their title to Emyvale

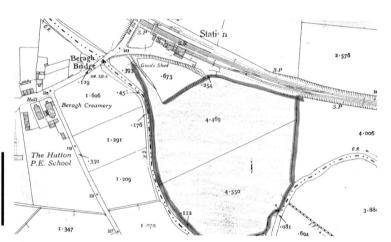

A map showing the ground purchased by the Beragh St Mary's in 1954.

of Monaghan the following year when the Grand Presentation took place at a Ceilidhe in St Mary's Hall on the night of the final.

By 1958 the schedule was well established and the appeal of the event was emphasised by the appearance of top teams like Stewartstown, Donaghmore, Urney, Clogher, Galbally and, of course, Carrickmore who were annual strong contenders. Clogher were the winners that year.

Clogher again won in 1959 when Pomeroy provided the opposition following another busy programme of matches. The organisers were complimented for their efforts as the competition continued to provide surprises and entertainment.

Club Secretary at the time, Sean Bennett, recalled the circumstances surrounding the purchase of the pitch, the beginning of the Tournament and other key events at the time.

"Myself and FH Rodgers were talking about things one day and he started saying about how bad it was that other clubs had pitches and we were always shifting around," remembers Sean Bennett.

"I said to him 'what about that holm of yours, would you take a notion of selling' and out of the blue he said yes. He was very interested in football and I remember him taking John Donaghy and myself to Dublin.

"After that there was a Field Committee appointed and each of them put up £100. Before that you were playing in back gardens one match and in the middle of rushes in the next. It was difficult to get pitches and McGirr's Holm was where we played after moving away from Deroar because the fields had to be ploughed up.

"The ground in Beragh cost £1500 and there were fifteen men involved in buying it. The Tournament was run every year and if you made £50 it was great. The Field Committee took it over and eventually paid off the debt.

"The ground was let out to cattle dealers like Hugh Boyle, Packie Mullan and a few others. But the cattle wrecked it and then it was let out to sheep. The pitch would be in terrible shape when there was a match.

"It was very handy for the Railway Station and some dealers would even have put their cattle in without anybody knowing. The pitch was let to raise money, the Field Committee did that and the football committee didn't have anything to do with it. Anyone that had given £100 was on the Field Committee, but we never knew how much the pitch was rented for."

Tullyneil Pipe Band

Parades by the Tulac Neill Pipe Band were a key feature of community life during the fifties when their success at a number of events culminated in them winning the All-Ireland title in 1950 at Lansdowne Road in Dublin. They came on top from 33 entries in the All-Ireland Pipe Band Championships, just reward for weeks and weeks of dedicated practice.

Prior to the final, which took place in August, the Band received the benefit of instructions from Major Robert Reid of Glasgow, a world champion, who was on holiday in Mick McGrath's and had been with the Sixmilecross players each evening.

One of the problems faced by them in the run-up to the final was the acquirement of new drums, the old ones having been blamed for their failure at a Pipe Band competition in Dundalk some weeks previously. However, the quality of drums was put right in time for the All-Ireland Final.

The band's pipe major at the event was Michael McCann, the Drum Major was John Brannigan and Maurice McGarrity was the leading drummer.

Some time after their success, the Band honoured the contribution of Mr Reid to their success at a function in the AOH Hall. He was unable to attend the All-Ireland Finals in Dublin, but was said to have learned of their success with much delight.

The guests at the event were welcomed by Packie McAleer, president of the Band Committee and other officers and members present were William Collins (Vice-President), Patsy Collins (secretary and treasurer), Michael

> Parades by the Tulac Neill Pipe Band were a key feature of community life during the fifties when their success at a number of events culminated in winning the All-Ireland title in 1950 at Lansdowne Road in Dublin

Many emigrants from Sixmilecross and Beragh are included in this photograph of those attending the Tyrone Society Dinner in June 1957 for the victorious Tyrone team of 1956.

WELCOMING BANQUET FOR
COUNTY TYRONE FOOTBALL TEAM
TENDERED BY
THE COUNTY TYRONE SOCIETY, INC.
HOTEL EDISON   JUNE 8, 1957.

McCann (assistant treasurer), John Brannigan, James Cleary, Gus McNamee and Terry McCann.

Members of the band, of course, often paraded visiting football teams to the pitches at Beragh, Sixmilecross and Deroar and one of their first engagements following their All-Ireland success was to lead the Beragh and Trillick teams prior to the 1950 Davis Cup Final.

The Fancy Dress Parade through Sixmilecross at the Sports.

Community events - the death of Pat Grimes

When Tyrone contested the 1953 Ulster Minor Final the lineout for the game included Pat Grimes of Clogherney. Then considered as an up and coming player of promise for the St Mary's, his career and life were cut tragically short by a car accident in 1955. Aged 20, he died at the end of November at Tyrone County Hospital from injuries received after being knocked down on Main Street, Beragh.

Another person with strong GAA connections who died during the decade was a former Chairman of the Sixmilecross Wolfe Tones club, James Slane. His obituary in the Ulster Herald stated that he had for many years been a prominent member of the Association both as a player and a legislator and, as well as keeping a well-informed interest in gaelic games, his house was a popular place for discussions and meetings.

Towards the end of 1958 retired chemist, 95 year old Hamilton McDowell, died after a fire broke out at his home in Main Street, Beragh, where the Bistro now stands. The fire was discovered by an Indian salesman, Daman Datt Takler, then resident above Mr McDowell's home and who was praised for his efforts to save his elderly neighbour. The fire broke out in the middle of the night and a later inquest heard that the body of Mr McDowell was recovered badly burned from the ground floor of the building.

Earlier in the decade concern was expressed about the state of many houses in the rural area of the Omagh District. A survey found that in Beragh 58 houses had no water laid on, 20 had water supplies, 29 had dry closets, eighteen had water closets and two had chemical closets. In

Sixmilecross 28 houses had no water laid on, 20 had water supplies, 29 had dry closets, 18 had water closets and two had chemical closets.

Dr Watson, though, complained that the water in Beragh and Sixmilecross was not of sufficient quality and there were complaints during the decade about the 'litter louts' of the two villages, with one member of Omagh Rural Council saying that litter bins provided were not being used.

Around the same time, in 1950, discussions were taking place among the members of the Tyrone Education Committee with regard to the building of a new school in Sixmilecross. It was felt that a new school was badly needed.

The committee was also concerned about the provision of new Intermediate Secondary Schools. According to a report in the Ulster Herald in 1951, Tyrone's Catholic Population was increasing and there were plans to erect new schools at a number of locations including Dromore and Ballygawley.

The state of the harvest at the time was also of pressing and immediate concern. In September 1953, a report from Sixmilecross stated that the corn and potato crops were excellent, but that fine weather was urgently needed to ensure their success.

"There has been little or no corn cut during the past fortnight because of rain, although much of it is over-ripe, the ears falling to the ground. In hundreds of fields, the grain has been flattened by rain and it will be almost impossible to use mowing machines.

At a meeting in the 'Cross, farmers were also being urged to ensure an immediate and substantial improvement in the quality of bacon pigs. The plea was made by Mr Reginald Loane, Tyrone representative on the Pigs Marketing Board.

Cycle races at Deroar Park during the Sports drew top riders from throughout Ulster

For some light relief, the Beragh Drama Society staged its first pantomine in 1952 with its production of 'Simple Simon' in the Hall. The cast, though, according to one reviewer, had one fault - "they paid too much attention to the audience."

Cast members included Sean Bennett, Maurice McGarrity, Elizabeth Collins, Josie Owens, Joan Mullin, Brendan McNamee, Michael Donnelly, Frank Hagan. The Chorus comprised Annie Conway, Rose Daly, Frances McElhatton,

Excited children put the finishing touches to their Fancy Dress costumes

Patricia Cleary, Maggie Daly, Jeannie Kelly, Aggie Owens, Sheila Woods and Nora Skeffington, the Fairies were Mary McGarvey, Claire Donnelly, Mary McQuade and Margaret McQuade while Mary Boyle and Rosaleen O'Neill were Angels.

A Ceili in St Mary's Hall in October 1958 was recorded by the BBC and included a selection of Irish dance music, comedy, songs and ballads. Beragh Amateur Dramatic Group productions included a pantomine, while the film shows in St Mary's Hall became very popular. The showing of Westerns and other features is still fondly remembered, with the technical expertise being the responsibility of projectionist, Francie Gallagher.

The Melody Aces played in the Hall on Friday July 30th, 1954 and such was the demand for facilities that in 1953, Fr McKernan applied for an extension to the Hall to make space for a Youth Club. The extension was subsequently completed.

And, of course, the Beragh and Sixmilecross Races were ever-popular on the Ballyhallaghan course. They took place on Easter Monday in the early part of the decade before slipping off the calendar.

Handball

One of the big developments of the late fifties was the formal organisation of handball locally under the banner of the Brackey Club. It was established in March 1958 as interest in the game grew steadily thanks to the involvement of a large number of enthusiasts.

The Ulster Herald reported that the alley was developed at the old school in Brackey where the game had been played for over thirty years. The ballcourt was described as having a main wall, two short side-walls and an excellent concrete floor which was built entirely by local voluntary labour.

"Interest in handball in the district has reached a high pitch. On Sunday's games are played from about 11 o clock in the morning until dusk, with competition being very keen," the correspondent said.

"This new club should be a welcome shot in the arm to Tyrone handball. Although last year was not exactly a bumper year, 1958 promises to be the greatest year ever for the game in the county. Already Michael Kelly has qualified for the Gael Linn finals and plans have been made for a major reconstruction scheme at Loughmacrory's four-walled court.

It's a pity that districts like Fintona, Dromore, Drumquin and Castlederg, where handball once flourished, and where you can still hear the older generation talk of games between men like Patsy Bradley, Mickey

Interest in handball in the district has reached a high pitch. On Sunday's games are played from about 11 o clock in the morning until dusk, with competitive being very keen

A group of handballers outside St Mary's Hall prior to its extension. The formation of the Brackey Club provided a focus for the game in the parish from 1958

Mick Kerr's contribution to Tyrone's fortunes that year cannot be over-emphasised either. For it was his outstanding display against Monaghan in the semi-final which really set Tyrone on their way

McCann, Tom O'Kane, Paddy Foley and Sergeant McGuinness of the RIC, to mention but a few, don't make an effort to revive handball."

The eagerness of the new players from Brackey to test their skills was also highlighted by the news that they were anxious for competition, especially from districts where handball has been revived or introduced."

A year later the Tyrone Gael Linn Finals took place in Brackey and the efforts during the later years of the 1950s were to reap the rewards at the start of the new decade when the sport really gained a solid and permanent foothold locally.

Inter-County activities

Complaints about what was perceived as a bias towards players from East Tyrone didn't prevent a number of Beragh players from making regular appearances on Tyrone teams during the 1950s.

But the club has very special reason to remember the historic Ulster title success of 1956. For the team included Mick Kerr at corner forward and had Jim McAleer among the substitutes for the final win over the then mighty Cavan. The win sent shockwaves through Ulster football that are still being felt into the 21st Century.

Victory over the mighty Breffni men opened the doors for a whole series of breakthroughs. Derry came with their first title in 1958, Down followed suit in 1959 and Cavan were never again a serious force on the championship front in the province.

Mick Kerr's contribution to Tyrone's fortunes that year cannot be over-emphasised either. For it was his outstanding display against Monaghan in the semi-final which set Tyrone on their way.

Representing the county at the time wasn't as high profile as today. Indeed, at only 19, Mick was just brought into the panel for the semi-final against Monaghan and made a sensational impact by scoring 1-1.

"As luck would have it Tyrone made a real find for the right corner forward position in Mick Kerr. This dynamic little two-footed player proved to everyone there that he was the Tyrone selectors meal ticket and after welcoming Mick to the team I hope he now wins an Ulster Championship medal," wrote Fearghal in the Ulster Herald.

Mick went on to line out at corner forward for the Ulster Final against Cavan, before making way for one of the county's longest serving players to come in for the second half, Hugh Kelly of Urney.

"The first time I knew about being selected on the Tyrone team in 1956 was when I saw my name in the paper. I wasn't sure if it was me, but then somebody asked did I know anyone else called M Kerr who played football," Mick recalled.

"It was an even bigger surprise to be selected for the match against Monaghan because I had been out watching the Minor game when Paddy O'Neill came and told me to get togged out.

"For the final we trained eight nights in two weeks at Pomeroy. I stayed in Donnelly's Hotel in Omagh the night before going to Clones. I don't think I was nervous or anything like that, apart from maybe just before the start.

"To be honest, I probably didn't realise how tough a game it would be – I was marking Brian O'Reilly in a full-back line that also had Phil 'The Gunner Brady.' But we won the match and the celebrations were nearly tougher than the match with people congratulating us and jumping on our backs. It was a big achievement."

Another member of the Tyrone panel that day was Beragh's Jim McAleer, who had represented the county with distinction on many occasions over the previous years. A key player for the St Mary's around that time, he made his senior championship debut for Tyrone in the 1954 Ulster Semi-Final against Cavan. That year also saw them line out against Donegal in the provincial Junior Final.

Pat Grimes, who so tragically died in a car accident in 1955, had also lined out for the Tyrone Minors when they reached the provincial final in 1953. His goal in the last quarter secured a 2-7 to 1-4 semi-final victory over Monaghan.

Ollie Slane, who returned from

Buy Your Feeding Stuffs From Your own Society at Millers' Prices

Home Milled Maize Meal	£25	0 0 ton
Home Milled Barley Meal	£24 5	0 ton
Barley Feeding Meal with Vitamealo	£22 10	0 ton
Pig Fattening Meal with Vitamealo	£23 10	0 ton
Sow and Weaner Meal with Vitamealo	£33 0	0 ton
Deep Litter Mash with Protein	£32 0	0 ton
Coarse Dairy Meal 18% Protein	£31 10	0 ton
'Cross Channel Dairy Cubes	£31 5	0 ton
Beef Fattening Nuts	£31 0	0 ton

Above Prices are for Prompt Cash in Ton Lots or 10cwt. to 10cwt., 6d per cwt. on 10cwt. lots 3d per cwt. extra.

Vitamealo is a careful selection of Proteins chosen to provide the widest range of Animo Acids, and supply the particular blend of Proteins, Minerals, Vitamins and Essential Elements required for each and all purposes of Stock Feeding. It provides against risk of nutritional deficiencies and the farmer better stock and highest production.

Sixmilecross and Omagh Co.-O and Agric. Society, Ltd.
and OMA

Carrickmore to Beragh at the beginning of 1952, lined out at corner back against Armagh in that year's championship. He made his debut for the county while playing for Carrickmore in 1945, played again in the 1951 Ulster Championship and was full-forward when Tyrone played Cavan in 1953.

Promise being fulfilled

Those associated with the Beragh St Mary's at the end of the fifties had justifiable reasons to feel optimistic for the future as they looked ahead to a new decade. Many of the officials involved provided the drive that saw noteworthy developments which put the club on solid foundations.

The players who featured on the winning St Enda's Cup team pictured at a presentation function in St Mary's Hall

St Mary's Park, purchased at the beginning of 1954, was an example of their ambitions while the fielding of teams at Juvenile, Minor and Senior level saw them join in the growth being experienced by the Tyrone GAA as a whole.

On the field, too, the club had enjoyed steady progress throughout the decade without ever fulfilling what many believed was their true potential. Occasional victories over top teams like Omagh and Dungannon hinted at the possibility of higher honours but these didn't come.

> Those associated with the Beragh St Mary's at the end of the fifties had justifiable reasons to feel optimistic for the future as they looked ahead to a new decade

But there were achievements by the players and officials of the time to reflect upon with pride. The Davis Cup success in 1950, the St Enda Cup win of 1956, and the progress of the Minors to the County Finals in 1950 and 1951 provided the impetus which culminated in the Senior semi-final appearance of 1955 and the Quarter Finals of 1956, 1957, 1958 and 1959.

Add in the holding of regular meetings and the staging of Conventions, the role of people like Sean Bennett, WJ Conway and Jack Woods on the West Tyrone Board, and it's clear that Beragh St Mary's were to the fore in GAA activities during an historic decade locally and county-wide.

Chapter Eight
1960 - 1970
Pushing a Youth Policy

Chapter Eight
1960 - 1970

HOPES were high entering the sixties that the Beragh St Mary's would be prominent in all aspects of GAA affairs. A new young team was gaining experience backed by the provision of improving facilities and there was sterling work being done by various people at youth level.

Like all clubs, however, they could point to the failure to complete competitions on time as having a detrimental impact on their fortunes. That was a point dealt with in depth at the 1960 County Convention when Tyrone officials met to plan ahead. The need to improve club football was stressed as being of the utmost importance.

Better organisation of the West Tyrone League offered the opportunity for teams such as Beragh to better fulfill their potential. However, at a time when the winning of competitions was seen as an important aim, things didn't go to plan for the St Mary's. While their youth teams continued to make their mark, the decade provided greater challenges than many could have envisaged but eventually it was marked by the arrival of some new faces who would drive it towards the modern era.

Ceile Old Time or Modern Dancing. Employ the Silver Star Band, Beragh. Fully amplified with Crooner and Skiffle Group. Distance no object. Injuries to Jerry Grimes, Co-Op Omagh or Pat McGirr, Roscavey

League competitions 1960-1965

Changes to the structure of the West Tyrone League were introduced for 1960 when the competition was sub-divided in an effort to ensure more regular games. Beragh took part in the southern section along with Carrickmore, Creggan, Clogher, Ballygawley, Pomeroy and Fintona.

Early games were against Carrickmore and Creggan. They beat Creggan by 3-4 to 0-4 on February 28th, but then lost to the St Colmcille's by 1-5 to 1-1 in April.

Matches also took place against Clogher and Pomeroy at the end of June and beginning of July. They defeated Clogher and also scored a deserved 3-5 to 2-4 victory over Fintona. But the mixed form of the team continued when the Pearses reversed the earlier result on a score of 2-7 to 0-4 in August.

Autumn time 1960 brought them better luck as they laid the foundations for a title bid. A 1-10 to 1-9 win over Pomeroy on September 18 was noteworthy for the strength of the defence, Augher were accounted for by 2-9 to 0-6 on October 9 and then a 2-4 to 1-6 win over Ballygawley was recorded. In that game the teams were level at 1-3 each at half-time, and

The teamsheet for the 1963 Senior Championship signed by the Secretary, Peter Bennett

the performances of Pat Fox in goals, Frank Rodgers at full-back, Liam McGrath at centre back, Nickle Grimes and Dessie McMahon at midfield and the returning John McSorley, Mick Kerr and Anthony McGrath, were mentioned as being crucial.

An unusual feature of a 1-8 to 0-3 win over Augher at the end of the month was the placing of Mick Kerr in goals. All of this helped Beragh top the South Section of the West Tyrone League with twenty points, two ahead of Fintona and with Pomeroy back in third. They now had a Top Three semi-final to decide who would meet Newtownstewart in the Final.

That semi-final tie saw them meet Pomeroy in Fintona at the beginning of March 1961. By then the momentum was missing and they lost by 3-3 to 1-4. Brian Grimes was among the top performers, scoring 1-2, but that March 1961 defeat was the end of their challenge.

It wasn't long after this that the 1961 League began with defeats by Carrickmore and Ballygawley in April. Carrickmore, who went on to win the County title later in the season, were winners by 1-10 to 1-6 while Ballygawley won by 2-7 to 2-6 in May.

An example of just how haphazard things were is shown by the fact that by September the Beragh team had still only played two matches. Their third game which resulted in a 2-2 to 0-2 win over the Ballygawley was described as follows:

Sean Bennett and John Donaghy were regular delegates to the West Tyrone Board during the decade

"The Beragh team at half-time made up their minds not to let any scores over or under the bar and this they did. The forward line of McCann, Donaghy and Owens gave one of their best displays. Rafferty and Kelly were sound at midfield, Kelly, Maguire and Heaney were the half-forwards, Hagan in goals, Donaghy, Bennett and Grimes in the full-back line and Donnelly, Montgomery and Scallan completed the lineout."

Carrickmore were defeated by 2-3 to 1-5 in the League in December as the 1961 competition ran into 1962. The game against Pomeroy was refixed for April 1st, but it seems that from then on Beragh's involvement switched to the current year's activities and it wasn't until the summer that the final of the 1961 League was held.

The slow pace continued in 1962 and by September Beragh had still only played two games and won one match in Section B. Things eventually improved, however, and by December they were in second place on the table with twelve points from seven games and two games in hand over leaders, Carrickmore.

However, at the subsequent West Tyrone Convention, delegates decided to declare Carrickmore the winners and to proceed with the 1963 competition in the new year. Consequently, it was a case wondering what might have been for the St Mary's if they had got fulfilling their quota of matches.

That may have contributed to their subsequent slump in form during much of 1963. By September, the League table showed them as having played three matches without a win. They had been scheduled to meet Urney and Omagh in May, Clogher in June and Carrickmore in September but for whatever reason they didn't do so.

The seeds of failure were catching root and in November they were given one last chance to prove themselves. The West Tyrone Board told them to field a team or be relegated to the Intermediate Division which had been established at the start of 1962. This threat prompted an appeal from club officials to co-operate and turn out for their remaining games.

The appeal was heeded and the following week they were 1-11 to 2-7 winners over newly crowned county champions, Omagh. This was all the more remarkable since the St Enda's had led by 2-4 to 0-3 at half-time before Beragh came back strongly to win

They beat Ballygawley the following week and in January 1964 they were above Omagh and Fintona on the table. It appears that this kept them clear of the relegation zone and secured them a place in senior ranks for another year.

There was an enthusiastic start to the 1964 season for games in April against Pomeroy, Ballygawley and Omagh. Their ability was exposed however in a 3-11 to 2-4 defeat at the hands of the St Ciaran's who were helped by two PJ McClean goals. They also lost to Pomeroy and while Omagh were defeated, the league table at the end of June showed them in bottom place with Carrickmore. The win over the St Enda's didn't spur a revival and by July Carrickmore's improved form had lifted them to leave Beragh bottom on their own.

Relegation to Intermediate ranks was once again a real possibility and by November six points from thirteen games highlighted their failings. The result was that a play-off match against Clogher would decide their status for 1965.

The fortunes of the team had by then declined to such a level that there was severe difficulty in getting the match played. It was scheduled for the end of February, but didn't take place when Clogher travelled to Beragh only to find the pitch deserted.

April 1960 - Large congregation at 40 hours devotion. High Altar most artistically decorated by Bertie McGarrity, the Sexton. Choir under the direction of Miss Ann Conway. Canopy bearers were F H Rodgers, Mr J McCullagh, Mr John Kelly and Mr Patrick Donnelly

The Ulster Herald reported that at 3.30pm, eighteen Clogher men took to the field fully togged out, but it wasn't until 3.55pm that Beragh finally appeared. However, there was no referee and the teams eventually decided to play a challenge match. "To say the least, it was poor consolation for the spectators who had shivered around from 3pm and would not be described as a boost for club games with ever failing gates," the report stated.

The game eventually took place on March 7th when three goals in the opening minutes from Joe McKenna sent Clogher on their way to victory. This loss left Beragh out of senior for the first time since 1950 and at a subsequent club meeting, Mick Kerr described the defeat as "extremely disappointing."

Intermediate League 1965-1969

Some indication of the problems being faced by the St Mary's as they sought to regroup for the new challenge of the Intermediate League is evident from the number of players missing from their ranks.

County players, Dessie McMahon and Liam McGrath had gone to Dublin clubs and John McSorley and Hugh Owens had transferred to Carrickmore. Other losses included Frank Rodgers to Irvinestown, Basil Neville to newly formed Killyclogher, Barney Horisk and Michael McGarvey to Ballygawley and Hugh Fitzpatrick back to his native Newtownbutler.

It was to this backdrop that Ollie Slane took charge of the team for 1965. He returned to training on a Monday night early in the year and expressed the hope of having the team 'fighting fit' for the championship.

> Concern of parents who have to rouse their children for 8am bus which arrived in Omagh at 8.25am, much to early for the lessons. Hope that bus shelters will also be erected

"With his experience and skill, Beragh should turn out a team to match any team. At a training session, he showed that even after a long absence, he has lost none of his skill," the Ulster Herald reported.

But the road ahead proved tough. Aghyaran were the winners by 3-9 to 0-4 at the beginning of April and later that month Leckpatrick scored a 2-7 to 2-4 victory over them after leading by 1-7 to no score at half-time. They were bottom of the table and later lost to Strabane by 8-9 to 2-2, after trailing by 5-9 to 1-0. The goal came from Mickey Heaney while Kieran Kelly and Dan Heaney got the other point. So, there was to be no quick return to Senior ranks and they finishing poorly in mid-table with nine points from ten games and plenty to work on for 1966.

Games against Augher, Leckpatrick and Pomeroy got the 1966 season going and among the players listed for a match against Gortin on March 6th were: Brian Donnelly, Kevin Grimes, Nickle Grimes, Benny Donaghy, Peter Donaghy, Dermot Meenagh, Tony Heagney, FH Owens, Brian Grimes, Liam McGrath, Aidan McGrath, Brian Gallagher, Ben McQuaid, Paddy Owens, Mickey Heaney, Hugh Ward, Kevin Maguire, Barney Owens, Kieran Kelly, Murt Kelly, Mick Kerr, Sean Callaghan, Dan Montgomery, Tony Baxter, Benny Hunter, Mickey Kelly, Eugene Horisk and Tony McGrath.

The wedding day picture of John Boyle in the early 1960s. This ended his direct involvement in the Beragh club

The St Patrick's defeated them a month later and in May the situation facing them was already one of survival as they had posted just two points on the League table. By October 1966 they had achieved eight points from ten games, well behind the leaders Augher and Gortin. The final table in December showed no improvement and they finished just above bottom-placed Fintona.

Those disappointing years generated a desire to secure improvements and this was evident at the beginning of 1967 when the Club Convention decided to initiate a course of physical training commencing in March and undertaken by Liam McGrath and Frank Rodgers who had transferred back to the club.

Early indications of the benefits of this appeared when Clogher were defeated by 3-9 to 2-2. Then, Ben McQuade, Christy Owens, Ben Donaghy and Frank Rodgers were among the scorers when Pomeroy were defeated on a score of 1-6 to 0-3 and Augher by 4-8 to 0-1 in subsequent matches.

Things were thus going to plan at the beginning of April until they lost to Leckpatrick by 2-7 to 2-3 and to Newtownstewart by 2-3 to 1-5. Despite that the pressure was maintained and one notable result was a 0-9 to 0-8 victory over the league leaders, Leckpatrick, in July. That left them just four points adrift of the north Tyrone team at the top of the table.

From then on, though, their league campaign drew almost to a halt. Things dragged on into the new year of 1968 and they remained on twelve points from nine games and short of promotion.

217

Players for the 1968 season included Kevin Nixon, Eugene Horisk, Brian Donnelly, Francie Grimes, Brian Grimes, Kevin Maguire, Noel Maguire, Murt Kelly, Kevin Grimes, Benny Donaghy, Liam McGrath, Dessie Donnelly, Anthony McGrath, S McGrath, Seamus McMahon, Mick Kerr, Frank Rodgers, Jim Gallagher, Jim Mulholland, Pat McCartan, Paddy Owens, Brendan Gallagher, FH Owens, Mickey McSorley, Mickey Kelly and Benny Hunter.

One of their first games in 1968 saw them lose to Carrickmore Seconds by 2-6 to 2-5 and a late goal from Ciaran Kelly failed to prevent a 2-6 to 1-7 loss at Donemana in their next game. However, wins over Newtownstewart and Donemana saw them top the table at the start of April.

Carrickmore Seconds were defeated on a score of 1-11 to 0-7, and then a few late scores saw Aghyaran rob them of victory, the teams finishing level on 3-5 each. Aghyaran then defeated them by 1-5 to 0-5 a month later and the challenge for league honours faltered.

In September, that challenge was almost over when Leckpatrick won by 1-8 to 2-4. The opening goal came from Mick Kerr after good work from Brian Donnelly and Kieran Kelly and the second was scored by Frank Rodgers, who capitalised on the efforts of Brian Donnelly and Gerry Owens.

A later league table showed them back in fourth place on fifteen points eleven behind the leaders, Tattyreagh.

Into 1969 and the recently relegated, Ballygawley, renewed rivalries with Beragh at the beginning of the season when they emerged winners by 2-4 to 1-4 in the League. So, even in the early weeks they were struggling and defeats by Donemana and Newtownstewart didn't help.

In April they lost to the league leaders, Aghyaran, by 2-11 to 2-4 when Ben McQuaid, Liam McGrath, Paddy Owens and Dessie Donnelly were the scorers, but later that month they beat Newtownstewart by 3-11 to 1-4.

However, all enthusiasm had disappeared by the summer when concerns were expressed about their failure to field in a game against Aghyaran. But they recovered to defeat Carrickmore Seconds by 1-5 to 0-2 in August and a mid-table position ten points behind the winners, Ballygawley, was the eventual result.

Sixties Championship action -
The 1962 Carrickmore game

In the Championship, apart from a few glimpses of hope, the decade was a story of missed opportunities, lost potential and a struggle to make the grade at both Senior and Intermediate level.

In 1960 some good league displays set them up nicely for the Senior Championship and a win over Dromore at Pomeroy on June 24 put them into the Quarter Final where they were to lose heavily to a Dungannon team that included Iggy Jones, Art McRory., Jimmy McCallion, Tommy Campbell and PJ Hughes in its ranks.

With the McMahon brothers, FH Owens, Frank Rodgers and Anthony McGrath, the St Mary's were expected to pose a strong challenge and they attacked in determined fashion in the early stages. However, things soon deteriorated. They trailed by 2-9 to 0-2 at half-time and ended up losing by a whopping 3-15 to 0-3. In 1961 the margin was smaller when they lost by 2-7 to 2-6 to Ballygawley in the second round.

But it's the 1962 clash against Carrickmore which has really gone down in local GAA folklore as one to remember. The St Colmcille's were reigning County Champions at the time and firmly expected to easily defeat their neighbours.

The first round game was fixed for the CBS Park in Omagh and the unfancied St Mary's really did give their more illustrious rivals a shock. The game was described as "being pulsating from start to finish," the climax being a great goal by Mick Kerr which earned Beragh a deserved replay.

Hopes were high that they would be capable of maintaining their challenge in the replay a few weeks later. And, 1-1 in the opening stages from Jack Heaney had their supporters dreaming of progressing. However, things went wrong from then on as the report of the game states:

"Even then Carmen seemed relaxed, the sign of a match fit team. Beragh's challenge fizzled out as Carrickmore, inspired by the artistry of Frankie Donnelly, took control. Their forwards combined well and Beragh's lead was nullified. Beragh tried hard in the second half, but all they could manage were two points." The final score was 0-14 to 1-5.

Francis McQuaid and Brian Magee playing near the old sewerage works at the Beragh end of SMX when jumped on manhole and went eight foot down. Thomas Devlin got rope to pull Francis out on the evening of weekend June 3rd, 1961

The following 1963 season saw them once again lose to Ballygawley on June 9. The second week of June also ended their involvement in 1964 when for the third year in four the St Ciaran's emerged winners. And, that marked Beragh's last appearance in the Senior Championship for a decade.

Relegation to Intermediate ranks provided a new challenge in 1965, but the outcome was more or less the same frustrating story as it had been at senior level. Only the opposition had changed and it was Aghyaran who ended their 1965 knock-out involvement on a score of 4-8 to 1-1.

Then, in 1966, Leckpatrick were defeated at Newtownstewart on June 19, setting up a Semi-Final tie against Eglish. Liam McGrath, Mick Kerr and FH Owens were described as being key men for the game along with promising young players, Peter Donaghy and Paddy McGarvey.

The East Tyrone side threatened strongly during the opening stages when the efforts of goalkeeper, Kevin Nixon, and Sean Montgomery at corner back were noted. They led by 1-3 to 0-3 at half-time, and the sending off of the full-back Frank Owens early in the second half was said to have ended Beragh's hopes of progressing.

Eglish eventually clinched their place in the final with a late second goal. The 2-6 to 0-5 result was disappointing for the Beragh team which and was also said to have been a 'distinct disappointment' to their supporters.

The tables were turned in 1967 when goals from Liam McGrath and Frank Rodgers helped earn a 2-9 to 1-4 win over Eglish in the first round. That victory put them through to play Pomeroy at Dunmoyle, but despite their high hopes they lost by 1-7 to 0-5.

They defeated Donemana by 2-6 to 1-8 in the first round of the 1968 Championship. However, the promise generated by that game evaporated at Omagh in the next round when Tattyreagh were the winners. There was no luck either when the 1969 championship saw them lose to Leckpatrick by 0-9 to 0-5 at Omagh on May 18.

Other competitions

Other competitions also proved to be a case of 'so near and yet so far' for Beragh teams. The newly introduced Junior League provided an opportunity for non-senior players to still get the chance to play matches. It was introduced in the mid-sixties and Beragh reached the semi-final in 1966 when they lost to Omagh by 3-7 to 2-4. Good performers on that

FH Owens,
player of 1950s
and 1960s

occasion were Jim Gallagher, Ben McQuaide, Mickey Heaney, the Darcy brothers, Sean McGrath and Paddy Owens.

The McElduff and St Enda Cups continued to demand attention, especially during the autumn and winter months. Beragh's best showing came in 1966 when they progressed to the semi-final before losing to Pomeroy on a score of 1-13 to 1-2 and they went on to reach the play-offs in 1969.

Club Tournaments were a big attraction at this time and the highlights for Beragh included reaching the final against Moy at Donaghmore in 1963. The teams drew first time out and then the Tir Na Ogs won the replay comfortably by 4-6 to 0-6. The Beragh team was: Pete McQuaide, Nickel Grimes, FH Owens, Barney Owens, Hugh Fitzpatrick, Pat Fox, Dan Montgomery, Liam McGrath and Dessie McMahon, Brian Grimes, Hugh Owens, John McSorley, Basil Neville, Mick Kerr and Seamus Heagney.

Another popular event at the start of the sixties was the annual series of matches involving teams from different regions playing for the Fr Peter Campbell Cup. Players selected from Beragh normally represented the Mid-West along with colleagues from the Ballygawley, Pomeroy, Carrickmore and Creggan areas and a highlight came when the club had a large contingent on the 1960 team which reached the final against the South East.

Dessie McMahon, Vin Donaghy, Frank Rodgers, Seamus McMahon, Pat Fox, Basil Neville, John McSorley, FH Owens, Hugh Owens and Mick Kerr were all in the panel due to take on opponents led by Iggy Jones.

April 1960 - Large congregation at 40 hours devotion. High Altar must artistically decorated by Bertie McGarrity, the Sexton. Choir under the direction of Miss Ann Conway. Canopy bearers were FH Rodgers, M r J McCullagh, Mr John Kelly and Mr Patrick Donnelly

A golden decade on the youth scene

Numerous West Tyrone titles in the Juvenile and Minor age groups emphasised how well Beragh were working at the development of youth football during the decade. The sixties were a time when the structures for the provision of underage competitions improved and the St Mary's were at the forefront.

As early as May 1960 a meeting was held to discuss the starting of summer youth competitions. Around the same time the Beragh U-15s took part in the South Tyrone League, a Juvenile team was also fielded and the Minors as usual enjoyed both league and championship competitions.

Beragh and Ballygawley qualified for the final of the South Tyrone Juvenile League for the St Colmcille Cup in 1960 and that same summer players from the club and also Omagh, Gortin and Newtownstewart were due to take part in a Minor Insurance Shield. The Beragh Players on that selection which won the Minor Insurance Shield were Dan Heaney, Dessie McMahon, Frank Rodgers and Hughie Owens.

An U-14 League was started in 1961, with all clubs taking part receiving a size four football. The teams played three home and three away matches. Beragh, Ballygawley, Carrickmore and Aughnacloy took part in the championship and the efforts to promote football among the boys saw John Donaghy being granted permission to organise a Juvenile Tournament on a Sunday in early August that year.

Later in the decade, a Parish Juvenile League was started between Sixmilecross, Roscavey, Drumduff and Beragh. Confined to players U-16 years of age, the event took place in March and April and was aimed at providing the chance to progress as the official competitions offered this opportunity to only a limited number. The event progressed apace and gave club selectors a chance to 'look at the games and take stock of the players.'

It was things like this which helped put Beragh among the top youth teams in Tyrone at the time. And, one match of note in 1962 saw the Juveniles, defeat Carrickmore by 1-2 to 1-1 in the League.

> In November 1964 Sixmilecross Court to close. The court had been held in Donaghanie Orange Hall for some years and the last defendant was fined £1 for not having a rear light in October 1964

The team, according to the report, included Neil Hagan who was great in goals, full-backs, John Scallan, Peter Bennett and Francie Grimes, Sean Montgomery, Ward and Mickey Heaney in the half-backs, Paddy McGarvey and Joe Rafferty at midfield, Dan McSorley, Peter Donaghy and Christy Owens in the half-forward line and Gerry McCann, Noel Colton, Brian Gallagher and McMenamin in the full-forwards. And, the scorers in a 4-5 to 2-5 win over Aughnacloy were Gerry McCann (2-0), Peter Donaghy (1-3), Kevin Maguire (1-0), Sean Montgomery and Dan McSorley (0-1 each).

Later that year a win over Ballygawley by 2-2 to 0-2 saw them become South Tyrone Juvenile Champions and a meeting of the South Tyrone Board congratulated them and praised the team manager, John Donaghy, for his enthusiasm and efforts.

In 1963 Beragh were in contention with Carrickmore and Loughmacrory for the title again. They progressed to the final where they lost an exciting tie to Loughmacrory by 1-1 to 0-2.

The Beragh Senior team of the early 1960s provided the inspiration for the successful youth sides of the middle part of the decade. This side played Omagh in the West Tyrone League

They also reached the League final against Augher which was due to take place in December 1963, but remained unplayed until the following summer. The game eventually finished level in a welter of excitement as first John McCarroll goaled for Beragh and then Ray McKenna equalised for Augher. Noel Colton, Dessie Donnelly, the McGraths, Mickey Heaney and Peter Donaghy also impressed. The replay took place in January 1964.

In 1964 the 'Black and Amber Wizards' were said to 'have done it again in the South Tyrone Juvenile League', winning it for the second year out of three. They defeated Augher and only sprung into action thanks to a great save from Peter Donaghy. Following the win, arrangements were put in place for the players to receive their medals on May 26th, two years after the competition began.

They also did well in 1965, winning the championship and going on to play Coalisland in the County Semi-Final where they lost by 4-8 to 0-8.

"Beragh gave of their best through the game," the Ulster Herald report of the match said. "Most of their players were small and beaten in the air for high balls, but made up for this by dash and the will to win, which kept the game very interesting to the end.

Prominent for Beragh were Michael Bennett and Ben McQuaide in defence, John McCarroll and Jim Gallagher at midfield and Sean McGrath and Mickey McSorley in the forwards.

It was a similar story in 1966 when the league decider between Beragh and Ballygawley at the end of June drew a large attendance in perfect conditions to St Mary's Park. Anthony Donaghy and Mickey McSorley combined to set up Dessie Donnelly for a Beragh goal and they led by 2-5 to 0-1 when Vincent McMackin made doubly sure with the third goal.

223

The double was secured in August that year when Carrickmore were defeated by 2-1 to 1-2. And, chants of 'easy easy' were said to have been chanted when they completed the 'three in a row' of South Tyrone titles in 1967. They defeated Carrickmore in the final by 4-7 to 0-5.

The Beragh Juvenile team which played in the South Tyrone League in 1961

Goals from Dessie Donnelly, Michael McSorley (2) and Anthony Donaghy set them on their way and afterwards the Cup was presented to the captain, Peter Hagan, by the Chairman of the South Tyrone Juvenile Board, Jack Woods. Anthony Donaghy, Seamus Maguire and Stephen Kelly were good for Beragh in defence, Brian McCullagh also impressed and Peter Hagan, Vincent McMackin and Dessie Donnelly excelled in the forwards.

Major Minor progress 1964-1966

Regular training sessions under coaches who included John Donaghy, Hugh Ward, Mick Kerr, Jack Heaney and Pat McCartan were having an obvious effect. They enjoyed great success in the Minor grade in West Tyrone between 1964 and 1967, without translating it onto the all-county scene.

The 1964 Minors defeated Omagh early in the championship and scored a fine 4-4 to 0-3 win over Ballygawley. This set up a semi-final against Trillick at Dromore which resulted in a 5-11 to 2-6 win. However, they failed completely in the West Tyrone Final when losing by 3-15 to 0-3 to Carrickmore.

But they came back strongly in 1965 to get to the West Tyrone Final again. Paddy McGarvey, Jim Gallagher and Mickey Heaney did well in the 3-3 to 1-4 semi-final win over Dromore to set up a final meeting against Omagh. Victory, though, once again eluded them in August at Dromore where Omagh were 2-10 to 2-5 winners.

They made amends in the League Final which didn't take place until late in the year and was a repeat of the previous season's decider with Dromore. Not surprisingly for the time of year, the match was played in a relentless downpour and gale force winds which made good play very difficult.

Beragh led by three points at half-time and victory was secured when Aidan McGrath finished a Peter Donaghy centre to the net. The report gave a rundown on how the team overall played.

"For Beragh, none played harder than the captain, Brian Donnelly, who along with Peter Donaghy kept them in control at midfield. In defence, Sean McGrath did well and not far behind him were Mickey Kelly and Ben McQuaide while Paddy McGarvey, Noel Colton and John Scallon all had their moments.

"In goal Neil Hagan looked very safe all the time. The Beragh attack played reasonably well, but seemed determined to get goals rather than points. Aidan McGrath's 2-1 was invaluable while Mickey Heaney time and again opened up the attack with fast solo runs. The three Juveniles in the attack, Jim Gallagher, John McCarroll and Mickey McSorley played some of the nicest football of the hour and Christy Owens got in some useful work on the right wing."

Team - Neil Hagan, Mickey Kelly, Peter Hagan, S Donnelly, Noel Colton, John Scallon, Ben McQuaide, Peter Donaghy, Jim Gallagher, Christy Owens, John McCarroll, Peter Hagan, Dessie Donnelly, Anthony Donaghy, Michael McSorley.

The following year, 1966, was also one to remember for the St Mary's Minors as they again made their presence felt in the league and championship. Omagh were narrowly defeated in the Championship Semi-Final at Cloughfin by 1-9 to 2-4 and in the Final played at Dunmoyle in August, they accounted for Mountfield in what was described by the Ulster Herald as a very exciting final. Peter Donaghy and Jim Gallagher were strong at midfield and a goal from Mickey McSorley saw them lead by 2-2 to 1-1 at half-time.

A further goal on the resumption looked set to seal the win for Beragh,

> Francis McQuaid and Brian Magee playing near the old sewerage works at the Beragh end of SMX when jumped on manhole and went eight foot down. Thomas Devlin got rope to pull Francis out on the evening of weekend June 3rd, 1961

The Beragh Juveniles from 1963

before they were hit by two great goals from Sean Meenan for Mountfield. And, the reporter at the game was in no doubt about the quality of the exchanges subsequently.

"The very large crowd was then treated to ten minutes of the most exciting football seen in West Tyrone for some time. Peter Donaghy moved to full-back for Beragh and this soon tightened up the defence. But although he got good assistance from Pat Hagan and Jim Mulholland, it took them all their time to keep Sean Meenan, Sean Treacy and company from getting scores." Beragh won the match by 3-5 to 3-1.

But their hopes of reaching the County Final were dashed by Dungannon who won the semi-final by 3-10 to 1-3 at Omagh. The St Mary's team lined out: Neil Hagan, Mickey Kelly, Peter Hagan, S Donnelly, Noel Colton, John Scallon, Ben McQuaide, Peter Donaghy, Jim Gallagher, Christy Owens, John McCarroll, Peter Hagan, Dessie Donnelly, Anthony Donaghy, Michael McSorley.

A night of celebration highlights a decade

Pictured at the night of celebration in 1966 are the Beragh Juveniles who won the South Tyrone Championship

In February 1966 over 500 people attended a special Presentation Ceili for the players and supporters in St Mary's Hall. Two of the club's four teams were honoured at the function, with the winning Juvenile and Minor players being presented with their medals.

The Juveniles had won the South Tyrone Championship and the Minors the West Tyrone League. Guest of honour was John McCusker of Dromore, Chairman of the West Tyrone Minor Board, who said he was impressed with the way Beragh took victory and defeat in the right spirit. He also had high praise for the Beragh club who he said paid so much attention to minor and juvenile football.

Amid great applause the trophies were presented to Brian Donnelly, the Minor captain and to other members of the team. The captain of the Juvenile team, Paddy McGarvey, was unable to be present and the St Colmcille Cup was presented instead to the Vice-Captain, Jim Gallagher.

Music on the night was supplied by the Old Cross Bandshow and the secretary Jack Heaney, thanked both the guests and the teams which included: Juveniles - Paddy McGarvey (captain), Jim Gallagher, Ben McQuaide, John McCarroll, Jim Mulholland, Sean McGrath, Michael McSorley, Michael Bennett, John Donnelly, Martin Donnelly, Gerry Owens, Seamus Maguire, Dessie Donnelly, Paddy Short, Patsy Daly, Vincent McMackin, Gerald McAleer, Charlie Daly, Sean Clarke, Brian Maguire, Anthony Donaghy and Eamon McQuaide.

The Minors were: Brian Donnelly (captain), Pat Hagan, John Scallon, Noel Colton, Mickey Kelly, Ben McQuaide, Paddy McGarvey, Sean McGrath, Peter Donaghy, Mickey Heaney, Aidan McGrath, Christy Owens, John McCarroll, Jim Gallagher, Mickey McSorley, Francie Grimes, Jim Mulholland, Joe Rafferty, Peter Bennett and Sean Montgomery.

The Beragh Minor, captained by Brian Donnelly, pictured with their West Tyrone League trophy

The Beragh Tournament

Large crowds from all over the country converged annually on St Mary's Park during the sixties as the club tournament provided top class action. It was recognised as one of the best around and regularly drew top teams from Donegal, Monaghan, Derry and Fermanagh.

Local teams were also strongly represented and in 1960 the competing clubs included Carrickmore, Pomeroy, Clogher, Ballygawley, Fintona, Beragh, Donaghmore and Ballinderry. The week-long event reached its climax on June 4 and there was an added incentive this year for the hosts as they reached the final only to lose to Fintona.

The organisers were also hoping for a few good evenings in 1961 when Omagh, who had beaten Beragh in the semi-final in a replay, won an exciting final by 4-5 to 1-7 over Fintona.

Children's Sports and a Fancy Dress Parade were held as part of the festivities in 1962. The highlights included R McCrystal taking part in the Fancy Dress parade as 'Miss 1970 and K Maguire, Sixmilecross as 'Small Farmer and the Common Market' in the Tiny Tots section. The

BERAGH ST. MARY'S G.F.C.

ANNUAL
FOOTBALL
TOURNAMENT

9th JULY, 1967 - 23RD JULY, 1967

FIRST ROUND GAMES

A	BALLYGAWLEY v TRILLICK	SUNDAY 9th JULY
B	AUGHER v BROOKBOROUGH	WEDNESDAY 12th JULY
C	DROMORE v DONAGHMORE	FRIDAY 14th JULY
D	TEMPO v CARRICKMORE	SUNDAY 16th JULY

MATCHES AT 8 O'CLOCK

SEMIFINAL GAMES

A v B	WEDNESDAY 19th JULY
C v D	FRIDAY 21st JULY

ADMISSION TO ALL GAMES   2/6

Tournament final was eventually won by Clogher, who defeated Donaghmore.

There was an exotic feel to things in 1963 when St Paul's of Belfast and Emyvale of Monaghan took part. Admission was 1/6 and all matches started at 8.30pm sharp between July 1st and 14th. Ballygawley emerged winners.

Paddy Devlin refereed all the matches in 1964 when Carrickmore defeated Ballygawley in the final by 2-8 to 1-8. The preview of the 1965 Tournament stated that Beragh would be "a mecca for all gaelic fans and that the winners would receive a magnificent set of trophies." They were eventually received by Carrickmore, the defending champions.

By the mid-sixties, the GAA Week had expanded to include the Summer Carnival. A Car Run for Treasure and Pleasure was organised, alongside old favourites like the Bonny Baby competition and more novel events such as an Open Clay Pigeon Shoot, Kiss of Life Demonstration by Omagh Red Cross Society and Irish Dancing.

Omagh's Jackie Martin began a long stint as Tournament referee in 1966 when surprise packets Tempo came through to win. The 1967 final between Carrickmore and Augher drew what was reckoned to be "a record crowd." The match didn't disappoint either and saw Augher win by 5-7 to 3-6 in a thrilling high scoring affair.

In 1968 Carrickmore were back as winners and evidence of just how seriously the event was taken can be gauged from the fact that the 1969 Final had to be postponed because of Carrickmore's involvement in a championship replay. They were due to play Augher in what was a repeat of that season's St Enda Cup Final.

Handball

★ 1969 BERAGH TOURNAMENT ★

Easter Sunday Final

At 6.15 p.m.

CARRICKMORE v. **AUGHER**

Winners of County Championship, All-County League and St. Enda Cup in 1969. Winners of Beragh Tournament in 1968.

Winners of St. Enda Cup in 1968. Finalists in 1969. Winners of Beragh Tournament in 1967.

Referee: Mr. JACK HEALEY, 1969 Co. Final Referee

| 5.15 p.m. MINOR LEAGUE BERAGH v. SIXMILECROSS Ref.: Mr. MICK KERR | ACCORDEON BAND (Drumnakilly) WILL ENTERTAIN AT THE INTERVALS |

ST. MARY'S PARK, BERAGH FOR YOUR EASTER SUNDAY ENTERTAINMENT

The promotion of handball had received a major boost with the formation of the Brackey Club in 1958 and the following ten years would see important progress being made. While Brackey remained a force in the game in Tyrone, the setting up of the Cloughfin Club and the erection of a 60x30 alley gave extra opportunities for players.

One of the main events in the handball scene at the time was the Gael Linn Tournament. In 1960 Brackey took part with players from Armagh, Belfast, Lurgan, Pomeroy and Loughmacrory. A fixture lists M McAleer, MJ Kelly and Jack Heaney as being competitors on at least one occasion.

Coverage of the sport remained scant in the pages of the Ulster Herald. But there is no doubt that a lot of handball was played during those years both at a competitive and recreational level.

The Brackey club was in full swing at the beginning of April 1961 when the hope was expressed that the players would "give as good account of themselves as had the stars of previous generations." That August draws were made for the Tyrone Senior Championship and, while it's unclear what Brackey players took part, a warm-up game in November for the Gael Linn Tournament listed the names of those in contention to play against Pomeroy.

The fixtures were: Hugh Owens v Thady McAleer, Mick Kerr v Barney Owens, Liam Heaney v Mick McAleer, Jim McAleer v Basil Neville, Dan Montgomery v Packie Murphy, Kieran Kelly v Kieran Murphy, Peter Daly v Jack Heaney and Jackie Ward for Noel Maguire. Brackey were drawn against Loughmacrory in the Senior and Minor Championships.

Amid concern that handball was not making the desired progress outside the three established clubs, Brackey organised a Doubles Tournament. The fixtures were: J Gormley, B Neville v K Kelly and Liam Heaney, Mickey Kelly and Hughie Owens v P Murphy and Jim McAleer, Sean Montgomery and F Owens v B Cunningham and K Murphy, J Ward and M McAleer v H McNamee and B Owens, M Owens and Pat Donnelly v T McAleer and TJ Kelly, C Woods and P Daly v M Kerr and MH Ward.

A Ceili took place in Brackey Hall on Tuesday January 30th to raise funds for prizes and at that year's Tyrone Convention, players were urged "to train more and take part in tournaments to improve their game." With this in mind, Brackey's players were offered the chance to use Loughmacrory's alley at the end of 1963.

That telling offer highlighted a serious problem with the provision of facilities. The lack of an alley led to the demise of the club during 1963 and 1964, but there was a revival of Brackey Handball Club in February 1965.

The man behind that effort was the new President, Paddy McCrumlish,

On March 23rd 1968 a case of anthrax was reported in Sixmilecross and the County Medical Health Officer reported that all possible precautions were being take to prevent its spread to humans

who received strong support locally. A committee was elected and the decision taken to adapt a new alley at Cloughfin, Omagh. The local potential was shown when Paddy McGarvey reached the Ulster U-15 Final, only to be beaten by his Cavan opponent. Along with Aidan Donoghue, he had earlier won the Tyrone Doubles title at Juvenile level.

Another key development in February 1965 saw the formation of a new club in Cloughfin. After two meetings, a committee elected and among the first decisions was to build an alley, for which a site had already been purchased.

"The club is expected to commence building after the Handball Congress in March and the committee has been assured of help from GAA clubs in Beragh, Ballygawley, Carrickmore, Killeeshil and Galbally," a report in the Ulster Herald stated.

What was described as an 'outstanding year' followed and the committee elected for 1966 was: Chairman - Pat Donnelly, Vice-Chairman, - Peter McNamee, Secretary - Terence McGarvey, Treasurer - Francis Donnelly. Committee - Neil McGarvey, Michael Kelly, Francis McGarvey, PJ McClean, Michael McGarvey and Patsy McCrory.

Work commenced on the site in March 1966, the foundations were dug and a subscription fund set up. Regular tournaments took place and a highlight was the winning of the Liam Magee Cup by Barney McNally, who defeated Francie McGarvey in the final. Sean McGinn defeated Sean Tierney in the Juvenile Final.

The Cloughfin Handball Committee which worked hard during the 1960s to ensure the completion of its new alley

Players from throughout the parish competed at Cloughfin and the 1969 Inter-Club Tournament included the following: Peter McNamee, Hugh McClean, Seamus Heaney, Francis McGarvey, Mickey Heaney, George Moore, Mick McCartan, Sean McGirr, Michael McGarvey, Paddy Ward, Pat Mullin, Pat McCartan, Pat Donnelly, Seamus Donnelly, Owen Nugent, Stephen Kelly, Sean Tierney, Neil McGarvey, Kieran Kelly, Francis Tierney, Barney McNally, Francis Donnelly, Paddy Montague, Mick Kerr, Mickey Kelly, Kieran Maguire, Johnny Kerr, Terence McGarvey.

It took time, however, to complete the alley. In February 1968, three years after the formation of the Cloughfin

club, there was an appeal for patrons to support the Handball Alley scheme which was described as a 'modern, roofed and floodlit facility,' destined to be one of the best in the country.

Camogie and Hurling

The thirty year period from 1937 to the mid-sixties had been barren ones indeed for camogie in Tyrone. That changed in the middle of May 1965 when a meeting in Dungannon formed a new County Committee and the efforts to promote the game filtered to Beragh by the beginning of 1968.

It is understandable that the girls should be anxious to have a recreational outlet. Afterall, as they said, "the boys had football and the girls nothing." Officials of the St Mary's Club were contacted and thirty nine girls attended the meeting to form the Camogie Club in mid-March.

A committee was elected and comprised the following: Chairman - Annie Owens, Deroar, Secretary - Ann Gallagher, Main Street, Beragh, Treasurer - Margaret Donnelly, Ballykeel. The decision was taken that the team would 'play in emerald green tonics and be known as Beragh St Mary's Camogie Club. There was no slacking as the girls immediately bought camogie boots and stick and collected enough money to get the operation on the road.

The Beragh Camogie team of the late 1960s

Registration was accepted at the County Board, and players from Eglish agreed to help with coaching. The first match was played on Sunday April 7 against Dromore in St Mary's Park. All the practice paid off when they won by six points and by May they were unbeaten before their run was ended by Eskra.

Time to reflect arrived in October when the many games that they played were recalled at the Tyrone Ceile in St Mary's Hall. Organised by the Beragh club, the event drew a large number of camogs from clubs involved at the time including Augher, Eglish, Ballygawley, Killeeshil, Pomeroy, Beragh, Dromore, Dungannon, Eskra and of Beragh itself.

The first Convention was held in February 1969 when members heard that Beragh had competed in the league and championship, held weekly training sessions, organised the raffle at the Tournament and promoted the very successful Ceili. Plans were finalised for a Keep Fit class and hopes expressed that the year ahead would prove successful.

The four Owens sisters pictured prior to a Camogie game in the late 1960s

They were drawn against Eglish in the knock-out competition and by June wins over Tattyreagh at home and away and a draw with Ballygawley had earned them vital points. They also defeated Galbally by five goals to nil in the Pomeroy Tournament when the team was: A Mulholland, S Owens, B Grimes, G Ward, A Donaghy, B Owens, L Donnelly, Margaret Donnelly, Annie Owens, M Colton, Lizzie Franey, M Mulholland.

As well as the active and successful revival of camogie, there were attempts made to start a hurling team in the parish which made some progress. The efforts were prompted at the beginning of 1965 when the club Chairman, Mick Kerr and Secretary, Jack Heaney, heard a lecture on the new hurling revival spearheaded at the time by Coiste Iomana.

It was intended to supply hurls to the schoolboys team, but another three years were to pass before the game again came to prominence locally. That was on May 5th, 1968, when twenty boys from Beragh attended the Coiste Iomana coaching session in Pomeroy

Club notes in the Ulster Herald recounted how the Juveniles were anxiously awaiting the start of the hurling revival. The aim was to begin with the present U-16 boys and progress from there. It was also reported that a former Cork hurler had agreed to introduce the young players to the basics of the game.

It isn't clear whether or not the Cork assistance had materialised in the following months, but by June the young club members had taken part in quite a number of coaching sessions. Indeed, six of them earned trials for the County Juvenile team and Dessie Donnelly gained a place on the Tyrone U-18 side.

Other club activities

Members who gathered at the 1960 Beragh Convention in April could hardly have foreseen how difficult the following ten years would be for the club. There were times, indeed, that things looked set to fall apart completely before urgent remedial action was taken.

The significance of the decade in terms of ultimate survival cannot be over-estimated. The GAA enjoyed a lot of growth in the 1960s and, while a number of new clubs were formed and others re-established, the organisation of activities was never easy.

And, that 1960 Convention heard the new Chairman, Fr Donnelly, pledge to carry out his duties to the best of his ability and hope for the full support of the committee. That body included a selection committee consisting of John Donaghy, Sean Bennett and Mickey Mullan, gatemen in John Brannigan, Hugh Colton and Matt Colton and Minor and Juvenile organisers, Jack Woods and Hughie McCann.

A total of 51 members attended the following year's Convention when more work was urged on youth football. By then Fr Donnelly had been transferred to Carrickmore, club meetings were to be held each Wednesday, with every third one in Brackey, Nickle Grimes was appointed the team captain and the committee included PJ Keenan, John McSorley and John Breen.

On to the 1962 Convention and at it younger members were urged to take a greater interest in the running of the club and it was agreed to give a subscription to Brackey Handball Club. A year later and the Convention agreed to have training for all players on Monday and Thursday nights. Paddy McCrumlish joined Sean Bennett and John Donaghy as a senior selector and among those on an eight-strong Minor committee were Benny Donaghy, Eugene Horisk, John Broderick, Peter McQuaide, Peter Bennett, Kevin Grimes and Dermot Meenagh.

But tough times lay ahead and things came to a climax at the beginning of 1965 when only seven of the registered members turned up at a meeting on January 1st. It was decided to hold another small meeting on the following Sunday and the message was sent out that "if sufficient

> On March 23rd 1968 a case of anthrax was reported in Sixmilecross and the County Medical Health Officer reported that all possible precautions were being take to prevent its spread to humans

233

Four Chairmen of the 1950s and 1960s. Pictured from left are Jack McCann, Tommy McGarvey, Terry Kelly and Mick Kerr

numbers don't turn up then everything will be scrapped. This will be the third to be called, as the other two had only a handful of members present."

Affairs were eventually put on a more solid footing, monthly meetings took place to organise administration and other matters and a big attendance of members was reported at the 1966 Convention. At it, the Secretary, Jack Heaney, praised the great sportsmanship which prevailed in the club and the Treasurer, Pat McCartan, reported on a 'most satisfactory' financial position.

Paddy Bogan began his long involvement with the club as Treasurer at the 1967 Convention and Frank Rodgers joined the committee as Secretary in 1968.

The launch of club membership saw an initial enrolment of 36 that year ten shillings being the fee. The selection of several club members on county committees, the start in the development of hurling and the appointment of a Field Development Committee were among the highlights mentioned at the 1969 Convention. Jack McCann presided at the election of officers and a motion was passed that the committee should have representation from all areas of the parish. The area representatives who were elected as a result were: Brackey - Barney Owens, TJ Kelly, Seskinore - Jim Gallagher, Jim Mulholland, Beragh - Frank Owens, Hugh Colton, Cloughfin - Pat Donnelly, Tommy McGarvey, Sixmilecross - Terry Kelly, Jack Heaney, Roscavey - Jim Franey, B Donnelly, Drumnakilly - M Kelly, Brian McCullagh.

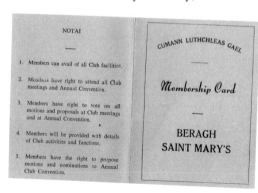

NOTAI

1. Members can avail of all Club facilities.

2. Members have right to attend all Club meetings and Annual Convention.

3. Members have right to vote on all motions and proposals at Club meetings and at Annual Convention.

4. Members will be provided with details of Club activities and functions.

5. Members have the right to propose motions and nominations to Annual Club Convention.

CUMANN LUTHCHLEAS GAEL

Membership Card

BERAGH
SAINT MARY'S

Finance

An interesting insight into the running of the club during the sixties can be got from the financial report presented by the Treasurer, Paddy Bogan, for the 1968 season. It showed income and expenditure of £878 with all the usual items included.

The main fundraiser was the Tournament, which in that year raised £250, gates at home match totalled £32 and the Bazaar brought in £209. On the outlay side travel accounted for over £51 of the total.

Materials for the highly successful bazaar came to £74, Juvenile jerseys cost £11 and £27 was spent on advertising. The renovation of the 'dressing rooms' came to £29. Field maintenance cost £4 and registration fees were £24.

Park Development

By the sixties St Mary's Park, as it had become known, was established as a neutral venue for various play-offs.

The annual tournament provided reason for a general tidying up and for improvement work. In 1960 the grounds were improved by what was described as a 'whole army of members.' Among the tasks completed by them was the erection of new goalposts and the fencing and marking of the pitch.

That growing acceptance of the need for ground improvement was emphasised in 1965 when the then grounds man, John Clarke, raised the issue of the state of the pitch at the monthly meeting in St Mary's Hall. He said he would like something done about cars driving in on the field at matches and cutting up the ground. After lengthy discussion, it was decided not to allow cars on the grounds at future matches.

At the time, affairs relating to the field were still controlled by the Field Committee, set up when the ground was purchased in 1954. This group had ultimate control over the use and development of the park and regularly 'let it out' for use by local farmers transporting livestock to and from the Railway Station.

With a number of new officials gradually gaining in know-how towards the end of the decade, tentative efforts were begun to raise the subject of "further development." These began in 1967 when a meeting between the Field Committee and the Club Committee took place.

Plans were made at the meeting to study the development of St Mary's Park, with the provision of dressing rooms as a first priority. Mick Kerr, Jack Heaney and Pat McCartan were co-opted onto the Field Committee and the way was clear for things to get moving.

Then the new 1968 Club Committee made a start by converting the old shed on the hill into temporary dressing rooms which were in use by April.

In November 1969 Omagh Rural Council told to quit the dump at Beragh which had been leased from the GNR for six months, but the ground had now been sold to a Cookstown woman. Council decided to write to the woman and gave her possession, but to deny liability for number of old cars that had been dumped there. Felt that the dump should never have been there

"

The closure of the
Railway Line in
1965 resulted in
what some say was
a missed by the
club. And, Sean
Bennett, who by
that time was no
longer centrally
involved, claims
that the large
Station site could
have been
purchased

"

The ambitions of the club with regards to facilities were revealed when the first Annual Dinner Dance coincided with the launch of fundraising for a major new development venture on the club's ground.

The Secretary, Frank Rodgers said: "Club officials are very much aware that present-day trends in the GAA are towards more and better facilities for players and supporters. The immediate aim in Beragh is a well-made pitch and dressing-rooms. Long term plans also include a handball alley, a putting green, tennis courts and an all-weather practice pitch.

"Naturally such a progressive venture calls for increased finance and in coming years many new and exciting money-making schemes are planned. The immediate start to the first plans is now being held up because of a drainage scheme pending on the river bordering the park," he said.

The closure of the Railway Line in 1965 resulted in what some say was a chance missed by the club. And, Sean Bennett, who by that time was no longer centrally involved, claims that the large Station site could have been purchased.

"The Railway Station was missed by the club and John Scallion who lived there at the time told me that he could have bought it but he didn't have the money," he said.

"It was one thing that was missed. If the Station had been bought it would have been great asset for developing the grounds."

Other events

In the Beragh notes in the Herald, sales of TV sets were reported to be on the up in the Beragh area but the weekly cinema screenings remained popular. The 'Foxes of Harrow' featuring Maureen O'Hara and Rex Harrison was shown around Easter 1960 when former Sixmilecross Wolfe Tones player, Barney Gormley, returned from England for a visit.

He may have been around to see how much football had changed from what it had been in the early part of the century. And, he could have watched the 1954 All-Ireland Final which was featured along with "The Vatican" in a special charity screening for the Salesian Fathers in St Mary's Hall.

Mr. and Mrs. W. Conway (centre), who have retired from the teaching staff of Beragh P.S., photographed at a presentation social in St. Mary's Hall, Beragh, last week. Also in the photograph are, from left, Miss A. Conway, Rev. S. McCartan, C.C., Dundalk, Mrs. V. Courtney, Rev. Fr. McOscar, C.C., Rev. Fr. Tercy, P.P., Mr. K. Conway and Miss Mary Cosgrove.

Beragh teachers retire after 37 years at local school

MR. and MRS. W. J. CONWAY have retired from the staff of Beragh Primary School. Mr. Conway arrived in Beragh in 1932 and Mrs. Conway came the following year. They were married in 1934

parents. In this respect the Conways were always a good example for all.

Father Terry said Mr. Conway had always taken a leading part in all activities in the

the shop was going as well as the teacher.

He said that as teachers the Conways had equipped all sorts of different people to lead very different lives well and the presentation he was about to make

tague and Shiela Owens who sang during the social.

He made special mention of Paddy Gormley and his band from Cavanh who provided the music.

Rev. Father James Cairns

The retirement of former club Treasurer and Secretary, WJ Conway, from Beragh school marked the end of an era

The winner of the Bazaar Star Prize at Beragh in 1965 had the choice of nine items, including a Chesterfield Suite, Hoovermatic washing machine, dining room suite, a trip for two to Lourdes, a bathroom suite, a TV set, a fitted Axminister carpet or a gas cooker with two years supply of gas valued at £75.

St Mary's Hall, of course, was used regularly at the time and among the biggest events in the early part of the decade were the weekly Whist Snowball Series. From humble beginnings with just £60 on offer in January, 1960, it event went from strength to strength. Thomas McGarvey, Patsy Collins, Pat Donnelly, Master McMahon, Pat McCartan and Jack McCann were among the weekly checkers for the Friday night event.

Guest teas were held as well and the hosts in Drumduff included Nellie Owens, EJ Kelly, Mrs Felix McAleer, Mrs Barney McCullagh and Mrs Mary Gallagher. All these efforts culminated in £825 being raised for the Beragh Parish School Building Fund. The money went towards the maintenance and building of primary and secondary schools in the area.

Parents of children attending those schools at the beginning of the sixties were concerned about having to rise their children for the 8am bus which arrived in Omagh before 8.30am and much too early for lessons. There were also calls for the erection of bus shelters. But getting to school at all was also a problem when an influenza epidemic struck at the beginning of

1961. One school was closed, carriers were going down everywhere and some rated it worse than the Avian Flu of 1957.

There was an end of an era, too, in 1967 when Mr. and Mrs. WJ Conway retired from the staff of Beragh School after 37 years. At a special reception in the Hall, Master Conway said he had many pleasant memories since he stepped off the train at Beragh many years earlier.

Roscavey School Opening

Another major event in the history of the parish came with the opening of the new school in Roscavey in May 1966. Complete with three classrooms, an assembly hall and kitchen, the building replaced the 100 year old school nearby which had been erected in 1867.

The Beragh
Pantomine of the
1960s was a
big attraction

The official opening was carried out by the newly installed Cardinal Conway, who said nothing but a fine school like it was good enough for the children. At a Mass to mark the occasion, he remarked upon "how important the primary school years were" and spoke of "the importance of parents making sure that their children attended school regularly."

A motorcade escorted the Cardinal from the main road and the welcoming party included the seventy pupils waving papal flags, parents and past pupils, led by Rev P Gallagher CC and Rev K McOscar CC.

Work on building the new school had been started by Fr Brady PP and Fr Terry had special thanks for the McSorley family, on whose land the school was built, the Ministry of Education and the Tyrone Co Committee of Education. He congratulated the architect, Alan Murnaghan, the contractor, Jack McCann, and the quantity surveyor, Mr McAvoy.

Meanwhile, over in Sixmilecross there were problems in 1965 when the Church of Ireland parents alleged discrimination in jobs. According to the Ulster Herald, the row centred on a clash between Presbyterian and Church of Ireland members of the County Education Committee which had come to a head over 'the method of appointment of teachers to County Schools.'

The report stated that when the new term commenced at Sixmilecross County Primary School 23 out of the 40 Church of Ireland pupils on roll did not attend. Next day there were sixteen absentees, before the boycott ended on the Wednesday when all the children turned up. A petition by parents aimed at getting an inquiry into the system for appointing teachers was eventually sent to the Ministry of Education.

Beragh Drama Group

Activities at St Mary's Hall increased following the appointment of a committee to organise functions and fundraising there. At a meeting in 1964, representatives from all parts of the parish enthusiastically discussed plans and the group appointed to forward them was comprised of Paddy Bogan (Chairman), John McCullagh (Secretary) and Rev Fr Gallagher (Treasurer). They were helped by a committee of fourteen and they would have been hoping to build on the success of the Drama Group which had been re-established a few years earlier.

Aughnaglea school group pictured in 1961

Frank Donnelly was in charge of the script for the successful staging of 'The Country Boy' in 1961. The troupe also scored successes with 'The Rugged Path' in May 1964. A packed St Mary's Hall witnessed that production, of a grim story of life in the Cavan mountains during World War Two. Produced by Frank Donnelly, the cast of fourteen included Billy Doonan, Jack Heaney, Margaret McKeown, Ann McAleer and Pat McCartan.

The annual Irish Concert drew a packed audience in January 1965 when the local performers were Joe McMenamin and Margaret Gallagher and Fr Terry thanked all the artistes for coming along and performing so well.

But in a changing decade, it was the new sound of the Showbands which was starting to draw the crowds and that month saw the first of the weekly Saturday Night Dances in the Hall with Omagh's Mark V Showband

Scene From Beragh Players' Production

providing the entertainment. Later in the year the Beragh Carnival '65 attracted the crowds with a week-long programme.

The highlight was the visit of the Rose of Tralee and the crowning of the Beragh Carnival Queen. The finalists included Christina Noble (Drumduff), Anne Hagan (Beragh), Patricia McMaugh (Eskra), Maureen O'Donnell (Strabane), Mona Donnelly (Ballykeel) and Frances McGee (Ederney). A cash prize of £20 was on offer to the winner.

> Birdie Sweeney and Frank O'Neill were also on the bill for the Carnival which got underway with a record crowd of dancers for Gerry and the Ohio

Birdie Sweeney and Frank O'Neill were also on the bill for the Carnival which got underway with a record crowd of dancers for Gerry and the Ohio. Frankie McBride and the Polka Dots, Brian Coll and the Buckaroos and Eileen Donaghy were other headliners as the Carnival drew the crowds in a decade to remember.

The Beragh Concert Group resumed its activities in 1966 after a lapse of seven years. Their programme was described as follows in the Ulster Herald:

"Seskinore is to the fore with a piano piece by Olive McElhatton and the popular monologues by Rosemary D-Arcy. From Sixmilecross, there is the Tulach Neill Singers, mouth organist, Paddy Lafferty, guitarist, Joe Rafferty with Malachy McNamee helping out everywhere on the drums.

"The Drumduff area has a large contingent of artistes, including the talented McMenamin family, Peter Maguire on the guitar, singers Sean Hutchinson, Pat Ward and Gerry Molloy and another accordion solo by John Gordon. Joe Rafferty comes all alone from Ballintrain.

"From Beragh there are songs by Paddy Montague, Anthony Donaghy and Mrs Gallagher and a La Yenka Trio. John and Sheila Owens from Deroar also sing well, while from the heart of the parish, Liskencon, comes that ever popular turn by Jim Campbell. From Clougherney and Roscavey we have the McMahon sisters, Kevin, Brendan and Peter Grimes, the Conway sisters and the McAleer duet."

The GAA also got in on the social entertainment act in 1968 with the introduction of a new All-Ireland Talent and Quiz competition, forerunner of Scor. Entertainment was divided into seven sections and trials held for the purpose of selecting a team to represent Beragh in the County Finals.

And, if that wasn't enough, there was also the chance to engage the Silver Star Band from Beragh, who in 1960 were fully amplified with crooner and skiffle group. Enquiries were to be made to Jerry Grimes, Omagh Co-Op or Pat McGirr, Roscavey.

Sewerage Scheme and Sixmilecross Co-Op

Farmers were again being urged to stand together when the progress of the Sixmilecross and Omagh Co-Op, which had amalgamated in 1956, was being reviewed in 1963. Shareholders and a number of visitors from neighbouring co-ops were told that small farmers were finding that profit margins were shrinking and that the level of government support for agricultural prices was not likely to rise.

Thomas McGarvey retired as Manager in 1965 after making what was described as a 'magnificent contribution' to the managerial success of Sixmilecross since 1927. And, the growth of the movement was highlighted with the opening of a new self-service supermarket in March 1968. This marked the latest development in a history stretching back to the establishment of the Co-Op in February 1916.

Tommy McGarvey receives a presentation to mark his retirement after many years from Sixmilecross Co-Op

In Beragh, meanwhile, plans were outlined for a £30,000 sewerage scheme by Omagh Rural Council. The need for this work was highlighted when two young boys, Frank McQuaide and Brian Magee, fell eight foot down a manhole in Sixmilecross and had to be rescued by Thomas Devlin. However, in relation to the Beragh scheme, concerns were expressed about the cost and it was said that any reduction would lead to intended development at the Omagh end of the village having to be cut.

Actors and actresses go through their lines for a Beragh Players Production of the 1960s

"The scheme as designed would take care of all the new building in Beragh," the Clerk, JP Robinson, told a meeting of Omagh Rural Council. He added that the scheme would be large enough to serve any new estates that might be built in the foreseeable future.

A few years earlier in 1960, four new houses in Sixmilecross were the first to be built since the War. However, the vesting of land for housing development proved to be a thorny issue a few months later. Omagh Rural Council eventually sought a vesting order for two acres of land at Beragh for eight houses following the refusal of the owner to sell.

Inter-County GAA Affairs

After the highs of the late fifties, Tyrone's fortunes at inter-county level took a nose-dive in the sixties. The only high points in a decade of defeats proved to be the success of the county Junior team in winning the All-Ireland title for the first time in 1968.

A number of Beragh players made their mark at various times in the decade, particularly on the Vocational Schools side which really came good by winning Ulster and All-Ireland titles.

Ollie Slane was a county selector at the beginning of the decade when Dessie McMahon nailed down a place in the Tyrone defence. He made his debit against All-Ireland Champions, Down, on July 15th, 1962 and was at corner forward for the 1963 meeting against Antrim.

That game also saw Liam McGrath named at corner back and he also went on to feature regularly in subsequent years. While he missed out the following year, he was in the half-back line for the 1965 tie against Down and again featured against them in 1966. Others who gained shorter term recognition on Tyrone teams in the sixties were FH Owens and Frank Rodgers.

At Minor level, to, a number of players represented the county with distinction. Most notable among them were Ben McQuaid and Paddy McGarvey who were on the Tyrone side of 1967 which won the Ulster title and lost to Cork in the All-Ireland semi-final at Croke Park.

Ben McQuaide also featured in the 1967 Tyrone Vocational Schools team which defeated Kerry to win the All-Ireland title for the first time. Neil Hagan was in goals on the historic side that lined out in Croke Park, while the strong Beragh representation was completed by Sean McGrath, Peter Hagan, Anthony Donaghy and Eamon McQuaide.

And, there was also a first for the club in the later part of the decade when Dessie Donnelly, who had played for the footballers also, lined out for the Tyrone U-18 Hurling team. He had, of course, gained his experience in the coaching sessions taking place at that time.

> After the highs of the late fifties, Tyrone's fortunes at inter-county level took a nose-dive in the sixties. The only high points in a decade of defeats proved to be the success of the county Junior team in winning the All-Ireland title for the first time in 1968

Reflections on the sixties

Dessie McMahon, second from the right, pictured playing for Tyrone against the then All-Ireland Champions, Down, in the 1962 Ulster Championship.

Every decade of activity has its defining moments, times when the GAA in Beragh took important steps forward. In a period where new clubs were being established throughout Tyrone, the Beragh St Mary's managed to keep things going when the promoting gaelic games was often extremely difficult.

A number of factors threatened to derail club activity completely for a brief spell. But things were confidently revived and the success of the youth teams in the 1964-1966 laid the foundations for future progress.

By the end of the decade affairs had once again been put on a solid footing ready to embrace the seventies with enthusiasm on and off the field.

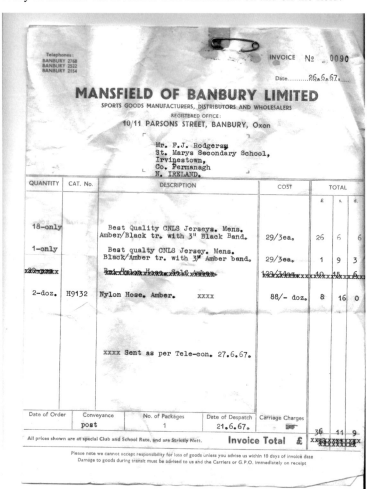

The receipt for the last set of Black and Amber jerseys purchased by Beragh St Mary's in 1967

Chapter Nine
1970 - 1980
Resurgence with new Red Knights

Beragh club
meeting in 1972
condemned the
occupation of
Casement Park and
enquired from the
Tyrone County
Board what protest
was to be taken

Chapter Eight
1970 - 1980

THERE was a new enthusiasm within the St Mary's as the seventies dawned with the club participating in a wide range of activities. Developments in the areas of football organisation at adult and youth levels, social events, plans for St Mary's Park, handball and camogie ensured that there were plenty of challenges for the decade ahead.

It meant that many of the concerns which had required attention during the previous ten years were being addressed. To the fore was the aspiration of making sure that the GAA club fulfilled its potential as a key organisation in the life of the community.

But it's fair to say as well that the quest for adult football success was a top priority. The promising youth achievements of the mid-sixties and the number of young players coming through the ranks provided the potential for progress.

League fortunes 1970-1975

Brian Owens
turns to celebrate
after registering a
crucial goal for
Beragh in a
relegation battle
against Edendork
in the 1970s

After being relegated from senior in 1964, the St Mary's spent the remainder of that decade at Intermediate level. And, that's where they were at the start of the seventies before their fortunes changed for the better in exciting fashion in 1972.

Challenge games as well as matches in the St Enda Cup gave the players some preparation for the 1970 West Tyrone Intermediate League. However, the poor form of the previous few years showed no signs of improving when Fintona comfortably defeated them by 3-6 to 0-8 in one of the opening games.

They were soon out of contention for promotion, even though they had one notable result in mid-summer when they beat Ballygawley on a score of 2-9 to 1-9. Dan McSorley, Francie Grimes, Martin Donnelly and Jim Franey were among the good defenders while Mick McSorley, Noel Colton, Peter Donaghy and Jim Gallagher were also to the fore in

The Beragh Red Knights team, with manager, Frank Rodgers, start out on their glorious 1972 run with a game against Fintona

attack. While relegation to the Junior grade was never really a threat, the fact that they finished just above Newtownstewart and the Carrickmore seconds on the table tell its own story.

They fared little better at the beginning of 1971. Killyclogher were easy winners over them by 2-13 to 0-4 and they also lost to Newtownstewart by 3-12 to 1-3. Ben McQuaide scored 2-6 in the 3-10 to 2-7 defeat by Ballygawley before they began showing improved form.

Fintona were comprehensively defeated on a score of 5-11 to 0-7, they beat Drumquin by 4-8 to 4-4 and the end of year statistics showed them with six wins and seven defeats from the thirteen league matches. But none of this gave any indication of the glories that were to come in 1972.

1972 - Promotion back to senior

Any look at the highly successful 1972 season has to take into account the background when a glorious time for the senior team on the playing front coincided with the Golden Jubilee celebrations, the timely change of name back to the Red Knights, Beragh, the introduction of a new all-red strip and a specially designed club crest.

All of this created a special aura for the Red Knights who under manager Frank Rodgers certainly made their mark on that season's West Tyrone GAA scene. The team's debut under the new name resulted in a 1-11 to 0-4 victory over Fintona and the lineout in that Red Knights debut match at Fintona on Sunday 12th March was: Eamon McQuade, Francie Grimes, Stephen Kelly, Brian McCullagh, Jim Franey, Colm McAleer, Murt Kelly,

Frank Rodgers,
Sean Montgomery
and Liam McGrath
pictured at a 1970s
Dinner Dance

Paddy McGarvey and Neil Hagan (capt), Brian Owens, Vincent McMackin, Harry Owens, Jim Gallagher, Mickey Kelly, Brian Maguire.

Subs - Liam Deazley, Arthur Doherty, Tommy McGarvey, Michael McCann, Brian Colton.

Scorers - Paddy McGarvey (1-4), Vincent McMackin (0-6), Harry Owens (0-1).

Their only League defeat came a week later when they lost to Newtownstewart by 1-8 to 0-5. From then on, though, there was no stopping the new Red Knights. They came back from six points down at half-time to beat Eskra by 2-7 to 2-2 and by April were four points clear at the top of the table.

With twelve of the team still U-21 they continually notched up some great scores and the marksmen in an easy win over Fintona in April were: Ben McQuaide (2-2), Vincent McMackin (1-3), Stephen Kelly (1-2), Brian Owens (1-1), Harry Owens (0-3), Arthur Doherty (1-0) and Neil Hagan (0-1).

An important win was the 4-10 to 2-4 result recorded over one of the challengers, Killyclogher. Beragh had led by 2-7 to 2-2 at half-time after Killyclogher had taken an early advantage. But it all came good in the second half when two goals from Jim Gallagher put the result beyond doubt.

Eventually, the quest for league honours came down to a match against one of the bottom placed teams, Drumragh, on August 27th. And, the win came in typically dramatic style when Vincent McMackin scored just before the end to secure a 0-12 to 2-5 win and promotion back to senior. The Ulster Herald report of the match stated that "those final five minutes seemed endless as both sides were striving for the winning score. Then a sudden Drumragh breakaway with Dessie Mullan and Pat McGlone to the

The 1978
Beragh team

fore, was only broken up an alert full back line of Liam Deazley, Jim Franey and Pete Owens.

"The winning score came after a good Eamon McQuaide clearance found Murt Kelly well placed. A pass to Brian Owens, whose shot was blocked down to Vincent McMackin, put the team's sharpshooter in a scoring position and he made no mistake. For the Red Knights, this dramatic victory proved a great climax to their league campaign.

The team that won that historic match was: Eamon McQuade, Liam Deazley, Jim Franey, Pete Owens, Brian Maguire, Colm McAleer, Murt Kelly, Paddy McGarvey and Brian Owens, Vincent McMackin, Neil Hagan, Stephen Kelly, Harry Owens, Jim Gallagher, Ben McQuaide. Sub - Tommy McGarvey.
Scorers - Vincent McMackin 0-3, Jim Gallagher, Ben McQuaide, Neil Hagan (0-2 each), Paddy McGarvey (0-1).

"Their panel of players, which included twelve eligible for U-21 football, played thirteen games in the league, with the loss of only three points. Many of the young players, however, are still lacking in expertise as their championship form showed, but they have youth on their side."

A quick relegation from senior

Novel ties against strong teams from the eastern end of the county provided a different challenge to Beragh at the start of 1973. And, an indication of how tough things would be came in the opening game when Derrylaughan defeated them by 2-4 to 0-8.

Better fortunes followed with wins over Edendork and Kildress being sandwiched between a defeat by Omagh. Brian Owens and Paddy Rodgers got goals in a 3-13 to 1-7 win over Edendork again at the end of April and they continued to show fairly good form as the season progressed.

In June a 1-7 to 0-2 win was recorded over Dungannon that was marked by the first senior appearance of Pete Owens at full-back. Vincent McMackin, Liam Deazley and Dessie Donnelly were again among the main performers. Beragh were now joint second on the table with Clonoe and Stewartstown and they maintained their place with a 2-9 to 0-4 win over Omagh.

The fairly good form continued and in August they were fourth behind Stewartstown, Clonoe and Dungannon and were expecting tough games

Elaborate defensive barrier at Montague's Bar, following second attempt to bomb it in six weeks

249

Receipts for the manufacture of the new club crest in 1972 and the trip to Dublin for the Senior team at the beginning of 1973

against the Harps, Ballygawley and the Rahilly's to conclude their campaign.

In 1974 Ann Gallagher won Best Actress at Ballyshannon Drama Festival. Mid-Ulster Drama Club's presentation of Mistress of Novices

But their efforts weren't good enough and the beginning of 1974 saw them meeting Stewartstown to decide which of them would remain in Senior football. Stewartstown won and Beragh joined Kildress and Edendork going down despite a number of appeals involving them and Omagh against the Harps.

Into February 1974 and Pomeroy defeated them in the first game of the West Tyrone Intermediate League, but that didn't stop them from topping the table by March along with Pomeroy and Greencastle. By May they were still top, one point ahead of Dromore. They extended their lead in June but Dromore had three games in hand.

The subsequent months saw them maintain their form and towards the autumn their position earned them a place in Division Three of the new

All-County League for 1975. They had completed a campaign of eighteen games, with only Dromore getting more points than them to gain promotion to Senior.

Beragh were joined in Division Three of the new ACL in 1975 by Clonoe, Killyman, Moy, Kildress, Strabane, Edendork and Mountjoy and they were mid-table by the half-way stage. Wins by 1-8 to 1-5 over Mountjoy and by 3-11 to 0-3 over Clonoe boosted their position to eleven points from eleven games in August. However, a later loss to Mountjoy saw them fall into the relegation zone again and their survival was only secured when Killyman defeated Mountjoy at the finish in October.

Defeats by Urney, Edendork and Clonoe resulted in a bad start to 1976. The first win came against Clogher before losses were recorded in the games against Kildress and Dungannon. All of this meant that they were again struggling against relegation.

However, matters took a turn for the better in the final game when they beat leaders, Kildress, at Kildress by 4-4 to 1-2. Frank Owens scored two goals and other important contributions came from Pat Donnelly, Paddy Grimes, Malachy Donnelly, Liam Deazley and Brian McCullagh in really dramatic fashion.

Things started well in the new 1977 season and a win over Dungannon by 1-15 to 2-5 in May saw the Red Knights go top of the Division Three table. But that month also saw the first defeat, by Omagh that sparked a decline in fortunes. They had dropped to third by July and, while they continued to challenge, the season ended with them well behind the leaders in the promotion hunt.

A Division Three lineup that included Stewartstown, Killyman, Drumragh, Pomeroy, Fintona, Gortin and Edendork provided the bread and butter action for the Red Knights in 1978. However, the slowing momentum of the previous couple of seasons continued as defeat followed defeat against teams like Drumragh, Fintona, Gortin and Pomeroy.

Ground was lost to such an extent that they fell to the bottom of the table at the beginning of November. However, they defeated Fintona by 2-6 to 2-5 to earn a play-off to stay in the division. It took place against Edendork at the end of November and they came from 2-3 to 0-5 down in the last ten minutes to win. A goal from Louis McNamee started the comeback, Vincent McMackin equalised and the winner came from Louis McNamee late on.

> Fire destroyed a hayshed and 800 bales of hay at the home of Mr M O'Neill of Osnagh, Beragh. Omagh Fire Brigade said the cause of the fire was a mystery

A motion sponsored by Beragh and Drumragh resulted in a new three-tier league for 1979. Beragh were placed in Division Two and were top of the table with full points after four games.

By July they had twenty points from eleven games, including a 2-6 to 0-5 win over Brocagh. Victory over Edendork by 3-5 to 2-2 kept them going before two defeats proved very costly. There was a close finish between Beragh, Cookstown and Killyclogher and in the end Killyclogher won promotion with the very last game of the season, leaving Beragh, Cookstown, and Owen Roes to fight it out for the other place in Division One. And, setting a precedent that was to be maintained on subsequent play-offs, the Red Knights lost to Cookstown by 2-9 to 0-5 to finish the seventies in the Intermediate grade.

Championship action

Pat Donnelly fists a point against Killyman in this action shot from the 1970s

After the excitement of the early sixties and those big games in the shake-up for the O'Neill Cup, the form of both the Beragh St Mary's and later the Red Knights in the Intermediate Championship left a lot to be desired. First round defeats were more often the norm as they struggled to progress to the later stages throughout the seventies.

The trend was set in 1970 when the first of a number of defeats by Pomeroy was recorded. The Plunkett's went on to lose in the County Intermediate Final that year and so were on hand again in 1971 to inflict another defeat on the St Mary's.

A revival of fortunes on the league scene following the name change to Red Knights also made a difference to championship form in 1972. They opened with a 3-13 to 1-5 win over Newtownstewart on May 21. Ben McQuaide scored 2-5, the performances of Paddy McGarvey and Stephen Kelly at midfield and Jim Franey, Pete Owens and Murt Kelly in defence being of note.

The Quarter Final finally saw them turn the tables on Pomeroy at Dunmoyle and the win set up a semi-final clash against Clonoe. And, the confident Red Knights got off to a dream start when points from Vincent

The Intermediate team from 1977 which won thirteen games out of twenty four played

McMackin and Stephen Kelly and goals from Brian and Harry Owens were registered.

But a disastrous ten minute period saw them throw away the momentum of their earlier dominance. Mis-understandings in defence let Clonoe in for quick goals. They led by the interval and really pressed ahead in the second half when Paul Doris and Peter Brady were among their main players.

But the 1972 West Tyrone League success had earned them promotion and it was the senior championship that attracted their attention in 1973. They could hardly have got a tougher assignment than to have to meet the 1972 defeated finalists, Stewartstown in the First Round. In the end, it was all so inevitable as the Harps, won by 0-11 to 0-2 despite the best efforts of Liam McGrath, Tommy McGarvey and Colm McAleer. Stewartstown had led by 1-4 to 0-1 at half-time.

Back to Intermediate action in 1974 and Pomeroy were yet again Beragh's opponents. And, they won again even though the Red Knights started well. The two of them met for the fifth time in six years in 1975 and finished level at Dunmoyle before the Plunkett's won the replay by 0-6 to 0-3. On to 1976 and the only thing that changed in 1976 was the scoreline, Pomeroy winning by 0-6 to 0-4 that year.

It was probably with a sense of relief as much as anything else that the two avoided each other for only the second time in the decade in 1977. Beragh took full advantage of the change to defeat Mountjoy in a first round tie that saw Adrian Nixon, Brian Owens and Paddy Rodgers excel.

While hopes were high for more of the same in the Quarter Final against Aghyaran, they just couldn't match the north Tyrone side, who dominated throughout, led by 0-4 to 0-3 at half-time and won by 0-9 to 0-3 as Beragh failed to score in the second half.

Last member of the Belmore family died. She was Lady Margaret Lowry-Corry, aged 92. Efforts being made to sell in the remaining land of the Belmore Estate in 1975

253

Old video footage survives of the 1978 Intermediate Championship tie against Killyman at Dungannon. And, while it doesn't show the whole game, a late goal secured a 1-5 to 1-3 win for Killyman.

So a decade of disappointing championship results came down to 1979 and another First Round meeting with Stewartstown which ended in a replay victory for Beragh. It was 4-4 each in the drawn game after Vincent McMackin got a late equalising goal. The other goals were scored by Tommy McGarvey, Liam Deazley and Brian McGarvey.

Pete Owens
about to clear his
lines at
St Mary's Park

In the replay Colm McAleer was missing due to a back injury but Malachy Donnelly starred at midfield. Pete Owens held Peter Mulgrew scoreless and the sharpshooting of Vincent Mackin, who scored four points, helped Beragh to a 0-6 to 0-5 victory. However, they exited a week later when Killyclogher were the comfortable victors on a score of 2-11 to 2-2 in the Quarter Final.

Other competitions

McElduff Cup Winners and Tournament successes

With promotion and the league title secured at the end of 1972, attention turned to the McElduff Cup. The competition began with a number of group games which Beragh comfortably won to progress to the semi-final where they defeated Strabane by 1-9 to 2-5 after trailing by 1-2 to 0-4 at half-time.

That game, which took place at the end of November, set up a final clash against their old rivals for league honours, Killyclogher. The match was

Council
Chairman, Paddy
Bogan, presents
Sport for All
trophies to the
Beragh team
in 1978

played in Omagh on March 18th 1973 and attracted a large attendance as the Red Knights went for the League and Cup double.

Stephen Kelly and Paddy McGarvey missed the match, but the replacements at midfield, Dessie Donnelly and Jim Franey proved their worth. Brian Maguire and Harry Owens were involved in setting up full-forward, Neil Hagan, for the crucial first goal that left the Red Knights enjoying a 1-5 to 0-1 interval advantage.

Eamon McQuaide made a couple of timely saves in the second half and Tommy McGarvey scored the second goal which made sure of the double on a score of 2-7 to 0-5. The McElduff Cup was presented to the captain, Neil Hagan, at the finish amid what were described as "scenes of jubilation among the supporters."

The McElduff Cup success of 1972 had climaxed a period of good performances in the subsidiary competition. They had lost to Ballygawley in both the 1970 and 1971 semi-finals by 0-11 to 0-6 and then by 1-10 to 0-5.

The claim that Beragh were in touch with the pacesetters in Tyrone football at the time was backed up by a number of fairly notable wins in the top Tournaments. Chief among them was the victory over the then reigning county champions, Ardboe, in the Carrickmore Tournament at the end of June 1972.

This was no makeshift O'Donovan Rossa side as they included their top county stars of the period. Kevin Teague, MJ Forbes, Frank McGuigan, Phelim Forbes and Sean Coyle all lined out and they started well. They led by 2-3 to 2-1 at half-time before the second half turned into a thriller.

Brian McCullagh, Murt Kelly and Colm McAleer were each to the fore as three goals from Neil Hagan, the team captain made the difference. In the end, Beragh won by 4-7 to 3-6, with Hagan's personal tally of 3-3 proving vital against opponents who later went on to win the second of three county titles in a row in 1972.

The team and scorers in the McElduff Cup Final victory were: Eamon McQuade, Brian McCullagh, Liam McGrath, Peter Owens, Brian Maguire, Colm McAleer, Murt Kelly, Dessie Donnelly and Jim Franey, Brian Owens, Vincent McMackin, Harry Owens, Tommy McGarvey, Neil Hagan, Ben McQuaide.
Subs - Michael McCann, Francie Grimes, Mickey Kelly.

Death of Paddy McCrumlish at the end of 1976 - A raconteur who had the history of the GAA in the parish at his fingertips. Never known to miss a match and even known to have cycled to Croke Park. Special interests were traditional music and handball

Scorers - Neil Hagan 1-2, Vincent McMackin 0-3, Tommy McGarvey 1-0, Harry Owens 0-1, Brian Owens 0-1.

But Beragh were not finished yet in the Carrickmore competition and went on to meet the Fermanagh champions, Tempo, in the final. Matters came to a head during the final five minutes with the Red Knights falling behind. However, Jim Gallagher equalised and then with just two minutes left Vincent McMackin grabbed the winning goal to secure the honours on a score of 1-12 to 0-12.

> Treasure Hunt by Cloughfin HC on Tuesday July 26 1977 to be followed by a Jamboree in the alley with music by the San Antones

A year later they returned to Carrickmore to successfully defend their title, this time defeating Ballygawley by 0-9 to 0-8 in the decider. It wasn't quite as dramatic as the year before but still exciting. The teams were level at 0-4 each at half-time and Harry Owens, Paddy Rodgers and Vincent McMackin got the important scores in the closing stages.

Efforts to provide a playing outlet for those not gaining first-team action at adult level continued in the 1970s with the introduction of a Junior grade. In the first half of the decade Beragh teams competed regularly and then in 1973 the club proposed that Reserve Leagues and Championships should be provided in the All-County system. This was accepted and was introduced for the following 1974 season and has proved to be a great success.

That year saw the Beragh Reserve team finish runners-up to Clonoe in their league division. The increased seriousness with which the level was being taken was highlighted when Eugene Bogan and Francie Grimes began their stint as team managers in 1977. The age-old problem, though, of players losing interest caused concern as the season progressed.

A group of U-14 players who took part in coaching sessions during the mid-1970s

Youth football

All-Ireland success for Tyrone Minors in 1973 as well as their progress to the final the previous year indicated the progress being made at youth level throughout the county during that period. In Beragh the introduction of a Parish Minor League, the progress of the Minors to the West Tyrone Final, the regular appearance of players on county teams and the starting of the Primary League were all signs that the club was doing good work at youth level.

Teams from Drumduff, Beragh, Sixmilecross and Roscavey competed in the Parish Minor League which involved around fifty players in 1970. It had been established in 1968 and within the next couple of years extended

The increase in youth coaching in the 1970s further boosted the promotion of gaelic football in the parish

to involve those in both the Juvenile and Minor grades. It aroused great interest around the parish and the 1976 final was between Emmetts, captained by Timothy Grimes and Rossas, captained by Pat Donnelly.

At this time, the U-16s played in the South Tyrone Juvenile League and the Minors, U-14s and U-12s in the West Tyrone Leagues. The U-16s reached the South Tyrone Final in 1973 and 1974 but lost in both. The 1976 Minors reached the West Tyrone Final, while the Juveniles lost out in the semi-final of their league to eventual winners, Omagh.

Among the people praised for their involvement in the organisation of youth teams in 1975 were Jim Franey, Tommy McGarvey, Pete Owens, Lawrence Connolly, Frank Rodgers and Jack Woods. In 1977 a trip to Termonfeckin in Co Louth, the native area of Fr Carroll was organised, and those looking after underage teams in the later part of the decade included Eamon McQuaid and Pat and Mick McCartan, PJ McClean, John McGlinn, Frank Rodgers, Kevin Maguire and Kevin Grimes.

The players pictured here featured in the 1972 West Tyrone Minor Final against Omagh at Dunmoyle

West Tyrone Minor Final 1972

Stories of misfortune often play a part in sporting life. So it was with the Beragh Minor team which proved to be strong performers in the 1972 season. But they lost narrowly to the eventual County Champions, Carrickmore, at the Quarter Final of the Championship and to Omagh in the West Tyrone League Final.

The Championship Quarter Final was described as one of the best Minor games of the year and it was only in the final few minutes that Carrickmore edged ahead. Beragh were leading by two points when their

opponents worked a goal against the run of play. And, that score made the difference as the St Colmcille's got two further points against a Red Knights team that fell away at the finish.

A final score of 2-7 to 2-4 ended Beragh's hopes and they later thought about what might have been when Carrickmore went on to take the county title by comfortably defeating Coalisland in the final.

Following that defeat, a good league campaign reached its climax towards the end of the year. Drumragh provided the opposition in the semi-final, with the first game finishing level at 1-8 for Beragh to 2-5.

Eamon Donnelly, Tommy McGarvey, Tommy Gartland and Lawrence Mulholland did well as did Malachy McCann, Paddy Rodgers. Leo Horisk and Brian McGarvey led the way up front. Drumragh were 2-2 to 0-1 in front at the break, before Liam Deazley and Colm McAleer led the revival in the second half. A late point from Liam Deazley was to earn them the draw. It was again closely contested in the replay on September 3 at Omagh. On that occasion Beragh finished strongest to win by 0-7 to 0-5.

This set up a final meeting against an Omagh team that included County Minors Oliver O'Neill, Justin O'Doherty, Sean Healy and former Beragh player, Charlie Donaghy. Dunmoyle was the venue for a match played on the same afternoon as the replayed All-Ireland Final.

The St Enda's led by 0-4 to 0-2 at half-time and Beragh missed a good chance to go into the lead on the resumption. A move involving Paddy Rodgers, Paddy Grimes and Mickey Walshe broke down on the edge of the square and Omagh counter-attacked to score at the other end.

Players breaking the pain barrier at training in St Patrick's Hall in the mid-1970s

While goalie, Tommy Fitzmaurice saved a penalty from Oliver O'Neill and Malachy McCann cut back the Omagh lead, the St Enda's stayed in front and a goal from O'Neill sealed the win on a score of 1-6 to 0-3.

The Beragh team lined out: Tommy Fitzmaurice, Brian Colton, Pete Owens, Malachy McCann, Tommy McGarvey, Liam Deazley, Tommy Gartland, Colm McAleer, Malachy McCann, Eamon Donnelly, Paddy Rodgers, Paddy Grimes, Gerry Ward, Frank McQuaide, Leo Horisk.

Subs - Mickey Walsh, Mickey Deazley and Malachy Donnelly.

The Cuchullain's U-21s

In the final, though, they lost out to the Emmetts, the Fintona and Trillick combination, on a score of 0-7 to 1-2

The U-21 grade in Tyrone was first introduced in 1973 and those first years saw Beragh and Ballygawley enter an amalgamated team. Known as Cuchullain's, they played three games and reached the semi-finals in the opening season only to lose in what were described as 'very unsatisfactory circumstances' to Killyclogher.

Players on the combined side that year included Vincent McMackin, Harry and Pete Owens, Tommy McGarvey and Colm McAleer from Beragh and Mickey Harte, Paul McCaffrey, Sean Loughran, Peter Farrell from Ballygawley. The knock-out nature of the competition saw them play only one match in 1974, two in 1975 three in 1976 and four in 1977.

But they did better in 1978 when they reached the semi-final. The team that lost by 2-7 to 1-3 was: Paul Colton (Beragh), Paddy Grimes (Beragh), Eugene Quinn (Ballygawley), Ciaran McCrory (Ballygawley), Louis McNamee (Beragh), Tommy McGarvey (Beragh), Barry Canavan (Ballygawley), Liam Farrell (Ballygawley), Pat Donnelly (Beragh), Paudge Quinn (Ballygawley), Barney Campbell (Ballygawley), Brian McGarvey (Beragh), Brian Quinn(Ballygawley), Seamus Quinn (Ballygawley).

They reversed that result in the semi-final in 1979 when recording a 2-7 to 0-8 victory. A goal from Adrian Nixon put them 1-6 to 0-6 ahead at a crucial stage and the defensive work of Ciaran McCrory, Barney Campbell, Barry Canavan and Pat Donnelly kept them on top in the second half. The game went into extra time when Malachy Donnelly and Liam Farrell raised the tempo.

In the final, though, they lost out to the Emmetts, the Fintona and Trillick combination, on a score of 0-7 to 1-2. Malachy Donnelly's long shot was dropped by the goalkeeper into the net midway through the first half, but Emmetts still led by 0-5 to 1-1 at the break.

However, the Cuchullains managed only one more score, an Adrian Nixon point right at the end and the good work of Ciaran McCrory, Finbar Grimes, Pat Donnelly and Stevie Canavan was to no avail.

Park Development - The Opening of St Mary's Park

The development work at St Mary's Park in the early seventies culminated in a number of improvements which made it one of the best in Tyrone.

At the start of the decade the work of the late sixties was continued with a number of options on the table for the construction of what was

> **By then the possibility of involving the newly formed Omagh District Council in the development of the spare ground as a community facility became a possibility**

The play facilities at St Mary's Park provided an added dimension to the role of the Beragh Red Knights in the community

described as a 'Sports Centre'. But these were held up at the time by the intention of the Drainage Department of the Ministry of Agriculture to carry out work on the river. However, an arrangement with the Drainage Department resulted in the entire playing area being levelled at a nominal cost in 1972. During that time matches were played at Carrickmore. Pat McCartan, Felix McCann, Hugh Hackett, Joe Franey, Hugh Colton and Jack McCann were among those on the Park Development Group who worked closely with Terry Kelly (Chairman), Frank Rodgers (Secretary) and Paddy Bogan (Treasurer) and the rest of the club committee members to turn the newly levelled ground into a fully fenced pitch with a superb playing surface that was ready for use in 1974.

By then the possibility of involving the newly formed Omagh District Council in the development of the spare ground as a community facility

The tin-hut on the hill, dressing-rooms for players until the mid-1970s

became a possibility. However, the move provoked a dubious response from a number of Councillors when it was discussed at their meeting in June 1974.

Councillor Joseph Anderson commented on a recommendation from the Recreation Committee to proceed with the development by saying that "traditions die hard and it is not a good idea to provide these facilities on land associated by tradition with one section of the community such as the GAA."

Councillor Stephen McKenna praised the club for their 'public spirited' approach, while Councillor Albert Cooper said it was up to the wider community to use the facilities available. The scheme was adopted on a majority vote.

The Official Opening of St Mary's Park

And so almost twenty years after it was first purchased by the Beragh club, the new and re-developed St Mary's Park was officially opened on Sunday July 21, 1974, with an exciting programme of attractions. They included children's sports, band parades, Irish Dancing, ballad singing, Juvenile and Adult football games and a seven a side Camogie competition.

Formal business on the occasion was carried out by the Chairman of the Tyrone County Board, Paddy Corey, who said "the ground was as good as he had seen anywhere in Ireland." He continued: "The provision of facilities like these enables the ideals of the GAA to be further developed and I am proud to say that Tyrone clubs are forging ahead at a magnificent rate with their new grounds."

Club President, Fr Terry, PP spoke of the foresight of those who had purchased the ten acre site for the GAA Club. "They have provided something in the community that will be a permanent amenity for years to come." He called for the youth of the area to be involved in the next phase of the development and expressed the hope that the highest standards would be displayed by those who played in Beragh.

County Chairman, Jimmy Treacy presents the Intermediate Cup to Fintona following the 1978 Final. Included are the McCann Brothers of Fintona who were later to be the main contractors on the re-development of the clubrooms in 2005-2006

PICTORIAL RECORD OF THE OPENING OF BERAGH G.A.A. CLUB'S PARK

Historic occasion for Beragh Red Knights

Pat McCartan, Chairman of the Park Development Group, paid tribute to the former Field Trustees, four of whom were deceased. He said that the next stage would be the development of a first-class recreational facility around the grounds.

But, of course, the highlight of the day for many people was the wide range of activities on offer. They included a large selection of sports events at which some of those competing were Colin McCann, Declan Colton, Eugene McCann, Sean Owens, Brian McGarvey, Pat Donnelly, Michael Slane, Patricia McCann, Clare Colton, Ann McAleer, Sinead McCartan, Patsy Farley, Brendan McMackin, Mairead McClean, Imelda McCann, Angela McHugh, Aidan McCann, Liam McClean, Anne McCann, Paul McCann, Gerard Donnelly, Caroline Mullan, Mary McKelvey, Anne Slane and Ann Owens.

A Ladies football match resulted in a 1-2 to 1-1 win for Mountfield over Beragh, while the £100 winner in the Park Development Draw was Peter McNamee (Junior) of Remackin.

It is interesting to note that in the period from 1972 until the opening of the Park four years later some £3000 was raised for the development through the annual 'Closed Draw.' A total of £600 was paid out in prizes.

Later in the year, work on the development of the spare grounds was enabled by the granting of £15,000 for the initial stages of the project.

This spare ground was leased by the club to the Council in 1975 for 35 years and Enterprise Ulster were commissioned to design and carry out the scheme

This spare ground was leased by the club to the Council in 1975 for 35 years and Enterprise Ulster were commissioned to design and carry out the scheme, with the first stages of which were due to be completed in 1976.

The club, incidentally, broke new ground by becoming the first to make such an arrangement for the development of recreational facilities for the wider community. The presence of Club Treasurer, Paddy Bogan, as a member of the Omagh Council helped in putting the arrangement in place.

By 1976 work on the recreation area and dressing rooms had begun, with plans also in place to provide a Handball Alley on the site. The riverside walk and playpark were eventually completed in early 1977, just in time for the summer when the facilities proved very popular with young and old. The dressing rooms were finished early in 1978.

Omagh Council's Recreation Officer, Vincent Campbell, said that it was hoped, subject to land acquisition, to make provision for other sports such as football and tennis on a site across the river from the present facilities, with access by means of a footbridge. That, however, never materialised

The end of the seventies brought yet another addition to the development when the tennis court was completed and final proposals were put in place for the building of the new 40x20 Handball Alley. The provision of a caretaker followed and Hugh Colton took up the post in 1978.

All of this contributed to making the ground a popular venue for big matches. Several top Senior Championship matches were hosted as well as the Intermediate Finals of 1978 and 1979 and the County Hurling Final on a number of occasions.

> A decade that was to see massive changes in the organisation and playing of handball began on a very optimistic note in the parish with the opening in 1971 of the 60x30 Alley at Cloughfin

Rev Fr Terry blesses the new handball at Cloughfin in 1971

Handball

A decade that was to see massive changes in the organisation and playing of handball began on a very optimistic note in the parish with the opening in 1971 of the 60x30 Alley at Cloughfin. Plans for the facility had begun following the formation of the club in the mid-sixties and finally reached fruition at a cost of £12,000.

Conor, Martin ,
Niall and Mick
Kerr pictured with
their handball
trophies in 1978.
All four played an
important role in
the development of
the game during
the decade

The building began and the work of fundraising was undertaken with much vigour. A series of bazaars, raffles, ballots and a range of other events were held, while the neighbouring clubs of Beragh and Ballygawley also took a big interest.

Spectator accommodation for an estimated 200 was provided and a modern lighting system ensured that the 150 handballers using the alley were served with the best of facilities. At the time of opening the alley was one of just 24 fully equipped covered alleys in Ireland.

Top priority for those gathered on Sunday May 9 was an exhibition by Joey Maher, the best handballer in Ireland, and a match between Harry Haddock and Tyrone's very own first All-Ireland Champion, MJ Conway from Loughmacrory. The local players weren't expected to get on court until later in the evening.

> By then the
> possibility of
> involving the newly
> formed Omagh
> District Council in
> the development of
> the spare ground as
> a community
> facility became a
> possibility

The correspondent in the Ulster Herald the following week was in no doubt about the significance of the completion of the alley. "How well the Alley looked for the big day. Newly painted by voluntary workers, this complex stands out as a landmark along with the nearby Bernish Glen, the Dunmoyle Church and the ancient relics of Shane Castle. The spacious carpark adjoining the alley was a good planning foresight, taking visitors' cars off the narrow roadways and cutting traffic hazards."

Speakers at the event were Fr Terry, who Blessed the building, the Chairman and Secretary of the Irish Handball Association, the Chairman of the Ulster Handball Council, Tom Walsh, West Tyrone Board Chairman, Pat McCartan and the Chairman of the Tyrone County Board, Paddy Corey.

After all that excitement, players representing the Cloughfin club continued to compete in the Gael Linn competition, the Magee Cup, their own inter-club events and the Tyrone Championships which were growing in popularity.

The 1971 Magee Cup got underway in October that year when the fixtures were: M Kelly v HJ Tierney, T Mullin v Francis Tierney, B McCallan v Francis McGarvey, Brian McCullagh v Paddy McGarvey, Eugene McGirr v Vincent McCullagh, Seamus Donnelly v Peter Nugent, Michael McGarvey v Sean Tierney, Peter McNamee v Justin Kelly, Pat Mullin v Johnny Kerr, Mick McCartan v Pat McCartan, Martin Tierney v Joe Mullin, Patrick McCrory v Brian McNally, Stephen Kelly v Mick Kerr, Hugh McClean v Brendan Kelly, Francie Donnelly v Seamus Nugent, Neill McGarvey v Pat Donnelly and Pat McCallan (bye).

Success was inevitable considering the number of players participating in that event. And, in 1972 Cloughfin won their first title at provincial level when they defeated Loughmacrory in the final of the Ulster section of the Inter-Club Novice Championship.

In the first game Hugh McClean was beaten by John McCullagh, but Mick Kerr and Brian McCullagh came back to beat John Smith and Joe McMahon. This put Cloughfin ten marks ahead, leaving everything down to the final match which saw Pat Donnelly come from behind to defeat 15 year old Eugene Maguire. The club was then due to play in an All-Ireland competition, but no record of this having taken place was available.

An improving proficiency was also evident in 1974 when the Brian McGarvey won the Tyrone U-16 title and Stephen Kelly was runner-up in the Junior grade. The County Minor title in 1975 was won by Eugene Maguire. He later went on to win the Ulster title and the impetus provided by the Cloughfin club ultimately led to the reformation of the Brackey club in 1977.

The Brackey
Handball
Committee of 1978

They had been out of existence for around ten years at the time, and the fresh efforts made to revive it proved fruitful. The club made the decision to play at McAleer's of Cloughfin, Killyclogher, an adult league was started and a schoolboys tournament planned under the guidance of Sean Clarke and Andy McAleer. The committee elected was: Chairman - Mick Kerr, Vice-Chairman - Basil Neville, Secretary - Brian McCullagh, Assistant Secretary - Sean Clarke, Treasurer - Basil Neville and Mick McAleer.

Indications of the good health of the game were becoming evident. At the County Handball Presentations at the end of 1977 players from both Brackey and Cloughfin were listed among the winners. That summer the Brackey Club took the momentous decision to proceed with the building of their own alley. Decisions had to be taken on the size and location, although within weeks the possibility of a new 40x20 alley in Beragh was on the agenda. The long negotiations were bearing fruit when Omagh District Council intimated its intention to ask the Department of Education to grant-aid an alley, which was estimated to cost around £23,000. And, while efforts to achieve this continued towards the end of the decade, players from both clubs continued to excel at a local, county and provincial level.

Camogie

The re-establishment of the Camogie club in the late sixties created a good impetus which was effectively maintained into the following decade. While the absence of a pitch for a number of seasons caused problems, the game continued to be enthusiastically promoted.

It was no wonder, then, that there was an air of optimism in the ranks of the girls as they gathered for their Annual meeting in January 1970. The previous year was described as one of progress that had seen them fulfil all their fixtures.

A committee was elected for the season ahead comprising the following: President - Annie Owens, Chairman - Sheila Owens, Vice-Chairman - Gloria Donaghy, Secretary - Mary Rodgers, Assistant Secretary - Lizzie Franey, Treasurer - Margaret Donnelly. Committee - Brigid Grimes, Marian Colton, Margaret Gallagher, Mary McCann, Bridie Woods and Patricia Tierney.

Briege McCartan challenges for possession for the Beragh Minor Camogie team

Plans were made for the coming year and there was great enthusiasm about facing the challenges ahead. But in April they lost by 2-0 to 1-0 to

The 1979 Beragh Minor Camogie team which reached the County Final

Edendork and the girls found that their lack of practice during the previous months was telling against them. However, twelve girls were called to the county trial in Dungannon a few days later and Bernadette Owens and Brigid Grimes gained selection.

Practices were held each Tuesday at the pitch, teams were fielded at Minor and Senior level and results included a defeat by Eglish in the senior championship. The panel to travel to Killeeshil for a game on Wednesday July 22, 1970 was: Brigid Grimes, Annie Owens, Geraldine Ward, Bernadette McKeown, Anne Mulholland, Bernadette Owens, Anna Brigid McSorley, Mona McCann, Aggie Rodgers, Margaret Gallagher, Margaret Franey, Veronica Donnelly, Jacqueline Nixon, Mary Rodgers, Kathleen Conway, Kathleen McCann, Kathleen O'Neill and Olive Owens.

For 1971 new officials included Dymphna Rodgers (Chairman), Deidre Mullan (Assistant Secretary) and Margaret Mullan (Treasurer). The usual schedule of games continued but the impending work on St Mary's Park was to lead to a fall-off in activity subsequently.

Interest at the meetings was poor, prompting a decision to hold a practice session to assess the level of playing support. The members made their view known that the lack of interest would lead to teams having to be withdrawn.

There was no sign of things improving and the club did not enter a team in 1972 when one of the reasons cited was the lack of a playing pitch. Players did continue their involvement in the game and Annie Owens was a member of the County Camogie Board.

The re-establishment of the Camogie club in the late sixties created a good impetus which was effectively maintained into the following decade

The coaching
was paying off
for the Beragh
Camogie players
in the late 1970s

The coaching
was paying off
for the Beragh
Camogie players
in the late 1970s

The decline in involvement which set in at the beginning of the decade lasted a lot longer than expected. Five years were to pass before the club again fielded a team, with the reformation taking place in 1978 and leading to the most sustained period of camogie activity ever in the area.

Those efforts to promote the game again were prompted by a meeting in St Mary's Hall at which a large number of girls attended. With quite a number of them teenagers, the decision was taken to enter a Minor team, while the older players were encouraged to join Eskra.

The committee elected was: President - Rev Fr Terry, Chairperson - Elizabeth Given, Treasurer - Briege McNamee, Secretary - Agnes Rodgers, Trainer - Kevin Grimes.

66

There was no sign
of things improving
and the club did
not enter a team in
1972 when one of
the reasons cited
was the lack of a
playing pitch

99

Players listed to play in a Minor match against Eglish later in the year were: Bridget Franey, Deidre Franey, Gabriel McAleer, Briege McClean, Caroline McCrystal and Jackie O'Neill, Ann Slane, Claire McCann, Siobhan McCrystal, Briege McCartan, Kathleen McNally and Rose McNamee.

That 1979 campaign saw the Minor girls progress to the Championship Final. On the way they defeated Carrickmore by 7-0 to 0-0 and Derrylaughan by 4-0 to 3-0. Hopes were high that the enthusiasm and skill of the girls would stand to them in the decider against Eglish.

However, things didn't quite go according to plan against the top team in Tyrone and Beragh ended up losing. But the efforts of Ann Slane, Jackie

O'Neill and Siobhan McCrystal were among those praised as the seeds of future progress in the eighties were sown.

The Beragh Tournament

One of the great attractions in the Beragh GAA Calendar in the 1970s was the annual Tournament. Held over a fortnight at St Mary's Park, the event continued to attract the crowds in the decade when the range of activities was extended to include sports, a camogie tournament and penalty kick and tennis competitions.

Carrickmore, of course, were the big favourites and their regular appearances at Beragh were always guaranteed to draw a large attendance and generate exciting matches.

Along with them, the teams in the 1970 Tournament were Irvinestown, Fintona, Ballygawley, Tattyreagh, Killyclogher and Omagh and it was eventually won by Carrickmore who defeated Omagh 2-8 to 2-2 in the final.

In 1971 Mrs Jack McCann looked after the catering arrangements when Jack Martin and Frank McClean were the referees and Carrickmore defeated Ballygawley in the decider.

Development work affected the competition in 1972, resulting in it having to be called off. Described by then as mid Tyrone's most popular tournament, the Ulster Herald reported that the event was in trouble when the opening games failed to take place because of the Carnival. It was then suspended until the reopening of St Mary's Park after development work.

Carrickmore's dominance continued when it was revived in 1975 and they defeated Fintona in that year's final. The following year saw them defeat Drumragh and they also won in 1977 and 1978.

A big effort was made to promote the event for its Golden Jubilee in 1979 and the end result was certainly positive. The games were supported by record attendance, and a special commemorative programme was produced for the final between two of the top teams in the county at the time, Carrickmore and Trillick.

The St Macartan's fielded players such as Brendan Donnelly, Joe McGrade, Pat King and John

Mick McCartan presents Mickey Gallagher with a Ciste Gael cheque. As well as the Tournament, Ciste Gael was a major fundraising activities during the decade

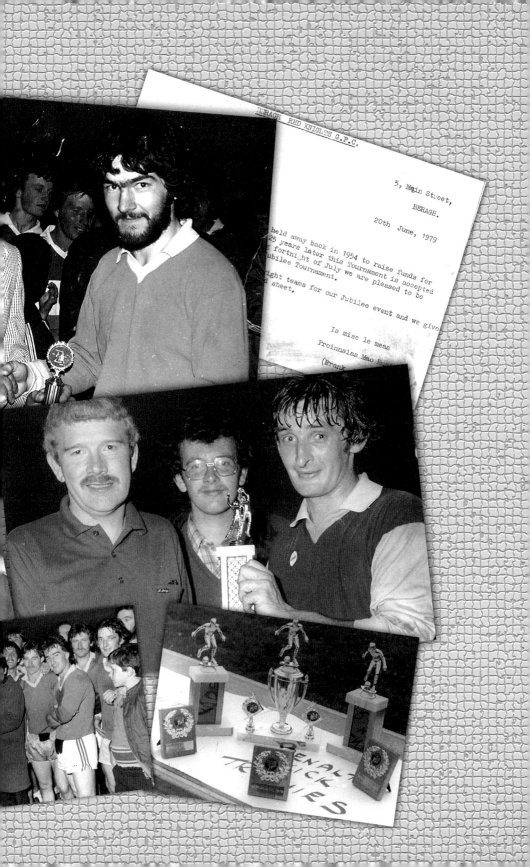

[Hand-lettered document reproduced in image:]

1976 | BERAGH RED KNIGHTS | 1976

PARISH YOUTH LEAGUE

G.A.A. | TEAM TROPHY AND INDIVIDUAL PLAQUES KINDLY DONATED BY MR. WILLIAM. C. MAGEE | G.A.A.

TONES	PEARSES
ANTHONY LITTLE (CAPTAIN)	JOHN MAC MAHON (CAPTAIN)
Malachy Donnelly	Brian Mac Garvey
Gerry Ward	Michael Mac Garvey
Finbar Grimes	Kevin Mac Cann
John Mac Cann	Sean Mac Haskin
Hugh Mac Aleer	P. J. Slane
Eugene O'Neill	Eamonn Cunningham
Brendan Cunningham	Gerard Devlin
Marty Colton	Sean Fitzmaurice
Aiden Donnelly	Malachy Owens
Tracy Curran	Mickey Mac Cullagh
Tony Cartland	Sean Haskett
Denis Mac Aleer	Martin Mac Bride
Ciaran Mac Cloan	Seamus Mac Cloak

EMMETTS	ROSSAS
TIMOTHY GRIMES (CAPTAIN)	PAT DONNELLY (CAPTAIN)
Louis Mac Nenoo	Gerry Maguire
Paul Colton	Gerard Kelly
Sean Owens	Mickey Slane
Martin Mullan	Michael Rodgers
Seamus Ward	Cornelius Colton
Martin Grimes	Declan Colton
Phillip Conway	T. Mac Burley
Seamus Boyle	Jim Gallagher
Mark Donnelly	Martin Kerr
	Mark Dillon
Seamus Collins	PAUL WARD
Sean Cunningham	Sean Bhaney
Mark Colton	Sean Cunningham

THE FIRST FIXTURES OF THE LEAGUE
SUNDAY 14th MARCH - TONES v PEARSES
RED KNIGHTS GROUND - 2.00
WEDNESDAY 17th MARCH: ST PATRICK'S DAY
TONES v EMMETS 2.00 p.m.

Donnelly, while there was no doubting Carrickmore's determination to maintain a decade-long unbeaten record when they fielded Sean Gormley, PJ Treanor and John Keenan. In the end, though, a goal from Brendan Donnelly early in the second half sent Trillick on their way to a 2-10 to 0-9 win. In the penalty kick section the winners were Donal McAleer (Open), Briege McCartan (Ladies) and Brendan Hegarty (Juvenile).

It is interesting to note the finances of the Tournament around that time. While the cost of various items such as trophies and refreshments came to some £65, gate receipts ensured a healthy profit. A total of £169 was lifted in 1970, that rose to £250 the following year and, while expenses rose to £130 when the event was revived in 1975, the gate receipts rose to £273. The takings were increasing year on year from £400 in 1977 to £620 in 1978 and to almost £1000 in 1979.

Other Activities

The 1970s were marked by a growth in the range of activities officially organised under the banner of the Beragh St Mary's and then the Red Knights from 1971. These included social functions, talent contests and, of course, the new Scor and Scor Na Og competitions.

Three Ceilis and a talent concert took place in 1970 when the policy of having area representatives on the general club committee was kept up. Refreshments were served at the interval at that first Convention of the decade, which saw WJ Conway, Peter McNamee and Thomas McGarvey

Club officials from 1979. Standing left to right are Paddy Bogan, Jim Franey, Kevin Maguire, Kevin Grimes, Barney Cunningham, Mick McCartan, John McGlinn, Jack Woods. At front are Finbar Grimes, Frank Rodgers (Secretary), Louis McNamee (Chairman), Paddy Grimes (Treasurer) and Eugene Bogan

elected as Honourary Presidents in recognition of their role in the purchase of St Mary's Park in 1954.

Later in the year the annual convention discussed the hot topic of the time - the removal of the Ban on Foreign games. The motion was carried on a day that saw Brian Donnelly, Jack Heaney and Terry Kelly all run for the post of Chairman. Brian Donnelly was elected while Frank Rodgers and Paddy Bogan were returned as Secretary and Treasurer.

Plans were put in place to organise Irish Dancing classes. In 1971 the members of the club joined together to condemn internment. A house to house collection was taken up and a fundraising concert organised by the club in February 1972 to help the dependents of those interned in Long Kesh, who included Beragh resident Paddy Joe McClean.

Over 400 people attended the concert and heard Mickey Lynch from Pomeroy tell of his visit to Long Kesh to entertain the internees. He spoke of the magnificent spirit shown by the men behind the wire in the face of their sufferings and mis-treatment. A draw was held, with souvenirs made by the internees as the prizes.

Those performing on the programme included Paddy Ward, the Wheelers Ballad Group from Carrickmore, Jackie Nixon, Mary Collins, Joe McMenamin (accordion), Peter Turbett, Bernadette McMenamin (recitation), Margaret Franey accompanied on the guitar by Sean Cleary, Dympna Rodgers (recitation) and the Lynch family and the Loughran sisters from Donaghmore.

The 1972 Convention heard the Secretary, Frank Rodgers, call for a wider range of social activities to be held and urged the club to concern themselves more with the general affairs of the parish. "We should be the driving force behind any effort to improve life in the area. I feel perhaps that we might even be doing something to encourage the setting up of some small local industry," he said.

Of course, getting people involved remained a priority highlighted at the

The 1970s were marked by a growth in the range of activities officially organised under the banner of the Beragh St Mary's and then the Red Knights from 1971. These included social functions, talent contests and, of course, the new Scor and Scor Na Og competitions

> On the talent front the regular internal club Scor events led to a lot of enjoyment over the years. The winners went on to represent the club in the Tyrone heats of the competition and, while titles were not won all that often, the involvement of many on the social side proved satisfactory

1974 Convention when the failings of the club were attributed to the absence of regular meetings. This, according to the meeting, led to jobs not being done and progress faltering as a result. Regular monthly meetings were eventually established as a feature of club business and for a time they were held at Aughnaglea School.

On the talent front the regular internal club Scor events led to a lot of enjoyment over the years. The winners went on to represent the club in the Tyrone heats of the competition and, while titles were not won all that often, the involvement of many on the social side proved satisfactory.

Another event which became extremely popular was the Talent Contests. The Beragh show was among the best around and won the Ballygawley Talent Contest and several other events on a number of occasions.

The Treasurer Reports presented at Convention also provide an insight into the workings of the club around this time. The usual running costs of equipment, registration fees and other expenses meant that expenditure rose from £1162 at the beginning of the decade to some £6579 ten years later.

Players injuries amounted to £20 in 1970, a new set of jerseys that year cost £10, £6 was spent on the organisation of the Talent Concert and £100 was put into a special grant fund for GAA Development. All-Ireland tickets for 1972 amounted to £15, £14 was spent on the renting of Carrickmore's park and £12 was paid to Ulsterbus for transport.

The 1974 account showed a profit of £503 and assets were put at £2601. Footballs cost £49 in total in 1976 and the total invested in the field by that time had amounted to £3969.

Winners again in the late 1970s were the Red Knights Talent team

Gate receipts brought in £728 in 1977 and £1050 the following year when the hosting of the Intermediate Championship Final was a big occasion. Grass cutting by then was costing £30 annually and the end of the decade accounts showed that £2605 had been raised through Ciste Gael, the GAA's own fundraising scheme of the time.

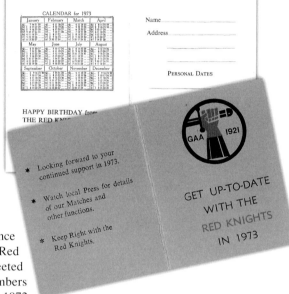

The Golden Jubilee Celebrations 1972

News that fifty years had passed since the formation of the original Red Knights Club in 1921 was greeted enthusiastically by current members when they sat down to plan for 1972. Under the planning of the Secretary, Frank Rodgers, this important year in the development of the GAA locally was marked by a number of significant events.

Perhaps the most important decision of all was the name change. Since the forties the club had been known as St Mary's. However, this changed when it was realised that it was 50 years since a club under the banner of the Red Knights had been formed.

The move to make the change was taken at the 1972 Convention. Weeks later the new club colours were adopted and the celebrations continued with an art competition for young people on the theme of Cuchullain and the Red Branch Knights.

The sense of excitement continued with the introduction of the club's very own crest to coincide with the change of club name and colours. The crest quickly became a recognisable feature throughout the county, being used on badges, notepaper, membership cards, carnival posters and all newspaper advertisements.

Coupled with a more successful season at senior level in 1972, the Red Knights of Beragh were now the new, young and vibrant face of the GAA in Tyrone. Their all-red strip, complete with togs, socks and even a kitbag

and improving fortunes marked them out as something special.

The big highlight was the Golden Jubilee Dinner in the Royal Arms Hotel in Omagh on Sunday February 20. Over 200 guests attended and included representatives from the various periods over the previous half century.

Guests pictured at the 1972 Golden Jubilee Dinner

The night was summed up by a report in the Ulster Herald which went: "Incidents from the past were discussed and enjoyed, but above all there was an air of enthusiasm and ambition about the future." Details were provided about the Jubilee functions, the present activities of the club and plans for the new clubrooms and social centre.

Mr Joe Martin, representing the County Committee and the West Tyrone Board, urged the club to aim for the highest honours and success was sure to come. His words of advice are said to have been particularly appreciated by the younger Red Knights and he had high praise for the all-round efficiency and for the efforts of the club to cater for the entire Beragh community by providing a wide range of activities.

The Honourary President of the Club, Rev Fr Terry, spoke of the fine achievement of those who had formed the Red Knights fifty years earlier. He referred to the difficult times in which the club was born and the efforts that must have been needed to keep it alive.

Messages of congratulations were read out by the Secretary, Frank Rodgers, among them one from Paddy Joe McClean in Long Kesh. His greetings came in the form of a linen-based illustration of the link between Cuchullain and the Beragh Red Knights Club.

Other messages came from the Ulster Council, the Tyrone County Board, West Tyrone Board, Omagh St Enda's, Carrickmore St Colmcille's, Ballygawley St Ciaran's, the South Tyrone Juvenile Board and Ulster Herald newspapers.

Another big event to mark the occasion was a GAA related Art competition which drew entries by pupils from all over the county. The young artists were asked to select any scene from the legends of the Red Branch Knights as their theme.

Cuchullain figured prominently with the two most frequent entries being based on the killing of the hound of Cullain and the death of Cuchullain. Indeed, the winning entry by Herbert O'Kane from Envaugh PS in Drumquin was an exciting modern interpretation of a battle scene.

Local winners included Niall Grimes, Anne Marie Boyle, Michelle McCrystal, Paula Nixon, Briege McCartan and Declan Maguire in age groups from 6 years to 7 years. Brigid Franey and Aelis McSorley of Roscavey PS were Highly Commended and each of the winners received certificates recording their success.

New jerseys as part of an all-red strip set the Red Knights apart for their Golden Jubilee season in 1972

One of the biggest events of all was the Carnival which ran between Friday June 9th and Tuesday June 27th and featuring such bands as the Zulus, Tommy Fee and the Cajun Sound and Dermot Henry and the Virginians.

The Ulster Herald preview of the summer extravaganza was in no doubt about the importance of the Red Knights in its Golden Jubilee season.

"Although fifty years in existence, the Red Knights are facing the future with an enthusiasm and drive only imagined in newly formed clubs and unequalled throughout Tyrone at the moment. Indeed, in many circles the Red Knights are being regarded as the club of the future - both on the playing fields and in its provision of amenities and activities for the community.

"Thus parallel with the current new image being created by the club teams, an impressive new sports complex is under construction on one of the finest sites in the county. Ideally placed in pleasant rural setting, convenient to the villages of Beragh and Sixmilecross, plans are being made to provide a community park with riverside walks, resting places and picnic areas, in addition to the sporting facilities already on the drawing-boards."

Cuchullain figured prominently with the two most frequent entries being based on the killing of the hound of Cullain and the death of Cuchullain. Indeed, the winning entry by Herbert O'Kane from Envaugh PS in Drumquin was an exciting modern interpretation of a battle scene

County Activities - other achievements

Photographs of long haired young players lining out at Croke Park are among the lasting images from a decade that saw Tyrone invariably

"

Captained by Frank McGuigan, Tyrone also won the Ulster Senior title for the first time since the breakthrough years of 1956 and 1957. And, both he and Colm McAleer were in the U-21 team that completed the treble of provincial triumphs by capturing the U-21 title

"

struggle at senior level. It had been almost twenty years since the county had won an Ulster title and the drought showed no signs of ending in the early part of the seventies. The later years were also notable for the struggles of the county in the National League and Ulster Championship.

But there were high points, not least the brief period of optimism generated in 1972-1974 and the dominance of the Minor teams throughout the decade. The county won Ulster Minor titles in 1972, 1973, 1975, 1976 and 1978 and many of the teams included players from the Red Knights.

Foremost among them was Colm McAleer. He was centre half back and a key player on the Minor side that reached the All-Ireland Final in 1972 - a panel that also included Pete Owens - and he was again prominent when Tyrone came through again the following year.

His performance at the centre of defence made an important contribution as Tyrone captured the Thomas Markham Cup for the first time since 1947. They defeated Kildare in the All-Ireland Final to put the seal on a famous year in the inter-county ranks.

Captained by Frank McGuigan, Tyrone also won the Ulster Senior title for the first time since the breakthrough years of 1956 and 1957. And, both he and Colm McAleer were in the U-21 team that completed the treble of provincial triumphs by capturing the U-21 title. Alongside them in the panel was another Beragh player, Vincent McMackin.

Pat McCartan was involved with the Minor team as a selector with Art McRory and Donal Donnelly. Colm McAleer's rise through the ranks continued when he captained the Omagh CBS team to win the McRory Cup title for the first time in 1974.

Pat McCartan receives a specially engraved clock to mark his term as Tyrone Chairman. He is pictured with Jimmy Treacey, Louis and Mrs McNamee and Jack Woods

Later that summer, he was selected at half back in the Tyrone senior side which lost its Ulster crown to Donegal. He gained some consolation by once again representing the county U-21s as they defended their title.

The middle of the decade was also marked by the ongoing success of the Tyrone Vocational Schools team. Tommy McGarvey represented them in the 1974 All-Ireland Final and he was joined in the team by his cousin Brian at full-forward in the side which lost the 1975 Final to Wicklow.

The level of All-Ireland success enjoyed by the Minors didn't reach the heights of 1973 again in the decade. However, Malachy Donnelly was in the team which captured the 1976 Ulster title and lost to Cork in the All-Ireland Semi-Final while Hugh McNamee was corner back in the team which progressed to the 1979 Ulster Final where they lost to Down.

Alan and Eamon Rodgers pictured with the Thomas Markham Cup won by the Tyrone Minor team including Beragh's Colm McAleer in 1973

Other events

Police searches at houses in Beragh, Carrickmore and Dungannon during August 1971 highlighted the heightened tension in the north at the time. The 'Troubles' were taking hold and the people of the Beragh area were not to be left untouched.

The Civil Rights campaign at the end of the sixties had been marked by a number of local events. One of the speakers at a demonstration organised by the Beragh-Carrickmore CRA in May 1970 was the newly elected Mid-Ulster MP, Bernadette Devlin. Others included Dr Conor Cruise O'Brien and Mid-Tyrone's Independent Stormont MP, Thomas Gormley.

Committee Chairman, Pat John Rafferty, said that there were many things wrong west of the Bann, including the unfair allocation of housing, discrimination in employment and the actions of corrupt councillors who he said did things to suit their own 'whims and fancies.'

Mr Gormley said the main problem with Omagh Council was their unfair allocation of jobs, while Miss Devlin said it was time for the people to put their feet down and campaign for their rights.

Reform of the housing allocation system was an important issue and in August the CRA said that the allocation of houses at Cooley, Beragh, would be a test case. Twelve houses were to be let and the committee said

Red Knights players who took part in a sponsored run for club funds in the late 1970s

that how the houses were allocated would indicate if the desire for reforms was sincere.

The introduction of internment in 1971 was to prove a critical event. Among those lifted was Paddy Joe McClean, who was taken at 4am, just after returning from sitting up with his mother in law, Mrs Hackett, who had died late on the Monday evening. It was to be some time before news of where he had been taken reached the family home at Main Street, Beragh.

Mrs McClean told the Ulster Herald of her agonising wait for news that her husband had been badly beaten and was in the hospital wing of Crumlin Road prison. She also told the Ulster Herald of the repeated refusal of security authorities or the Ministry to give her any news.

Nora Connolly-O'Brien attended a function in St Mary's Hall to welcome Mr McClean home in May 1972. Later that year the Corner Bar was the target for the first of a number of bomb attacks. The premises were owned by Paddy Montague at the time and the village was sealed off for several hours.

The start of 1973 was marked by a rocket attack on the RUC Station in Beragh, which missed and instead hit the premises of Josie Owens.

Later in the decade there was widespread shock when Jimmy McKee of Kirk Crescent was shot dead while driving a school-bus at Creggan

Crossroads in 1978. He was 61 years of age and was delivering school meals when he was targeted.

Life, of course, had to go on and the development of the community continued throughout the seventies in what was overall a fairly lively period. Fr McOscar left the parish in 1973 and presentations were made to him at a function in the Hall in December of that year.

Mrs A Donnelly, B Daly, Mrs C Devlin and John McCullagh received Fifty Year Pioneer Pins in March 1974 and that year also saw the opening of Beragh Credit Union. Applications for membership were being encouraged and the new President was Jack McCann, with Liam Magee as Vice-President, Paddy Bogan as Treasurer and Jack Woods and Pat McSorley as Secretaries. Shares of £12,000 were raised in the first year and a working profit of £163 recorded.

A new management committee was appointed to control the six schools in the parish. Fr James Carroll arrived as curate in the early part of 1974 and in the years which followed was to make a considerable impact on several fronts.

One of the first big events of his time was the holding of a Mass at Clogherney Mass Rock. Many people walked to the special ceremony, which held particular significance for Mrs Mary Ann Donnelly who had a life-long wish to have Mass celebrated on her farm. She said she remembered Fr Rodgers marking out the spot where the Mass Rock was situated.

Fr Carroll was also involved in great efforts to improve the quality of life for young people locally. The Beragh Youth Club was formed in October 1974 in St Mary's Hall and that year saw the first of many discos. Admission was 25p and it provided a last chance to hear DJ Franklin Lee, a popular disc-jockey of the time. Members held a 24 hour fast and football as well as a fashion show in the autumn of that year.

In May 1976 the Fr Carroll Perpetual Trophy for Club Member of the Year was presented to Anthony Lyttle and prizes were also presented to the draughts, chess and football winners.

There was also the establishment of the new cross-community magazine called 'Link.' It carried weekly announcements concerning activities in the area, with news items and photographs recording local events. Incidentally, the Link name and logo was created by Beragh school pupil, Gerry Boyle.

The Ulster Herald reported that one of the most fascinating features introduced by Link was the 'photo of the week.' It went on to report that

> Mr Gormley said the main problem with Omagh Council was their unfair allocation of jobs, while Miss Devlin said it was time for the people to put their feet down and campaign for their rights

281

Secretary, Frank Rodgers and Vice-Chairman, Mick McCartan make the draw for All-Ireland tickets outside the chapel in 1977

the people behind Link were Fr Carroll as Editor and his two regular assistants, Pat McSorley and Mick Grimes.

Facilities for winter activity were provided in St Mary's Hall, and the completion of a Children's Play Area in Beragh in April 1976 was welcomed. It cost £29,000 and included swings, climbing frames, sandpits with chutes, slides, see-saws, tyre walls, a kick-about area and seats, picnic tables and areas for parental supervision.

The Parish Sports in 1978 were held in fine weather conditions. Lisa Lyttle, Majella Owens, Raymond McClean, Celine Grimes, Kevin McMahon and Catherine McQuillan were among those in the Bonny Baby competition, Sinead Gorman and Tracy Grimes were top in the Most Topical section of the Fancy Dress, while Mr and Mrs Tommy Fitzmaurice won the Granny and Grandad Waltzing event. There was also Tug O'War, Irish Dancing, a sack race, throwing the wellington and a penalty kick competition.

The Parish Tug O' War was won by the team representing Brackey which comprised: John McGlinn, Barney Cunningham, Barney Owens, Brendan McNally, Pat Bonner, Brendan Gallagher, Hughie McCrystal and Noel Maguire.

At the end of the decade the visit of Pope John Paul II to Ireland generated a lot of excitement and interest. Two coach loads young people from the parish left the Chapel for the Youth Mass in Galway. The group stayed in Tuam on the Saturday night and one young pilgrim wrote in Link of the excitement of the visit and the night before.

"Despite the cramped limbs and and tired eyes, sleep was entirely out of the question. This was a night for joy and happiness and we wanted to enjoy it as best we could. Some chatted with their friends, others joined in some rousing ballads, while another group played some arduous games with cards. The helpers became somewhat exasperated when they eventually did doze off only to be disturbed minutes later by the Gardai calling to check an electrical fault in the hall. It certainly wasn't their night!"

The matter of house building as always caused concern and in 1978 the people of Sixmilecross claimed that the village could die if new homes were not built. It was a fear echoed in Beragh and Seskinore as well.

Changes to the educational structures in the parish during the decade resulted in the closure of the old schools at Aughnaglea, Beragh, and Cloughfin and the opening of St Oliver Plunkett's.

Archisbishop O'Fiaich, blessed the new St Oliver Plunkett's School on June 4 1979 in the presence of teachers, pupils and hundreds of parishioners. Five teachers were appointed and there was an initial enrolment of 130.

A Mass was celebrated to mark the occasion at which the Liturgy of the Word was read by Mick Keenan and Martin Kerr and the Responsorial Psalm by Frances Conroy. Representatives of local voluntary community groups led the Prayers of the Faithful while the Offertory Gifts were borne to the Altar by Sally McNamee and Geraldine Conroy.

The setting up of the Credit Union provided another new dimension and it got a permanent home in October 1979 with the opening of premises at Main Street, Beragh. Margaret J Mullin unveiled the commemorative plaque and among those in attendance was the President of the Irish League of Credit Unions, John Sunderland.

> In May 1976 the Fr Carroll Perpetual Trophy for Club Member of the Year was presented to Anthony Lyttle and prizes were also presented to the draughts, chess and football winners

Conclusion

The close of the 1970s signalled the end of one era and the beginning of another for the Beragh GAA Club. Achievements on the playing field, efforts in the promotion of Irish culture through Scor and Scor Na Og and the development of facilities marked the Red Knights as a club going forward from a sound base.

But there was also cause to reflect during the decade as three of those involved since the earliest days of the Association in the parish passed

The Beragh team which blazed a trail during 1972 and 1973. This was the side that defeated Killyclogher to win the McElduff Cup

away. Long-time Treasurer, WJ Conway, died in 1972, former player and official James McMahon in 1974 and Paddy McCrumlish, Brackey's 'Father of the GAA' in 1976. They were typical of the many who had contributed to the development of a vibrant GAA club which was confidently entering its eighth decade under the Red Knights banner.

The new teachers for St Oliver Plunkett's Primary School, opened in 1978 were Jack Woods and Hugh Ward (Principal) at back pictured with colleagues Claire Rodgers, Vera McCann and Phyllis McAleer

The introduction of Reserve football was a new innovation in the 1970s. This was the Beragh Reserve team for 1979 with the team manager, Eugene Bogan

Chapter Ten
1980 - 1990
Good Work Showing Results

Chapter Eight
1980 - 1990

SOME encouraging highs mixed with disappointing lows perhaps best sums up an eighties decade of considerable achievement on a range of fronts for the Beragh Red Knights Club. Each of these contributed to ensuring that every aspect of GAA activity was catered for, something which was reflected upon with pride even though there was no resting on the laurels of progress.

On the footballing front the Junior successes of 1981 and 1988 provided the prelude to a sustained push for promotion to Senior ranks. A significant breakthrough came with the capturing of the Tyrone Juvenile title in 1985, while the involvement in hurling, camogie handball and cultural activities, as well as the winning of numerous awards and the recognition for several members on an individual basis, gives an indication of just what a vibrant unit the Red Knights was throughout the 1980s.

Hugh McNamee about to score the goal which so nearly clinched promotion to Senior ranks for the Red Knights in 1983

All this progress also came at a time when the GAA in Tyrone was also confidently embracing the modern era. Centenary Year celebrations in 1984, the reaching of the All-Ireland Senior Final for the first time in 1986 and the winning of several Ulster titles gave a new lease of life which was certainly very evident in the Beragh parish and specifically around its GAA home, the developing St Mary's Park.

League Football 1980-1989

It is a fact of life on the gaelic football scene that the success or failure of the club's main adult team is often seen as the yardstick by which every other activity is measured. And, in the 1980s, the mixed fortunes enjoyed by Beragh saw them rebound dramatically from the brink of senior football to the lower reaches of the Junior ranks more than once.

Confidence was justifiably high entering that first season

of the decade, especially considering how close the Red Knights had come to winning a place in Division One at the end of 1979. A 0-7 to 0-5 win over Edendork in the first match of the season set them on the right road, before things took a demoralising backward step. The slide began with a 2-6 to 0-9 loss to Brackaville at the end of March. A month later Beragh had just two points from four games and a series of defeats did little to improve morale. In September only Galbally and Pomeroy were lower in Division Two, Beragh entered a play-off with promotion-chasing Castlederg from the Junior grade and a comprehensive 2-7 to 2-1 defeat tells its own story.

The Beragh team of 1983 pictured prior to their decisive League tie against Aghyaran

The performances of Tommy McGarvey, Hugh McNamee, Colm McAleer and Malachy Donnelly were among the bright spots on a dismal day that condemned the Red Knights to Division Three. But the presence of players with inter-county experience in the previous decade indicated the potential of the team and the determination to quickly bounce back. This was duly achieved, Beragh went top of the table by the beginning of April and never really looked back. While Pomeroy overtook them at one stage, the confident Red Knights had two games in hand and were back on top at the end of August with 22 points from eleven games. They only lost one game in the whole league season and clinched the title by virtue of a walk-over against Strabane on September 13.

The Intermediate Division beckoned again in 1982 when, under team managers Mickey Heaney and Kevin Maguire, Beragh soon moved up the table. They were second in early April and remained there despite a 3-7 to 2-5 defeat by Dungannon at the end of the month. One notable result was a 2-8 to 1-4 win over Coalisland and, although they slipped back mid-season, the lost ground was comfortably regained. Everything came down to a three way play-off with Clonoe and Edendork. Beragh were unable to repeat a 3-4 to 1-7 earlier victory over the O'Rahilly's and lost by 0-5 to 0-4 in the semi-final before suffering a 2-11 to 1-4 defeat at the hands of Edendork.

Some believed that Beragh's run in 1982 deserved better and that the confidence and experience gained would reap the rewards the following year. Suffice to say that the feeling of disappointment was far more acute after that 1983 season. "It was with our Intermediate and Reserve teams

It is a fact of life on the gaelic football scene that the success or failure of the club's main adult team is often seen as the yardstick by which every other activity is measured

Martin Grimes and Pat Donnelly displaying the type of tenacious defending which was a characteristic of their performances during the early 1980s

that we had our greatest successes and greatest disappointments in the past season," remarked Frank Rodgers in his Secretary's report for 1983.

Once again, though, those great disappointments saw Beragh pipped at the post. They were joint top with Brackaville on nine points from five games entering June, they dropped back a bit by July before going top within weeks with 17 points and two games in hand. Affairs were now heating up at the top of the table and a 1-4 to 0-3 win over Killyman in September, put Beragh joint second with Cookstown on 21 points, just behind Edendork on 22.

"We have three matches to win now and every player is prepared to give everything in a bid to win them," remarked team mentor, Fr McParland. "I know too well what the disappointment is like so we have to make it this year," added Mickey Heaney. They were talking ahead of the Clonoe game which Beragh lost by 2-11 to 0-12, although the title was still within reach and would come down to the home match against Aghyaran.

A goal from Hugh McNamee just before half-time boosted them and they were on the verge of victory with time up and league chairman, Tony McKenna getting ready to present the trophy. Out on the field, though, referee John Hackett, added three minutes extra time, culminating in a last gasp equaliser from Ciaran McGarvey which earned the St Davog's a draw and denied a deflated Beragh the title.

Defeat in the subsequent play-offs was perhaps inevitable and resulted in a loss to Edendork in Carrickmore at the end of November. This ensured that the Red Knights would remain in the Intermediate grade for 1984.

After the exertions of the previous three years, the next three would see Beragh on a downward spiral which began in Centenary Year. While a place in Division Two was retained, they finished well down the table in eleventh place in 1984.

Two wins at the beginning of 1985 suggested that things were getting back on track. Owen Roes and Glenelly were both defeated before their poor form was heralded by a derby 1-7 to 0-7 loss at the hands of Ballygawley. From then on it was a disastrous run culminating in relegation back to Junior ranks and

> It is a fact of life on the gaelic football scene that the success or failure of the club's main adult team is often seen as the yardstick by which every other activity is measured

Tommy McGarvey, Club Chairman and experienced player of the 1980s

an overall playing record of just seven wins from 25 games during a season which finally marked the end of a competitive Intermediate spell.

That first season since 1981 back in Division Three showed just how much Beragh had fallen. As early as June they were mid-table with ten points and the situation improved little by the end of the season when they were still mid-table, with nineteen points from a programme of seventeen matches.

> New structures within the club combined with the arrival of a host of new young players to make 1987 a better year.

New structures within the club combined with the arrival of a host of new young players to make 1987 a better year. Many of those who had been on the championship-winning 1985 Juvenile team were now making their mark at adult level. The result was that Beragh's challenge for promotion improved and they finished in third place behind the winners, Derrytresk and Newtownstewart.

A look through the 1988 team indicates how well the blend of youth and experience worked. The presence of players such as Malachy Donnelly, Pete Owens, Hugh McNamee and Tommy McGarvey provided the backbone to a young and vibrant team. attendance at training regularly exceeded 45 and the result was a sustained challenge in Division Three. At the halfway point Beragh and their great rivals from that season, Brackaville, were out in front on twelve points. Further wins saw Beragh go clear in June with twenty points from eleven games and just one defeat and the situation remained in focus in August when four points separated them from Drumquin even though the Wolfe Tones had two games in hand.

Mickey Heaney, Colm McAleer, Paddy Grimes and Kevin Maguire put the finishing touches to preparations for the 1981 Junior Final

Eventually the race for the title went right to the wire. Beragh defeated Drumquin by 1-7 to 0-7, to go two ahead, followed this up with an important 2-6 to 0-5 away win over Brackaville. Then, they met Drumquin in a direct play-off for the Division Three title.

That game was played in Trillick on November 13 and began badly when Beragh went 1-1 to no score behind. But a goal from Mickey McCann and points from Patsy Farley, Adrian Donnelly, Gerry Ward, Eamon Rodgers and Mickey McCann put them ahead at the break.

The 1989 team which lost in the promotion play-off.

They led by 1-5 to 1-1 entering the final quarter and held on to complete the double on a score of 1-5 to 1-3. The team was: Pete Owens, Stephen Farley, Brian McGarvey, Aidan Grimes, Sean Donnelly, Paul Donnelly, Eamon Hackett, Malachy Donnelly, Sean Grimes, Eamon Rodgers, Hugh McNamee, Patsy Farley, Adrian Donnelly, Gerry Ward, Mickey McCann.

Sean Owens and Brendan Gallagher keeping a close eye on proceedings in a match at St Mary's Park

Subs – Fergal Grimes for E Hackett, Barry McCartan for M McCann. Panelists – Gerry Owens, Malachy Owens, Joe Franey, Gerry Ward.

Of a panel comprising 48 players in 1988, 21 of them were under 20 and this drive towards introducing more younger members into the adult ranks continued in 1989. There was also a continued focus on player development in terms of dedication to training and skills practice which contributed to a continued progress during the year as Beragh surprised many by making such a strong bid for Intermediate and Division Two honours.

At the mid-way point of the campaign they were top on thirteen points with a game more played than second placed, Moortown. A 2-3 to 1-6 draw with Gortin saw them drop only their second point and by the beginning of June the trend was set with Moortown on top and the Red Knights in second. But the gap was widening and the quest for the title was as good as finished in September when the east Tyrone side led by five points and went on to take the title. Beragh entered the promotion play-off, where a 1-7 to 0-8 defeat by Moy continued their terrible run in play-offs and left them still searching for the big breakthrough.

Championship action 1980-1989

A defeat on a score of 2-6 to 0-4 in the 1980 Intermediate Championship gave an indication of how Beragh's fortunes were declining at the time. However, they bounced back in the Junior grade in 1981 when a first championship final since 1947 was reached.

Double-winners for 1988. At left is the victorious championship final winning panel and at right the team which clinched the League title

Their campaign that season got underway with a 2-4 to 1-6 win over Greencastle and in the Quarter Final they drew 1-8 each with Drumquin at Tattyreagh on May 24. A 0-13 to 0-2 victory was recorded in the replay before Eskra were confidently defeat in the semi-final at Augher. Colm McAleer, Brian McGarvey and Gerry Ward were among the stars in a 1-13 to 2-5 win. The teams were level at half-time and Beragh took a big step towards the final when Louis McNamee goaled entering the final ten minutes. Pat Donnelly, Tommy McGarvey and Finbar Grimes held out as the Red Knights clinched their final place.

O'Neill Park in Dungannon was the venue for the decider against Brocagh, and team managers, Mickey Heaney and Kevin Maguire, were both confident that the win would be secured. "We haven't had things

In training for the 1981 Junior Final are Brian McGarvey, Martin Kerr, Frank Owens, Barney Cunningham, Gerry Maguire and Gerry Ward

easy in any of our matches up to this, so we're not expecting anything easy on Sunday," Mickey Heaney told the Ulster Herald.

His forecast of a tough outing came through as they found the going hard right from the start. Beragh just couldn't get going, Brocagh led comfortably by 1-5 to 0-2 at half-time and it was only in the last quarter that the Red Knights staged a revival. A few switches, including the moving of Tommy McGarvey to the forwards, worked well, Pete Owens registered a point and a penalty goal from Hugh McNamee left the score 1-10 to 1-5. Brian McGarvey added another point and there was only two between them when Aidan McMullan finished a Colm McAleer '45 to the net. However, time ran out for Beragh as the Emmetts held out.

It was the Intermediate Championship and a 2-5 to 0-7 defeat at the hands of Coalisland for Beragh in 1982, but they bounced back a year later. Edendork were defeated on the low scoreline of 0-3 to 0-1 in the Quarter Final at Dungannon May 29th to see Beragh through to their first Intermediate semi-final since 1966.

They looked to be on their way to the final at the expense of Clonoe when taking a four point lead at the start of the second half. Pete Owens' success in curbing Kevin McCabe was crucial as they led 0-4 to 0-3 at half-time. Just after the resumption, a goal from Seamus Collins appeared to set them on the way. But they failed to score again, the sides were level in the 21st minute and Paddy McKee got the winner five minutes from the end.

The team and scorers was: Colm Ward, Martin Grimes, Pete Owens, Paul McGlinn, Pat Donnelly, Mickey Slane, Tommy McGarvey, Colm McAleer, Hugh McNamee, Barry Donnelly, Gerry Ward, Seamus Collins, Finbar Grimes, Brian McGarvey, Mickey McNally. Scorers – Seamus Collins 1-3, Mickey McNally 0-1.

Centenary Year saw a first round defeat by Aughabrack on a score of 2-5 to 2-0 but they got off to a good start with a win over Glenelly in the first round of the 1985 Intermediate Championship. But there was great disappointment when they lost the Quarter Final to Edendork on a score of 2-5 to 1-5. Beragh led by 1-2 to 0-2 at half-time – the goal being scored by Declan Grimes – and Seamus Collins added further scores before they fell away in the closing stages.

A 0-10 to 1-4 defeat once again highlighted Beragh problems when they returned to the Junior Championship in 1986, although things improved a year later when Aghaloo were defeated on a score of 1-9 to 1-4 in the first

Centenary Year saw a first round defeat by Aughabrack on a score of 2-5 to 2-0 and Beragh got off to a good start with a win over Glenelly in the first round of the 1985 Intermediate Championship round Greencastle provided the opposition in the Quarter Final and then won by 1-7 to 1-5 at Omagh.

What had been a decade of mixed fortunes on the championship scene took a dramatic turn for the better during the last two years. The winning of the Junior title in 1988 and then reaching the Intermediate Final in 1989 cast aside the earlier disappointments.

The first outing in 1988 resulted in a 1-4 to 2-1 draw with Dregish, Beragh comfortably won the replay on a score of 2-8 to 0-6 and then defeated Urney on a score of 1-9 to 0-8 in the Quarter Final. This set up a semi-final meeting against Brackaville and the Red Knights progressed to the final thanks to what was described as "a slick performance".

Goals from Tommy McGarvey and Adrian Donnelly helped them to a 2-8 to 0-5 victory and put them into the final against Strabane who had

> Afterwards, the trophy was presented to the winning captain, Hugh McNamee, the game was described as a memorable won for Junior football in Tyrone and the County Chairman, Tony McKenna, praised the dedication of the Red Knights players and officials

Kevin Maguire and Mickey Heaney give a relaxed teamtalk during 1980s training at St Mary's Park

defeated Aghaloo in the second semi-final and were expected to provide tough opposition. And, the pairing lived up to expectations in a fairly high scoring encounter at Carrickmore on Sunday September 11th.

Beragh led early on, but two goals in quick succession brought the game alive. Strabane got the first from a penalty before a long ball into the danger area by Sean Grimes was latched on to by Gerry Ward who made no mistake with a low shot to help leave Beragh 1-5 to 1-2 ahead at the break.

A second goal soon after the resumption saw Eamon Rodgers send a left footed shot to the net. Beragh looked to be on top and on course, but they were again pegged back. With Paul Donnelly and Brian McGarvey doing well in defence and Patsy Farley and Sean Grimes on form at midfield,

Some shooting practice for the 1980s players during training

they seemed set for a comfortable cruise to the final whistle. However, Strabane had other ideas and a goal left them back in touch with time to make their mark. Pete Owens had to be on his toes to save another effort as Beragh held out for a first Junior title since 1947.

Afterwards, the trophy was presented to the winning captain, Hugh McNamee, the game was described as a memorable one for Junior football in Tyrone and the County Chairman, Tony McKenna, praised the dedication of the Red Knights players and officials.

Intermediate Final 1989

Promotion to Intermediate ranks for 1989 could have presented a daunting task for the young Red Knights. However, they showed no signs of nerves when racing up the Division Two League table ahead of an opening championship clash against Aughabrack in May. A 1-11 to 1-5 win was recorded to set up a Quarter Final against Derrytresk.

They led by three points at half-time, but points from Gerry Boyle, Mickey McCann and Barry McCartan helped Beragh back on track. A goal from Barry McCartan put them in front, Derrytresk responded and looked like winners until Patsy Farley popped up with the equalising point on a 1-5 to 0-8 scoreline. Beragh made no mistake in securing a 3-6 to 1-9 win in the replay and really turned things around in the semi-final at Dungannon at the end of July.

They trailed Galbally by 1-6 to 0-3 at half-time and went even further behind at the start of the second half before responding with a fine comeback. A goal from Barry McCartan got them started as a tally of six points in the final quarter, culminating in the winner from Gerry Ward, saw them through narrowly by 1-10 to 1-9.

Beragh were now into their first ever Intermediate Final., with Gortin standing between them and that much sought after place in Senior ranks. And, their dreams of taking the title appeared to be on course when a goal from Seamus Collins helped them into a 1-2 to no score lead.

The Ulster Herald reported that Beragh looked to be the more composed outfit, with Stephen Farley, Brian McGarvey, Shane Fox and Patsy Farley

The Beragh team
which lined out
against Gortin in
the 1989
Intermediate Final
at Pomeroy

on top in defence and Malachy Donnelly and Hugh McNamee dominant at midfield. However, Gortin fought back, they led by 1-4 to 1-3 at half-time and extended it on the resumption.

The tie remained extremely tight as Gerry Ward and Patsy Farley responded for the Red Knights to set things up perfectly for the closing stages. A point from Barry McCartan, after he was set uop by Eamon Rodgers, got them back on track, although missed chances by Malachy Donnelly and Hugh McNamee thwarted efforts to go ahead.

Instead, it was Gortin who came strong at the finish and two late points saw them take the title on the final score of 1-9 to 1-7.

Beragh – Pete Owens, Stephen Farley, Brian McGarvey, Aidan Grimes, Shane Fox, Sean Donnelly, Patsy Farley, Malachy Donnelly, Hugh McNamee, Gerry Boyle, Barry McCartan, Adrian Donnelly, Gerry Ward, Seamus Collins, Mickey McCann.
Subs – Eamon Rodgers for G Boyle.
Scorers – Patsy Farley (0-4), Seamus Collins (1-0), Barry McCartan, Gerry Ward and Mickey McCann (0-1 each).

It was a game that ended the decade on an optimistic note despite the defeat. And, all involved hoped that the experience gained from this first ever Intermediate Final appearance would stand to them as the quest for a place in the top flight continued into the nineties.

Other competitions

Regular action in the Jim Devlin Cup and numerous other competitions, including Tournaments and the Ceannaras and Centenary Cups, provided extra matches for the adult first team during the eighties. Their form in each of these seemed to mirror their fortunes at league and championship level, while the decade also saw the Reserve team hold their own in great fashion in both the Division Two and Division Three Leagues and Championships.

Jim Devlin Cup wins over Augher, then one of the top teams in the county, highlighted the potential within the Red Knight in the earlier part of the eighties. One notable achievement was the reaching of the Jim Devlin Cup Final in 1982 when Omagh St Enda's provided the opposition at Carrickmore.

The County Town side led by 0-4 to 0-2 at half-time and the scores remained tight until the closing stages when Omagh raced ahead to win by 0-10 to 0-5. The Beragh scorers were Hugh McNamee (0-2), Brian McGarvey (0-2) and Gerry Ward (0-1) and the team lined out: Gerry Maguire, Paul McGlinn, Martin Grimes, Martin Kerr, Brian Owens, Mickey Slane, Pat Donnelly, Colm McAleer, Pete Owens, Brian McGarvey, Malachy Owens, Hugh McNamee, Louis McNamee. Sub – Frank Owens for M Owens.

But it was the Reserves who really came into their own during those years. They challenged well for honours in 1980 and picked up the

Centenary Year saw a first round defeat by Aughabrack on a score of 2-5 to 2-0 and Beragh got off to a good start with a win over Glenelly in the first round of the 1985 Intermediate Championship

The Reserves from the early 1980s held their own in Division Two

Injuries to a
number of key
players for the
1984
Intermediate
Championship had
a knock-on
beneficial effect
for the Reserves

Division Three title with plenty to spare in 1981, once again under the management of John McGlinn and Pete Owens. A challenge for the League in 1982 wasn't maintained to the finish and they finished fourth in 1983 under the management of Francie Grimes and Eugene Bogan.

Injuries to a number of key players for the 1984 Intermediate Championship had a knock-on beneficial effect for the Reserves. Gerry Owens and Frank Owens were the joint managers as they blazed a trail. Wins over Killyclogher, Coalisland, Cookstown and Edendork saw them win the championship title, with Anthony Lyttle the team captain.

They retained the title in 1985 when Edendork were again defeated on a score of 1-8 to 2-3 in the final at Donaghmore. The teams were level at half-time and a point by Patsy Farley proved decisive. Afterwards, the Cup was presented to the Beragh captain, Seamus Boyle, who had been married the previous day but postponed his honeymoon to play in the final.

The team was: Brian McGarvey, Aidan Grimes, Martin Grimes, Anthony Lyttle, Malachy Owens, Mickey Rodgers, Finbar Grimes, Colm Ward, Barney Cunningham, Gerry Boyle, Patsy Farley, Seamus Boyle, Adrian Nixon, Frank Owens, Eamon McClean. Subs – Niall Grimes for F Grimes, Gerry Ward for G Boyle.

Those double triumphs in the Reserve Championship were to be repeated later in the decade as well. In 1987 the team captained by Anto Duffy, defeated Owen Roes in the final, with the skipper expressing the hope for 'more trophies.' He got his wish, too, as Beragh came back the following year to defeat Owen Roes on a score of 1-4 to 0-4, Gerry Owens captaining the team on that occasion.

The winning
Reserve
Championship
team of 1984

Add in successes for the senior team in the Drumragh Tournament in 1982, Killyclogher Tournament in 1988 and the Augher Tournament in 1989 and it's clear that Beragh's teams were certainly heading in the right direction.

Youth Football

Titles won at various grades as well as the ability of teams to compete at the highest level within Tyrone marks the 1980s as probably the club's most successful decade in youth football. While the highlight was obviously the winning of the Juvenile title in 1985 – the first and to date only Top Grade competition won by a team from the club – the overall level of activity also increased dramatically throughout these ten years.

The visits of clubs from other counties provided a major boost to youth football in Beragh during the 1980s. Here members of the Roscommon Gaels mix with the Beragh girls in 1987

A number of major developments aided this progress and the introduction of the Primary League in 1980 was a crucial factor. Teams were fielded from U-14 right through to Minor level and the introduction of an U-12 League in 1982 also marked a significant development. There was also a growing acceptance of the need for regular coaching and the revamping of the club's structures in the middle part of the decade coincided with a big drive towards the promotion of gaelic football among young people.

Some indication of the ability of Beragh's teams to hold their own came in 1980 when the Juveniles defeated Omagh in the West Tyrone Final played at Pomeroy at the end of August. The Red Knights controlled the game from the moment scores from Eamon Hackett, Paul Ward and Mark Colton put them ahead. They were 2-3 to 0-4 in front at half-time and a late second half goal from Fergal Grimes clinched a 3-6 to 0-5 win.

This victory saw them through to the all-county final against Dungannon. But the Clarkes proved far too strong and the match was marred by fighting in the second half which prompted a sharp rebuke from the Beragh club. In a letter sent subsequently to the County Secretary, the club apologised for the behaviour of its players described their actions as disgraceful and pledged to carry out a full internal inquiry. Things eventually settled and at the end of the year members preferred to concentrate on the achievement of reaching the final rather than the incidents which spoiled the match.

Players who took part in the Parish Minor League at the beginning of the decade

The players involved in that team were:Martin Kelly, Jerome McCann, Conor Kerr, Declan Grimes, Seamus McClean, Mickey McNally, Enda McClean, Seamus Collins, Paul Ward, Declan Maguire, Mark Colton, Eamon McClean, Fergal Grimes, Eamon Hackett, Colin McMackin. Subs – Kieran O'Neill, Dermot McAleer, Timothy Donnelly, Gerard Donnelly, Paddy Owens.

A total of forty games were played by club youth teams that year and in 1981 the U-16s again made their mark by reaching the West Tyrone Final. The number of matches increased again in 1982 to 45 and the among the highlights in 1983 was the first youth trip when a party of forty from Skyrne in County Meath spent a weekend in the parish.

The trip was organised through Beragh native, John McSorley, and followed what was to become a familiar pattern for the young players of the time. After arriving on the Saturday, games took place between the respective U-12 and U-14 teams, the visitors were hosted by families throughout the parish, a disco was held and that particular trip concluded with an excursion to Omagh Leisure Centre before departure on Sunday afternoon.

A record 52 matches took place involving teams in 1984 when the U-12s

One of the teams which took part in the popular Parish Minor League which was held each winter and pre-season

won their League section and the U-14s and Minors reached the County Quarter Finals. And, the U-12s and U-14s made the return trip to Skyrne in August, attended the All-Ireland Semi-Final between Kerry and Galway at Croke Park the following day. Later in the year they visited St Paul's in Lurgan, the Chairman of which was ex-Beragh man, Philip Mellon.

The year 1985 was especially busy. Trips were undertaken to Enniskillen, Lurgan, Roscommon, Belfast, Termonfeckin, Dublin and Ballinascreen and the growing ability of teams was highlighted by the success of the Juveniles in winning that year's Tyrone Championship title. Carrickmacross, Cavan, Monaghan, Newtownbutler, Kells Donagh and Croke Park were the venues for a series of one-day and weekend trips in 1986. Roscommon Town was added to the list of venues for visits in 1987 as the policy continued to provide worthwhile social and games benefits for players and officials.

All of this continued to have an impact on the club's fortunes. The final of the Juvenile Supplementary League was reached in 1985, the Minors won the West Tyrone League and progressed to the championship semi-final in 1986, the U-14s were narrowly defeated in the Championship semi-final in 1987 and the Juveniles won their League section in 1988 and progressed to the County Semi-Final.

By 1988 Beragh's youth teams were playing around 68 matches a year, although concerns about the drop-out after U-16 and Minor remained. In addition, a programme of recruitment, coaching, training and the development of the young players was yielding the desired dividends, leading the Secretary, Frank Rodgers, to reflect on 1986 in the following terms.

"It has now reached the stage where practically every boy in the parish is being involved in gaelic football and that state of affairs has to be good. The work put in by the players and by those in charge was reflected in the performances of all our under-age teams in the new Grade A competitions. All of them held their own against the stronger teams with whom we just couldn't compete a few years ago."

> The year 1985 was especially busy. Trips were undertaken to Enniskillen, Lurgan, Roscommon, Belfast, Termonfeckin, Dublin and Ballinascreen and the growing ability of teams was highlighted by the success of the Juveniles

Tops in Tyrone

By then and under the management of Brian Donnelly, Mick Kerr and PJ McClean, the U-16 team had certainly proved the point. It was soon clear that they were on the right track in 1985 when a fine sectional campaign in the league was finished with a 2-4 to 0-7 win over Shamrocks to take the title.

They reached the final in August through an unbeaten run which included wins over Augher, Carrickmore, Clogher, Fintona, Owenkillew, Aghaloo and Fintona and an early goal from Barry McCartan gave them the edge in the League section final.

But it remained tight, points from Eamon Rodgers and Adrian Donnelly brought them level before Paddy Maguire clinched the win with a late goal. However, the tables were turned when the teams met again in the League Final a few weeks later and the Shamrocks emerged comfortable winners by 1-8 to 0-1.

Beragh trailed by 1-5 to 0-0 at half-time and their only point came from team captain, Mickey McCann, following an early spurt on the restart. However, they couldn't sustain this and slumped to an inevitable loss. The team was: Mark McCartan, Brian Walshe, Sean McNamee, Liam McClean, Kieran Owens, Stephen Farley, Kevin McClean, Sean Donnelly, Paddy Maguire, Damien Grimes, Paul Donnelly, Adrian Donnelly, Eamon Rodgers, Barry McCartan, Mickey McCann.

Now was the time
for them to really
produce the goods
and they responded
emphatically

Nevertheless, the real character of the side shone through in the championship which looked to be all over for Beragh when they lost to Shamrocks in the semi-final after initial wins over Castlederg and Owenkillew. But the victory by the Shamrocks in the Quarter Final was subsequently appealed when it was revealed that they had played ineligible players.

The appeal was won by Beragh, who defeated Newtownstewart by 6-13 to 4-2 to progress to meet a fancied Omagh team in the decider at Loughmacrory on September 29th 1985. Each of the 'big town' teams had dominated the Juvenile Championship since its establishment and Beragh's 2-5 to 2-3 win after a thrilling encounter proved to be a breakthrough that was fully capitalised upon by other rural clubs.

Two goals for Omagh in the opening half left the large support from Beragh fearing the worst. They trailed by 2-2 to 0-1 approaching half-time before their challenge was transformed by a Mickey McCann goal with the last kick of the half.

"That reduced the gap to four points and when Paul Donnelly opened the second half scoring with a point in the first minute the Red Knights were back in business," the Ulster Herald report of the game stated. With Paddy Maguire and Sean Donnelly taking a grip at midfield, a smashing goal from Eamon Rodgers left just the minimum between them.

Now was the time for them to really produce the goods and they responded emphatically. Paddy Maguire equalised and Eamon Rodgers put them in front for the first time on a score of 2-4 to 2-3. Omagh searched for a way, back, but the defending of Kieran Owens, Stephen Farley, Sean McNamee, Brian Walshe and Kevin and Liam McClean kept them at bay. Mark McCartan also pulled off a number of important saves as Mickey McCann pointed in the last minute to reward the earlier efforts of Adrian Donnelly, Barry McCartan and Damien Grimes.

The team was: Mark McCartan, Brian Walshe, Sean McNamee, Liam McClean, Kieran Owens, Stephen Farley, Kevin McClean, Sean Donnelly, Paddy Maguire, Damien Grimes, Paul Donnelly, Adrian Donnelly, Eamon Rodgers, Barry McCartan, Mickey McCann(captain).
Scorers - `Mickey McCann (1-2), Eamon Rodgers (1-1), Paul Donnelly, Paddy Maguire (0-1 each.)
Other panel members – Eugene McCrystal, Shane Kelly, Kevin Grimes, Sean McCrory, Barry Grimes, Sean Montague, Shane Fox, Joe McClean, Stephen Donnelly.

And 'Link' the following week was in no doubt about the sense of satisfaction after a match which the Chairman of the Youth Board, Paddy Devlin, described as being the best Youth Final of 1985.

"It was great to see so many followers there on Sunday night. In fact, all areas of the parish were represented on the terraces just as they were represented on the team. It was fitting that that should be the case on a unique occasion like Sunday.

"But of course the heroes of the night were the young players and their trainers, Brian Donnelly, Mick Kerr and PJ McClean. Their months of dedicated work bore fruit and they won the title with style. It wasn't easy by any means, but as the match wore on, the knowhow of the Beragh boys become more and more obvious."

It was great to see so many followers there on Sunday night. In fact, all areas of the parish were represented on the terraces just as they were represented on the team. It was fitting that that should be the case on a unique occasion like Sunday

303

A cavalcade of vehicles headed by the team bus passed through the villages of Sixmilecross and Beragh and highlighted the joy of all concerned while a specially organised presentation night and video showing of the match rounded off the year perfectly.

Defeated at the final hurdle

Much was expected of the 1988 Minors as the team included many players from that successful 1985 Juvenile team. The team was managed by Pat McCartan and Brian Donnelly and proved its worth by reaching both the championship semi-final and the league final.

In 1988 the Beragh Minors, pictured left, reached the League Final where they lost to Castlederg. This was the panel pictured prior to the Championship Semi-Final, also against Castlederg

In the Championship they defeated Omagh by 0-11 to 1-5 in the first round and then easily accounted for Urney in the next game on a score of 4-12 to 1-3. However, their bid to reach the final was thwarted by the team of the year, Castlederg, at Carrickmore. Played before a large attendance, Castlederg won by 2-9 to 2-5, with Beragh missing a number of chances near the end to get back into the game.

However, the side was challenging strongly and got a chance to avenge that loss in the league final. The game marked the culmination of a league campaign which had seen them come second to Carrickmore in their section. They then defeated Coalisland by 4-9 to 3-6 in the Quarter Final and Carrickmore by 2-4 to 0-9 in the semi-final after withstanding great late pressure from opponents who contained six members of that year's Tyrone Ulster title-winning team.

Drumquin was the venue for the decider which saw Castlederg complete the double on a score of 2-7 to 0-7. Beragh never really got going in the game, they trailed at half-time and struggled to find their form in the second half as the St Eugene's came strong at the finish.

Some of the same players were on board for the Juveniles the following year, 1989, when they reached the League Final. Beragh comfortably topped their section in the competition, a 4-15 to 0-3 victory over Carrickmore being among the highlights and they went on to defeat Owen Roes in the Quarter Final.

A 4-5 to 0-5 win was recorded over Cappagh, who had earlier defeated them in the championship, and they went full of hope to the final against Dungannon in Galbally at the end of November. On this occasion, though, they were well defeated on a score of 3-7 to 0-5.

The team was: Paul Kelly, Damien Donnelly, Stephen Mullan, Damien Given, Barry McGuinness, Brendan Barrett, Terry McKenna, Sean Owens, Niall Farley, Darren Baxter, Mike Cathcart, Colm McClean, Alan Rodgers, Liam Kelly, Stephen Owens.
Subs – Gerard Conroy, Michael Montague, Dominic Donnelly, Seamus McCrory, Colin Grimes, Colm McCann, Eamon McHugh, Stephen Mullin, Gerard Conroy.

One of the most innovative developments of the late seventies and early eighties was the introduction of the Primary League, spearheaded by the Club Secretary Frank Rodgers

Primary League

One of the most innovative developments of the late seventies and early eighties was the introduction of the Primary League. Spearheaded by the club Secretary, Frank Rodgers, in conjunction with the three schools of the parish, the event grew steadily from its small beginnings and eventually included a number of teams from neighbouring areas.

Recarson, Eskra and Garvaghey were among the first 'outsiders' to enter and the competition assumed a familiar format. A Shield and individual trophies were awarded to the winning team after a busy schedule of matches.

In 1982 a total of twenty games were played over the course of several weeks and the winners were Recarson who defeated Roscavey in the final. Credit was given to the teachers, pupils, referees and club officials who contributed to the success and it was a list that included the three Principals of the parish schools – Paddy Bogan, Hugh Ward and Vincent McCullagh and the usual referee, Eamon Mullin. St Oliver Plunkett's in Beragh fielded two teams and won the competition for the first time in

1984, while the trophy for the larger schools was renamed the Skryne Trophy in 1985.

Of course, the event culminated what was planned to be an active coaching structure within the schools. The provision of coaches in the parish schools took place for the first time in the early eighties, although by 1986 there was a realisation that much more needed to be done. While the introduction of various competitions on a county-wide basis for Primary Schools provided additional matches, the Primary League remained a popular attraction.

This can be clearly seen from the lineup for the ninth School's League in 1989. It followed the usual format with games at two levels and the emphasis, according to the Ulster Herald, being on the provision of fun, enjoyment and entertainment. All games were played on the shortened pitches and the teams taking part were Mountfield, Garvaghy, Beragh A and Beragh B, Drumduff, Loughmacrory, Carrickmore and Carrickmore B, Fintona, Ballygawley, Recarson, Eskra, Garvallagh and Altamuskin.

Camogie and Hurling

Efforts to promote camogie received a great boost with the reformation of the team in the late seventies. This prompted a renewed drive which helped to make the eighties a very successful time for the game locally with teams participating at U-14, Minor and Senior level.

Many of the players who fielded on the team which reached the Tyrone Minor Final in 1979 continued to participate. This ensured that Beragh fielded regularly in league and championship competitions, providing a chance for as many girls as possible to learn the skills of the sport.

A wedding day guard of honour for Briege McNamee from her Beragh Camogie teammates

In 1980 the various teams enjoyed a busy year which saw the Minors narrowly miss out on a county title. At inter-county level, Kevin Grimes, managed the Tyrone team which reached the All-Ireland Junior Final and the following season, Rosaleen McCann, Deidre Slane and Kathleen McNally were all part of the Tyrone Minor team.

Jacqueline O'Neill gained selection on the county senior side for a number of seasons and it is interesting to note the names of the players who were taking part during those years in the early eighties.

Minors – Elaine Grimes, Monica Donnelly, Nuala Franey, Ann McAleer, Maura McClean, Eilish McClean, Elaine McCann, Avril Grimes, Ann O'Neill, Mairead Donnelly, Imelda McCann, Pauline McCann, Helen Kerr and Ann McCartan.

Seniors – Bernie McMahon, Gabrielle McAleer, Deidre Franey, Bridget McElhinney, Margaret McCartan, Aggie Rodgers, Lizzie Given, Mairead McClean, Rosaleen McCann, Briege McCartan, Avril Grimes, Anne Slane, Patricia Owens, Sheila Owens, Dympna McMenamin,

Lizzie Given receives the Camogie Tournament trophy from Tommy McGarvey in 1982

Dolores Slane, Jacqueline O'Neill, Kathleen McNally, Sharon Maguire, Rose McNamee, Caroline McCrystal, Siobhan McCrystal, Imelda McCann.

Sometimes, though, the going was tough and in June 1983 a game against Ballygawley was lost because of the unavailability of a number of senior players. But, while a number of wins for the Minors proved encouraging, the failure of players to turn up was clearly frustrating.

Minor players for 1984 included Ann Colton, Denise McCann, Orla McClean, Angela Cathcart, Martina McDonald, Roisin McCann, Pauline McCann, Mairead Donnelly, Michelle Heaney, Dawn Heaney, Tara Heaney, Elaine Grimes, Shelly Grimes and Karina Grimes, Oonagh

The 1989 Beragh Senior Camogie team, one of the last to represent the club at that time

The 1982 Beragh
Senior Camogie
team, pictured
prior to that year's
Tournament Final

McCann. While the Seniors lost to Ballygawley in the Intermediate semi-final, the Minors went one better by defeating Derrylaughan at the penultimate stage and going on to meet Eglish in the final. However, their hopes of upsetting the odds were dashed as Tyrone's top team defeated them narrowly.

Players from both Beragh - and Carrickmore and Eskra - who had no team at the time - represented the club in 1985. They had some success in the championship, defeating Pomeroy in the first round before going on to contest the final at Donaghmore where they lost to Eglish.

Of course, the activities of the club were not just confined to the playing of games. Members also actively promoted a range of other events, including fundraising discos, participating in events run by the wider GAA club and each year organising the Camogie Tournament.

It was with a good sense of optimism that they attended the 1986 Convention in the Youth Centre at which the hope for further progress was expressed. Officers elected were Chairperson – Rose McNamee, Secretaries – Briege McCartan and Ann Meegan, Treasurer – Gabrielle McAleer and PRO – Marion McAleer. Kevin Grimes was appointed manager for the coming year, Rose McNamee was delegated to contact the GAA club to obtain a night for training and it was decided to enter teams in the Division Two League, Intermediate Championship and All-County League.

Victory in the Division Two League saw them win promotion for 1987, a special function was held for the presentations and the new challenge of facing into the Senior League and Championship was being relished.

The Minor team in 1986 included: Orla McClean, Rose McNamee, Gabrielle McAleer, Aggie Rodgers, Briege McCartan, Lizzie Given, Avril Grimes, Ann McCartan, Elaine Grimes, Dawn Heaney, Claire McGuinness, Angela Cathcart, Lorraine Hall and Denise McCann.

There was further progress in 1988 when the U-14s, who had been introduced just the previous year, reached the County Final where they lost narrowly to Eglish. The players involved were Mary Farley, Shauna

McGuinness, Eilish Kelly, Mairead Nixon, Oonagh Maguire, Marie Owens, Madeline McCann, Helen Rodgers, Regina Donnelly, Ciara Donnelly, Roisin Gallagher, Roisin Donnelly, Catherine McGlinn and Karen Mullin.

Officials for 1987 were Hugh Colton (Chairman) and Avril Grimes (Secretary) and others involved at an organisational level at the time were Aggie Rodgers, Lizzie Given, Briege McCartan and Mary Donnelly.

Efforts to start a hurling team at underage level had been ongoing since the beginning of the decade without success. But the attempts eventually got off the ground for the 1983 season when the decision was taken to enter an U-14 side. With the help of coaches from Carrickmore, Omagh and Killyclogher, players got a first taste of both the skills of the game and match action.

One of the first games came against Omagh at Beragh on April 30th when goals from Sean Montague and Anthony Hamilton came in a 4-2 to 2-0 defeat. Hurleys were put on sale for £4, coaching was organised each week, a sponsored run took place and by the end of the season Beragh were listed as being in joint third place on the U-14 table behind Omagh and Carrickmore.

By then the numbers participating were beginning to grow and in the GAA Centenary Year the evidence of further progress was highlighted when they defeated Killyclogher to go through to the Feile Na nGael semi-final. Stephen Farley and Eamon Rodgers competed in the Poc Fada

> It was with a good sense of optimism that they attended the 1986 Convention in the Youth Centre at which the hope for further progress was expressed

The U-14 Camogie team which reached the County Final in 1989

and the summer coaching sessions at St Mary's Park were also well attended during July and August.

Under the guidance of Secretary, Frank Rodgers, hurling officer, Peter Grimes, and the players themselves, a total of ten matches were played in 1984. Five players, Stephen Farley, Eamon Rodgers, Sean Montague, Paul McClean and Barry Grimes, attended the Tyrone Training course and the growing confidence and experience led to the fielding of both U-14 and U-16 teams in 1985.

History was made in 1986 when a hurler from Beragh, Eamon Rodgers, lined out at Croke Park for Tyrone in the All-Ireland Grade Three U-16 Final. And, the memories from that year include a number of very competitive games against the Coalisland and Clonoe combination of Naomh Colmcille.

By 1987 much of the work involved in organising things was being done by youth member, Alan Rodgers. Around 38 hurlers competed in training and matches and a big highlight was an overnight stay in Lavey. A party of around twenty travelled to the South Derry club where coaching took place on the Friday evening under the watchful eye of the well-known hurling enthusiast from the area, Tom Magill. The players also enjoyed a talk from Henry Downey and went on to win the Slaughtneill Tournament with the help of some of Lavey players.

> By 1987 much of the work involved in organising things was being organised by youth member, Alan Rodgers. Around 38 hurlers competed in training and matches and a big highlight was an overnight stay in Lavey

It is interesting to note those who were taking part in hurling at the time. They included: U-14 – Sean O'Neill, Gerard Conroy, Colm McCann, Shane Munroe, Damien Coleman, Ciaran McCallan, Ciaran Cox, Damien Given.
U-16/U-18 – Patrick Conroy, Darren Coleman, Shane McCarney, Barry McClean, Barry Grimes, Paul McClean, Eamon Rodgers, Cathal Grimes, Stephen Farley, Paul Kelly, Barry McGuinness, Alan Rodgers, Niall Farley.
Others – Eamon McHugh, Declan O'Neill, Brendan Barrett, Mark McCartan, Sean Montague, Justin McClean, Raymond McClean.

But poor numbers at training and matches ensured that the task of putting hurling into a position of strength was never easy. Over-age players often had to the fielded with the agreement of the opposition and there were times as well when players from the other team lined out. The main aim, of course, was to provide players with the chance to learn the skills and to this end the names of those involved during with the 1989 U-14s are again worth recording.

Ciaran McHugh, Sean Donnelly, Stephen Montague, Brendan Montague, Barry Donnelly, Kevin McMahon, Shane Donnelly, Martin McMahon, Ciaran Cox, Brian O'Neill, Malachy Maguire, Shane Kelly, Raymond McClean, Sean Donnelly, Dominic Donnelly, Gerard Loughran, Stephen Maguire, Damien Given, Gary Donnelly, Stephen Nixon, Adrian Harley, Colin Grimes and Niall Owens.

That year the club also fielded a Minor team and the players involved included: Colm McCann, Barry Donnelly, Eamon Rodgers, Patrick Conroy, Gerard Conroy, Cathal McCann, Alan Rodgers, Barry Grimes, Mickey McCann, Barry McGuinness, Barry McCartan, Sean O'Neill, Damien Given, Paul Kelly, Ciaran McHugh.

Young handballers for the Brackey club in the early 1980s

Regular matches against visiting teams, including Keady and Carrickmacross, added an extra dimension to hurling affairs during an eighties decade that saw the club contribute in good measure to the overall fairly healthy state of the game in Tyrone.

Handball

Several factors combined to make the 1980s probably the most successful decade of all for handball in the parish. Under the auspices of the Brackey Club, local players made their mark on the Tyrone, Ulster and All-Ireland scenes, while the completion of the new modern-sized 40x20 alley at St Mary's Park provided a focus that attracted new players from townlands not traditionally associated with the game.

Nevertheless, in 1980 it took two players firmly rooted in handball and who had come through the ranks to blaze a trail. Martin Kerr and Mickey McCullagh won the Ulster Minor doubles title and went on to represent Tyrone against Clare in the All-Ireland semi-final. However, their hopes of making the final were dashed at Croke Park where they lost in straight games, 21-16, 21-16.

Martin and Conor Kerr contested the Tyrone Minor Singles, a game which Martin won comfortably, and the success of the club continued that year when Conor Kerr and Paul Clarke captured the Ulster U-16 doubles title.

Activity was also continuing in the 60x30 alley at Cloughfin. Hugh

Sean Clarke presents the latest awards to Brackey players, Gerry Ward and Mickey McNally

"

By then, of course, the benefits of regular coaching under Mick Kerr were beginning to tell at youth level especially. The following years until the end of the decade would see players from the club maintain the momentum at Ulster level and make the breakthrough to All-Ireland success

"

McClean and Brian Grimes (senior) and Paul Tierney and Leo Devlin (Minor) represented the club in the Tyrone Championships while Brian Tierney, Aidan Tierney, Terry Mullin and Francie Mulgrew play-off for the Junior and Novice titles. The club's doubles final in 1980 was contested by Pat Donnelly and Francie Mulgrew and Noel Owens and Hugh McClean .

Gradually, though, the focus was switching increasingly to the new alley at Beragh, although delays in having it completed caused great concern. So much so that the Tyrone Handball Board expressed its displeasure at the failure of Omagh District Council to finish the job, with the floor being among the problems.

"In its present state, as well as being a waste of taxpayers money, it deprives people in the Beragh area – in which there are two handball clubs – of the facilities needed to play the game and necessitates travelling to Drumquin and Loughmacrory for those who wish to continue playing the game," the letter stated.

Nevertheless, Brackey held their own on the competitive front and in 1981 its 'B' team were runaway winners of the South Ulster League involving teams from Tyrone and Monaghan. They recorded 65 points from a possible 70, with Cloughfin A in second place and Pomeroy and Drumquin next. The Brackey A team was comprised of Sean Clarke, Brian McCullagh, Martin Kerr and Justin Kelly, while the B team included Mick Kerr, Pat McCrystal, Conor Kerr and Paul Clarke.

On an individual basis the haul of titles continued with wins for Niall Kerr and Peadar Curran in the Ulster U-13 Doubles and Stephen Clarke and Paul Murphy in the U-14 Doubles and history was made in 1982 when Conor Kerr and Paul Clarke reached the All-Ireland Minor Final and Martin Kerr the U-21 Final after first defending his provincial crown. The games took place at the Beechmount Leisure Centre in Belfast where all three suffered losses at the hands of their Clare opponents.

Martin Kerr, Conor Kerr, Paul Clarke and Stephen Kelly captured the South Ulster League in 1983 when Martin Kerr gained a notable achievement by dethroning Hugh Duff to take the Tyrone Senior title. It was Brackey's first ever Senior title and saw Kerr beat his older and more experienced opponent in a classic tie, 12-21, 21-17 and 21-16.

Brian and Mickey McNally and Gerry, Paddy and Colm Ward won the GFC League in 1983 and Beragh retained it the following year with the three Ward brothers being joined by Seamus Maguire. The handball competition played as part of the Tournament was also very popular.

Stephen Clarke won the Ulster U-16 Doubles title in 1983 and followed this up with the Minor title in 1984. He followed in the footsteps of Martin Kerr when he won the Tyrone Senior title in 1986 after previously coming out top in the Ulster Minor title in 1985 and being joined by Tony McElduff in winning the U-21 Doubles a year later. That year also saw Mick McCartan and Mickey John Kelly win the Golden Masters crown. At county level, too, the club was regularly to the fore, with Stephen Clarke adding the U-21 singles to his senior title in the space of a week in 1986.

A Brackey Handball committee from the mid 1980s. Pictured are standing, Paul Clarke, Hugh Colton, Sean Clarke, Seamus Maguire, Pat McCartan, Brian McCullagh, Malachy Ward, Stephen Clarke and Mick Kerr. Seated are Barney Cunningham and Stephen Clarke

By then, of course, the benefits of regular coaching under Mick Kerr were beginning to tell at youth level especially. The following years until the end of the decade would see players from the club maintain the momentum at Ulster level and make the breakthrough to All-Ireland success.

Sean Owens and Alan Rodgers won the Ulster U-13 Doubles in 1986, Stephen Clarke and Tony McElduff won the U-21 Doubles in 1987, Stephen paired with his brother Paul to win the Ulster U-21 title,

Paul McClean and Fergal McNally captured the U-15 provincial title and Mick McCartan and Mick Kerr won the Over 40s pairs.

While the Cloughfin Handball and Social Club continued to provide plenty of activity in the 60xc30 alley there, players from throughout the parish took part in the Brackey Club League and Heaney Handicap competitions.

Stephen Clarke maintained his great form by winning the Ulster U-21 title in 1988 and the decade ended in style when Ciaran McCallan and Stephen Conway captured the U-14 Doubles and Gerard Conroy won the U-15 singles title. He progressed to the All-Ireland Final before narrowly missing out on a national breakthrough that was now imminent.

> Jack refereed the 1969 Tyrone Final between Carrickmore and Coalisland and also took charge of the 1976 decider between Augher and Ardboe

Whistler Jack on the All-Ireland stage

Steady progress through the ranks since he began refereeing back in the late sixties marked the career of Beragh whistler, Jack Heaney. Numerous National League and Ulster Championship matches established a reputation for fairness and authority that was soon to be rewarded on the highest stage of all.

Jack refereed the 1969 Tyrone Final between Carrickmore and Coalisland and also took charge of the 1976 decider between Augher and Ardboe. But it was in the early eighties that he really hit the big time. In 1981 he was honoured to be chosen to take charge of the Ulster Senior Final between Armagh and Down, an appointment which he believed was on the cards. "I felt that I was in line for a final, but it was still a surprise when it actually came my way," he remarked at the time. "I'm delighted about it and regard it as an honour to referee in the whole county as well as to myself."

That same year he took charge of the All-Ireland Minor Semi-Final between Cork and Mayo and the biggest appointment of all came just over a year later when he received the call to be the 'man in the middle' for the All-Ireland Minor Final in 1982 between Kerry and Dublin.

It marked the culmination of a lifelong ambition to referee at All-Ireland Final level and he recounted in that year's Tyrone Gaelic Games Annual how he had received the news first from Club Secretary, Frank Rodgers and then the GAA PRO, Pat Quigley, and of the weekend itself.

"On the eve of the match my wife Colette and I travelled down to Dublin.

My umpires, John McGlinn, Neil McGarvey, Barney Cunningham and Barney Owens, who assist me at all games travelled down on the Sunday morning. Colette and I had received a number of invitations to several functions on the weekend.

"It was an early start to Croke Park and on arrival I was presented with a new strip and carrier bag. The time soon came for me to go onto the pitch, the teams warmed up, the coin was tossed and Kerry won the toss, the game flowed and was a joy to referee as both teams were prepared to play good open football.

"Monday was a very enjoyable day as Colette and I were invited to a reception in the Gresham Hotel for all the teams minor and senior officials, Press, Radio and TV Reporters were also there. It was a great opportunity to meet so many great names attached to the Association. For example, seated alongside my wife and myself were Michael and Mrs O'Hehir, a very friendly and interesting couple."

As well as that illustrious career at county, provincial and All-Ireland level, Jack was also chairman of the Tyrone Referees Board. Following the achievement of taking charge of the Minor Final in 1982, he continued to referee for a number of seasons before gradually retiring from the job.

Red Knights Awards

Involvement in a wide range of GAA activities marked the Beragh Red Knights out as a forward-thinking unit during the early years. The fact that these were covered so well by the Secretary, Frank Rodgers, for the Annual Convention each year earned him the accolade for Best Secretary's Report in Ireland on 1979 activities.

The award was presented in the Tara Towers Hotel in Dublin by ex-President of the GAA, Seamus Ryan, the GAA President, Paddy McFlynn and Liam Mulvhill, the new Secretary General. And, the judges were in no doubt about the quality of the report.

"The Beragh Report is comprehensive, factual, colourful and well written. Fourteen carefully selected photographs cover all club activities. There is an interesting review of the Seventies showing all club progress and attainments. Easily the most presentable and readable report we got for 1979. It is a model and an example of how a little thought and work can produce a report which stands out among many other fine efforts."

The award was presented in the Tara Towers Hotel in Dublin by ex-President of the GAA, Seamus Ryan, the GAA President, Paddy McFlynn and Liam Mulvhill, the new Secretary General. And, the judges were in no doubt about the quality of the report

315

Beragh officials pictured at the reception marking their achievement in winning the Centenary Merit Award in 1984 for ground development

Officials and guests of the club attended a subsequent presentation Banquet in the Royal Arms Hotel in Omagh at which the President, Paddy McFlynn, said "Your club has set a head line and is now known all over the island for its dedication and loyalty to the Association."

Another honour arrived in 1982 when the Club was presented with the Club of the Year in the Grade C section. The entry for the awards provided a detailed insight into the organisation of gaelic games and culture in the locality and the club's success in the Tyrone section was rewarded with a special presentation dinner at which the club was presented with the AIB trophy, an AIB Certificate of Merit and a cheque for £200.

These were handed over to the Chairman, Louis McNamee and Secretary,

Frank Rodgers, while the cheque was presented to the Treasurer, Paddy Grimes. Guests at the dinner were the club officials, committee members and team managers who contributed to the winning of the award.

Club Treasurer, Mary McCarney, receives the Tyrone Club of the Year Award for 1988

Centenary Year saw the club gaining the Special Centenary Merit Award for ground development. Club officials attended the presentation ceremony in Monaghan while later, in 1988, the club earned the Tyrone Award for Club of the Year. This was the first year of the awards and the magnificent crystal trophy was presented to the Treasurer, Mary McCarney at a special function in Cookstown.

Other activities

Relegation to Junior ranks in 1985 prompted an overall review of the organisation of the Red Knights which led subsequently to a complete overhaul of the management structure with a view to preparing for the challenges ahead. Central to this was the setting up for 1986 of a ten member Executive committee and four sub-committees responsible for Games, Finance, Development and Social and Cultural affairs.

Throughout the coming seasons people involved in these groups worked to try and put the club on a firmer footing. Their respective roles included the promotion of games, the organisation of fundraising activities, the completion of work on St Mary's Park and the organisation of Scor and Scor Na Og and other social and cultural events.

Among the objectives was to ensure that all members work towards meeting the aims of the club and not just filling out an application form and paying the membership fee. And, the message at the 1987 Convention was clear:

"1988 must be the year when the members of Beragh Red Knights GAA Club start living up to their responsibilities in whatever area they find themselves. If they don't, then our teams won't make their true impact, our sub-committees won't operate to their full potential, our members won't gain anything as individuals and worst all our community will continue to be one in which carping criticism and lack of initiative will continue to be the order of the day."

By the end of the following year the adult teams had begun to realise their potential and plans were in place for a £10,000 draw to raise funds for the further development of St Mary's Park. Under the chairmanship of Sean Owens, the Development Committee prepared plans for new dressing rooms, meeting area, social facilities and other amenities with a view to enabling the club to face the nineties and beyond with confidence.

Work such as this had been ongoing through the decade, beginning with the completion of the handball alley and committee room in 1981. But possibly the biggest achievement was the building of the covered stand in

The award was presented in the Tara Towers Hotel in Dublin by ex-President of the GAA, Seamus Ryan, the GAA President, Paddy McFlynn and Liam Mulvhill, the new Secretary General. And, the judges were in no doubt about the quality of the report

317

Teenage guests pictured at a Dinner Dance in the mid-1980s

1983 at a cost of £30,000. Work was carried out under the ACE scheme and those involved included Briam Grimes, Sean McMackin, Michael Grimes, Eamon Cunningham, Mickey Kelly, Martin Colton and Paddy Joe Keenan, while a lot of administrative work was completed by Kevin Grimes and Tommy McGarvey. The new facility was filled to capacity for the 1983 Tyrone Intermediate Final and Replay between Clonoe and Aghyaran and was to be widely used as the club hosted numerous high profile Senior and Intermediate Championship matches in that period.

Once the job was finished a specially-commissioned, Centenary Plaque, was unveiled at the entrance to the stand to mark 100 years of the GAA. An extension to the dressing rooms took place in 1985 and the later part of the decade saw further maintenance and other work being carried out under the auspices of the Development Committee, chaired by Sean Owens.

Top priority for it was the maintenance of the pitch and the provision of new facilities. The playing surface was drained during late 1987 following

Martin McCrory, whose rendition of the 'Homecoming' was a popular feature of Scor during the decade

a Ground Maintenance Training programme for all clubs in Ulster and the first steps were taken to identify the needs of the club for the future. And, of course, there were the immense contributions often beyond the call of duty by Hugh Colton until his retirement in 1986 and then TJ Kelly.

On the Social and Cultural front the highlight was undoubtedly the success of the Novelty Act in winning the Tyrone title in 1980. It was the club's first success in the event and the team members were Mick Grimes, Pat

Youth footballers eyeing up the talent rather than the camera at a 1980s disco

Donnelly, Pat McCartan, Dympna Rodgers and Anne Gallagher. Later, the Two Pats – Pat McCartan and Pat Donnelly – and Kevin Grimes, almost made it an Ulster win as well when they were narrowly defeated.

They retained the title in 1981 when the club had a large number of competitors as well in the Tyrone Scor Na Og event. Martin McCrory was runner-up in the Recitation section in both 1983 and 1984 and in 1985 Kevin Grimes, Martin Montague and Sean McNamee won the Scor Na Og Question time section.

Other highlights included the annual parish sports, regular dancing and Irish Language classes, the established of a 35 member concert group which put on shows in Roscommon and Donagh and the annual presentation dinners, which in the eighties proved very successful in honouring past teams like the 1947 Tyrone Junior Champions.

All-Ireland Final 1986

Years of struggling to make the grade at inter-county level were finally ended when Tyrone's fortunes took a dramatic upward turn in the eighties. An Ulster Final appearance in 1980 was followed by a provincial title in 1984 that will, of course, be remembered for Frank McGuigan's eleven point tally from play.

On the Social and Cultural front the highlight was undoubtedly the success of the Novelty Act in winning the Tyrone title in 1980

319

> Years of struggling to make the grade at inter-county level were finally ended when Tyrone's fortunes took a dramatic upward turn in the eighties

Tyrone manager, Art McRory, pictured with Beragh youth members, Declan O'Neill, Martin Gallagher and Niall Farley at the Centenary Year Tournament Final on the evening of Tyrone's Ulster title success that year

Two years later the county again captured the Anglo Celt Cup with victory over Down. The All-Ireland semi-final over Galway was won thanks to Kevin McCabe's penalty goal and for the first time ever players, officials and supporters were preparing for an All-Ireland Final. Standing in their way was the all-conquering Kerry team then going for an eighth Sam Maguire Cup triumph in just eleven years. And, in Beragh, too, the excitement reached fever pitch in the build-up to the big game.

Beragh girls Mary Donnelly, Diane Kelly, Jane Kelly and Claire Connolly pictured with Tyrone star of Centenary Year, Patsy Kerlin

Central to the sense of anticipation was the search for tickets. In order to ensure the fair distribution of the precious pieces of paper, it was decided to organise a sponsored run to give the general membership a chance to secure their ticket for the big match. Stands tickets were to be allocated to paid-up members and club workers who had made a contribution and involved themselves in club affairs.

Eventually the club received 150 tickets and officials, members and supporters somehow managed to attend a match which saw Tyrone lead shortly after half-time before injuries to key players coincided with a winning Kerry revival.

An Ulster title was won again in 1989 and the decade also saw players from the club continue to make their mark on various county teams. In 1983 Mickey Slane was on the Junior side which won the provincial title, Pat McCartan, contributed as selector to the Tyrone teams from 1980-1986 and in 1988 Paul and Adrian Donnelly were on the Minor team which won the Ulster title for the first time since 1976.

Both of them, along with Cathal Grimes, won All-Ireland Vocational Schools medals in 1988 and 1989, Barry McCartan and Joe McClean were on the St Patrick's Omagh team which won the All-Ireland Vocational Schools title in 1988 and Eamon Rodgers was a member of the Tyrone Minor Hurling team which won the All-Ireland C title in 1988 following Croke Park defeats in 1986 and 1987.

Beragh Tournament

Many abiding memories stand out from the Beragh Tournaments during the event's last golden period. There was the large attendance at the 1982

Beragh's Mickey
Slane on the
Tyrone Junior team
which won the
1983 Ulster title

Final on the same night as the World Cup Final, there was the visit of the winning Tyrone team with the Anglo Celt Cup following the 1984 Ulster Final and the various other activities which were organised alongside the main action on the field.

A major development in 1980 was the beginning of the Camogie Tournament, played as curtain-raiser to the football matches. Eglish, Kildress, Beragh and Carrickmore were the competing teams, with Eglish coming through as expected.

Ballygawley were awarded the new Cuchullain Perpetual Trophy when they defeated Carrickmore in the 1980 Final by 3-9 to 0-7. Top scorer during that year was Damien Kavanagh, who registered 4-5, while others on form were those who won the Tennis, Target Golf, Penalty Taking and Darts competitions.

Special presentations were made to the referees, Jackie Martin and Brendan McAleer in 1981 when Kildress won the camogie title with victory over Omagh and Carrickmore were back on top in the football with a 1-4 to 0-4 victory over Trillick.

Handball was added to the growing range of competitions in 1982 when the sponsors for the event included On the Spot Trophies, Sixmilecross Co-Op, Kelly Freight, McGarvey Insurance and the Whistler's Inn. And, this time it was Trillick who won the Tournament with a 2-5 to 1-3 victory over Carrickmore.

But Carrickmore were back in 1983 to win the Football and Camogie double, Cuthbert Donnelly and Mick McCullagh helped out with the refereeing and Jimmy McCloghan finished top scorer with 0-14.

Centenary Year was always going to be special, although few in the Red Knights could have imagined just how memorable the highlight of the annual Tournament would be. Now in its 30th year, the event had grown to be the main stopping-off point for the Tyrone team following their victory over Armagh to take the Ulster title for the first time in eleven years.

Guest appearances at St Mary's Park by Art McRory, Ciaran McGarvey and Patsy Kerlin made that night in July 1984 one to remember. It was also extra-special for Fintona who won the title and Carrickmore who retained the camogie crown.

Killeeshil, Clogher, Moy and Dromore were among the competitors in 1985 when the wet weather failed to dampen the overall enthusiasm. Trillick won the title and a new dimension was added in 1986 when youth games were played as curtain-raisers to the Tournament ties.

Ballygawley won then and were succeeded by Carrickmore in 1987. Income for the event during those years remained fairly constant at around £1000, but the days of the traditional format had by then passed their high point.

With so many other competitions at youth and adult level to be played, an increasing emphasis on the completion of regular league and championship games at club level and better fortunes for Tyrone's teams, the days of the Tournament were numbered.

Trillick won the title in 1988 and Clonoe followed suit in 1989 as it became clear that the Tournament was beginning to lose the widespread appeal which had made it one of the most popular in Tyrone from the 1950s.

Community Events

Numerous building projects concentrated the attentions of the people of Beragh during the 1980s as first the Youth Club, then the new Chapel and the completion of renovations to St Mary's Hall were on the agenda.

Other construction work included the erection of new houses along the Fintona Road in Beragh, to be known as Springwell Drive and in the mid-eighties, Tullyneill Court in Sixmilecross.

Centenary Year was always going to be special, although few in the Red Knights could have imagined just how memorable the highlight of the annual Tournament would be

323

Club Chairman, Paddy Bogan, makes a presentation to members of the Skyrne club following their visit to Beragh Red Knights in 1983

Activities in the Youth Club at the old school finally got underway in September 1980, while another body celebrating around that time was Beragh Credit Union. At the All-Ireland Convention in May 1981, they won the Credit Union Cup for the first time, having been placed fourth in 1979 and second in 1980.

The competition included all Credit Unions in Ireland and was especially pleasing for Beragh as the savings approached the £150,000 mark. The President, Louis McNamee said: "We were keeping our fingers crossed that we could finally pull it off, but until the actual announcement was made we had no idea who had won."

Years of struggling to make the grade at inter-county level were finally ended when Tyrone's fortunes took a dramatic upward turn in the eighties

Another group in the record books for a marvellous achievement was Kelly Freight. At Christmas 1981 one of their refrigerated lorries, driven by Eugene Cunningham, took 20 tons of frozen beef from Newbridge in Co Kildare to Kuwait – the furthest any Irish lorry had ever travelled overland. Roger Kelly said at the time that the company was also transporting electronic and building materials to Iraq and Libya.

Beragh was tops in 1982 when the village was named the 'most improved small town' in the Omagh District Council Best Kept Awards.

One man who was probably very much relieved in the autumn of 1980 was local rugby star, Willie Anderson, as he made his way home three months after being arrested in Argentina. Then 25, he had been held in Buenos Aires after being accused of stealing an Argentinian national flag. He was given bail, but told not to leave the capital city and was eventually given a two year suspended jail sentence and told to go home immediately.

Among the big events of the mid-eighties was the construction and opening of the new Church of the Immaculate Conception. Work started in June 1983 with the ceremonial cutting of the first sod.

Officially opened on Sunday July 29th, 1984 at a cost of some £400,000. Officiating at the Ceremony was Cardinal O'Fiaich who spoke of the immense work which had gone into completing the Church, spearheaded by Fr Francis Quigley and Fr Peter McParland and the band of fundraisers whose work during the previous few years had helped to clear outstanding debts prior to the official opening.

Drama also made a welcome return to Beragh after a number of years, with the staging of 'Many Young Men Twenty' in 1986 and 'The Far Off Hills' a year later. Among those involved in the Drama Club at a the time, and who took part in these and other plays were: Cast Paddy Montague, Diane Kelly, Michelle Heaney, Denise McCann, Martin McCrory, Eamon Mullan, Claire Rodgers, Dermot Hagan, Mary McCann, Pearse McCann, PJ McClean, Cathal McCann, Hugh McAleer, Kathleen O'Neill, Una McGrory, Goretti Donnelly and Michael Curran. Back Stage: Anne Gallagher, Fr John Travers, Dermot Meenagh, Brendan Grimes, Eamon Mullin, Siobhan O'Neill, Kevin Grimes, Jennie McCann, Jane Kelly, Kay Ward.

Also drawing the crowds during the eighties was Drumnakilly comedian, Kevin McAleer. He was making a name for himself on the London cabaret scene. The Ulster Herald in March 1985 reported that his act was unique and involved "Kevin doing droll and often surreal voice-overs before projector slides of, for example, cows in a field. A London magazine said he was well known for his pauses, which "sometimes last for days".

The Beragh club Centenary Plaque pictured on the altar at the opening of the new Church of the Immaculate Conception on July 29th, 1984

But the weather was causing problems for many farmers in 1985 when hay farmers were urged not to panic at the end of August despite the continuing rain preventing the usual seasonal work.

325

The Chief Agricultural Officer, Mr TA Larmour, described the summer as 'disastrous,' especially for those who were dependent on hay. He expressed the hope that a second cut of silage may be possible, while Cardinal Tomas O'Fiaich got the priests of the Archdiocese to offer prayers for good weather at all Masses so that the harvest could be saved.

Conclusion

Solid foundations for the future were laid by the GAA activities of the 1980s. Progress at youth level, plans for the continuing development of St Mary's Park and the drive to increase the numbers of people involved on both the playing and administrative fronts marked a new phase in the development of the Beragh Red Knights.

Successes came on a regular basis to provide a boost to these efforts. By the end of the decade the club was very much to the fore in all aspects of the GAA in Tyrone and competing at a high level at the various youth grades.

Now the task ahead was to sustain this process and ensure that the adult teams reached their potential. Evidence of how this could be achieved was provided by the club's ability to compete so strongly at Intermediate level. Now the task of making the final push for a place in Senior ranks would be a priority alongside the job of preparing for a tenth decade of gaelic games and culture in the area.

The completion of the new stand was one of the achievements of the 1980s. Here, it is packed to capacity for the 1983 Intermediate Final between Clonoe and Aghyaran

BERAGH LIFE *in colour*

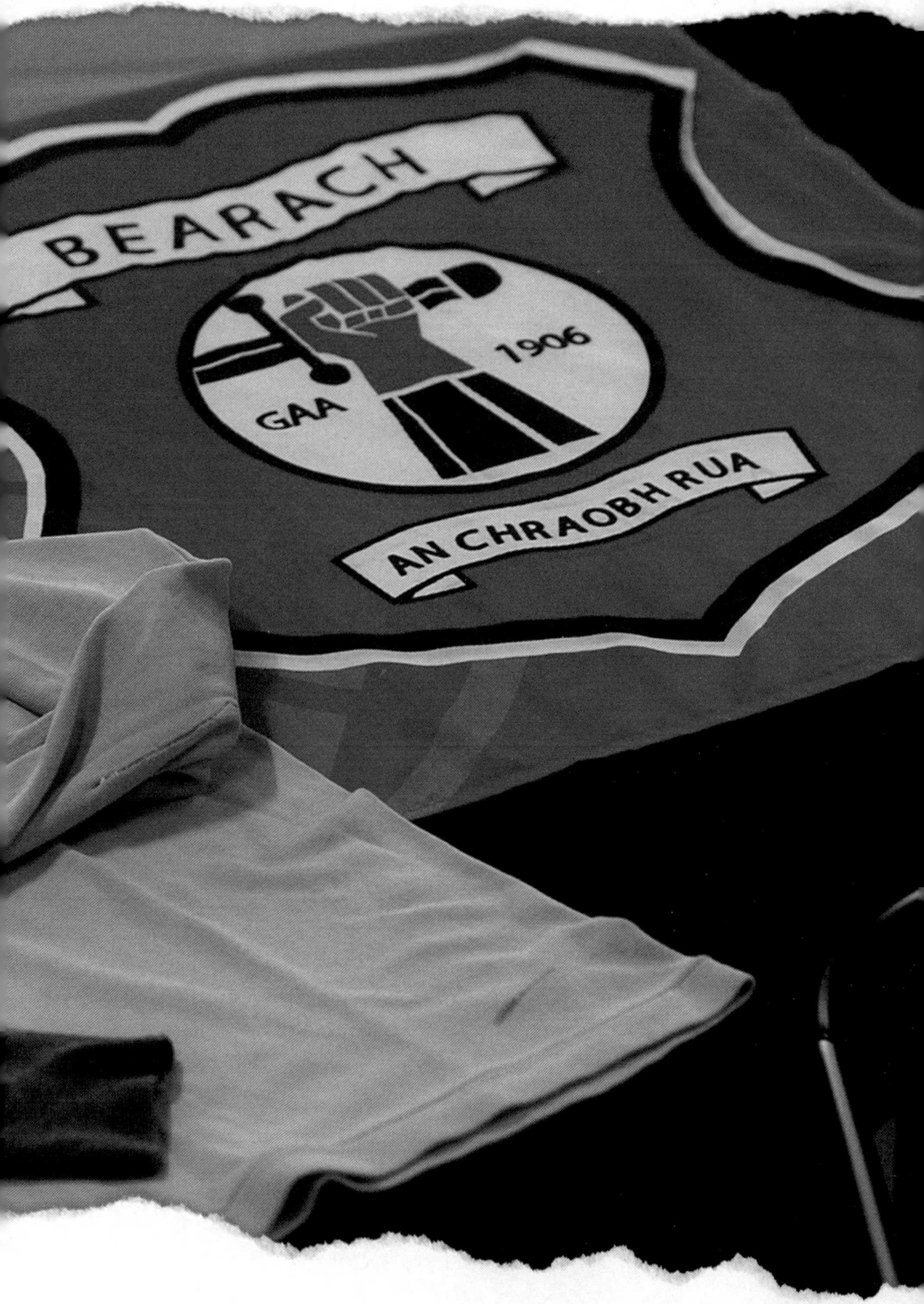
BEARACH
GAA
1906
AN CHRAOBH RUA

❶

❷

3

4

1 - Making history were the hurlers of the eighties

2 - The U-14 Camogie team of 1989 which reached the County Final

3- Beragh's Junior team which progressed to the County Final in 1981

4 - Champions for the second time - the Reserve side of 1985

The winning Juvenile team of 1985. Pictured back row left to right are Mick Kerr, Kevin Grimes, Sean McNamee, Paddy Maguire, Brian Donnelly, Damien Grimes, Sean McCrory, Kevin McClean, PJ McClean. Middle row left to right are Paul Donnelly, Sean Donnelly, Ciaran Owens,

Eamon Rodgers, Mark McCartan, Mickey McCann (captain), Eugene McCrystal, Barry McCartan, Adrian Donnelly, Stephen Farley, Liam McClean. At front from left are Brian Walshe, Sean Montague, Shane Kelly, Barry Grimes, Shane Fox, Joe McClean and Stephen Donnelly

1 - Commemorative tapestry presented to the club by PJ McClean in 1972

2 - Red Knights pennant from the late seventies

3 - Ulster Final Referee, 1981, Jack Heaney pictured with the Armagh and Down captains

4 - Beragh Juveniles, Tyrone League Finalists from 1989

5 -Seamus Boyle receives the Reserve Championship trophy in 1985

6 - The Minor panel which reached the 1988 League Final

1

2

1 - The U-14s, with a few U-12s,
pictured with their managers
in 1981

2 - A Reserve team from the
mid-eighties

3 - Kieran Murphy, a youth player
with the Beragh St Mary's
in the fifties

6 - Mickey Kerr, member of the
historic Tyrone team of 1956,
long-serving player, handball
champion and former
club Chairman

1

2

3

4

1 - Vincent McCullagh and a Drumduff Primary League team from the early eighties.

2- The Beragh Blues from around 1988 pictured prior to one of their Primary League games

3 - Lining up for the presentation from Club Treasurer, Mary McCarney.

4 - Primary League organiser, Frank Rodgers, presents the Shield to the
  winning Roscavey captain.

5 - Another successful Primary Schools League reaches its climax for the Red Knights club as
  Shane Donnelly gets the Shield from Mary McCarney

1 - The 'Big Draw' for club development is launched at the 1989 Dinner

2 - Recreational facilities include the tennis court and riverside walk

3 - Ongoing work on the new stand is completed in the early eighties

4 - Development Chairman, Sean Owens, completes some routine work on St Mary's Park

5 - Peter Grimes presents the Art competition prizes to Regina Donnelly and Ciaran Cox

6 - Kieran McCartan, Paul McCartan, Gerry Boyle and Gerard Colton at work on the pitch

1 - The Brackey Handball Committee from the early eighties

2 - A successful year for the Red Knights and the Games Committee of 1988

3 - Club officials and supporters pictured at the unveiling of the Centenary Plaque in 1984

Chapter Eleven
1990 - 2000
Top Rung Reached and Lost

Chapter Eight
1990 - 2000

that place in senior ranks was continuing to prove elusive as the club entered the 1990s

CLEAR challenges presented themselves to the members of the Beragh Red Knights as they entered the nineties full of optimism for the future. Promotion to senior ranks with a young team was a positive on the adult football scene. The youth teams that had proved so competitive in the eighties were aiming to make an even bigger mark while it was hoped that participation in hurling and camogie would gain in strength.

On the handball scene, too, the Brackey Club looked to success at All-Ireland level as a key aim after players from the club had showed signs of making the breakthrough in the previous few years.

But there were the usual difficulties on and off the field which characterise every decade of involvement. And, while the nineties were to prove to be an immensely satisfying decade in many ways, a number of shortcomings meant that the level of achievement wasn't sustained.

League Football 1990-1999

Indications of Beragh's potential to make the grade at Intermediate level were certainly very much in evidence at the end of the eighties when the adult first team reached the Championship Final and made a strong bid for promotion in the league.

Players of the Year pictured at a 1990s Dinner Dance

But that place in senior ranks was continuing to prove elusive as the club entered the 1990s. And, early form in the decade suggested that the team was destined to struggle in this regard, just as it did at the start of the previous decade.

Defeats by Edendork and Ardboe got them off to a disappointing start in 1990. But by May they were in joint third place and were showing good form. A 3-4 to 0-6 victory over Pomeroy in July put them joint top of the Division and the race for the title eventually came down to an important home tie against Derrylaughan. In that one, however, a 1-12 to 2-7 loss at home in front of a large attendance dealt a decisive blow.

As always, though, there were the play-offs to fall back on and a 1-10 to

1-8 win over Killyclogher set up a tie against Donaghmore for a senior position. But the poor record in play-offs continued when Donaghmore emerged comfortable winners by 0-11 to 0-4. Patsy Farley missed a penalty in the first half, the Red Knights trailed by seven points at the break and, while Cathal Grimes and Barry McCartan reduced the deficit, chances for Eamon Rodgers and Brian McGarvey were missed and so was promotion.

The disappointments of the 1988-1990 period seemed to take their toll in 1991 when Beragh failed to make any real impact. By April they were in mid-table and though they moved into third behind Killyclogher and Galbally in June, the momentum wasn't maintained. A 1-11 to 2-6 defeat by Eglish saw them slip back, they were ten points adrift of the leaders in September and they eventually finished fourth.

It was to be a similar story the following year and by July they were well down the table with just six points from six games. A good run in the championship boosted morale for a while but they had improved only slightly by the finish of their league programme.

A series of fine victories near the end of the 1993 season highlighted the very positive impact of winning a first Intermediate title. With the sought-after spot in Senior football secured, a late League spurt saw the Red Knights race up the table to finish in second.

Survival was the aim in 1994 as a first year in senior ranks since the seventies presented a whole new set of high profile and novel ties. They included games against teams which hadn't provided opposition since the early sixties, including neighbours Carrickmore, Errigal Ciaran and Omagh.

But the first game on their return brought a stark reality check as Moortown were the winners at home on a score of 1-10 to 1-5. But encouraging wins over Ardboe and Pomeroy followed and there was a point courtesy of a 0-8 draw with Moy. Galbally were then defeated on a score of 0-12 to 0-10 and by August they were on seven points on the Division One table.

However, the three derby games against neighbouring teams all resulted in defeat. It was tight and tense as Carrickmore won by 0-8 to 0-4 in a match that saw Cathal Grimes register Beragh's only score of the second half. Omagh scored a 1-8 to 0-9 victory and Errigal Ciaran emerged well on top at Beragh by 3-10 to 1-6. These and a vital 2-9 to 2-8 defeat by

A good run in the championship boosted morale for a while but they had improved only slightly by the finish of their league programme

Clonoe left Beragh struggling against relegation but three points secured on the first weekend of October eased the pressure.

Barry McCartan (0-7), Eamon Rodgers (0-4), Cathal Grimes (0-4) and Gerry Ward (0-3) were the scorers in a 0-18 to 1-4 win over Dungannon, while an equalising point from Eamon Rodgers did the trick in an away tie against Coalisland which finished 1-10 to 2-7. But relegation was still a threat and the season eventually climaxed with a Division 1/2 play-off against Killyclogher. That game started well for Beragh as goals from Barry McCartan and Cathal Grimes and the performances of Sean Owens, Aidan Grimes (Deroar) and Sean Donnelly helped them into a 2-4 to 0-4 lead at half-time.

Killyclogher, however, fought back after the break, to equalise before Paul Donnelly added two points and Eamon Rodgers one to secure a 2-8 to 1-8 win.

There was little time to contemplate the achievement of reaching the Senior League semi-finals for the first time in sixty years as the 1994 league began again on March 31st. And, once again a memorable victory over Errigal Ciaran saw the Red Knights off to the perfect start

After just managing to stay in Division One in 1994, there was a determination to make a better impression during 1995. Under the new management of club chairman, Gerry Owens, they got off to the perfect start at Dunmoyle on April 9. A tally of 2-4 from Eamon Rodgers helped them record a shock 2-7 to 0-7 win.

"Beragh led by 1-3 to 0-4 at half-time before the introduction of Peter Canavan by Errigal Ciaran put them under pressure in the second half. The game was in the balance going into the final quarter when the second goal secured the win," reported the Ulster Herald.

A 1-9 to 0-5 win over Omagh saw them go top of the table and, while the leagues were delayed due to Tyrone's progress towards the All-Ireland Final, they remained to the fore. Although Carrickmore defeated them easily by 2-15 to 0-8, they came back with a flourish of wins. Dungannon were defeated on a score of 1-15 to 0-11, Trillick by 0-10 to 0-6, Dromore by 2-7 to 1-6 and Coalisland by 1-13 to 0-13 as they clinched a play-off with Dungannon to reach the semi-finals. They won that on a score of 2-13 to 3-8 and progressed to meet Carrickmore.

That game was played at Clogher on January 14th 1996 and with Patsy Farley, Paul Donnelly and Sean Owens to the fore in defence, Beragh gave their all during a closely contested opening half. The teams were level in the 38th minute with Beragh playing well. But they managed only two more points while a goal eleven minutes from the end put Carrickmore on top and on the way to victory despite some late Beragh pressure.

Terry McKenna
in determined
action in the
Tyrone Senior
Championship

The team was: Paddy Grimes, Stephen Farley, Gary Donnelly, Stephen Donnelly, Patsy Farley, Paul Donnelly, Sean Owens, Terry McKenna, Seamus Grimes, Ciaran Cox, Niall Farley, Barry Grimes, Mickey McCann, Eamon Rodgers, Barry McCartan.
Subs – Aidan Grimes for Gary Donnelly, Cathal Grimes for Mickey McCann, Mickey McCann for Barry Grimes.

There was little time to contemplate the achievement of reaching the Senior League semi-finals for the first time in sixty years as the 1994 league began again on March 31st. And, once again a memorable victory over Errigal Ciaran saw the Red Knights off to the perfect start.

Peter Canavan was back after injury, but first half dominance saw Beragh lead by 0-12 to 0-6 at half-time. A Martin McCaffrey goal threatened to derail them but they held on to win by 0-17 to 1-9. The scorers were: Cathal Grimes (0-8), Eamon Rodgers (0-5), Terry McKenna (0-1), Ciaran Cox (0-1) Barry Grimes (0-1).

It was a case of trying to build on that fine result. Edendork were defeated on a score of 1-10 to 1-8, but they lost to Omagh by 1-7 to 1-4 before defeating Galbally by 1-13 to 2-6. By July they were in joint third place and wins over Trillick and Dromore left them second on 19 points behind leaders Carrickmore on 28 points. That secured a place in the playoffs, but

Adrian and
Donnelly and Barry
McCartan, two of
the regular senior
players who made
their mark during
the decade

their hopes of reaching the Final were emphatically dashed at the semi-final stage as Errigal Ciaran reversed the earlier result with a 3-6 to 0-5 win at Fintona on December 8th. Three goals either side of the break proved decisive as the Ballygawley side, who led by 1-3 to 0-3 at half-time, were always in control when they struck twice in quick succession on the resumption.

On to 1997 and perhaps the opening result of the season provided an indication of the troubles ahead when Beragh lost to Errigal at St Mary's Park. They struggled in the first half and trailed by 1-6 to 0-4 at half-time. Barry McCartan goaled on the resumption, Paddy Grimes pulled off a number of good saves from Peter Canavan but an equaliser from Terry McKenna was only the prelude to a late Errigal rally which culminated in a disappointing defeat.

A 2-8 to 0-14 draw with Galbally, a win by 0-11 to 1-5 win over Donaghmore generated hope that the senior status could be maintained. But by September the situation was becoming bleak after defeats by Coalisland and Dungannon, left them needing almost full points to survive. Then a 3-14 to 1-10 defeat at Moortown and a 5-8 to 0-5 defeat by Ardboe sealed their fate.

So, it was back to Intermediate ranks for the 1998 season and early form proved disappointing before a five match winning run midway through the season seemed to have got things back on track. But then came a change in form and the end result was a direct play-off against Aghaloo for a place in the new Division 1B.

Again the playoffs didn't deliver and a 0-13 to 1-10 draw was followed by a 3-4 to 0-8 defeat on November 22nd at Dromore which left Beragh back in Intermediate ranks.

Time was moving on by the end of the decade. Many of the players who had spearheaded the race for promotion in the late eighties and early nineties were nearing the end of their careers and their experience and abilities were badly missed as a decade which had proved so successful in so many ways closed with a 1999 derby-tie far removed from those which had attracted attention in the 1993-1997 period.

After an encouraging start to that 1999 campaign, a couple of narrow defeats proved costly. The season eventually came down to a play-off to avoid relegation to Junior. There was relief all-round when Tattyreagh were defeated on a score of 0-14 to 0-7 to stay Intermediate - in a year which saw Beragh win the Division Two Disciplinary Award.

> Time was moving on by the end of the decade. Many of the players who had spearheaded the race for promotion in the late eighties and early nineties were nearing the end of their careers

Championship Football

It has been seen how League football provided so much in the way of thrills and spills for followers of the Red Knights during the nineties. And, it was the same on the championship scene which provided a number of very memorable moments in a real decade to remember.

Just as in the League, things took a little time to warm-up to the heat of the middle part of the decade. A comfortable 0-16 to 1-3 win over Killyman put Beragh through to the Quarter Final of the 1990 Intermediate Championship. They led by 0-7 to 0-1 at half-time and, with Brian McGarvey doing well at full forward, also dominated on the resumption.

But the Quarter Final tie against Ardboe on July 1st at Donaghmore proved a lot more difficult. The loughshore side were anxious to make a quick return to senior ranks and were boosted by a goal in the third

Highfielding action as Beragh lead the way in Senior ranks

Terry McKenna, seen here in action against Trillick in the 1996 Senior
Championship, played for Tyrone in the 1998 Ulster Championship

minute. Points from Mickey McCann and Cathal Grimes and a goal from Hugh McNamee raised hopes until Ardboe's second goal made all the difference and ended Beragh's 1990 championship hopes.

June 1991 will be recalled for an exciting three match installment, not between Dublin and Meath in the Leinster Championship, but between Beragh and Galbally in the Tyrone Intermediate Championship. Beragh led early on by four points in the first game at Clogher on June 2nd after Patsy Farley had converted the rebound from a penalty saved by Joe Cassidy. They looked to be heading for victory when leading by five in the second half, before Galbally fought back to draw - Beragh 2-7 Galbally 1-10.

Beragh struggled in the opening half of the replay as Galbally led at one stage by 2-1 to 0-2. Barry Grimes got a goal to reduce the deficit to 2-4 to 1-2 at half-time and an Eamon Rodgers goal brought them level at 2-4 each.

It was still all square at the end of normal time on a score of 2-6 each and a goal from Hugh McNamee and points from Eamon Rodgers, Shane McCarney and Barry Grimes gave the Red Knights a six point lead for the second period of extra time. However, Galbally made all the running in the final period as only a Patsy Farley equaliser saved Beragh's bacon on a score of 3-11 each.

But Beragh's luck ran out in the second replay when Galbally held their nerve to progress. Something had to give and the Pearses were on their way to the win when leading by. The dismissal of Eamon Rodgers dealt a blow as despite their best efforts they went out on a score of 2-8 to 1-7.

> It was still all square at the end of normal time on a score of 2-6 each and a goal from Hugh McNamee and points from Eamon Rodgers, Shane McCarney and Barry Grimes gave the Red Knights a six point lead for the second period of extra time

On the road to Intermediate title 1992-1993

Demoralising defeats had characterised Beragh's championship efforts at Intermediate level since 1989. But 1992 gave hope that the breakthrough towards the title was imminent as a Final appearance that year provided vital experience for a last big push the following season.

More direct football did the trick in the opening round of that 1992 championship against Urney on June 1st. Stephen Farley and Sean Donnelly led the way in defence, as Beragh recovered from the dismissal of Paul Donnelly and a missed penalty from Eamon Rodgers. The score was 0-6 to 0-5 at half-time and the 1-8 to 0-8 win was clinched by a Mickey McCann goal near the end.

In the next round some excellent point-scoring was vital in a 0-17 to 0-6 win over Killyclogher. Beragh led by 0-7 to 0-3 at half-time and Aidan Grimes handling of Noel McGinn made a key contribution in the second period as Adrian Donnelly, Barry McCartan, Barry Grimes and Mickey McCann rounded of a fine display.

In the semi-final late goals from Barry Grimes and Sean Owens sealed a 2-10 to 1-7 victory over Aghyaran in Drumquin at the end of July. Aghyaran had led by 1-3 to 0-4 at half-time and it was only the defending of Stephen Farley, Terry McKenna and Aidan Grimes which kept the Red Knights in touch.

But they looked to be on their way out when they trailed by 1-7 to 0-4 with just ten minutes remaining. They rallied, however, 1-1 from Barry Grimes got them going and, when Sean Owens goaled with five minutes remaining, they were in front for the first time at 2-5 to 1-7.

They stepped up a further gear after that and points from Hugh McNamee (2), Mickey McCann and Sean Donnelly and a vital interception by Terry McKenna sealed a great recovery.

And, so the Red Knights were now preparing for their second Intermediate Final, this time under the management of Kevin Maguire and Mickey Heaney. "So far we have shown great character in the championship and taken our chances. In the league we have missed chances and have been hit by injuries and absentees," was the comment from Mickey Heaney prior to the final against Eglish.

66

the Red Knights
were now
preparing for their
second
Intermediate
Final, this time
under the
management of
Kevin Maguire and
Mickey Heaney

99

"We will take the final as another game, just as we have done in every round. It's a case of our players giving their best on the day," he added. Among the possible absentees from the two finalists were Tyrone players, Paul Donnelly and Matt McGleenan. Both, though, were introduced during the course of the game at Carrickmore which saw Beragh miss out on the Paddy Cullen Cup for the second time.

A goal set Eglish on their way early on and, while Stephen Farley, Shane McCarney and Fergal Grimes, worked hard in defence, Beragh were 1-3 to 0-3 behind at half-time. The deficit was doubled within eight minutes of the restart and the Red Knights looked to be heading for a heavy loss.

But points from Mickey McCann and Barry Grimes briefly got them going again. Then, the sending off of Paul Donnelly proved decisive and consolation points from Fergal Grimes, Barry McCartan and Adrian

Donnelly only put a more respectable look on the final scoreline of 1-10 to 0-8.

The losing Beragh team in that 1992 Final was: Cathal Grimes, Stephen Farley, Aidan Grimes, Terry McKenna, Fergal Grimes, Shane McCarney, Patsy Farley, Sean Grimes, Sean Donnelly, Barry McCartan, Adrian Donnelly, Barry Grimes, Sean Owens, Hugh McNamee, Mickey McCann.
Subs - Paul Donnelly for P Farley, Paul McGlinn for S Grimes.

Scorers - Mickey McCann (0-3), Barry Grimes (0-2), Fergal Grimes (0-1), Barry McCartan (0-1), Adrian Donnelly (0-1).

The winning 1993 Intermediate Championship panel pictured with the Paddy Cullen Cup

Whether or not the 1993 year was a make or break one for the Beragh team of the time is hard to gauge but one thing for certain is that their success in that year's Intermediate Championship erased the disappointments of many previous seasons.

It began well for them when what was described as a fine team display resulted in an emphatic 2-12 to 1-5 win over Castlederg at Omagh on May 23rd. This set them up for a Quarter Final tie against Urney on July 4th at Carrickmore.

Perfect conditions provided the backdrop to a match that the Red Knights never looked like losing. Shane McCarney along with Patsy and Stephen Farley led the way in defence as the dominance of Paul Donnelly and Terry McKenna at midfield set Beragh on the road. A total of 1-7 without reply - the goal coming from Mickey McCann - sealed the win even though the complacency of the second half caused concern.

There was certainly no room for complacency against Drumquin in the semi-final on July 25th at Omagh. A 0-6 to 0-5 half-time scoreline highlights the closely fought exchanges and it wasn't until Barry McCartan bundled the ball to the net midway through the second half that Beragh really looked like winners. That left the score 1-7 to 0-6 and a couple of late points gave them vital breathing space for the final stages.

Edendork were to provide the opposition in the final which was preceded by headlines such as "Beragh bidding for overdue championship glory."

And, after the disappointments of 1989 and 1992 they really were. The prospect of finally making the breakthrough inspired the players who were now under the management of Sean O'Kane and Frank Martin.

The Ulster Herald preview was clear about the choices facing the Red Knights players. "On the face of it, the turn of Beragh to lift the Intermediate title should be at hand, but in sport titles aren't handed to deserving cases. They have to be won on merit on the day and that's where the onus rests on the Beragh players. They have done all they had to en-route to the final, so now they must produce the goods."

Produce the goods they most certainly did in a Final that fulfilled all expectations for the Red Knights. All fifteen players contributed much to a victory that finally realised the dream of promotion to senior ranks.

Of particular note was the defensive play of Sean Donnelly, Aidan Grimes and Patsy Farley, while Terry McKenna and Paul Donnelly cancelled out the threat of the Edendork pairing at midfield. Up front Eamon Rodgers and Cathal Grimes shared nine of the twelve points but overall it was a team display which clinched the victory.

Wind advantage helped Beragh to a good start as Barry McCartan, Paul Donnelly, Eamon Rodgers and Cathal Grimes all scored points. However, their resolve was tested when Edendork struck back with a goal.

It was clear that a tough match was on the cards, although the Red Knights proceeded to take control and points from Cathal Grimes, Patsy Farley

This panoramic action shot from the 1993 Intermediate Final against Edendork shows nine of the Beragh players who lined out that day

and Eamon Rodgers left them with a valuable 0-9 to 1-0 cushion for the second half. But two early points reduced their lead to just four points and urgent action was demanded from Beragh. The efforts of Patsy Farley and Aidan Grimes steadied them and the Ulster Herald report described the final stages in these terms:

"As the game entered its final phase, Edendork's wastefulness, coupled with good defending by the Beragh backs made many believe that the Red Knights were on the verge of an historic victory. Hugh McNamee, who up to now had been quiet, produced some inspirational play and a pointed free from Cathal Grimes made it 0-11 to 1-6.

"The title was sealed when, in their last attack, Eamon Rodgers fielded a great ball and shot high for the insurance point and a famous Beragh victory. The final whistle signalled the start of the celebrations to mark the return to Senior Football after a 20 year absence. Happy supporters, especially trainer, Sean O'Kane, and, of course, the players made it an occasion to remember."

Those celebrations included a victory cavalcade through the villages of Beragh and Sixmilecross and a special night as the full impact of what had been achieved sank in. A first Intermediate title had been safely secured and the winning team and panel was:

Paddy Grimes, Stephen Farley, Aidan Grimes, Niall Farley, Patsy Farley (captain), Sean Donnelly, Sean Owens, Terry McKenna, Paul Donnelly, Eamon Rodgers, Hugh McNamee, Cathal Grimes, Mickey McCann, Barry McCartan, Barry Grimes.

Subs - None used. Other panel members - Seamus Grimes, Gerry Ward, Aidan Grimes, Michael Montague, Stephen Hall, Kevin Connolly, Stephen Mullan, Martin Grimes, Gary Donnelly, Stephen Donnelly, Fergal Grimes, Paul McGlinn.

A missed opportunity - Errigal Ciaran 1994

High profile Senior championship games in the mid-nineties did not come any bigger than meeting Errigal Ciaran or Carrickmore. Beragh could hardly believe their fortune when the draw for the 1994 Championship pitted them against the then Tyrone and Ulster Champions and above all their neighbours from Errigal Ciaran.

It was a match in which probably few outside the immediate panel expected anything other than a tough introduction to the challenges of the

> The title was sealed when, in their last attack, Eamon Rodgers fielded a great ball and shot high for the insurance point and a famous Beragh victory

The Beragh Red Knights team which came so close to cause the shock of the decade against the reigning Tyrone and Ulster Champions, Errigal Ciaran

Even at the vantage point of over a decade, the events of that balmy Friday evening are difficult to comprehend. The facts speak for themselves about how Beragh came so close to downing their mighty opponents

Senior Championship for the new boys from the Red Knights. Carrickmore at 8pm on Friday May 20th was the venue date and time for a derby tie that held so many potential hazards for the previous year's Intermediate Champions.

"The Canavans, Quinns, Eamon McCaffrey and company are currently flying high in the League, while Beragh, without their Tyrone player, Paul Donnelly, are presently finding the going tough. In the circumstances, then, it's not surprising that Errigal Ciaran are the hottest of favourites to cruise to the Quarter Final with something to spare," was how the Ulster Herald preview saw things.

Even at the vantage point of over a decade, the events of that balmy Friday evening are difficult to comprehend. The facts speak for themselves about how Beragh came so close to downing their mighty opponents.

According to the report, this match of immense drama had everything which could be expected from a championship tie and more. An attendance of 2000 was enthralled from the moment Adrian Donnelly goaled to give Beragh a dream start to the time that Martin McCaffrey's last gasp equaliser saved Errigal Ciaran's titles.

Beragh led by 1-1 to no score after ten minutes as stout defending from Sean Donnelly, Terry McKenna and Stephen Farley was needed to keep the threat posed by Peter and Pascal Canavan and Owen Gormley at bay. Eamon McCaffrey goaled for Errigal, although a point from Eamon Rodgers left Beragh enjoying a 1-5 to 1-3 interval lead.

Further scores from Cathal Grimes and Terry McKenna extended the lead to 1-7 to 1-3 early in the second half. Sean Donnelly, Stephen Farley and Sean Owens continued to defend well and trouble the champions. However, a ten minute spell midway through the second half got Errigal back on track and they scored 1-3 to lead for the first time, 2-5 to 1-7.

Eamon Rodgers pointed and for the first time there was the realisation that a shock could be on the cards. But, missed chances curtailed their impact to an Adrian Donnelly point which made it 1-9 to 2-5 in the dying minutes. Still, they looked to have done enough until Errigal Ciaran came with a last gasp rally described in the following terms by the Ulster Herald.

Action from the meeting of Beragh and Errigal Ciaran in the opening round of the 1994 Tyrone Senior Championship at Carrickmore

"The Tyrone and Ulster Champions produced their trump card with the very last attack of the game. A sweeping move starting with goalkeeper, Cathal McAnenly, saw Peter Canavan gain possession. His pass found Eamon McCaffrey in front of goal and shooting for victory.

"But Beragh goalkeeper, Paddy Grimes, made the save of his life. The ball rebounded to Martin McCaffrey who pointed from close range to become the hero of Errigal Ciaran and the player who saved their titles. Seconds later came the kick-out and the final whistle from referee, Donal O'Neill...and now for the replay."

It was perhaps inevitable that the replay failed to live up to the excitement generated by the drawn tie. Forewarned is forearmed and the benefit of

357

hindsight shows that Errigal were never going to slip-up when given the second chance.

An increased attendance of 3000 arrived back at Carrickmore expecting to see more heroics from the Red Knights. What they got was a strong message of defiance from Errigal that their titles were not going to be so easily relinquished.

Beragh on the defensive against Errigal Ciaran

However, the opening quarter looked to be following the trend of the opening tie. Despite missing the injured Barry McCartan and Stephen Farley and the suspended, Paul Donnelly, they held Errigal to a two point lead before the champions raced to score 1-11 without reply in the next fifteen minutes. They piled on the agony on the resumption, although a goal from Paddy Maguire made it 1-15 to 1-1 entering the final quarter. Errigal finished with further goals from Peter Canavan and Eoin Gormley to seal the easiest of wins on a final score of 3-16 to 1-2. And, later in the season they retained their title with a win over Carrickmore in the final.

In 1995 it was back to normality for Beragh in the championship when a first round defeat by Cookstown proved very disappointing. At Dungannon on May 14th, they lost out on a score of 1-8 to 1-7, the goal coming right at the end and too late to save them. Wasteful shooting cost Beragh dearly throughout and they struggled until the final minutes when a foul on Sean Owens resulted in a close-in free which Cathal Grimes hammered to the net.

1996 Senior Semi-Finalists

Appearances at the semi-final stage of the Senior Championship have been a rare treat for followers of the GAA in the Beragh area since 1906. But a third year in the top flight in the mid-nineties meant that the team of 1996 had the necessary experience and ability to add to the list which already included 1924, 1936 and 1955.

So, the Red Knights were tipped to progress against Trillick in the opening round of that 1996 race for the O'Neill Cup. They duly did just that, although only after being given a real fright from the championship specialists of the previous two decades.

But Beragh came strongly in the end, a foul on Eamon Rodgers resulted in a penalty which Cathal Grimes slotted home

Only in the last ten minutes did they finally impose their authority on proceedings. A rather fortunate goal from Eamon Rodgers, whose sideline ball sailed all the way to the net, put them level on 1-4 to 0-7 at half-time. Paddy Grimes had to be on his toes in the second half as Trillick led by three points entering a crucial stage.

But Beragh came strongly in the end, a foul on Eamon Rodgers resulted in a penalty which Cathal Grimes slotted home and further points from Grimes and Stephen Donnelly sealed the win.

A prolonged delay in the championship due to Tyrone's progress to the All-Ireland semi-final meant that it wasn't until the beginning of September that Beragh got the chance to play Drumquin in the Quarter Final. Both were relative newcomers to Senior ranks and anxious to make their mark.

Drumquin looked to be on form when they led by 0-5 to 0-1 in the early stages. However, a quick-fire move started by Paul Donnelly resulted in Ciaran Cox firing home a goal to leave them level at 1-2 to 0-5 at half-time.

Action from the meeting of Beragh and Errigal Ciaran in the 1996 Senior Championship Semi-Final

Eamon Rodgers moving ahead for Beragh during the 1996 Senior Semi-Final against Errigal Ciaran

Eamon Rodgers hit the crossbar after good work from Cathal Grimes and a couple of points from them failed to make any real impression on Errigal's lead

Paddy Grimes was to the fore in saving a Drumquin goalbound effort as Beragh bounced back with an Eamon Rodgers goal and then went three ahead thanks to Cathal Grimes. Sean Owens, Paul Donnelly and Niall Farley worked hard to keep Drumquin in check and the issue wasn't decided until late on when Terry McKenna knocked home a Cathal Grimes cross to complete the five point win on a score of 3-4 to 0-8.

This set-up a semi-final date with destiny against Errigal Ciaran just five days later. A keenly contested tie was expected, but the favourites proved too strong for their neighbours and underdogs.

Points from Cathal Grimes and Eamon Rodgers kept things tight in the first quarter. But Errigal pressed ahead and were five points to the good at the interval, 0-7 to 0-2. Grimes reduced the deficit on the resumption before Errigal took a decisive step forward thanks to an Eamon McCaffrey goal.

From then on the game was effectively over as a real contest. Eamon Rodgers hit the crossbar after good work from Cathal Grimes and a couple of points from them failed to make any real impression on Errigal's lead as they emerged winners on a final score of 1-13 to 0-7. Errigal Ciaran went on to lose to Carrickmore in the 1996 County Final.

The Beragh team was: Paddy Grimes, Stephen Farley, Sean Owens, Shane McCarney, Gary Donnelly, Paul Donnelly, Niall Farley, Terry McKenna, Adrian Donnelly, Ciaran Cox, Sean Donnelly, Stephen Donnelly, Eamon Rodgers, Barry Grimes, Cathal Grimes.
Other panelists – Barry McCartan, Hugh McNamee, Mickey McCann, Patsy Farley, Barry McMahon, Martin McMahon, Aidan Grimes, Peter McNamee, Barry McNamee, Ciaran Donnelly, Michael Montague, Paul Meenagh, Barry Conroy, Dominic Donnelly, Seamus Grimes.
Scorers – Cathal Grimes 0-4, Eamon Rodgers 0-3.

Cathal Grimes giving chase in the 1996 Senior Championship Semi-Final

Carrickmore on top - Championship action 1997-1999

One final swansong for the Red Knights during a golden period at senior level came in 1997 when they faced Carrickmore in the first championship meeting between the clubs since 1962. Three decades earlier Beragh had caused the champions a real fright and were determined to repeat the feat against the O'Neill Cup holders on June 1st at Omagh.

It was described as a 'tense and taut' sixty minutes, as space was at a premium. Eight minutes had elapsed by the time of the first score and points from Martin McMahon, Cathal Grimes and Barry McCartan helped Beragh into a 0-4 to 0-2 interval lead.

There was thus reason to hope that the efforts of Patsy Farley and Ciaran Cox in defence and Paul Donnelly at midfield would see the Red Knights cause a shock in the second half. However, it was Carrickmore who called on a lot of their championship experience to come from behind. They were soon level as Beragh were left ruing the absence of a left-footed free-taker. Misses proved costly and three late scores saw Carrickmore through by two points on a score of 0-6 to 0-4.

The Beragh team lined out: Paddy Grimes, Stephen Farley, Sean Owens, Dominic Donnelly, Ciaran Cox, Michael Montague, Patsy Farley, Niall Farley, Terry McKenna, Martin McMahon, Paul Donnelly, Barry Grimes,

Patsy Farley in
determined mood
against
Carrickmore in
the 1997 Senior
Championship

Barry McCartan, Shane McCarney, Cathal Grimes. Subs - Adrian Donnelly for M McMahon. Scorers - Cathal Grimes 0-2, Martin McMahon 0-1, Shane McCarney 0-1.

Relegation at the end of 1997 meant that it was Intermediate Championship action which involved Beragh in 1998. Newtownstewart provided the opposition at Omagh where the Red Knights got off to a dream start thanks to a Ciaran Cox goal. However, Newtownstewart responded in kind to lead by 1-5 to 1-3 at the interval.

Eamon Rodgers fired over a couple of points for Beragh who still trailed entering the closing stages. Ultimately, two late points from Barry Grimes and then Rodgers with a last gasp equaliser secured a 1-8 each draw.

Everything fell apart in the replay on June 21st at Omagh where Newtownstewart came strong in the second half. An Eamon Rodgers goal left the sides level at 1-5 each at half-time and a Niall Owens point put

Beragh in front at the start of the second half. Barry McCartan, Stephen Farley and Sean Owens tried hard for Beragh but a late goal secured Newtownstewart a 3-7 to 1-8 win.

The Beragh scorers were: Eamon Rodgers 1-4, Niall Farley 0-1, Adrian Donnelly 0-1, Niall Owens 0-1, Sean Owens 0-1.

In the 1999 Intermediate Championship good play from Stephen Farley, Dominic Donnelly and Gary Donnelly in defence, Terry McKenna at midfield and Niall Farley, Ciaran Cox and Patsy Farley helped Beragh into a 0-5 to 0-2 lead at half-time against Brackaville.

Regular goalkeeper during the 1990s, Paddy Grimes, saves this shot against Drumquin

Niall Farley extended the lead and Beragh remained ahead entering the final quarter but disaster struck when four goals in the last ten minutes saw Brackaville emerge winners by 4-6 to 0-9.

Other competitions

Progress to the later stages of the championship and league as well as double-title successes in the McGarrity and McElduff competitions at the end of the decade ensured that the Red Knights were formidable opponents on a range of fronts in the nineties. There were also the efforts of the Reserve team which reached the finals of the Division Two Championship in 1990 and 1993.

Victory over Killyclogher by 1-14 to 1-11 in the Jim Devlin Cup gave Beragh a confident start to the new decade. That win put them through to the semi-final, although a 3-6 to 2-4 loss at the hands of Gortin was their lot.

But there was better fortune towards the end of the season when they reversed this defeat with a 3-9 to 2-8 win in the Quarter Final of the McGarrity Cup. A 1-9 to 1-4 win over Moortown followed in the semi-final to set up a glamour decider against a Trillick team still containing many of the players who had marked a glorious era for the club in the seventies and eighties.

Healy Park in Omagh was the venue for the game on December 9. However, it wasn't to prove a particularly satisfying day for the Red Knights who lost by 1-7 to 0-7. A penalty goal proved decisive in the

> Successes in the McGarrity and McElduff competitions at the end of the decade ensured that the Red Knights were formidable opponents on a range of fronts in the nineties

game which saw Beragh miss a number of goal chances from Eamon Rodgers, Cathal Grimes and Mickey McCann.

At the time the Cup competitions provided plenty of pre-season preparations for Tyrone clubs. And, in 1994, Beragh's confidence as they headed into senior ranks for the first time since the seventies was boosted by a 3-7 to 0-12 win over Ardboe in the Frank O'Neill Cup. They went on to top their group, before losing by 1-10 to 2-6 to Moortown in the semi-final towards the end of March.

Within two years, Beragh had developed into one of the strongest teams on the senior scene. This was reflected in the league, championship and their reaching of the 1996 McGarrity Cup Final - the second of the decade.

They defeated Omagh by 2-8 to 1-9 in the semi-final, a win which came after they had trailed by 1-6 to 1-4 at half-time. A goal from Mickey McCann got them going and they never relinquished that lead.

Easter Monday at Fintona was the date and venue for the final against Dromore. However, understandable confidence was hit by the withdrawal through injury of Sean Owens, an early goal and the dismissal of Ciaran Cox.

> Within two years, Beragh had developed into one of the strongest teams on the senior scene. This was reflected in the league, championship and their reaching of the 1996 McGarrity Cup Final - the second of the decade

Beragh rallied to reduce the deficit to just three points at half-time before being hit by the sucker punch of a second Dromore goal on the resumption. The only response was when Cathal Grimes hammered the ball to the net late on following a sweeping movement, but the 2-9 to 1-6 final scoreline shows that the game was up a good bit prior to the final whistle.

Relegation from Senior ranks at the end of 1997 meant new challenges in 1998, including a different Cup competition. This time the Division Two teams provided the opposition and Beragh progressed to the Frank O'Neill Cup semi-final where a 1-17 to 0-10 win was recorded over a Clann Na nGael team containing Brian Dooher and a young Stephen O'Neill in their lineout.

This set up a final against Loughmacrory and in an exciting tie, the teams finished level at 3-9 to 2-12 in May. But a replay sometime later saw the St Teresa's emerge winners.

There was, however, to be an exciting end to the decade in terms of the Cup competitions as Beragh completed 1999 and the twentieth century on the highest of notes with a McGarrity and Frank O'Neill double in the autumn of that season.

The Frank O'Neill Cup decider was a real classic encounter as it took three hours to separate Beragh and Brackaville. The Owen Roes were favourites going into the opening game in front of a large attendance but the accuracy of Barry Grimes from frees helped Beragh into a 0-5 to 0-4 interval advantage.

Aidan Grimes receives the Paul Montague Memorial Trophy in 1994 with Stephen and Sean Montague among those looking on

He extended that lead on the resumption as affairs remained finely balanced. By the end of normal time, the teams were level at 0-10 each and Beragh got a dream start to extra time when Sean Owens set up Ciaran Cox for a goal. They led by 1-12 to 0-12, but slipped back as Brackaville grabbed a 0-16 to 1-13 draw.

There was more thrilling action in the replay on the last Sunday in October when goals from Mickey McCann and Patsy Farley gave Beragh the edge. There were also fine displays from Barry Grimes (0-9), Sean Owens (0-4), Stephen Donnelly (0-2) as they emerged winners on a score of 2-15 to 2-10 after extra time.

Afterwards, the Beragh captain, Terry McKenna, received the Cup and the team was celebrating again following a hard-earned victory over Fintona in the McGarrity Cup Final. Beragh had reached the final courtesy of a 2-16 to 2-9 win over Killyman. In the decider some good scoring in the second half did the trick for them after the Pearses had held a slender half-time lead. The final score was 0-15 to 2-6 in favour of the Red Knights.

High points for the team at Senior level were replicated to some extent by the fortunes of the Reserves who made some progress in Division Two in the early part of the decade and held their own in Division One during the four year stint there from 1994 to 1997.

They reached the championship final in 1990 against Galbally in a game played at Carrickmore. Beragh led by 1-4 to 1-3 at the break, the goal coming from Seamus Boyle, and continued to make much of the running in the second half when Frank Owens, Sean McNamee, Gerry Boyle and Gerry Ward were to the fore. The game finished 1-7 each and in the replay their hopes of taking a third title in six years were dashed when Galbally emerged winners by 2-4 to 0-5.

The Beragh players and supporters who travelled to Birmingham for the Paul Montague Memorial Tournament in 1994

That year also saw them finish runners-up in the Division Two Reserve League and the next big event for them arrived in 1993 when they once again progressed to the Division Two Reserve Championship Final. A 3-13 to 2-8 win was recorded over Drumquin in the semi-final, but their

hopes were again dashed at the last hurdle when they lost to Edendork in the final at Eglish by 2-13 to 0-8.

There were notable moments on other fronts as well. In 1993 the Over 30s team won the Eskra Tournament while the holding of the Paul Montague Memorial Tournament provided an enjoyable weekend in Birmingham in early October 1994.

That Tournament was organised to commemorate, Paul, a youth player with the club in the 1980s who had died suddenly while at University in Birmingham in 1992. A thirty strong party travelled to the event which saw the Beragh team take a break from the rigours of senior football to win the second running of the Tournament. Incidentally, the Paul Montague Trophy is now awarded to the Player of the Year in the British Universities Championship.

Youth Football

> The indications were good as a party of 54 travelled to Roscommon in March 1990 to take on the local Gaels team in U-14 and U-16 Challenge matches

It would have been understandable for those coming through the ranks of the Beragh youth teams in the nineties to expect to make a strong bid for honours at various levels in Tyrone Grade One competitions. After all, the successes of the 1980s at Juvenile and Minor level suggested that the Red Knights were on the right track in terms of maintaining their place among the top clubs on the underage scene.

The indications were good as a party of 54 travelled to Roscommon in March 1990 to take on the local Gaels team in U-14 and U-16 Challenge matches. They were among the top teams in Connaught at the time and went on to win numerous titles at county and provincial level, yet their matches against the Red Knights teams were extremely competitive.

But a look through the statistics for this period indicates that the progress made in the eighties was coming to a halt. No finals were reached, youth teams generally struggled to make their mark in Grade One during the early part of the decade and the end result was a drop to Grade Two where the fortunes failed to show any improvement.

Everything seemed so different at the beginning of 1990 when the facts spoke of ever-increasing numbers in the underage ranks and a call for more coaches. But the early part of the decade saw the club struggle to compete in Grade One despite occasional encouraging signs.

In 1996 the club's youth teams totally failed to mark their mark. For the

Youth teams of the 1990s who enjoyed their participation in gaelic football

second year running the U-14s finished their league with no wins from seven games, it was a similar story at Juvenile level where Beragh also played seven and lost seven and only the Minors in Grade Two salvaged something when they finished on eight points in their section.

Unsurprisingly, there was a lot of soul-searching at the end of the year when the question of whether to drop a grade was raised 'to raise standards of performance and increase the motivation of younger players.' This was done and, while the teams were more competitive, they still failed to make the desired impact until the end of the decade.

Of course, the bare facts do not acknowledge the efforts made by so many people during the decade in looking after teams and organising trips. Events such as the U-12 Mini-Tournament in 1993, a trip by the U-12s to the 1995 All-Ireland semi-final, the coaching day provided in 1998 and taken by Anthony Rainbow of Kildare, Kevin Walsh of Galway, Derry Foley of Tipperary, Brendan Devenney of Donegal and John Kenny of Offaly.

And, there was the Shield competition commemorating Mickey McGuinness who had been a dedicated club official until his tragic death at the end of 1989 in a construction site accident. A special Shield was presented by his workmates in McCallan Brothers and, appropriately enough, the Beragh Minors were the first winners when they defeated Dromore in the final.

> There was the Shield competition commemorating Mickey McGuinness who had been a dedicated club official until his tragic death at the end of 1989 in a construction site accident

Presenting the Shield to the winning captain, Mickey's son, Barry, Club Secretary, Frank Rodgers, said that "the Tournament was a great tribute to the work that Mickey McGuinness had done for the GAA in Beragh." Following this, a cheque for £200 was presented to the local Branch of St Vincent De Paul by Mickey's wife, Bernie.

The Tournament fell by the wayside after a number of years, joining the Primary League as one of the annual events no longer organised. So, while the Senior teams made their mark at the highest level in Tyrone with high profile matches, the fortunes of these competitions and youth teams generally during the nineties provided a warning for the future.

Bernie McGuinness presents the Mickey McGuinness Shield to the winning Dromore captain in 1992. Club Chairman, Seamus Boyle, is among those looking on

Handball

Problems with the deteriorating 40x20 Alley at St Mary's Park failed to prevent the Brackey Handballers making a big impact at Ulster and All-Ireland level during the nineties. A breakthrough at All-Ireland level combined with continued success on the county and provincial scenes came at a time when the need for improved facilities was becoming clear.

But that was far from the minds of officials at the beginning of the decade when they set about organising a Novice Tournament and the Brackey Invitational event. Officials for that year included Chairman - Patrick Conroy, Secretary, - Damien Given, Treasurer - Paddy Ward, Vice-Chairman - Mick Kerr, Assistant Secretary - Nuala McCartan, Assistant Treasurer - Stephen Hall.

On court, Stephen Clarke retained his Tyrone Senior title, while the following year, 1991 finally saw a player from Brackey win an All-Ireland title. The honour went to Damien Given, who teamed up with Rory Grogan to win the U-17 Doubles. They beat the Wexford pairing 15-13, 6-15 and 15-14 in the final, a kill-shot by Damien Given, clinching the title.

Other Ulster winners included Justin McClean, with Ciaran Curran, in the U-19 Doubles, Mark McCartan in the U-21 60x30 Doubles, Mark

Handball action
in the Beragh
alley during
the decade

McCartan and Patrick Conroy in the U-21 60x30 Doubles and Stephen Clarke in the 60x30 Junior Singles and Doubles.

Michael Maguire followed this up by winning the U-17 Ulster Singles title in 1992 and going on to take the All-Ireland as well when he defeated his Westmeath counterpart. Stephen Clarke completed a three in a row of Senior titles in Tyrone.

Players from Brackey won three provincial titles in 1993 when Justin McClean captured the U-21 Singles, Martin McMahon and Stephen Nixon triumphed in the U-15 Doubles and Peter McNamee and Ciaran Cox won the U-16 doubles.

The middle year of the decade, 1994, was definitely one to remember as in March Peter McNamee and Ciaran Cox won the U-17 All-Ireland Doubles title. They defeated the Cork pairing in straight games in the final at a time when Niall Kerr and Ciaran McCallan narrowly missed out on success in the All-Ireland Novice Final.

Niall bounced back, however, to take the All-Ireland Novice Singles title by defeating Pat Quail from Wicklow in the final. A master serve and kill-shot won the title for him while Peter McNamee joined Eunan Donnelly in capturing the All-Ireland Vocational Schools title.

A highlight of 1995 was the success of the Brackey Club in capturing the All-Ireland Intermediate title. The team included Paul Clarke, Conor Kerr, Stephen Clarke and Niall Kerr. They beat Rossa of Belfast to reach the semi-final in which saw they defeated Liscarroll.

This put them through to the final against Garda and it started well when Stephen Clarke won the initial singles game. Conor Kerr and Paul Clarke were the doubles pairing and going into the final game Brackey led by 96-85. Niall Kerr won 21-17 in the singles to leave them needing only seven points to take the title and it was safely secured when he went 7-0 ahead in the final match.

Eunan Kelly joined Ciaran Meenagh in coming top with victory in the 1996 All-Ireland 60x30 U-16 title in a year that saw Barry McCartan defeat Stephen Kelly in the Tyrone Intermediate Final. And, those victories provided the preclude to a good start to 1997 when Stephen Clarke and Justin McClean defeated Paul Clarke and Conor Kerr to win the Tyrone Senior Doubles title. Conor and Niall Kerr went on to win the Ulster Junior title before being narrowly beaten in the All-Ireland Final, while Peter McNamee and Ciaran Cox won the provincial U-21 Doubles

> The middle year of the decade, 1994, was definitely one to remember as in March Peter McNamee and Ciaran Cox won the U-17 All-Ireland Doubles title

371

crown and Ruairi Kelly the U-12 singles.

Conor and Niall Kerr went on to win the Ulster Junior doubles again in 1998 and they also contested the Junior singles final, with Niall coming out on top against his brother. Niall went on to contest the All-Ireland Handball Final, narrowly losing in his bid to win a second title.

Mick Kerr receives another award, this time from Mary McCarney, Club Treasurer as the Secretary, Frank Rodgers, Chairman, Paddy Bogan and Gerry Ward look on

The final year of the decade was to provide a high level of activity on the Tyrone Handball scene, including plenty for the Brackey Club even though the problems with the Alley persisted. On the Ulster and All-Ireland fronts, Stephen Clarke lost narrowly in the Junior Singles after capturing the provincial title, while Ruairi Kelly's Ulster win was not built upon as he narrowly missed out on an All-Ireland Final place after a great tussle. At 60x30 level, Niall Kerr lost in the All-Ireland Final.

With the 40x20 Alley in Beragh in urgent need of repair during the decade, efforts were made to revive Cloughfin Club from 1997 onwards. A committee was formed with people from the area and local clubs, the court was made playable again and a committee of the following elected: Chairman - Sean Clarke, Secretary - John Smith, Treasurer - Seamus Nugent, Members - Martin McCann, Martin Mullan, Aidan McMullan, Brian Somerville, Roger O'Sullivan, Brian Gormley and two delegated from the Brackey Club.

This renewed activity helped to revive 60x30 Handball locally and had a dividend when the club was only just beaten in the Novice and Junior All-Ireland Semi-Finals. The participants were Seamus Hussey, Martin Mullan, Con Smith, Niall Kerr and Ciaran McCallan.

Ladies Football

When a small group of enthusiasts gathered in Beragh Youth Club at the beginning of 1994 to form a Ladies team they could hardly have anticipated just how fruitful their efforts would be over the next few years. Their work came at a time of sustained growth for the game in Tyrone culminating in girls from the Red Knights Ladies subsequently making their mark at club, county and university levels.

Many of the players participating took the chance to become involved in gaelic sport again following the demise of camogie a few years earlier. A senior team was entered in Division Two for that 1994 season and one of the first games was against Castlederg in the League. The team that lined out was: Alisha McQuaide, Cabrini Owens, Ann McCartan, Cathy Montague, Shelly Grimes, Tracey Grimes, Briege White, Nuala McCartan, Caroline Donnelly, Helen Rodgers, Louise Donnelly, Carmel Grimes, Celine Grimes, Aine McCann, Ann Donnelly. Subs – Mary Farley, Sinead Donnelly, Dolores Donnelly, Ann McCarney, Maeve McKenna, Bronagh Gallagher, Orla Donnelly, Bronagh Grimes, Cara Franey, Donna Donnelly.

They defeated Trillick in the first round of the championship by 5-11 to 6-5 and, while the title eluded them, a second placing in Division Two provided grounds for hope.

At the first Annual Meeting in December, the officers elected were: Chairperson - Caroline Donnelly, Vice-Chairperson - Aine McCann, Secretary - Nuala McCartan, Assistant Secretary - Gabrielle McAleer, Treasurer - Cabrini Owens, PRO - Ann McCartan, Registrar - Tracey Grimes.

Barry Grimes, Ciaran Cox and Mickey McCann agreed to take the Senior team for the following 1995 season which was to prove a memorable one. Training and matches demanded the time of the players, whose commitment began to pay off when they defeated Aghyaran by 5-7 to 1-8 in the first round of the championship. Drumquin were defeated on a score of 1-8 to 1-6 in the semi-final to set up an Intermediate Final meeting against Trillick.

The Final was played on August 6th at Omagh and saw Beragh comfortably take the title. They led by 2-8 to 0-0 at half-time, Ann Donnelly getting the first two goals. But the wind made a difference and it was just 3-4 to 2-2 midway through the second half. However, a third goal from Ann Donnelly proved decisive in clinching the Thomas McGarvey Cup for the Red Knights.

The team was: Bronagh Grimes, Cathy Montague, Tracey Grimes, Sinead

Many of the players participating took the chance to become involved in gaelic sport again following the demise of camogie a few years earlier

Caroline Donnelly and Nuala McCartan have their success with Tyrone Ladies recognised by the Beragh club and Peter Canavan in 1995

Donnelly, Shelly Grimes, Briege McGarvey, Louise Donnelly, Nuala McCartan (captain), Caroline Donnelly, Louise Heagney, Aine McCann, Ann McCartan, Lisa Rodgers, Ann Donnelly, Cabrinia Owens. Other panelists - Pauline McCann, Emma Ward, Marie Donnelly, Bronagh Gallagher, Gabrielle McAleer, Orla Donnelly, Siobhan Owens.

What a moment it was for the Red Knights when Nuala McCartan lifted the Cup on the Hogan Stand to become the second-last captain to do so before the historic stand was demolished

While success in the league eluded them when Trillick came out on top, the team progressed with confidence to Division One as the growth of the game in the parish continued. This was especially significant in 1996 when for the first time a number of teams were fielded at underage level. Pauline Lyttle, Geraldine Donnelly, Gerry Donnelly and Nuala McCartan were among those mentioned for their efforts as the club entered competitions at U-12, U-14, U-16 and U-18 grades in 1996 and also retained their senior status.

The first success at youth level arrived in 1998 when the Juveniles, captained by Roisin McNelis and managed by Caroline and Ann Donnelly, won the Championship title. The players involved were: Ciara Maguire, Siobhan McSorley, Claire Montague, Donna Donnelly, Tracey Rodgers, Paula McMahon, Roisin McNelis, Emma Montague, Aishling Hagan, Josephine Rodgers, Edel McEnhill, Helena McSorley, Catherine Donnelly, Joeline Coleman, Tracey McClean, Claire Donnelly, Cathy Donnelly, Cathy Cox, Julie Conroy, Sarah Munroe, Aishling Lyttle, Paula Donnelly, Colleen McSorley and Lisa Mullin.

This was followed up a year later when many of the same players were

374

involved in the Minor team which won the League title by defeating Galbally in the final. And, with the Seniors maintaining their Division One status, the outlook was certainly bright entering the new century.

So bright in fact, that five people from the club were involved in the Tyrone team which won the All-Ireland title for the first time. What a moment it was for the Red Knights when Nuala McCartan lifted the Cup on the Hogan Stand to become the second-last captain to do so before the historic stand was demolished.

Her never-to-be-forgotten moment made up for the disappointments of 1995 and 1997 when herself and Caroline Donnelly endured defeat at this stage. Nuala's joy in that 1999 Final was shared by colleagues, Caroline Donnelly, Ann Donnelly and Ciara Donnelly, assistant manager, Barry Grimes, family, friends and a good representation of supporters from the club.

Camogie and Hurling

Pressure from other demands meant that the nineties saw the demise of both hurling and camogie in the parish after over a decade of encouraging and at times sustained progress. And, this was despite the fact that more young players than ever were getting the chance to participate in Ireland's national sport.

Gabrielle McAleer receives the Clubperson of the Year award in 1995 as the various Ladies Players of the Year awards are presented

The growth of Ladies football was highlighted by the introduction of youth teams in the later part of the decade. This was the 1999 Minor side

It was in the early part of the decade that the two finally fell by the wayside. Efforts were made to field a Camogie team during 1990 and 1991 and Beragh entered a number of competitions.

Teams were fielded in the U-16 and Minor grades and the adult side also took part in a number of games. But the decline that was taking root at a county-wide level was permeating through the ranks and, despite the best efforts of those involved, the demands in terms of equipment, personnel

This Omagh hurling team of the 1990s included three Beragh players in Ciaran Cox and Alan and Eamon Rodgers, pictured far right on the opposite page, in action for the Tyrone Hurlers in the 1996 All-Ireland Junior Final

and time proved too much.

But a number of players did continue their involvement, including Briege McCartan who won an Intermediate title with Tattyreagh.

Hurling, too, was abandoned. Without the backing of the Games Committee, which had proved effective in the period from the mid-eighties, the decision was taken to give up on the project of establishing hurling within the club.

The unfortunate fact for those involved was that this came following the busiest season ever in hurling. In 1990 teams were fielded in the U-14, U-16 and Minor grades and, although the going was tough at times, the players did compete well.

The difficulty in attracting adult members remained and the job of recruiting players, organising fundraising activities and coaching was left to Alan Rodgers, with help at that time from Patrick and Gerard Conroy.

So acute was the situation that the Tyrone Annual in 1990 contained this accurate summary of hurling health in Beragh. "The future of hurling in this club is hanging by a thread. Only for the determined efforts of one individual - and that's an U-18 member - hurling would have been long out of operation here despite making brave attempts over the past four years to get the game established at underage level.

"Basically, the lack of manpower is the biggest obstacle facing the Red Knights and unless there is much great improvement all around here and perhaps better 'outside' assistance being made available, it would be no great surprise to see hurling disappear completely. In the event of such, the game in Tyrone will suffer a sad and needless loss - clubs are already too few to allow another one to fold."

That bleak outlook came true at an Executive meeting on September 5th, 1991, when the decision was taken to withdraw and tribute was paid to Alan Rodgers "whose initiative, determination and effort was largely responsible for hurling in Beragh from 1983 to 1991."

Nevertheless, players from the club continued to participate. Patsy and Stephen Farley hurled with distinction in the colours of Carrickmore Eire Ogs, Brian O'Neill and Ciaran Cox won Minor and U-21 medals with Omagh St Enda's and represented Tyrone, Alan and Eamon Rodgers played for Omagh at adult level and Terry McKenna represented Carrickmore in the youth ranks.

One highlight was the involvement of club player, Eamon Rodgers, in the Tyrone Junior team which won two Ulster titles and eventually won the All-Ireland title in 1996. He played at midfield in the team which defeated Hertfordshire in the historic 1996 final and it was a sense of great pride for the Red Knights to have him and three other players with connections to

> " The future of hurling in this club is hanging by a thread. Only for the determined efforts of one individual - and that's an U-18 member - hurling would have been long out of operation here "

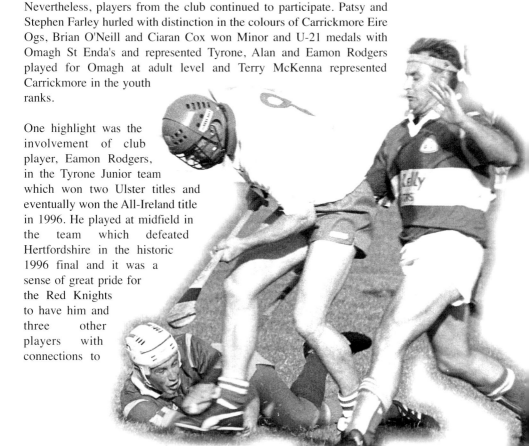

Dessie's design set in stone

Alan Rodgers,
Brian McGarvey,
Patsy Farley and
Frank Rodgers get
an insight into the
new Croke Park
Design from the
Architect, Dessie
McMahon, in 1991

Regular visits to the Croke Park of the late nineties generated great pride for members of the Red Knights as they reflect upon the fact that the stadium was designed by Beragh-born architect, Dessie McMahon.

A partner in the Dublin architectural firm of Gilroy/McMahon, the firm held off stiff competition to be chosen to carry out the redesign of the stadium described by the GAA President at the time, Peter Quinn, as the most challenging project of its kind ever undertaken in Ireland.

Dessie obtained his early education at Roscavey Primary School and afterwards attended the CBS in Omagh. After qualifying as a teacher he taught Art for a while as an art teacher in St Patrick's Secondary School in Dungannon. But he left to become an architect and after graduating set up the firm of Gilroy/McMahon in 1972. His partner, John Gilroy, later died in a car accident and by the time the Croke Park design contact was awarded, the company had 25 employees.

The firm was awarded the Sunday Tribune Building of the Year award in 1989 for the redesign of the Dublin College of Technology and the purchase of £200,000 of computers was crucial to the completion of the Croke Park project.

"To manually draw and redraw eighty thousand seats would have taken too long. In purchasing the computers, we saved a lot of time, time which we were then able to spend concentrating on the design," Dessie told the Ulster Herald in a 1991 article.

Stadiums were visited throughout Europe and the United States and on many occasions, Dessie travelled to the base of the H.O.K Sports Facilities Group in Kansas to research and design a stadium which would meet the requirements of the GAA. The result was a design for the biggest sporting organisation in Ireland beyond what even the most optimistic GAA follower could have hoped for.

And, speaking prior to the 2003 All-Ireland Final, he reflected on his memories of playing football in Beragh and the significance of what turned out to be a successful bid for All-Ireland glory by Tyrone.

"For me, Sunday will be an unbearably emotional occasion because of my roots in Tyrone. If we win I'll be thinking of all the people who have worked so hard to keep the Beragh club going over the years.

"Hard workers like John Donaghy, the Hagans, Mick Kerr, Frank Rodgers, the Donnellys, McCartans and so on. Childhood shapes your life and also victories, defeats and all the happy memories of waiting for the teamsheet to be pinned up on the chapel wall and going to West Tyrone Board meetings will be running through my head on Sunday."

The redevelopment was finished ahead of schedule and by the end of the 1990s was becoming the magnificent world-class stadium designed by a Beragh man with a unique place in GAA history.

Other activities and events - Early Nineties turmoil

Difficulties associated with the running of GAA clubs come in a range of different guises. In the early nineties those associated with the Beragh Red Knights had their share of problems as a number of burning issues came to a head.

The problems centred on the club structures which were established in the

Stadiums were visited throughout Europe and the United States and on many occasions, Dessie travelled to the base of the H.O.K Sports Facilities Group in Kansas to research and design a stadium which would meet the requirements of the GAA

> "
>
> It was a time that prompted the long-serving Secretary, Frank Rodgers, to issue a downbeat assessment of a 1991 season, which was to prove to be the last of his 24 in the post
>
> "

The 1995 Club Executive, with Chairman, Gerry Owens

mid-eighties. Sub-committees were set-up to look after aspects of club affairs, including development, games, social and cultural events, finance and communications. But it was the differences over team-selection and disciplinary matters which would prove the key stumbling blocks.

The Club Executive committee spearheaded this policy during the late eighties. It introduced a structure of internal disciplinary hearings for those deemed to have stepped out of line and match reports complete with statistics and comments on the team and player performance. Some felt that this was unnecessary and wanted to have the match reports done away with and the affairs of the senior team looked after by one "outside manager."

Matters came to a head during 1991, sparked among other things by an incident involving a referee at St Mary's Park, the resulting disciplinary hearings and the failure of a number of players to turn up for a subsequent Cup match in Ballygawley. The repercussions led to a year filled with recriminations and climazwed with a well-attended Club Convention in January, 1992.

It was a time that prompted the long-serving Secretary, Frank Rodgers, to issue a downbeat assessment of a 1991 season, which was to prove to be the last of his 24 in the post.

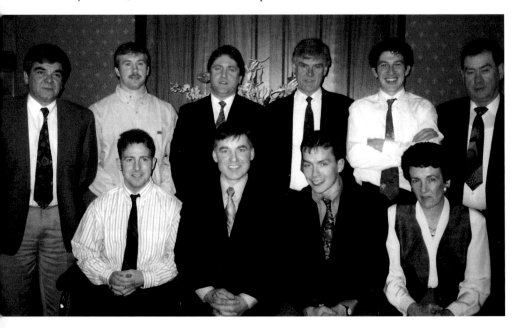

"The early season happenings resulted in the entire work of the previous six years being undermined. The sub-committee system ceased to operate and among those that fell by the wayside was the Games Sub-Committee that had achieved so much and was achieving so much.

Back for a re-union at the 1990 Dinner were the trailblazing players of 1972-1973

"We were back at the old system of one-man management and no central co-ordination of effort. The results of that are obvious from the tables etc of the year. And, it could get worse - for bear in mind that the importing of an 'outside manager' to look after ONE adult team will not be the answer to anything.

"Also out went the other sub-committees, so that there was no fundraising, no Scor, no Club Dinner, no members nights, no Park Development apart from the essential maintenance work.

And, resigning his position as Secretary after three decades, he added: " I have always done my best for the promotion of the GAA in the Beragh parish. I was privileged to be involved with a multitude of fine players and officials. Finally, I thank those on the 1991 Committee who made such a good effort to hold things together in the face of such disruption and lack of support."

It was a disappointing end to a prolonged contribution. Nevertheless, things moved on. New officials emerged with a determination to make the most of their opportunities and the success on the field during the following years eventually helped to put the events of that year of turmoil into perspective.

Other activities

Among the main priorities for the nineties was the provision of enhanced facilities at St Mary's Park in Beragh. Under the continued chairmanship of Sean Owens in the early part of the decade efforts continued to put together a plan for the renovation or reconstruction of clubrooms to meet the needs of the new decades.

Finance was, of course, a priority and the Members Draw in 1990 went some way towards providing the money necessary to do some work. Teams of sellers travelled around Ulster and further afield selling the £10 tickets, with the result that a total of around £13,000 was raised for development work.

New catchment nets were erected behind each goals, a security wall was built at the entrance to the dressing rooms and new dug-outs erected. However, the planned work on the dressing-rooms remained on the long finger.

However, a clearer picture was emerging of what was needed. In 1998 the message was sent out loud and clear that two extra male and female changing and shower rooms, toilet facilities for disabled spectators and participants were urgently needed.

The Novelty Act teams of the late 1990s produced some memorable shows

And, the failure to provide them saw the position of St Mary's Park as an attractive venue for top domestic matches diminishing. While Carrickmore v Errigal Ciaran in 1992 and Omagh v Killyclogher in 1995 were among the Senior Championship matches played there, the number of games hosted had declined to a trickle of low-profile youth games by the end of the decade.

Of course, none of this reduced the need for maintenance work which continued. The pitch was extensively drained in the early part of the decade ensuring that it remained one of the driest around even at times of persistent rain.

Malachy, Pete, Gerry, Brian, Dermot and Christy Owens pictured in 1994. Each one represented Beragh at both youth and adult level

The work that was carried out in the subsequent years was aided by a variety of fundraising activities. The Inter-Link draw and later the Club Lotto, which was established in the mid-nineties and drawn each Sunday night as part of what became known as 'The Sunday Club,' provided income on a regular basis. There were events such as the annual 'Night at the Races' and monthly discos in St Mary's Hall which were well supported and provided a significant contribution to meeting the rising running costs.

And a new way of raising finance in the 1990s was by jersey sponsorship and by selling advertisement hoardings around pitches. Rules allowing this were introduced for the 1991 season and it wasn't long before all clubs began using it as a source of income for themselves and advertising for local companies whose support for the GAA locally was welcome.

This was certainly the case in Beragh where the sponsorship of jerseys at all levels was appreciated, as the Club Secretary, Patsy Farley, explained in his 1995 report to Convention.

"We recognise that without the financial support of our sponsors, the running of the club would be much more difficult and our activities more limited. With the money received, the club has been able to provide new kits for our youth teams and we hope that the investment of sponsors will ensure the continued success of the club in the future."

Membership also showed a general increase during the decade. The number of adults enrolled stood at 67 in 1986, it had risen to 90 by 1990,

Finance was, of course, a priority and the Members Draw in 1990 went some way towards providing the money necessary to do some work

All those people
could follow the
activities of the
club through the
pages of 'News
and Views,' the
club news sheet
published between
1990 and 1992

to 156 by 1995 and record 207 by 1998. This was due to a more vigorous recruitment policy and to Tyrone's progress to the later stages of the All-Ireland Championships at Minor and Senior level when ticket allocation was tied to membership.

All those people could follow the activities of the club through the pages of 'News and Views,' the club news sheet published between 1990 and 1992. It covered matters relating to games, social events and historical items and other matters of interest, including a report in 1991 on how the Tyrone Minor team had used St Mary's Park as their base on the way to an Ulster Final appearance and another on Mick Kerr's success in winning the Tyrone GAA Special Merit Award in 1990.

On the Scor front, involvement was revived by the drive of Mickey McCann in the mid-nineties. Talented performers continued to avail of the opportunity to compete and did so with some success.

In 1999, County Scor Finals were reached in the Recitation (Martin McCrory) and Novelty Action (Niall Farley, Eoghain McKenna, Denise McCann, Maeve Grant, Sean Munroe, Barry Grimes and Ciaran Cox) while in Scor Na Og Sean Munroe, James Rodgers and Brian Mullin won their way through to the Quiz Final in 1998 and in 1999 Tracey Rodgers

(Solo Singing) and Briege Nugent (Recitation) reached the County Finals.

There was also death and tragedy. Barney O'Neill, a well known and dedicated supporter died at Easter 1991. Some of the last links with the early days of the Red Knights in the 1920s and 1930s also passed away. Among them were Felix Owens, Jack McCann, Mickey Gallagher, Packie Mullin and Mackle Grimes.

But no one can forget the events of August 15th 1998 when among those killed in the 'Omagh Bomb' were Mary Grimes, her daughter, Avril Monaghan and baby Maura and also Avril's unborn twins. All of the Grimes family had been involved with the Red Knights both as players and officials over the years and Avril herself contributed much to the promotion Camogie and Scor as well as serving on the Games Committee in the late eighties.

Some of the 1990 Minors with team manager, Gerry Owens, and the Mickey McGuinness Shield

Inter-County Affairs

History was made on September 17th 1995 when Paul Donnelly became the first player from the Beragh Club to line out for Tyrone in an All-Ireland Senior Final. He was introduced in the second half of the decider against Dublin to complete a steady rise through the inter-county ranks in the previous few years.

While he first came to prominence for Tyrone in the late eighties, it was in the early nineties that his real ability became apparent. Playing in the half-back line, his surging runs forward and ability to link up with Peter Canavan was a key asset.

He played on the Tyrone U-21 team which lost the All-Ireland Final to Kerry in 1990 and was back the following year when they defeated the same opposition to take the national title. A graduation to Senior ranks was inevitable and he made his championship debut against Derry in 1992 after earlier featuring in the side which reached the National League Final for the first time.

As Tyrone's fortunes improved dramatically, their Beragh star became a sort of 'cult hero,' with one of his most impressive performances coming against Donegal in the semi-final of the 1994 Ulster Championship. The incident with James McCartan in that year's Ulster Final remains a memory and, while he lost his starting place in 1995, his presence continued to be highly significant.

Paul Donnelly (front left) and Eamon Rodgers (back left) pictured on the Tyrone team of early 1996.

Paul's display against Derry in that year's Ulster Semi-Final was central to victory and a 'popular view' is that Tyrone 'might have won the Sam Maguire Cup for the first time if he had been introduced earlier against Dublin.' He remained part of the panel for a number of years after that and played against Meath in the 1996 All-Ireland Semi-Final.

Other players from the club to represent Tyrone during the decade were Eamon Rodgers, Patsy Farley and Terry McKenna. Terry captained the U-21 team in 1995 and went on to represent the Seniors in the National League before making his championship debut against Down in 1998.

At Minor level, too, a number of players gained representation. They included Cathal Grimes, who played in the 1990 Championship and Ciaran Cox, who played in 1995. Others featured on winning Tyrone Vocational teams.

There was also some success for players on their school teams, most notably the contingent from the Red Knights who featured on the Ballygawley St Ciaran's side which won the All-Ireland U-16 title in

1993. They were Barry Conroy, Ciaran Cox, Shane Donnelly, Michael Franey and Barry Donnelly (Cloughfin).

And, in 1999, two former players, Eamon Rodgers and Ciaran Donnelly were part of the Leeds Hugh O'Neill's team, which won the All-British Club Championship. The side was captained by Ciaran Donnelly and it later lost to a Crossmolina team spearheaded by Ciaran McDonald in the All-Ireland Club Quarter Final.

Conclusion

A look through the events of the nineties shows just how mixed the fortunes of the Beragh Red Knights really were. It was a decade that gave a glimpse of what could be achieved while at the same time providing a warning against complacency.

The progress of the Senior team to a high level in Senior and Intermediate ranks was a definite plus, balanced by the demoralising lows like the failure of youth teams to make an impact, the decline of hurling and

> " As Tyrone's fortunes improved dramatically, their Beragh star became a sort of 'cult hero,' with one of his most impressive performances coming against Donegal in the semi-final of the 1994 Ulster Championship "

camogie and the struggle to promote other club activities. Then, there was the growing dismay at the declining state of club facilities as the decade progressed.

Of course, the main aims of the Association were sustained and the numbers involved in youth and adult football, ladies football and handball provided satisfaction. In addition, the efforts of the usual band of dedicated workers ensured that the Red Knights remained to the forefront of parish and county sporting activity.

It was a decade that gave a glimpse of what could be achieved while at the same time providing a warning against complacency

Unsurprisingly, the need for improvement on so many fronts was clear as 1999 gave way to a new year, a new century and a new millennium. And, with the Centenary Year of the GAA in the Parish approaching, the Secretary's Report, presented by Alan Rodgers, for that last season of the 20th Century provided a focus.

"In six years we will celebrate the Centenary of the Association in the parish and throughout the past 100 years those involved in promoting gaelic games and culture can feel proud of their contribution.

"In 1999, the efforts of our members once again showed that the GAA in Beragh continues to thrive and prosper. But, while our memorable achievements are acknowledged and remembered, the service of all within the club and more is needed now as much as ever."

Chapter Twelve
2000 - 2006
New Facilities Match the Best

Chapter Twelve
2000 - 2006

AT the start of the 21st Century members of the Beragh Red Knights could look back with pride on their contribution to the GAA while at the same time look ahead with some confidence to the future. On and off the field the club was an active unit, fielding teams at all levels of Ladies and Mens football, participating in various cultural activities, including Scor and Scor Na Og, and generally providing top class recreational activity.

It was a scene, though, which required improvement. The performances of club sides at all levels demanded attention, and the deteriorating state of facilities at St Mary's Park was threatening to have a detrimental effect on the promotion of field games as well as on the fortunes of Brackey Handball Club.

There was definitely no room for complacency, then, as a second century of involvement in the GAA dawned. Many issues required attention while the ongoing daily responsibilities of team organisation, park maintenance, fundraising and a range of other jobs continued.

Intermediate Champions 2000

The experience gained during the previous decade meant that the Red Knights were capable of launching a serious challenge for adult honours in the first season of the new decade. But the big question centred on whether they would be able to regroup following the blow of suffering successive relegations at the end of the nineties.

the big question
centred on
whether they
would be able to
regroup following
the blow of
suffering
successive
relegations at the
end of the nineties

They appeared to be struggling at the start of 2000, before the arrival of Palor McNulty from Urney as manager helped to turn things around. A series of fine league wins set them up for the championship in which a magnificent run was to culminate in a second Intermediate title.

Killyman provided the opposition in the first round. The teams were evenly matched during the opening quarter before scores from Terry McKenna, Patsy Farley, and Barry Grimes helped Beragh into a 0-8 to 1-1 interval lead.

Killyman, however, staged a revival on the resumption when the dismissal of Martin McMahon hit the Red Knights. And, they looked to be in serious trouble when Killyman goaled entering the final quarter. But then the superior play of Dominic Donnelly, Sean Owens, Niall Farley and

Paddy Kelly about to win possession in the 2000
Intermediate Final against Gortin

The Beragh team which won the Division Two League at the start of the new decade

Paddy Kelly revived them as a goal from Ciaran Cox and points from Cathal Grimes and Sean Owens put them through on a final score of 1-13 to 2-6.

That win set up a Quarter Final meeting against Rock and as expected there were plenty of closely fought exchanges in that one. The St Patrick's side raced ahead before Beragh hit back and a goal from Ciaran Cox helped them to lead by 1-3 to 0-5 at half-time. A second goal, this time from Sean Owens, within twenty seconds of the throw-in extended their lead. A third goal from Ciaran Cox helped complete the final scoreline of 3-6 to 0-8.

It was all one-way traffic in the semi-final against Pomeroy in Dunmoyle. A series of well-taken points from Patsy Farley, Ciaran Cox, Terry McKenna, Niall Farley and Niall Owens put the Red Knights into a commanding 0-9 to 0-2 interval lead and the game was effectively over when Niall Owens goaled soon after the break. A second goal from Paul Donnelly, set up by Ciaran Cox, ensured an easy 2-15 to 0-5 win.

And, so to the Final where, appropriately enough considering the number of eagerly contested matches between the clubs in the previous decade, Gortin provided the opposition. It was played at Carrickmore on August 27th and proved to be dour and uncompromising.

Beragh got off to a good start through points from Ciaran Cox, Patsy Farley and Sean Owens. With Paddy Kelly, Niall Farley and Paul Donnelly working hard, a 0-6 to 0-1 lead provided grounds for optimism.

"

The teams returned to Carrickmore on September 10th when Gortin got the start that Beragh had enjoyed during the drawn game

"

Paul Donnelly shot narrowly wide and Sean Owens also had a goal chance saved as they threatened to overrun the St Patrick's.

But then things took a dramatic turnaround. Gortin fought back to leave just one point between them, 0-6 to 0-5 by half-time. They levelled on the resumption and the game remained very even right to the finish even though Beragh edged three ahead with ten minutes left. However, Gortin held most of the aces subsequently and three points in a row saw them secure a replay on a final score of 0-11 each.

The teams returned to Carrickmore on September 10th when Gortin got the start that Beragh had enjoyed during the drawn game. Stephen Farley, Barry McMahon and Paddy Kelly were called upon to make a number of vital interceptions as Beragh faced a determined initial storm from them. They weathered it to lead by 0-5 to 0-3 at half-time, the fact that they had to face the breeze in the second half meant that the odds were against them to some extent. The extra challenge brought out the best in the team and points from Barry Grimes and Ciaran Cox kept them just in front 0-7 to 0-5 as they approached the finish.

Dominic Donnelly battles for possession as Stephen Farley awaits developments

Then came the final decisive score. Smart thinking from Paul Donnelly resulted in him taking a quick free to Barry Grimes whose deft flick to the net set the Red Knights on the road to a second title. While Gortin tried hard to come back, Beragh held their composure to emerge winners on a final scoreline of 1-7 to 0-5.

Team - Cathal Grimes, Stephen Farley, Paddy Kelly, Barry McMahon, Martin McMahon, Dominic Donnelly, Niall Farley, Sean Owens, Terry McKenna, Stephen Donnelly, Gerard Loughran, Niall Owens, Paul Donnelly, Ciaran Cox, Patsy Farley.
Subs - Barry Grimes for N Farley. Other panelists -
Scorers - Barry Grimes 1-1, Patsy Farley 0-2, Ciaran Cox 0-1, Paul Donnelly 0-1, Niall Owens 0-1, Stephen Donnelly 0-1.

The 2000 Intermediate Champions

Following this victory Beragh went on to represent Tyrone in the Ulster Tournament organised at that time by the Clontribret club in Monaghan. However, a first round victory over the Armagh champions failed to herald a prolonged run and they lost to Craigbane of Derry in the next round.

Championship action 2001-2006

Senior Championship action the challenge for Beragh in 2001. Poor league performances, however, meant that they were really facing an uphill task by the time they met Clonoe on Sunday May 6th in Carrickmore.

The O'Rahilly's were a firmly established Senior team and wasted no time in emphasising their superiority. Only seven minutes had elapsed when Cathal Grimes was rounded for the opening Clonoe goal and Beragh were effectively out by the end of the first quarter when they trailed by 2-4 to 0-2. That lead was extended to 3-7 to 0-2 by half-time, leaving them with a mountain to climb in the second half.

To be fair, Terry McKenna, Seamus Grimes and Dominic and Paul Donnelly upped the pace before the dismissal of Paddy Kelly hit them hard. Barry Grimes, Stephen Donnelly, Niall Owens and Paul Donnelly got the scores which put a slightly more respectable look on a 4-12 to 0-8 final scoreline which said it all about the one-sided nature of the exchanges.

Intermediate again in 2002 and an attendance of just fifty arrived for the start of the Championship meeting with Gortin at Fintona on Sunday June

16th. Both teams had been relegated from Senior at the end of 2001 and the match clashed with Ireland's involvement in a World Cup tie.

Beragh led by 0-5 to 0-2 at one stage in the first half through Cathal and Barry Grimes, before being pegged back to a point by half-time. It remained close on the resumption with neither side capable of grabbing the initiative. Gortin did make much of the running and seemed to be on course for a win on a score of 0-9 to 0-7. However, Cathal and Barry Grimes got late points to bring Beragh level as the efforts of Niall Farley, Niall Owens and Sean McMahon paid dividends.

In the replay, things began to go wrong for them almost immediately as defender Paddy Kelly went off injured. Recent meetings between Beragh and Gortin had been close but there was no doubting Gortin's complete supremacy when they scored an impressive 1-19 to 3-4 win over the Red Knights.

It was effectively all over by half-time thanks to a brilliant spell of scoring from Gortin. Beragh's only score came from Cathal Grimes and they were facing an uphill struggle to retrieve the situation on a scoreline of 1-9 to 0-1.

Gortin continued to dominate on the resumption even though Sean Owens, Stephen Donnelly, Sean McMahon and Barry Grimes worked hard for Beragh's cause. Then, they were rewarded with a goal from Niall Owens and a comeback briefly looked possible.

Instead, Gortin stretched their lead to fifteen points and they remained in control even though late goals from Cathal Grimes put a better look on the scoreboard which read 1-19 to 3-4 at the finish.

"Poor league performances, however, meant that they were really facing an uphill task by the time they met Clonoe on Sunday May 6th in Carrickmore"

Sean Owens meets his Gortin counterpart at the start of the 2000 Intermediate Final

The 2002 Intermediate Championship bid was thus a disappointing one and the League was to be something similar when it ended in relegation to the Junior ranks for the 2003 season.

Fifteen years had elapsed since Beragh's last outing in the Junior Championship when they took on Stewartstown in the opening round of the 2003 competition. And, they marked their arrival back there with a well-earned 1-7 to 0-6 victory. A goal from Mickey Franey in the seventeenth minute set them on the road as the performances of Niall Farley, Adrian Donnelly and Sean Owens were of note.

The score was 1-2 to 0-2 at half-time but Beragh upped the pace substantially in the second half and the sending off of Mark Daffy five minutes from the end didn't derail their challenge.

This set up a quarter final meeting against Fintona which proved to be a real ding-dong tussle at Eskra. Dominic Donnelly received a straight red card along with his opposite number from Fintona as the sides went in at the break 0-6 each. Beragh trailed for a period in the second half before a goal from Sean Owens put them ahead. Fintona came back, however, to level and force a replay.

Most of the drama in the replay the following Thursday night, July 10th, came in the closing stages. With Niall Meenagh, Sean Owens and Paddy Kelly doing well, Beragh led by 0-7 to 0-5 at the break, but failed to build on this in the second half.

It was Fintona, therefore, who held control towards the finish. Beragh, however, fought back with scores from Michael Ward and Cathal Grimes to lead by 0-14 to 0-12 approaching the end of normal time. But then disaster struck when Fintona got a late goal to win on a 1-12 to 0-14 scoreline.

On to 2004 and wet and windy Galbally was to be the venue for the end of Beragh's Junior Championship hopes at the first hurdle on Sunday August 8th. The Red Knights enjoyed the perfect start against Stewartstown with

> The teams returned to Carrickmore on September 10th when Gortin got the start that Beragh had enjoyed during the drawn game

Palor McNulty, manager of the 2000 Intermediate Champions

points from Michael Ward and Martin Nixon and a goal from Mickey Franey putting them in front.

But two Stewartstown goals saw that advantage wiped out by the break. Beragh got back on level terms early in the second half and continued to battle well as but a second yellow card resulted in Barry McMahon being sent off and the Red Knights went out to a Harps side that went on to win the title and to later reach the All-Ireland Junior Final.

Action from the 2001 Senior Championship clash against Clonoe

The 2005 season and yet another good start prior to a dismal finish was Beragh's championship lot. A goal from Michael Franey got them going well against Brocagh on July 3rd at Coalisland when he shot home the rebound from a Damien Meenagh shot to raise their hopes.

But they failed to build on it. They trailed by 1-5 to 1-1 at half-time and found the going tough in the second half. Despite the best efforts of Barry McMahon, the sending off of Dominic Donnelly hit them hard and the game was well over before they eventually lost by 1-9 to 1-5.

The possibility of a Centenary Year title was thought about when the 2006 Championship got underway in Newtownstewart against Glenelly and Beragh defied their mixed league form to produce a determined display. Spearheaded by Dominic Donnelly, Terry McKenna, Daniel Boyle and top scorer, Michael Ward, they led by 0-8 to 0-4 at half-time and continued to dominate proceedings thanks to scores in the second half from Michael Ward. They also recovered from the dismissal of Sean McMahon and were leading 0-11 to 0-9 with time almost up.

However, a serious injury to Terry McKenna caused a fifteen minute delay and when a Glenelly player also went down a halt was called to proceedings almost one hour after the start of the second half.

In the replay, Beragh managed to reproduced the form of the drawn tie. With Enda Donnelly doing well at midfield, they led by 0-5 to 0-2 and, while Glenelly levelled early in the second half at 0-6 each, goals in the

The Beragh team which competed in Division 1B in 2001

final quarter proved decisive. Martin McMahon got the first and the second from Michael Ward right at the end was the insurance score.

Hopes were now rising high that the Red Knights could make their Centenary Year mark. But it was not to be. Newtownstewart provided the opposition in the Quarter Final at Fintona and two goals for them made the difference. Niall and Damien Meenagh, Terry McKenna and Barry McMahon worked hard, but Newtownstewart goaled early on to take the upper hand.

But Beragh fought back and were back on level terms, 1-3 to 0-6, at half-time. However, the St Eugene's took control again on the resumption when a further goal and a number of points left Beragh struggling to stay in touch before going out on a score of 2-9 to 0-11.

The team was: Cathal Grimes, Niall Boyle, Paddy Kelly, Damien Meenagh, Barry Conroy, Niall Meenagh, Dominic Donnelly, Barry McMahon, Terry McKenna, Niall Owens, Michael Ward, Sean McMahon, Conor Donnelly, Daniel Boyle, Martin McMahon.
Subs - Gerard Owens for B Conroy, Michael Franey for C Donnelly.
Scorers - Michael Ward 0-8, Niall Boyle 0-1, Terry McKenna 0-1, Sean McMahon 0-1.

An anxious Red Knights dug-out at the start of the decade

League action 2000-2006

Whatever promise was generated by the impressive exploits of the Red Knights in winning the Intermediate League for the first time in 2000 quickly degenerated as the decade developed into one of poor performances, play-off defeats and frustrating outcomes.

A winning sequence in that first year was not matched as the subsequent seasons resulted in relegation from Division 1B in 2001, a further drop at the end of 2002 and a gradual decline within the Junior ranks until the Centenary season, 2006.

Beragh's 2000 League campaign opened with a 3-2 to 0-6 defeat by Newtownstewart but few could have anticipated then what was to follow as they rallied after that to clinch the title with eleven wins, two draws and just that opening day setback to spoil the unbeaten record.

A 2-14 to 2-3 victory over Aghaloo at the beginning of July put them top of the table and other important wins were recorded against Killeeshil, Greencastle and Tattyreagh as they entered the final run-in with the double firmly in their sights. Fintona were defeated on a score of 1-10 to 0-6 on October 1 to set up a final clash against Newtownstewart for the title a week later.

In the title decider, Cathal Grimes missed a penalty, but that didn't stop Beragh from leading 0-6 to 0-1 at the break

Celebration time for Brian McCartan, Dominic Donnelly, Stephen Farley and Michael Montague

The 25 player squad in the 2000 Intermediate Championship title success. Pictured above are back row from left: Ciaran Donnelly, Martin McMahon, Barry Grimes, Shane Donnelly, Brian McCartan, Dominic Donnelly, Paddy Kelly, Mickey McCann. Middle row: Stephen Donnelly,

In the title decider, Cathal Grimes missed a penalty, but that didn't stop Beragh from leading 0-6 to 0-1 at the break. Newtownstewart had hoped to close the gap with the wind on the resumption, but were hit as Beragh maintained their momentum to clinch the title on a score of 0-12 to 0-3.

Promotion to Division 1B for the 2001 season presented a tough challenge for the Red Knights. Surviving in senior ranks was always going to be difficult and a number of factors made it even tougher. Tyrone's increased inter-county involvement meant that the league was divided into two phases and the changes had a disastrous knock-on effect.

The safety net of the second phase certainly didn't work for Beragh after many seemed content in the knowledge that the first eleven games hardly mattered. Four points was all that they had to show and, while there was hope of a revival in the next phase, a win over Gortin was the only one of the decisive campaign.

In that one Cathal Grimes proved to be the key figure with a total of 1-8 as Beragh won by 1-11 to 0-12. The goal came in the second half and the

John Donnelly (official), Terry McKenna, Niall Farley, Paddy Grimes, Michael Montague, Stephen Franey, Gerard Loughran Niall Meenagh. At front from left: Ciaran Cox, Paul Donnelly, Patsy Farley, Sean Owens, Stephen Farley, Niall Owens, Barry McMahon, Barry Conroy.

win moved Beragh off the bottom of the table. But defeats by Loughmacrory, Edendork and Brackaville meant that everything came down to a make or break clash against Strabane to retain a place in Senior ranks for 2002.

However, apart from a brief moment when Niall Meenagh's goal brought Beragh to within three points of them, Strabane never looked like losing. They led by 1-5 to 0-3 at half-time and a goal before the final whistle confirmed Beragh's relegation back to Intermediate ranks.

A restructuring of the Leagues heightened the pressure on all teams in Division Two during 2003 and Beragh's failure to make their mark over the whole of the season severely hit their hopes. Just down from Senior, the season got off to a good start with victory over Newtownstewart but it was downhill from then on.

Narrow defeats resulted in the dropping of valuable points and losses to Rock, Killyman, Fintona and Tattyreagh sealed their fate. In the end, Beragh finished with ten points, just ahead of the bottom placed teams,

Promotion to Division 1B for the 2001 season presented a tough challenge for the Red Knights

Newtownstewart, Stewartstown and Dregish and relegated along with them to Division Three.

New guidelines from Croke Park on the provision of matches at club level led to a higher number of games during 2003. A total of 22 were scheduled and hopes were high that Beragh could make a quick return to Intermediate ranks following the disappointment of being relegated at the end of the previous year.

However, defeats by Newtownstewart, Stewartstown, Glenelly and Drumragh early in the season effectively ended their challenge. Some good displays and wins were recorded later, but in the end they finished well adrift of the leading pack in a mid-table position. A total of 20 points was seventeen less than the winners, Owen Roes on a table in which Drumragh and Glenelly were the bottom teams.

In 2004, better performances under manager, Terry McCann, ensured that they made an improved impression on Division Three. A comfortable 0-10 to 0-3 win over Castlederg in April moved them into second place on the table and by the mid-point of the season they were among the main challengers Killyman, Drumragh and Stewartstown.

Double wins at the beginning of June over Stewartstown and Urney boosted their hopes further, although a gap was beginning to open between them and the top teams. However, a 0-14 to 1-4 win over the leaders, Newtownstewart, helped to close the gap and Beragh continued to compete for the automatic promotion slot.

But Drumragh eventually claimed the title, leaving Beragh to challenge for the step-up via the play-offs after finishing in third place on the table. They fell short, however, to Fintona when they lost on a score of 0-14 to 1-8, the goal coming from a Mickey Ward penalty five minutes from the end.

After the encouragement provided by the 2004 campaign, the hope was that Beragh could build on this the following season. And, the progress of the previous year was matched when they finished in third place to set-up a play-off against Urney.

Held at St Mary's Park, the extent of the challenge facing them was clear when they trailed by 0-7 to 0-6 at half-time. An early point from Enda Donnelly kept them in touch going, but it was Urney who finished the stronger to win by 0-11 to 0-8.

Former players, Sean Owens and Niall Farley, took over the role of

> Double wins at the beginning of June over Stewartstown and Urney boosted their hopes further, although a gap was beginning to open between them and the top teams

managers for the 2006 Centenary season. Almost immediately, though, the team faded from the title-race when a number of early losses saw them slip down the table. Rock, Greencastle, Brocagh, Owen Roes and Glenelly all provided tough opposition and a bad run of defeats during the summer meant that by September they were languishing fourth from the bottom and out of the race for both promotion and the play-offs.

Other competitions -
Reserve Leagues and Championships

The change in the competition structure for clubs resulted in more games being provided through the All-County Leagues had a knock-on impact on the number of games for Reserve teams.

Beragh had always competed well in the subsidiary Cup competitions and in the Reserve Leagues and Championships. But their involvement in the Reserve competitions was called into question when the initial years of the decade were dogged by poor commitment, disappointing performances and a generally lack-lustre approach.

Concerns were raised annually about the small number of players over the age of 21 who were taking part, the failure of others to attend training on a regular basis and the fact that it was difficult to know who exactly would be turning up for the weekend games. As a result, the Beragh Reserve teams regularly struggled to field and finished well down the tables in 2000, 2001 and 2002 and in 2003.

The winning Reserves of 2004 and 2005

The Reserve
competitions
continued to provide
activity players into
the 2000s

But then there was a turnaround in 2004. Victory over Stewartstown put them into the Semi-Final of the Championship and, while they lost to Fintona on a score of 0-12 to 0-11, the team rarely put a foot wrong in the league. Out of 21 games played, they won twenty and drew one to finish the season as title winners with the impressive total of 41 points.

Now the call went out for the championship to be added to the league title in 2005 and, under the management of Martin Hegarty and Niall Farley, the players responded well. They progressed through the League campaign and by the summer were ready to launch a serious onslaught in the championship.

A victory over Brocagh put them into the semi-final where Newtownstewart were confidently defeated on a score of 5-10 to 0-7. They then played Urney in the final at Killyclogher at the beginning of September when a good display of pointscoring saw them emerge with a first championship title at Reserve level since the mid-eighties on a score of 1-15 to 0-6. Two weeks later a comfortable nine point win away at Newtownstewart saw them add the league title for the second year running to complete the double after another marvellous season.

Youth football

An awareness of the need to raise the level of commitment on the part of both players and management began to yield slight improvements in the fortunes of the Beragh youth teams at the beginning of the decade. This, combined with the promotional boost provided by Tyrone's inter-county successes and the increased emphasis on coaching led, to a new all-round spirit and enthusiasm.

In 2001 the U-14s became the first Red Knights team since 1989 to reach a County Final when they qualified for the Grade Two League decider. They got through thanks to a number of good sectional wins and then they defeated Moortown by 3-12 to 3-3 in the Quarter Final and Galbally by 7-10 to 5-8 in the semi-final.

The final was at Killeeshil on July 3rd against a Derrylaughan team who had earlier defeated them in the championship semi-final. A closely contested tie eventually resulted in a 1-11 each draw, Beragh coming close to snatching the winner just on the call of time. However, their hopes of going one better in the replay were dashed as the Kevin Barry's went on a goalscoring spree to emerge very comfortable winners by 7-10 to 1-7.

The players involved, under the management of Paddy Rodgers and Cathal Grimes were: Mark McGirr, Brian Gartland, Colm Kelly, Noel Donnelly, Peter Meenagh, Karl McAleer, Ciaran Mullin, Shel Munroe, Conor Donnelly, Niall Boyle, Conor Donnelly, Ryan Donnelly, Pauric Grimes, Declan Fitzmaurice, Martin Rodgers. Subs – Daniel McSorley, Stefan Munroe, Kevin Owens, Paddy Owens, Ciaran Ward, Denvir McMahon, Cormac McMullan.

Further progress was made in 2004 when the U-14s reached the semi-final of the championship, where they lost to Donaghmore. They also competed in the All-Ireland Feile held in Tyrone to coincide with the county's Centenary Year. St Mary's Park was the venue for matches against St Loman's of Westmeath, Greencastle and the eventual defeated All-Ireland Finalists, Moyle Rovers from Tipperary.

> An awareness of the need to raise the level of commitment on the part of both players and management began to yield slight improvements in the fortunes of the Beragh youth teams at the beginning of the decade

The 2000 U-12 panel of players

While the Beragh boys failed to reach the qualifying stages, their participation in the Feile Parade provided fond memories for both the players and officials. And, there was an added bonus for them when a member of the team, Martin Rodgers, went on to win the All-Ireland Skills title.

He had progressed from heats among the Beragh players to the finals which took place in Healy Park, Omagh, on the day of the All-Ireland Feile Finals. Completing an obstacle course designed to test the all-round ability of those participating, he emerged with enough points to narrowly edge out the other competitors and record a very notable achievement.

The U-14 team which progressed to the final of the 2001 Grade Two League

In 2005 the club's U-13 team reached the final of the Grade Two Championship against Cookstown. They came close to winning the title when they drew 1-1 to 0-4, but they missed out in the replay on a score of 1-9 to 1-6.

However, under the management team of Martin Hegarty, Paddy Rodgers and Pete Owens, this group of players continued to develop and were to make their mark in the 2006 Centenary season. After progressing confidently through their league section, they eventually lost to Cookstown in the semi-final, but they bounced back in the championship where a semi-final win over Naomh Mhuire put them into the final against Galbally.

Beragh had always competed well in the subsidiary Cup competitions and in the Reserve Leagues and Championships

Playing at Aghaloo on Saturday July 1st, the young Red Knight players produced an impressive performance. A good start was secured through scores from Stephen McNamee, Darren Hegarty and Christopher Devlin and the work elsewhere of team captain, Christopher Devlin, Fergal McMahon, Emmett Gartland and Lee McCrystal helped Beragh into a 2-7 to 1-2 interval lead.

They continued to dominate in the second half when further goals from Christopher Devlin and Lee McCrystal secured an emphatic 4-12 to 1-5 win that saw them become the first team from the club to win a youth title since the breakthrough success at Juvenile Grade One level in 1985.

The team was: Cathal Donnelly, Hugh Franey, Fergal McMahon, Paul

Owens, Shane McDaid, Emmett Gartland, Martin Mullin, Ryan McNally, Christopher Devlin, Niall Owens, Lee McCrystal, Colm Mullin, Stephen McNamee, Darren Hegarty, Cathal Owens.

Subs - Ryan O'Keefe for C Owens, Gerard McCabe for N Owens. Other panelists - Cathal McAleer, Sean Caffrey, Kevin Gorman, Aaron Duffy, Simon Duffy, Ryan Heaney, Eamon Donnelly, Matthew Campbell, Dalton Mellon, Dean McDaid.

Ongoing development at youth level includes regular coaching sessions, the hosting of special coaching days for young players, a focus on the all-round preparation of individual players and teams and the annual Tyrone Summer Camps. The Paddy Bogan Memorial Primary Schools Tournament has also been revived and is regaining its standing as one of the top local tournaments. All of these initiatives are helping to consolidate the interest which now exists among the youth of the area in developing their skill and confidence as players.

Ladies showing the way

Several successes for Beragh Ladies teams have made the period 2000-2006 especially memorable. It has been a time of major development in both the growth, organisation and standing of the sport in Tyrone, not least among the Red Knights where the numbers taking part have grown beyond all expectations.

Now fielding teams at every level from U-12 right to senior, the growth of Ladies football in Beragh has been steady. And, the proof of their worth has also been highlighted by the production of title-winning teams at U-14, U-16, Intermediate and Junior levels during the current decade.

The 2004 Feile team on a visit to Croke Park after returning from a weekend trip to Moyle Rovers in Tipperary

During the later part of the nineties there was a major drive to provide the girls of the area with the chance to represent the club at underage level. This was to yield initial dividends in 2001 when the adult team, which had been relegated at the end of 2000, went on to win the Intermediate title for the second time and on this occasion add the crown to the league honours which had already been secured.

They progressed well through to the decider against Trillick on Saturday August 25th. However, they started very poorly in the Final and looked to be in trouble when Trillick led by 2-4 to 0-4 at the end of the first quarter.

Colleen McSorley
on the attack
during the
2001 Ladies
Intermediate Final

But then a goal from Julie Conroy got them going again, as Carmel Grimes, Josephine Rodgers and Ann Donnelly all excelled.

An exciting finale was on the cards when the sides were level at 2-5 each early in the second half and, with Nuala McCartan and Aishling Hagan to the fore, Beragh went on a scoring spree subsequently. A third goal from Josephine Rodgers and good attacking play from Colleen McSorley, Tracey Rodgers and Lisa Rodgers clinched the win on a score of 3-15 to 2-7.

Afterwards, there were jubilant scenes as the Beragh captain, Aishling Hagan, received the Tommy McGarvey Cup and the winning team was: Celine Grimes, Claire Donnelly, Aishling Hagan, Catherine Donnelly, Tracey Rodgers, Nuala McCartan, Orla Donnelly, Emma Ward, Ciara Strain, Lisa Rodgers, Anne Donnelly, Josephine Rodgers, Carmel Grimes, Julie Conroy, Colleen McSorley. Sub - Cathy Donnelly for L Rodgers.
Scorers - Anne Donnelly 1-3, Carmel Grimes 0-4, Josephine Rodgers 1-1, Cathy Donnelly 0-3, Julie Conroy 1-0, Lisa Rodgers 0-2, Ciara Strain 0-1, Colleen McSorley 0-1.
Other panelists - Cara Franey, Bronagh Mullin, Donna Donnelly, Roisin McNelis, Louise Donnelly, Caroline Donnelly, Denise McCann, Cathy Cox.

Following this victory, Beragh proceeded to the Ulster Club Championship where they defeated the Donegal champions. This set up a semi-final meeting away to the Cavan champions, Mullahoran. The teams were level at the end of normal time and the game remained tight into the added period before three goals in the space of six minutes ensured that Mullahoran won on a score of 4-13 to 2-14.

Despite this, the team was confident of doing well at Senior level in 2002. But their hopes were hit by the departure of a number of players. Although they suffered a heavy defeat by Carrickmore in the championship, the team rallied to comfortably maintain their place in Division One. But their two-year stint there ended in 2003 when Beragh fulfilled only three fixtures at adult level and lost out to Aodh Ruadh in the championship.

Things proved just as tough in Division Two in 2004 but they held on. However, they really struggled in 2005 and a drop to Division Three and Junior status followed. Nevertheless, this provided a renewed focus for the team who quickly took steps to bounce back.

With training beginning towards the end of December 2005, the girls, under the management team of Hugh McNamee, Paddy Mullin and Barry Grimes, left little to chance. A tough win over Ardboe in the first round of the championship was followed by more comfortable victories over Killeeshil in the Quarter Final and Pomeroy in the semi-final to see them through to the final.

This game was played at Greencastle on September 1st and saw Beragh dominate for the most part. The good play of Catherine Donnelly, Aishling Hagan, Aideen Meenagh and Nicola Boyle in the defence was aided by the link-work of Sabrina McNally and Noleen Owens at midfield.

Early scores from Josephine Rodgers, Colleen McSorley and Noleen Owens settled them with the wind and they were ready to press ahead when Lisa Rodgers goaled. But their impact was severely hit by too many wides and two first half goals ensured that the issue was still very much in doubt on a half-time score of 1-5 to 2-1.

Nothing less than a big effort was demanded on the resumption when the Red Knights continued to gain the greater share of the possession and two points from Colleen McSorley kept them just ahead, although the tension was heightened whenever Galbally attacked.

> " During the later part of the nineties there was a major drive to provide the girls of the area with the chance to represent the club at underage level "

Claire Donnelly moving forward for the Beragh Ladies

In the end, though, the final whistle brought relief and then celebrations for the Beragh girls. They later competed in the Ulster Club Championship with the hope of enjoying a good run to lay the foundations for a fresh onslaught in Intermediate ranks for 2007.

The team was: Helen Ward, Nicola Boyle, Tracey Rodgers, Cathy Cox, Catherine Donnelly, Aishling Hagan, Aideen Meenagh, Sabrina McNally, Noleen Owens, Michaela Donnelly, Josephine Rodgers, Colleen McSorley, Lisa Rodgers, Ciara Donnelly, Claire Donnelly.

Subs - Claire Ward for Ciara Donnelly, Sarah Owens for Cathy Cox, Michaela McCann, Bronagh Mullan, Eilish Owens, Roisin McNeilis, Kerri McCann, Roisin McSorley, Julie Conroy, Derbhla Mullan.

There was good progress at youth level as well and their commitment to coaching sessions and games resulted in a number of fine achievements. The 2002 U-14s came close to clinching the double only to lose out to Glenelly in both the League and Championship Finals.

> "In the end, though, the final whistle brought relief then celebrations for the Beragh girls"

The Beragh Ladies pictured in 2002 after returning to Senior ranks

But many of the players responded in the best way possible when they formed part of the U-14 team which captured the Grade 2 Championship and League Double in 2003. The team was managed by Lisa Rodgers and Helen Ward, and captained by Adela Donnelly and the players involved were: Leanna Owens, Jackie O'Neill, Catriona Grimes, Aideen Meenagh, Claire Donnelly, Sabrina McNally, Michaela Donnelly, Anna Lisa Donnelly, Nicola Boyle, Elle Caffrey, Sarah Owens, Adela Donnelly, Eilish Owens, Roseanna McSorley, Claire McDonald, Orla Conroy, Jayne Owens, Jane Ward, Claire Heaney, Claire Ward, Shauneen Breen, Ellen Franey, Leonna Owens.

On to 2004 and the progress of the group was maintained at Juvenile level when, under the management of Ciara and Christopher Donnelly, they again won the League and Championship double. The squad was: Leanne Owens, Andrea Mullan, Jackie O'Neill, Michaela Donnelly, Kerri McCann, Shauneen Breen, Sabrina McNally, Elle Caffrey, Derbhla Mullan, Charlene Lyttle, Claire McDonald, Catherine McNelis, Adela Donnelly, Aideen Meenagh, Orla Conroy, Sarah Owens, Nicola Boyle, Nicola Nugent, Helen Ward, Nadine Snow, Catriona Grimes, Lisa Marie

Colton, Kerri McNelis, Jayne Owens, Claire Ward, Ann Marie Franey, Roisin McSorley, Leona Owens, Jane Ward, Eilish Owens.

And, a tremendous treble of success was completed in 2005 by the U-14s under the management team of Tracey Rodgers, Catherine Donnelly, Colleen McSorley and Cathy Donnelly. They defeated Donaghmore in both the League and Championship Finals.

Ladies pictured taking a break from training in 2000. Pictured are Denise McCann, Catherine Donnelly, Barry Conroy, Eoghain McKenna, Lisa Rodgers and Josephine Rodgers at back. At front are Tracey Rodgers, Colleen McSorley, Claire and Cathy Donnelly

The players who shared in that success were: Nicola Boyle, Sarah Boyle, Jane Ward, Claire Heaney, Ann Marie Franey, Lisa Marie Colton, Shauna McNelis, Claire Ward, Aishling Gartland, Aishling Mullan, Orla Conroy, Claire McDonald, Nikita Donnelly, Kerri Strain, Louise McNamee, Roisin McSorley, Cora Breen, Jayne Lyons, Nuala McAleer, Emma Toal, Caoimhe Lyttle, Rachel McNelis, Aimee Owens, Leona Owens, Bronagh McAleer, Kelly O'Neill, Karen Gorman, Shaylynn McNally.

Recent years have also seen the Mens and Ladies sections of the Red Knights lead the way in terms of integration. Guidelines issued by the GAA are aimed at bringing both Associations under the one umbrella, a move completed in Beragh in 2003. Since then the affairs of the two have been administered by the one Executive Committee, with the efforts of all concerned helping to ensure a smoother operation.

Needless to say, the abilities of the Beragh players was recognised by their selection for various county teams during the decade. Aishling Hagan and Ciara Strain were on the Tyrone team which won the Ulster Senior title for the first time in 2000, while Barry Grimes was part of management team.

Other players represented Tyrone at various levels during the decade and were involved in the winning of a number of provincial and All-Ireland titles. They included Nicola Boyle, Roisin McSorley, Claire Heaney, Jane Ward and Claire McDonald who were part of a Tyrone U-14 team which won All-Ireland honours. Julie Conroy was a member of the Queen's University team which won the Dowd Cup inter-varsity title in 2005.

Handball

Ongoing concerns about the condition of the 40x20 Handball Alley in Beragh didn't prevent players from the Brackey Club from continuing their participation in the sport in the 2000s. While many of the highs achieved during the nineties were not matched, there was still no doubting the club's foremost role in the game both in Tyrone and Ulster.

This was evidenced in 2000 when they reached the All-Ireland Novice Final, losing by only one ace in the final. That year also saw Niall Kerr complete a marvellous All-Ireland Junior double in both the 40x20 and 60x30 courts. He joined up with his brother, Conor, to win the Ulster Junior Doubles title as well, while other provincial winners included Stephen Clarke in the Junior Doubles and Padraig McGlinchey at U-12.

He added the U-13 Doubles title in 2002 when Ruairi Kelly won the U-16 Singles and Mark McCartan reached the final of the Waterford Crystal National Novice competition. Niall Kerr continued his progress in 2003 by progressing to the All-Ireland Intermediate Final where he lost narrowly to the favourite from Mayo.

Niall and Conor then combined to win the Ulster Intermediate title while Mark McCartan and Conor captured the Tyrone Senior Doubles title, with Mark losing out in the Singles decider. In 2003 saw Niall Kerr and Stephen Clarke win the Ulster Singles and Doubles Intermediate titles respectively, both losing out in the All-Ireland Final. Also that year Cormac McMullan partnered Brian Donaghy of Loughmacrory to win the Ulster U-16 Doubles and Barry Devlin captured the provincial U-17 crown. He added the U-18 Singles and Doubles titles in 2005 when Niall Kerr emerged winner of the Ulster Intermediate Doubles and Singles. However, both lost out narrowly in their respective All-Ireland Finals.

In 2006, Shane O'Neill was an unfortunate loser in the All-Ireland novice singles final while Brackey player, Stephen Clarke, joined up with Barney Cororan to win the Tyrone Senior Doubles title.

> While many of the highs achieved during the nineties were not matched, there was still no doubting the club's foremost role in the game both in Tyrone and Ulster

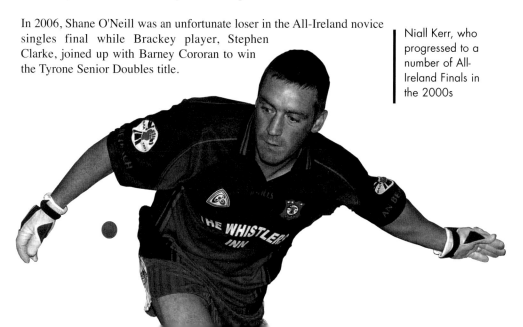

Niall Kerr, who progressed to a number of All-Ireland Finals in the 2000s

World Champions

> In the end, though, the final whistle brought relief then celebrations for the Beragh girls

Those hoping for success to mark the Centenary of the founding of the GAA in the parish were rewarded in rich measure when two Brackey handballers captured titles at the World Handball Championships held in Canada in 2006.

Before embarking on their trip to the event, Shane O'Neill and Ruairi Kelly completed their preparations in the new state-of-the-art alley in Beragh. And, their effort paid off when they took part in the Men's C Grade and won both Doubles and Singles honours.

Shane O'Neill was crowned Singles champion after an exhausting six day marathon, overcoming some tough opposition on the way. He defeated opponents from Spain, Canada, the United States, Mexico and Ireland and won the final convincingly by 21-1 21-6 over fellow countryman, David Walsh.

He then partnered clubmate Ruairi Kelly in the doubles, with the two of them beating an experienced partnership to take the World C title. And, they subsequently came home to a welcome fit for World Champions at the new Sports Pavilion at St Mary's Park.

Hurling

World Champions, Ruairi Kelly and Shane O'Neill, pictured with Barry Devlin, who also competed at the Championships

Efforts to ensure that all GAA activities are promoted under the umbrella of the Red Knights took a step forward in 2006 when the club renewed its involvement in hurling and camogie. Following the promptings of Club Executive member, Sean Clarke and the work of Alan Rodgers, regular coaching sessions built on the attendance of some 80 children at the Tyrone Hurling Summer Camp.

Coaches at these sessions have included Shirley Roberts, Niall Boyle, Gretta Donnelly, Barry McGuinness, Shane O'Neill and James Rodgers among others and the team took part in a number of blitzes, with the hope being that these will be consolidated into the future.

But there have also been other involvements in the game, including Niall Boyle's success in scoring the winning goal for Carrickmore Eire Ogs when they took the Ulster Minor Championship in 2004. A number of other players also represented other clubs in the period from 2000.

Other activities

Running club activities during the 21st Century has become increasingly varied. Fundraising events, social nights, cultural competitions and celebrity nights are all fitted into the schedule of matches and coaching sessions to complete the scene for the Red Knights during the period following the dawn of the new millennium. While the Annual Dinner Dance provides an important outlet for relaxation, a number of other similar occasions give members and supporters the chance to reflect on topical events of the day.

The winning Scor Novelty Act team with Ciara McKeagney, Barry Grimes, Denise McCann, Niall Farley, Eoghain McKenna, Stephen Donnelly and Sean Munroe

A night with a difference saw Adrian Knight come to St Mary's Hall with his hypnotist act in 2000, although the talents of the home-grown novelty act almost outshone the professional performer. Barbecues, Golf Days, the visit of the Sam Maguire Cup to St Mary's Park and other local venues following Tyrone's All-Ireland successes in 2003 and 2005, a Wild West Disco, the annual Night at the Races, the drawing of prizes in the Fundraising Draw and the Talk Show organised prior to the All-Ireland Final in 2005 have proved to be successful and enjoyable.

A notable achievement was the winning of the Tyrone Scor Novelty Act title in 2001. The performers were Eoghain McKenna, Stephen Donnelly, Sean Munroe, Ciara McKeagney, Barry Grimes, Denise McCann and Niall Farley. Their sketch took an amusing look at the GAA in Tyrone and beyond and was very well received on the way to the Tyrone title and subsequently in the semi-final of the Ulster Scor.

The level of finance required to run the club in the 2000s is ever-increasing and a multitude of fundraising ventures must be organised. Alongside special events, the weekly club lotto and membership fees remain important. The club has also been proactive in raising money and organised events for a number of charities. The annual St Stephen's Day Charity Match and donations to other worthy causes have been much appreciated.

Former caretaker,
TJ Kelly, his son,
Gerard, a noted
Brackey handballer
and his grandson

Red Knights jerseys, kitbags and sportswear are popular items of merchandise which help to promote the club name far beyond parish boundaries. While the club was the first in Tyrone to sell kitbags, badges and other such items back in the seventies and early eighties, the market for such goods has surpassed the expectations of the forward-thinking officials of thirty years ago. Now fleeces, replica jerseys, togs, socks, flags and a range of other goods are snapped up almost immediately by players and supporters of all ages who are always eager to have the latest fashions in sportswear.

This was especially so in Centenary Year when the production of a whole new set of commemorative jerseys and sportswear marked the milestone. Specially designed for the occasion by Fionnula Nixon, the jerseys combined the traditional red and amber colours of the club, with an updated club crest and the 'Reaching Out' logo and a depiction of Cuchullain to highlight the connections with the Red Branch Knights in Irish mythology.

St Mary's Park Re-development

Praise from all quarters for the top class facilities opened at St Mary's Park in the Centenary Year, 2006, marked the culmination of an immense amount of work during the previous few years. Evidence of the deteriorating state of the grounds was clear as the nineties progressed, leaving the Red Knights membership with a big re-development challenge at the beginning of the 2000s.

New fencing was erected at the hillside of the ground in 2000, while in 2001 the setting up of the St Mary's Park action group comprising Sean Clarke, Terry Kelly, Frank Rodgers, Patsy Farley, Gerry Owens and Gerry Donnelly got the ball rolling. Investigations were carried out into the implications of the 1975 Lease Agreement between the club and Omagh District Council. This in turn led to the provision of a second Training Pitch to replace the tennis court and playpark in 2002 before a new Development Committee took the work further for the start of 2003.

Under the Chairmanship of Gerard Treacy, the Committee gained approval for the appointment of Consultants to carry out a feasibility study into the best use of St Mary's Park. This in turn resulted in the finalisation of plans for a major re-development at an estimated cost of £750,000.

The raising of finance was crucial and the sourcing of grant-aid coincided with the launch of a major fundraising draw, coordinated by Gerard Treacy and Michael Montague, in the autumn of 2003. Teams of sellers covered all parts of the parish before moving out to target Tyrone, Ulster and elsewhere to raise a total of almost £300,000.

This combined with the grant-aid received from a number of different sources meant that the work was ready to proceed and it began with the demolition of the older clubrooms in May 2005 with McCann Brothers of Fintona as the main contractors. It was eventually completed by March of the Centenary Year and it incorporated the facilities needed to cater for the requirements of the Red Knights in the 21st Century. Among the amenities officially opened as part of the launch of the club's Centenary Year celebrations on St Patrick's Day, 2006, were four dressing rooms with associated toilet and showering facilities, a committee room, referee's changing room, an office, a fitness/weights room, a community and function room and a handball alley with a viewing gallery which can accommodate up to 60 people. Incidentally, the completion of the new facility came after the deaths of Trustee, Sean Owens, and former Chairman and Treasurer, Paddy Bogan, who had been centrally involved at an early stage in the development.

> Praise from all quarters for the top class facilities opened at St Mary's Park in the Centenary Year, 2006, marked the culmination of an immense amount of work during the previous few years

Centenary Year Celebrations - A very special birthday

It was thus with understandable pride that those associated with the Beragh Red Knights GAA Club approached the Centenary Year in 2006. Work on marking the historic milestone began towards the end of 2004

417

A special moment as the Club Chairman, Mickey McCann, assists the President of the GAA, Nicky Brennan and the President of the Ladies GAA, Geraldine Giles, in unveiling the commemorative plaque marking the official opening of the new Sports Pavilion and Clubrooms on July 30th, 2006

BEARACH

This build
was officially
by
Mr. NICKY BR
Uachtarán Cumann L
on 30ᵗʰ July
as part of the
Centenary Year ce

Guests including
the President of
the GAA, Nicky
Brennan and
Tyrone Chairman,
Pat Darcy, view
the ice-bath in the
new Pavilion

with the setting up of an organising Centenary Committee and yielded a wide range of specially organised events which proved immensely successful.

Under the theme of 'Reaching Out,' a Centenary Calendar was published at the end of 2005. It comprised professionally commissioned photographs and other images from club archives to illustrate each month as well as giving details of the major events planned for the 2006 season.

Exactly 100 years since the formation of the Sixmilecross Wolfe Tones Club on January 22nd 1906, their successors gathered to commemorate the event on Sunday January 22nd, 2006, in the Whistler's Inn in Sixmilecross.

Copies of the first Ulster Herald report of the first meeting aroused much interest while the Chairman, Mickey McCann, said those present were carrying on a proud tradition. "It is very appropriate that we are back here in Sixmilecross on the very date that the first meeting was held back in 1906 and it's important that we mark the role played by so many throughout the last ten decades."

In the end,
though, the final
whistle brought
relief then
celebrations for
the Beragh girls

Refreshments were provided courtesy of the hosts and music was provided by members of the Dromore and Galbally CCE Branches. Also speaking at the event, Alan Rodgers, called on those present to be proud of the fact that the Sixmilecross Wolfe Tones were among the very first clubs in Tyrone and that the present members and supporters were continuing to keep the alight flame lit in 1906.

Official launch of Centenary Year

Hundreds of people thronged Beragh village for the official launch of the Red Knights Centenary Celebrations on St Patrick's Day. Beginning with a parade to St Mary's Park, a wide range of events included the staging of a variety concert, the opening for use of the new facilities, the staging of a Centenary Exhibition and the launch of the club w e b s i t e , beraghredknights.com.

Drumduff, Roscavey and Beragh Primary Schools participated in the Parade led by St Macartan's Youth Band. Imaginative floats depicting various aspects of club activity and Irish culture added a splash of colour.

Events then continued at St Mary's Park where club Chairman, Mickey McCann, had the honour of turning the key to the front door of the new facility to the cheers of delight from an assembled attendance of some 400 people which included many from neighbouring localities. All were in agreement that the excellent amenities were a credit to the efforts of club members.

The exhibition of club memorabilia in the new Handball Alley provided the opportunity to reminisce about the players and teams of years gone by while the latest technology was on hand for the launch of the club's website. Prepared by Stephen Mullan, the pages available on-line covered all aspects of the GAA in the area, provided numerous photographs for viewing and proved a massive hit especially among the younger members. Hits on the website quickly approached 100,000 and continue to rise.

The successful Commemorative Centenary Calendar, produce to co-incide with the 2006 celebrations

In the evening, musicians, dancers, singers and recitations formed part of a highly enjoyable Variety Concert in the new community room. They played out to a capacity audience with the night being rounded-off by a folk concert.

Homecoming Weekend and Official Opening

Club supporters mixed with many of Tyrone's top inter-county stars from the nineties as well as dignatories from the GAA world and funding bodies for the Homecoming Weekend and Official Opening of the new Sports Pavilion at St Mary's Park between July 28th-July 30th.

It proved to be an immensely satisfying weekend for all associated with the Red Knights Club as a series of activities over the course of three days marked the culmination of months of careful planning. An exhibition of club memorabilia and a concert in the Community Room formed part of the Friday night proceedings before things really got off the ground on the Saturday.

Brackey Handball Club hosted a top class exhibition match featuring four of Ireland's best players. Eoin Kennedy from Dublin, the Cavan pair of Paul Brady and Michael Finnegan and Ricky McCann from Antrim used the match as preparation for the World Championships in the United States.

A packed attendance in the new fully air-conditioned alley watched as the players produced almost two hours of quality play. They were presented with new Brackey Handball Club strips to mark the occasion.

2006 Kerry All-Ireland star, Kieran Donaghy, pictured with his father, Oliver and grandfather, John, on a visit to St Mary's Park earlier in the decade

This was followed by a special re-union football match between the Tyrone team which reached the All-Ireland Final in 1995 and the Beragh side which progressed to the Senior Championship semi-final in 1996. None of that Tyrone side from eleven years ago is now involved in the current county set-up, but with many of them still playing domestically for their clubs, the standard of football on show from them remained high. Peter Canavan turned on the style with a few great scores, and the chance to see the past county and club heroes was greatly enjoyed.

The chance to meet and greet colleagues from a decade ago was relished by players and officials alike. Speaking after the game, Carrickmore's Ronan McGarrity praised the initiative of the Red Knights in organising the game. He also praised the efforts of the Beragh club in completing such an ambitious development scheme.

"It's fair to say that this must be the best facility in Tyrone and perhaps even Ulster at the moment. Young people in the area now have a great incentive to continue their involvement in gaelic games and culture," said the former Tyrone defender.

The Fancy Dress Parade as part of the Homecoming Weekend generated a lot of imaginative costumes

66

Club supporters mixed with many of Tyrone's top inter-county stars from the nineties as well as dignatories from the GAA world and funding bodies for the Homecoming Weekend and Official Opening of the new Sports Pavilion

99

The high point of the weekend was the Official Opening of the new Sports Pavilion and Clubrooms by the GAA President, Nicky Brennan on the Sunday. He joined the Ladies GAA President, Geraldine Giles and other dignitories for the unveiling of a specially commissioned commemorative plaque.

The Kilkenny native was making his first official visit to Tyrone and he paid particular attention to the fact that the club was now promoting hurling and its role through architect, Dessie McMahon, in the new Croke Park.

"This magnificent building should act as a focus for the continued promotion of GAA activities. To that end, I am pleased to hear that a Hurling Summer Camp is beginning here at St Mary's Park. Clubs throughout the Association have provided top class facilities and my hope is that the Beragh Red Knights will go from strength to strength."

Geraldine Giles, President of the Ladies Association, echoed comments by Mr Brennan regarding the integration of GAA clubs and their colleagues in the Ladies Association by saying: "Coming here today and seeing so many young people, both boys and girls, gives me great pleasure because the future of our games lies in attracting young people and facilities like this are a big help."

Tyrone Chairman, Pat Darcy, whose mother was from the parish, called on clubs to become more pro-active in 'Reaching Out' to people, especially to the immigrant community. "One area that this can happen is through the promotion of gaelic games among the immigrant community and I noticed that at the recent Primary Schools League organised by the Beragh club that this is already happening."

The Red Knights Chairman, Mickey McCann, said that the club could stand with the best GAA units in the provision of all activities of the Association, including football, hurling, handball, camogie, ladies football and Scor and Scor Na Og. "Our challenge for the future is to ensure that our efforts in achieving our aim of catering for all young people and providing them with the chance to participate in all GAA activities are successful. My vision is to see this happening," he said.

A letter of best wishes from the President of Ireland, Mary McAleese, was read by club Executive member, Ciara Donnelly.

Fun and games at the Homecoming Weekend and Official Opening of new Sports Pavilion

> Our challenge for the future is to ensure that our efforts in achieving our aim of catering for all young people and providing them with the chance to participate in all GAA activities are successful

Red Knights Reaching Out

A century ago in January 1906 a group of likeminded people gathered at the Market Hall in Sixmilecross to form Tyrone's newest GAA club - the Sixmilecross Wolfe Tones. They were inspired by a desire to see gaelic games, culture and Irish ideals promoted in their locality at a time when these aims were being actively developed in only a small number of parishes throughout the county.

Looking through the pages of history gives an idea of how the hopes and dreams of that far distant evening have been realised. It's a story which began in humble circumstances earlier on that cold winter's day at the beginning of the 20th Century. Now in the 21st Century the latest milestone is a glittering Gala Banquet highlighting the pride of the modern Beragh Red Knights in their gaelic heritage.

Some say that the more things change, the more they stay the same. Those first Wolfe Tones played a central role in the development of the GAA in Tyrone during the first two decades of the twentieth century. It was their example in the period between 1906 and 1920 which often spurred others into action when gaelic games and culture were struggling to survive.

The formation of the first Beragh Red Knights in 1921 took place when there was virtually no organised GAA in either Tyrone or Ulster. Yet, in the households of Beragh, Sixmilecross and Brackey, the talk was of starting a GAA team and getting others to follow. They were 'Reaching Out,' urging support and challenging others to follow their lead. Hardly surprising, then, that when the Association in West Tyrone was finally put on a firm footing in the 1930s, it was the Beragh officials who took the reigns.

> The formation of the first Beragh Red Knights in 1921 took place when there was virtually no organised GAA in either Tyrone or Ulster.

And, the flame of hope always flickered even when it wasn't easy combining GAA activity with the demands of everyday life in that period. The Beragh St Mary's were a stronghold in the fifties and sixties when playing football, fielding teams or running a club wasn't a priority or the popular choice that it is today.

In the modern era the Red Knights has been and is one of the most thriving clubs of all - Reaching Out and leading the way in the development and other initiatives in the seventies, the introduction of

Executive member Catherine Donnelly and Club Chairman, Mickey McCann, lead the Parade down Main Street in Beragh as part of the Centenary Celebrations.

GAA administrative structures in the eighties and most recently in employing the latest technological advances in wind energy and the development of facilities.

This is boomtime for the GAA in Tyrone, a time when gaelic games and culture are the activities of choice. In Beragh, the golden era is reflected in the numbers of boys and girls attending coaching sessions in gaelic football, hurling and handball, playing on teams and enthusiastically taking part in other club events.

But behind all this lies a task just as challenging to the club of today as those faced by past generations. Players, coaches, officials and supporters must believe in their very special role as members of a club with an illustrious past, a proud present and the promise of more great times ahead.

There can be no short-cuts to the top in the quest for long term gain. **'Down from the 'Cross'** tells the story of the first 100 years. Now the rewards are there to be grasped in a future in which the Red Knights membership has the opportunity to participate fully in the widest range of GAA activities while its teams and players reach their potential by competing and winning at the highest level at both underage and adult competitions.

The 2006 Executive Committee of the Beragh Red Knights GAA Club and Trustees with GAA President, Ladies GAA President, Ulster President and County Chairman

Beragh Red Knights
GAA Officials since 1906

GAA Officials 1906-2005

Year	Chairman	Secretary	Treasurer
1906	Jim Corrigan	Patrick Rodgers	HK McAleer
1907	HK McAleer	Jim McGillion	HK McAleer
1908	Bernard Rodgers	HK McAleer	HK McAleer
1909	Bernard Rodgers	Jim McGillion	HK McAleer
1910	**No organised GAA in Tyrone**		
1911	**No organised GAA in Tyrone**		
1912	HK McAleer	Patrick Rodgers	Jamie Slane
1913	HK McAleer	Barney Fitzsimmons	Jamie Slane
1914	HK McAleer	Barney Fitzsimmons	PJ Mallon
1915	Jamie Slane	HK McAleer	PJ Mallon
1916	Jamie Slane	Patrick McGirr	Felix Devlin
1917	Jamie Slane	Patrick McGirr	Felix Devlin
1918	Jamie Slane	Peter McNamee	Felix Devlin
1919	Jamie Slane	Peter McNamee	Felix Devlin
1920	Jamie Slane	Michael Donnelly	Felix Devlin
1921	Jamie Slane	Jamie Hagan	Harry Owens
1922	Jamie Slane	Jamie Hagan	Harry Owens
1923	Jamie Hagan	Harry Owens	FH Rodgers
1924	Jamie Hagan	Harry Owens	FH Rodgers
1925	Jamie Hagan	Harry Owens	FH Rodgers
1926	James McMahon	Harry Owens	FH Rodgers
1927	James McMahon	Harry Owens	Harry Owens
1928	Jamie Slane	Felix Hughes	Barney Farrell
1929	Frank Rafferty	James McMahon	Frank Kerr
1930	James McMahon	Frank Kerr	Frank Kerr
1931	Frank Rafferty	Jim McGurn	Frank Kerr
1932	James Magee	Michael McCaffrey	Frank Kerr
1933	Frank Rafferty	Jack Kerr	Frank Kerr
1934	Frank Rafferty	WJ Conway	WJ Conway
1935	Frank Rafferty	WJ Conway	WJ Conway
1936	Paddy McCrumlish	Frank Maguire	Felix Owens
1937	Paddy McCrumlish	Frank Maguire	Felix Owens
1938	Paddy McCrumlish	Frank Maguire	Felix Owens
1939	Jack McCann	Paddy McCrumlish	Felix Owens
1940	Jack McCann	Paddy McCrumlish	WJ Conway

Year	Chairman	Secretary	Treasurer
1941	Jack McCann	Francie Gallagher	WJ Conway
1942	Jack McCann	Francie Gallagher	WJ Conway
1943	Ollie Slane	Packie Owens	Patsy Collins
1944	Paddy McCrumlish	Sean Bennett	WJ Conway
1945	Paddy McCrumlish	Sean Bennett	WJ Conway
1946	Terry McCann	Sean Bennett	WJ Conway
1947	Terry McCann	Sean Bennett	WJ Conway
1948	Terry McCann	Sean Bennett	WJ Conway
1949	Terry McCann	Sean Bennett	WJ Conway
1950	Terry McCann	Sean Bennett	WJ Conway
1951	Terry McCann	Sean Bennett	WJ Conway
1952	Tommy McGarvey	John Boyle	WJ Conway
1953	Terry McCann	John Boyle	WJ Conway
1954	Tommy McGarvey	Sean Bennett	WJ Conway
1955	Tommy McGarvey	Sean Bennett	WJ Conway/J Boyle
1956	Jack McCann	Sean Bennett	WJ Conway
1957	Jack McCann	Pat McCartan	WJ Conway
1958	Terry Kelly	Pat McCartan/J McMahon	WJ Conway
1959	Ollie Slane	Sean Bennett	WJ Conway
1960	Fr Donnelly	Sean Bennett	WJ Conway
1961	Terry McCann	Sean Bennett	Terry Kelly
1962	Terry Kelly	Dessie McMahon	Sean Bennett/John Donaghy
1963	Jack Heaney	Peter Bennett	Sean Bennett/Liam McGrath
1964	Jack Heaney	Peter Bennett	Sean Bennett/Liam McGrath
1965	Mick Kerr	Jack Heaney	Pat McCartan
1966	Mick Kerr	Jack Heaney	Pat McCartan
1967	Mick Kerr	Jack Heaney	Paddy Bogan
1968	Mick Kerr	Frank Rodgers	Paddy Bogan
1969	Mick Kerr	Frank Rodgers	Paddy Bogan
1970	Mick Kerr	Frank Rodgers	Paddy Bogan
1971	Brian Donnelly	Frank Rodgers	Paddy Bogan
1972	Brian Donnelly	Frank Rodgers	Paddy Bogan
1973	Brian Donnelly	Frank Rodgers	Paddy Bogan
1974	Terry Kelly	Frank Rodgers	Paddy Bogan
1975	Terry Kelly	Frank Rodgers	Paddy Bogan
1976	Terry Kelly	Frank Rodgers	Paddy Bogan
1977	Louis McNamee	Frank Rodgers	Paddy Bogan

Year	Chairman	Secretary	Treasurer
1978	Louis McNamee	Frank Rodgers	Paddy Bogan
1979	Louis McNamee	Frank Rodgers	Paddy Grimes
1980	Louis McNamee	Frank Rodgers	Paddy Grimes
1981	Tommy McGarvey	Frank Rodgers	Paddy Grimes
1982	Tommy McGarvey	Frank Rodgers	Brendan Grimes
1983	Tommy McGarvey	Frank Rodgers	Brendan Grimes
1984	Kevin Maguire	Frank Rodgers	Brendan Grimes
1985	Kevin Maguire	Frank Rodgers	Brendan Grimes
1986	Paddy Bogan	Frank Rodgers	Brendan Grimes
1987	Paddy Bogan	Frank Rodgers	Mary McCarney
1988	Paddy Bogan	Frank Rodgers	Mary McCarney
1989	Paddy Bogan	Frank Rodgers	Mary McCarney
1990	Louis McNamee	Frank Rodgers	Mary McCarney
1991	Seamus Boyle	Frank Rodgers	Mary McCarney
1992	Gerry Owens	Fergal Grimes	Mary McCarney
1993	Gerry Owens	Fergal Grimes	Mary McCarney
1994	Gerry Owens	Patsy Farley	Mary McCarney
1995	Gerry Owens	Patsy Farley	Mary McCarney
1996	Gerry Owens	Patsy Farley	Mary McCarney
1997	Gerry Owens	Patsy Farley	Anto Duffy
1998	Gerry Owens	Nuala McCartan	Anto Duffy
1999	Gerry Owens	Alan Rodgers	Anto Duffy
2000	Gerry Owens	Alan Rodgers	Anto Duffy
2001	Mickey McCann	Alan Rodgers	Anto Duffy
2002	Mickey McCann	Alan Rodgers	Anto Duffy
2003	Mickey McCann	Barry Conroy	Anto Duffy
2004	Mickey McCann	Barry Conroy	Michael Montague
2005	Mickey McCann	Barry Conroy	Michael Montague
2006	Mickey McCann	Barry Conroy	Michael Montague

Beragh Red Knights
Statistics

Tyrone County Board Officers

Chairman –

HK McAleer - 1909-1910 and 1913-14

Pat McCartan -1975-1977

Treasurer – HK McAleer -1907-08

County GAC Board

Secretary -

Frank Rodgers 1980-2000

West Tyrone Board Officers

Chairman –

Pat McCartan - 1969 and 1971

Secretaries –

Jim McGurn – 1931-32

Sean Bennett – 1952-1954

Jack Woods – 1958-59

Treasurers –

Frank Kerr – 1931-35

WJ Conway – 1952-54

County Referees Board

Jack Heaney served as Chairman in the 1970s and 1980s

Camogie Officers

First Tyrone Co Board 1934 included Mrs Rafferty (Beragh) as Treasurer and Bernadette Owens as Delegate to Congress. Nora Devine played on 1936 Tyrone team in Ulster Championship.

Kevin Grimes served as County Chairman in the late seventies and early eighties.

County Handball Board

Pat Donnelly and Sean Clarke have served terms as Secretary while Mick Kerr has served a number of terms as Chairman.

Ladies Officials

President of the Ulster Council -

Mary Donnelly

County Senior Final Referees

Jim McGillion – 1908-09

FH Rodgers – 1924

James McMahon – 1936

Ollie Slane – 1953, 1954. (1951 while with Carrickmore)

Jack Heaney – 1969, 1975. (Ulster Senior Final Referee 1981, All-Ireland Minor Final 1982.

Ladies –Co Senior Final

Jim Gallagher – 2001

Ulster Club Final

Jack Heaney – 1980

Ladies Jim Gallagher - 2002

2006 Beragh Red Knights Executive Committee

Mickey McCann (Chairman), Barry Grimes (Vice-Chairman), Barry Conroy (Secretary), Lisa Rodgers (Assistant Secretary), Michael Montague (Treasurer), Stephen Farley (Registrar), Seamus Boyle, John Donnelly, Shane McCarney, Alan Rodgers, Sean Clarke, Catherine Donnelly, Hugh McNamee, Paddy Mullan, Christopher Donnelly, Ciara Donnelly, Tracey Rodgers, Pat McCartan, Stephen Mullan, Niall Farley.

Beragh Red Knights Club Trustees

Frank Rodgers, Louis McNamee, Gerry Owens, Danny Murphy (Secretary Ulster Council), James Treacy (Tyrone County Board).

Tyrone Players in Senior Football Championship

Ned McGee – 1924

Harry Owens – 1925, 1926, 1927, 1929.

PJ Shields – 1926

Jim McMahon – 1926, 1927, 1930, 1931, 1933, 1935

Mick Keenan – 1941, 1942 (while with Carrickmore).

Ollie Slane – 1945, 1951 (while with Carrickmore), 1952 and 1953 (while with Beragh).

Jim McAleer – 1954, 1955, 1956.

Mick Kerr – 1956

Dessie McMahon – 1962, 1963.

Liam McGrath – 1963, 1964, 1965, 1966.

Colm McAleer – 1974

Malachy Donnelly – 1977

Paul Donnelly – 1992, 1993, 1994, 1995, 1996

Terry McKenna – 1998

Ulster and All-Ireland Medal winners with Tyrone

Minor –

JJ Donnelly – 1948 (Ulster and All-Ireland)

Ben McQuaide – 1967

Paddy McGarvey – 1967

Jim Gallagher - 1967

Pete Owens – 1972

Colm McAleer – 1972 and 1973 (Ulster and All-Ireland)

Malachy Donnelly – 1976

Paul Donnelly – 1988

Adrian Donnelly - 1988

U-21 –

Colm McAleer – 1973

Vincent McMackin – 1973

Paul Donnelly – 1990 and 1991

Senior –

Mick Kerr 1956

Jim McAleer – 1956

Paul Donnelly – 1995 and 1996

Junior –

Mickey Slane - 1983

National League -

Jim McMahon – 1931 National League Division Two

Vocational Schools – All-Ireland winners

1967 – Neilly Hagan, Anthony Donaghy, Ben McQuaide, Peter Hagan,
Sean McGrath, Eamon McQuaide.

1988 – Paul Donnelly and Adrian Donnelly

1989 – Cathal Grimes

NB – Tommy and Brian McGarvey played on teams defeated in 1974 and 1975 Finals.

Hurling –

Eamon Rodgers – 1995 and 1996

NB – Teams also included Vinny Owens, Martin Hegarty and Tony McCrory.

Camogie –

Jacqueline O'Neill National Junior League 1982.

Ladies Football –

Nuala McCartan – 1995, 1997 and 1999

Caroline Donnelly – 1995, 1997 and 1999

Nuala McCartan, Ann Donnelly, Caroline Donnelly, Ciara Donnelly were members of the Tyrone team which won the All-Ireland Junior title for the first time in 1999.

Ashling Hagan was a member of Tyrone team which won Ulster Senior Ladies titles in 2000 and 2001.

Managerial Achievements

Tyrone Selectors – 1920s-1940s - FH Rodgers, Jim McMahon and Ollie Slane.

Pat McCartan selector with Tyrone team which won Ulster titles in 1984, 1986, 1995 and 1996 and reached All-Ireland Finals in 1986 and 1995. Also member of selection panel for 1972 and 1973 All-Ireland Minor teams.

Fr Gerard McAleer selector with Tyrone teams which won All-Ireland Minor title in 1998, All-Ireland U-21 titles in 2000 and 2001 and Ulster titles in 2003 and 2005 and National League title in 2003. Also a selector with Tyrone team which won historic All-Ireland Senior titles in 2003 and 2005.

Kevin Grimes manager of Tyrone Camogie team which reached the All-Ireland Junior Final at Croke Park in 1980.

Barry Grimes, joint manager of Tyrone Ladies team which won All-Ireland Junior title in 1999 and Ulster Senior title in 2001.

Co Senior Medal winners

Jim McMahon – 1926 and 1931 (with Ballygawley)

Mick Keenan – 1940, 1943 (with Carrickmore)

Frank Owens – 1947 (with Carrickmore)

Ollie Slane – 1943, 1949 (with Carrickmore)

Terry McKenna – 2003 (with Killyclogher)

County Finals Played in Parish

Senior –

Sixmilecross - 1907-08 (and Replay), 1908-09, 1913-14.

Intermediate –

St Mary's Park - 1978 and 1983.

Hurling –

St Mary's Park - 1977 and 1982

Beragh Tournament Winners 1954-1991
For the Cuchulainn Trophy

Carrickmore (13) – 1964, 1965, 1968, 1969, 1970, 1971, 1975, 1976, 1977, 1978, 1981, 1983, 1987.

Clogher – (5) 1956, 1958, 1959, 1960, 1962.

Ballygawley – (3) 1963, 1980, 1986.

Trillick – (3) 1979, 1982, 1985

One each - Beragh (1955), **Emyvale** (1957), **Omagh** (1961), **Tempo** (1966), **Augher** (1967), **Fintona** (1984), **Clonoe** (1989).

Mickey McGuinness Shield (Minor Football) – Beragh (1991), Dromore (1991 and 1992).

Results of note

1916 – Sixmilecross top West Tyrone League. Kilskeery protest leads to them being awarded County Final place without playing Semi-Final against the Wolfe Tones.

1924 – Stewartstown 2-5 Beragh 2-3

1933 – Omagh 0-6 Beragh 0-1

1935 – Omagh 0-2 Beragh 0-1

1955 – Coalisland 1-8 Beragh 0-3

1996 – Errigal Ciaran 1-13 Beragh 0-8

Intermediate –

1989 – Gortin 1-9 Beragh 1-7

1992 – Eglish 1-10 Beragh 0-8

1993 – Beragh 0-12 Edendork 1-6

2000 – Beragh 0-11 Gortin 0-11 (Replay – Beragh 1-7 Gortin 0-5)

Junior –

1938 – Edendork 1-4 Brackey 2-6 (Brackey disqualified)

1939 – Mountjoy 4-1 Brackey 0-2

1947 – Beragh 0-4 Washingbay 0-3

1988 – Beragh 2-8 Strabane 2-4

Reserve (Titles won) –

Championship – 1984, 1985 (Div 2), 1987, 1988, 2005 (Div 3)

League – 1981, 2004, 2005 (All Div 3)

Minor –

1950 Championship – Coalisland 5-1 Beragh 1-5

1952 Championship – Coalisland 3-11 Beragh 0-4

1988 League – Beragh 0-7 Castlederg 2-7

Juvenile –

1980 League – Beragh 1-5 Dungannon 2-11

1985 Championship – Beragh 2-5 Omagh 2-3

1985 League – Beragh 0-1 Shamrocks 1-8

1989 League – Beragh 0-5 Dungannon 3-7

U-14 –

2001 League – Beragh 1-7 Derrylaughan 7-10 Replay (Draw 1-11 each)

2006 Championship – Beragh 4-12 Galbally 1-5

Reflected Glory

* Peter McDermott who won All-Ireland Senior medal with Meath in 1949 married to Bridie Kelly of Sixmilecross.

* Mickey Harte, who managed Tyrone's All-Ireland winning teams, married to Marion Donnelly of Aughnagar. Their son Mark, winner of All-Ireland medals in 2003 and 2005.

*Ollie Murphy, who won All-Ireland Senior medals with Meath in 1996 and 1999, married to Regina Donnelly from Clogherney.

*Kieran Donaghy, the star of Kerry in winning the 2006 All-Ireland title, son of Oliver and grandson of long serving Beragh player and official, John of Beragh village.

Beragh Red Knights
Team Lists 1906 - 2006

TEAMLISTS 1906-2006

1906 – Sixmilecross v St Patrick's, Killyclogher Mid-Tyrone League 2/12/06
Thomas Gormley, Michael Tierney, Michael Tierney, Owen Mullin, J McGarrity, M Owens, John Owens, Hugh Donaghy, J Maguire, M Mullin, John Devlin, C Brown, Mat Gormley, Owen Haverin.

1907 – Sixmilecross v Letteree 20/1/07
Thomas Gormley, Mickey Owens, Peter Owens, Johnny Owens, Jas McGarrity, Owen Mullin, John Mullin, Jamie Slane, Mick Tierney, Hugh Tierney, Mick Tierney, Matt Gormley, Bernard Rodgers, Willie Shields, P Martin, John Devlin, Hugh Donaghy.

1908 – Sixmilecross v Pomeroy in Dungannon District League –
Frank Cleary, James Cleary, James Slane, Bernard Rodgers (captain), Patrick Rodgers, Hugh Donaghy, Mick Tierney (Owen), Mick Tierney (Hugh), Felix Devlin, John Devlin, James Bradley, Patrick Gormley, Owen Mullin, John Owens, Peter Owens.

1909 – Thomas Gormley, Mick Tierney, Jas McGarrity, Owen Mullin, Bernard Rodgers, Mick Tierney, Peter Owens, Hugh Tierney, John Mullin, Felix Devlin, Patrick Rodgers, James Slane, Willie Shields, Matthew Gormley, Johnny Owens, John Devlin, Hugh Donaghy, Thomas McLarnon, Robert McQuade, Patrick Kerr, Mick McCann and William McAllister.

1912 – Sixmilecross - James Cleary, Bernard Rodgers, Jamie Slane, McCabe, Johnny Mullin, Tom Mullin, John McGarrity, Patrick Rodgers, Ned Rafferty David Mullin, Hugh Rodgers, Frank Cleary, Johnny McNamee.

1914 – Sixmilecross v St Kieran's
James Cleary, Ned Rafferty, Hugh Rodgers, Bernard Rodgers. Jamie Slane, Kane, Patrick Rodgers, Felix Devlin, John Rodgers, John McGarrity, David Mullin, Johnny McNamee, Peter McNamee, Hugh Rafferty.

1916 – Sixmilecross v Fintona
J Connor, Bernard Rodgers, John Mullin, Felix Devlin, Ned Rafferty, Johnny McNamee, Peter McNamee, C McClenaghan, Hugh Rafferty, John Rodgers, Packie Farrell, J Farrell, Felix Hughes.

1917 – v Fintona in West Division League 7/1/17
Johnny McNamee, Peter McNamee, Hugh Rafferty, Ned Rafferty, Packie Farrell, Felix Hughes, John Rodgers. Felix Devlin, Frank Maguire, Jamie Slane, Jas Montague Jim McNamee, Bernard Rodgers, Jim Cleary, Tom 'California' Mullan.

1921 – Frank Cleary, Jamie Slane, Tom Kelly, Mickey Conway, Jamie Hagan, Johnny Donaghy, Paddy Donaghy, Matthew Rodgers, Packie Mullan, Felix Owens, Felix Hughes, Jim McMahon, Harry Owens, Jimmy Donaghy, John Owens (capt), Cecil Meehan, Packie McAleer, Micksie Boyle, Jim McCann.

1922 – Beragh v Dungannon
Jamie Hagan, Matthew Rodgers, McGirr, Doyle, Harry Owens, Pat Owens, Mick McGrath, Paddy Donaghy, Johnny Donaghy, Tom Kelly, Gerry McWilliams, Dan Woods, Mickey Owens, Joe Donnelly, Mickey Conway, Jim McGillion, Joe Colton, Felix Hughes, Barney Gormley.

1924 – Beragh v Stewartstown Co Semi-Final on 6/4/24 –
Frank Cleary, Harry Owens, Jamie Slane, Jim McMahon, Ned Magee, Packie Farrell, Jimmy Donaghy, Peter Mulgrew, Pat Owens, Pat Shields, Mick O'Hanlon, Gerry McWilliams, Felix Hughes.

1925 – Francie Cleary, Cecil Meehan, Jack Donnelly, Felix Owens, Joe Colton, Micksie Boyle, Harry Owens, Paddy Donaghy, Jim McCann, Peter McGarrity, Joe Donnelly, Packie McAleer, Jim McCann, Pat Shields, Felix Hughes.

1926 – Beragh v Fintona on 3/10/26 –
Francie Cleary, Johnny Donaghy, Cecil Meehan, Joe Donnelly, Packie McAleer, Harry Owens, Paddy Donaghey, Joe Colton, Jim McCann, Micksie Boyle, Felix Hughes, Jackie Gilmartin, Felix Owens.

1928 – Sixmilecross v Dungannon in Senior Championship
Patrick McGirr, William O'Hanlon, Barney Farrell, James Mulgrew, Ned McGee, Felix Hughes, JJ Kelly, T McCann, Joe Donnelly, Jim McCaul, Gerard McWilliams, Frank Farrell, Packie Farrell.

1929 – Beragh v Fintona in Junior League
Patrick Donaghy, Patrick Shields, James Mulgrew, Patrick McGirr, Jas McCann, Felix Owens, Frank McMahon, Frank Kerr, Peter McGarrity, P Kelly, Micksey Boyle, Joseph Colton.

1931 – Beragh v Altamuskin West Tyrone League 6/12/31 –
Patrick McMackin, Jim McCann, Francis Mellon, Patrick McCrystal, Felix Owens, Dan McSorley, Michael McCaffrey, Peter McGarrity, Peter McMahon, Frank Kerr, Frank Rafferty, Joe Colton, Micksie Boyle.

1932 – Beragh v Carrickmore West Tyrone League 16/10/32 –
Micksie Boyle, Peter McMahon, Joe Kerr, Owenie McMahon, Jim McCann, Frank Rafferty, Frank Kerr, James McMahon, Peter McGarrity, Harry McKernan, Johnny Ward, Mackle Grimes, Felix Owens.

1933 – Beragh v Omagh West Tyrone Championship Final (Co Semi-Final) - 18/6/33 –
Micksie Boyle, Mackle McCaffrey, Harry Owens, Frank Rafferty, Joe Kerr, Jim McCann, Owen McMahon, Jim McMahon, Frank McMahon, Jas Rodgers, Dan McSorley, Frank McMahon, Mackle Grimes, Francie Maguire, Johnny Ward.

1934 – Beragh v Dromore West Tyrone League 2/12/34 –
Barney Farrell, Mackle McCaffrey, Patrick McMackin, Mackle Grimes, Peter McMahon, Joe Kerr, Dan McSorley, James McMahon, Frank McMahon, Tom Mullan, Frank Hagan, Felix Owens, Jim McCann, Leo Kelly, Frank Kerr, Peter McGarrity, Johnny Ward

1935 – Beragh v Aughnacloy West Tyrone League 6/10/35 –
Barney Gormley, Barney Farrell, Mackle McCaffrey, Jim McCann, Jim McMahon, Johnny Mullin, Jas Rodgers, Leo Kelly, Johnny Ward, Dan McSorley, Tommy Mullin, Frank Hagan, Joe Kerr, Sonny Owens.

1936 – Beragh v Omagh 2/2/36 West Tyrone Championship Final – (Co Semi-Final)
Barney Gormley, Mackle McCaffrey, Barney Farrell, Frank Rafferty, Jim McCann, Jim McMahon, Jack Mullan, Peter McMahon, Frank McMahon, Dan McSorley, Laurence Kelly, Felix Owens, Johnny Ward, Frankie Farrell, Peter Montague.

1937 – Brackey v Tummery Junior League 5/9/37 –
Packie Owens, Frank Maguire, Willie Barr, Patrick Garrity, Patrick Kelly, John Kelly, Jas McGale, Eugene McCann, Frank Mullan, Frank Rafferty, Harry Kerr, Harry McCrory, Johnny Ward, Peter Daly, Michael Daly, Frankie Owens,

1938 - Brackey v Killyclogher Herald Cup Final 15/5/38 -
Packie Owens, Barney Farrell, John Kelly, Dan McSorley, Harry Kerr, Barney Gormley,
Johnny McAleer, Felix Owens, Johnny Ward, Frankie Owens, Laurence Kelly, Frank Hagan,
Frank Mullin, Peter Daly, Michael Daly.

1939 – Junior Final (1938) Brackey v Edendork 12/3/39
Packie Owens, John Kelly, Harry Kerr, Dan McSorley,Laurence Kelly, Peter Daly, Johnny
McAleer, Frank Hagan, Mick Keenan, Jas Rodgers, Frank Mullin, Peter Daly, Frankie
Owens,

1940 - Beragh v Dungannon Senior Championship –
Johnny McAleer, John Kelly, Harry Kerr, Peter Montague, John Donaghy, Frank Hagan,
Packie Daly, Dan McSorley, Frankie Owens, Johnny Mullan, Johnny Ward, Francie Gallagher,
Packie McKernan, Mackle Grimes, Kieran McCann.

1941 – Beragh v Omagh West Tyrone League 17/8/41 –
James Collins, Packie Owens, Johnny McAleer, John Kelly, Harry Kerr, Mackle McCaffrey,
John Donaghy, Frank Hagan, Ollie Slane, Johnny Mullan, Francie Gallagher, Packie
McKernan, Kieran McCann, Peter Montague, Mick Daly.

1942 – Beragh Tournament Panel
Packie Owens, Vincent Lafferty, John Donaghy, John Kelly, Mackle McCaffrey, Dan
McSorley, Harry Kerr, Johnny Mullin, Frankie Owens, Francie Gallagher, Frank Rafferty,
Jim McCann, Frank Hagan.

1943 – Beragh/Sixmilecross v Carrickmore Green Cross Tournament - 24/10/43
Packie Owens, Frank Hagan, Vincent Lafferty, John Donaghy, John Kelly, Peter McDermott,
Barney Farrell, Dan McSorley, Frankie Owens, Ollie Slane, Francie Gallagher, Jim McCann,
Packie McKernan, Leo Kelly

1946 – Seven a side at Sports 11/7/46 -
Frank Hagan, Vincent Lafferty, Frankie Owens, Louis McNamee, Harry Kerr, Dan McSorley,
Jack 'Attie'Mullan, James Colton, Peter Daly, Charlie Montague, Jack McEnhill, John
Donaghy, Sean Bennett, Jack McCann, Leo Kelly, Packie McKernan.

1947 – Junior Championship Panel
Frank Hagan, John Donaghy, Frankie Owens, Vincent Lafferty, Louis McNamee, Peter Daly, Tommy Owens, Harry Kerr, Jim McAleer, Vincent McCaughey, Jack McEnhill, James Colton, Jack 'Attie' Mullan, Dan McSorley, Charlie Montague.

1948 – Beragh v Washingbay JFC Final
Frank Hagan, Frankie Owens, Vincent Lafferty, John Donaghy, Louis McNamee, Peter Daly (capt), Peter Meenagh, Harry Kerr, Jim McAleer, Tommy Owens, John Donnelly, Jack 'Attie'Mullan, Vincent McCaughey, Charlie Montague, Dan McSorley.
Subs – Jack McEnhill, Kevin McNally, James Colton.

1949 – v Carrickmore in West Tyrone SFL 6/3/49 –
Frank Hagan, John Donaghy, Frankie Owens, Vincent Lafferty, Louis McNamee, Peter Daly, Peter Montague, Tommy Owens, FH Owens, Jim McAleer, B McAleer, J McCaughey, Barney Mullan, Terry McCann, Charlie Montague. Others - Brian Murphy, John McCann Gusty McMackin, Peter Meenagh, Kevin McNally.

1950 – Beragh v Cappagh West Tyrone SFL 6/5/50
Frank Hagan, John Donaghy, Frankie Owens, Peter Doherty, Vincent Lafferty, Jim McAleer, Brian McCann, John McAleer, Peter Daly, Kevin McNally, Tommy Owens, Joe McCann, B Mullan, Roche McGovern, Gusty McMackin, Phil Campbell.

1950 – Beragh v Trillick Davis Cup Final 8/10/50 - Panel - John Donaghy, Jim McCann, Johnny McAleer, Jim McAleer, David Mullan, Vin Donaghy, Brian Mullan, Johnny McAleer, David Mullan, Brian Mullan, Brian McAleer, Frankie Owens, Brian McCann, Tommy Owens, FH Owens, FH Lafferty, B Doherty, Roche McGovern, Kevin McNally, Terry McCann.

1951 – Tommy Owens, Peter Daly, Jim McAleer, Joe McCann, Peter Doherty, Frankie Owens, John McAleer, Jim McAleer, Roche McGovern, Tommy Owens, Maurice McGarrity, Phil Campbell, Gusty McMackin, Kevin McNally, Brian McCann, David Mullan, Brian Mullan, Vincent Lafferty, John Donaghy, Sean Canavan, Eugene McCann, Brian McAleer, Vin Donaghy, Terry McCann.

1952 – Beragh v Trillick SFC 1st Round 11/5/52 -
Peter Daly, David Mullin, Kevin McNally, Jerry Kavanagh, John Donaghy, Ollie Slane, Vin Donaghy, Mick Kerr, Joe McCann, Hugh McCann, Tommy Owens, FH Owens, Terry Kelly, Jim McAleer, Terry McCann, Phil Campbell. Phil McAleer, Ollie Slane,

1953 – Beragh v Newtownstewart SFC 10/5/53 –
Patsy Breen, John Donaghy, Vin Donaghy, Hugh McCann, Matt McNamee, Joe McCann (Capt), Terry McCann, Terry Kelly, Jim McAleer, John McAleer, Mick Kerr, Ollie Slane, FH Owens, Pat Grimes, P McAleer, Jerry Kavanagh, Maurice McGarrity, Sean Kelly, Basil Neville.

1954 – Beragh v Carrickmore West Tyrone SFL – 21/3/54 at new grounds –
Patsy Breen, John Donaghy, Hugh McCann, Ollie Slane, Matt McNamee, FH Owens, Joe McCann, Jim McAleer, Terry Kelly, Mick Kerr, Terry McCann, Pat Grimes, S Colton, Ian McCool, Frank McKenna, Basil Neville, Seamus Heagney, Roche McGovern, Mick McCartan, Mickey McGale, Sean Kelly, Gus McNamee.

1955 – Senior Championship Semi-Final v Coalisland
Jim Breen, John Donaghy, FH Owens, Pat Breen, Hughie McCann, Vin Donaghy, Antony McGrath, Jim McAleer, Terry Kelly, Joe McCann, Mick Kerr, Pat Grimes, Tommy McCann, John McSorley, Basil Neville. Subs – Mick McCartan, Frankie Owens, Tommy Owens, Sean Kelly, Ollie Slane, Gus McNamee.

1956 – Beragh v Carrickmore West Tyrone SFL 27/5/56
Barney Horisk, John Donaghy, FH Owens, Frank Rodgers, Nickle Grimes, Vin Donaghy, Seamus McMahon, Mick Kerr, Jim McAleer, Anthony McGrath, Basil Terry Kelly, Hugh McCann, Jack Heaney, Joe McCann, Basil Neville.

1957 – Beragh v Tattysallagh St Enda Cup 2/6/57
Barney Horisk, John Donaghy, Nickle Grimes, Vin Donaghy, Seamus McMahon, Mick Kerr, Terry Kelly, Anthony McGrath, Frank Rodgers, Basil Neville, Hugh McCann, Jack Heaney. Others – John McGlinn, Brian Grimes, Dessie McMahon, Mickey McCann, Pat Grimes, Barney Owens, Patsy Farley, John Breen, Mick McCartan, JJ Colton, Kieran Murphy, Sean McCartan, Pat McCartan.

1958 – Beragh v Carrickmore St Enda Cup Final
Barney Horisk, Frank Rodgers, FH Owens, Barney Owens, Anthony McGrath, Hughie Owens, Seamus McMahon, Dessie McMahon, Nickle Grimes, Mickey McCann, Mick Kerr, Joe McCann, Liam McGrath, Brian Grimes, Basil Neville. Others – Kieran Murphy, Seamus Coyle.

1959 – Beragh v Derrylaughan 30/8/59
Pat Grimes, John Donaghy, Hugh McCann, Barney Owens, FH Owens, Nickle Grimes, Anthony McGrath, Mick Kerr, Liam McGrath, Terry Kelly, Hughie Owens, Basil Neville, Frank Rodgers, Dessie McMahon, Seamus Coyle, Brian Grimes. Others – Dan Montgomery, Gerry Donnelly, Vincent McCullagh, Pat McCusker.

1960 – v Ballygawley West Tyrone League 14/10/60
Pat Fox, Barney Owens, Frank Rodgers John Donnelly, Hughie Owens, Liam McGrath, M Donnelly, Nickle Grimes, Dessie McMahon, Vincent McCullagh, Basil Neville, Mick Kerr, Barney Cunningham, John McSorley, Anthony McGrath. Others – Terry Kelly, Seamus McMahon, Brian Grimes, Hugh McCann, Fr Donnelly, Michael Murphy, Seamus Coyle, Jack Heaney, Pat McCusker, Anthony Heagney.

1961 – v Pomeroy West Tyrone League Semi-Final (1960) 26/2/61
John Breen, FH Owens, Frank Rodgers, Nickle Grimes, Dessie McMahon, Seamus McMahon, Liam McGrath, Mick Kerr, M Donnelly, Hughie Owens, Basil Neville, J Donnelly, John McSorley, Brian Grimes, Vincent McCullagh. Others – Barney Horisk, Michael Murphy, Kieran Murphy, Sean Callaghan, Hugh Ward, Barney Cunningham, Dan Montgomery, Noel Maguire, Kieran Kelly, Jack Heaney, Sean McCann, Kieran McCann, Seamus Heagney, Peter Baxter.

1962 – v Carrickmore Senior Championship
Barney Horisk, Brian Grimes, FH Owens, Barney Owens, Mickey Donnelly, Seamus McMahon, Hugh Fitzpatrick, Dessie McMahon, Hughie Owens, Nickle Grimes, John McSorley, Seamus Heagney, Jack Heaney, Mick Kerr,

1963 – v Ballygawley SFC 9/6/63
Barney Horisk, Barney Owens, FH Owens, Hugh Fitzpatrick, Anthony McGrath, Liam McGrath, Seamus McMahon, Dessie McMahon, Nickle Grimes, Hughie Owens, Mick Kerr, Dan Montgomery, Brian Grimes, Frank Rodgers, Basil Neville. Others – Kevin Grimes, Benny Donaghy, Seamus Heagney, Pete McQuaide.

1964 – v Kildress West Tyrone League 16/2/64
Pat Fox, Frank Rodgers, FH Owens, Barney Owens, Hugh Fitzpatrick, Liam McGrath, Hughie Owens, Nickle Grimes, Dessie McMahon, Seamus McMahon, Mick Kerr, Kevin Grimes, Basil Neville, John McSorley, Cahir Woods. Others – Brian Donnelly, Benny Donaghy, Dermot Meenagh, Mickey Donnelly Francie Heagney, Anthony Heagney, Pete McQuaide, Brendan Gallagher, Dan Montgomery, John Broderick, Michael McGarvey.

1965 – v Dromore St Enda Cup 20/3/65 –
Dermot Meenagh, Murt Kelly, Brian Donnelly, Barney Owens, Pete McQuaid, Hugh Fitzpatrick,   Brian Hunter, Eugene McClenaghan, Pat McCusker, Kieran Kelly, Mick Kerr, Sean Callaghan, Kevin Grimes, Brendan Gallagher, Basil Neville. Others – Kevin Nixon, Kevin Maguire, Tony Baxter, Tony Livingstone, Mickey Heaney, Ben McQuaide, Noel Maguire, Pat Grimes.

1966 – v Pomeroy McElduff Cup Semi-Final 23/11/66
Kevin Grimes, Francie Grimes, Brian Donnelly, Murt Kelly, Kevin Maguire, Dominic Darcy, Pat Hagan, Kieran Kelly, Jim Gallagher, Mickey Heaney, Mick Kerr, Tony Baxter, Jim Darcy, Ben McQuaide, Christy Owens, Eugene Horisk. Others – Liam McGrath, Paddy Donaghy, Jack Heaney, John McCarroll, Mickey Heaney, Mickey Kelly, Dan Montgomery, Sean McGrath.

1967 - v Clogher Intermediate League 18/6/67
Kevin Nixon, Pat Hagan, Brian Donnelly, Sean McGrath, Seamus McMahon, Liam McGrath, Pat Hagan, Frank Rodgers, Mick Kerr, Ben McQuaide, JimGallagher, Brian Gallagher, Murt Kelly, Benny Donaghy, Kevin Grimes, Kevin Maguire, Mickey Kelly, Eugene Horisk, Pat Hagan, Aidan McGrath, Christy Owens.

1968 – v Leckpatrick Intermediate League 1/9/68
Kevin Nixon, Francie Grimes, Brian Donnelly, Paddy Owens, Noel Maguire, Kieran Kelly, Stephen Kelly, Seamus Maguire, Dessie Donnelly, Jim Franey, Gerry Owens, Frank Rodgers, Vincent McMackin, Jim Gallagher, Mick Kerr, Paddy Owens. Others – Mickey Donnelly, Seamus Donnelly, Jim Mulholland, Brian Grimes, Mickey Kelly, Tommy Livingstone, Seamus McMahon, Stephen Deazley, Anthony Donaghy, Liam McGrath, Anthony McGrath, Ben McQuaide, Neilly Hagan, FH Owens, Benny Donaghy, Murt Kelly, Benny Hunter.

1969 – v Killyclogher Intermediate League 29/6/69
Kevin Nixon, Francie Grimes, Brian Donnelly, Martin Donnelly, Paddy Owens, Kevin Grimes, Mickey Kelly, Noel Maguire, Kieran Kelly, Mick Kerr, Jim Gallagher, Murt Kelly, Dessie Donnelly, Brian McCullagh, Ben McQuaide, Vincent McMackin. Others - Mickey Kelly, Mickey Heaney, Dan McSorley, John Tunney, Jim Mulholland, Brian Grimes, Liam McGrath, Seamus Maguire, Brian Colton, Brian Maguire, DJ Gormley.

1970 – v Pomeroy IFC 24/5/70
Eamon McQuade, Francie Grimes, Jim Gallagher, Brian Maguire, Kevin Maguire, Murt Kelly, Mickey Donnelly, Paddy Dillon, Paddy Donaghy, Dessie Donnelly, Noel Maguire, Vincent McMackin, Mickey Heaney, Paddy Owens, Jim Franey. Others – Arthur Doherty, Benny Hunter, Frank McQuaide, Dan McSorley, Harry Owens, Brian Owens, Noel Colton.

1971 – v Pomeroy IFC 13/6/71
Eamon McQuade, Mickey Donnelly, Francie Grimes, Brian McCullagh, Kevin Maguire, Jim Gallagher, Dan McSorley, Neilly Hagan, Vincent McMackin, Brian Maguire, Ben McQuaide, Harry Owens, Murt Kelly, Noel Maguire, Brian Owens. Others – Colm McAleer, Arthur Doherty, Colm Ward, Stephen Kelly, Jim Gallagher, Tommy McGarvey. Liam Deazley, Colm McAleer, Dan McSorley, Kevin Grimes, D Crozier.

1972 – v Drumagh Intermediate League 27/8/72
Eamon McQuade, Liam Deazley, Jim Franey, Pete Owens, Brian Maguire, Colm McAleer, Murt Kelly, Paddy McGarvey and Brian Owens, Vincent McMackin, Neil Hagan, Stephen Kelly, Harry Owens, Jim Gallagher, Ben McQuaide. Sub - Tommy McGarvey.

1973 – v Stewartstown Senior Championship 17/6/73
Eamon McQuaide, Murt Kelly, Pete Owens, Brian Maguire, Tommy McGarvey, Liam McGrath, Jim Franey, Colm McAleer, Dessie Donnelly, Brian Owens, Vincent McMackin, Harry Owens, Stephen Kelly, Liam Deazley, Paddy Rodgers. Subs – Jim Gallagher, Brian McCullagh, Tommy Fitzmaurice, Colm Ward.

1974 – v Pomeroy Intermediate Championship 19/5/74
Tommy Fitzmaurice, Brian Maguire, Pete Owens, Liam McGrath, Tommy McGarvey, Stephen Kelly, Murt Kelly, Colm McAleer, Dessie Donnelly, Brian Owens, Vincent McMackin, Liam Deazley, Brian McCullagh, Neilly Hagan, Frank Owens. Subs – Brian McGarvey, Colm Ward, Paddy Grimes.

1975 – v Clonoe ACL Div 3 9/3/75
Eamon McQuaide, Brian Maguire, Pete Owens, Jim Franey, Tommy McGarvey, Stephen Kelly, Murt Kelly, Colm McAleer, Malachy Donnelly, Vincent McMackin, Liam McGrath, Ben McQuaide, Kevin Maguire, Neilly Hagan, Frank McQuaide.

1976 – v Pomeroy Intermediate Championship 23/5/76
Tommy Fitzmaurice, Pat Donnelly, Pete Owens, Tommy McGarvey, Paddy Grimes, Jim Franey,
Kevin Maguire, Colm McAleer, Frank Owens, Brian McGarvey, Malachy Donnelly, Brian
Owens, Paddy Rodgers, Neilly Hagan, Adrian Nixon.
Others – Kevin Maguire, Barney Cunningham, Peter McSorley, Louis McNamee, Timothy
Grimes, Hugh Franey, Eugene O'Neill, Robert Colton, Anthony Lyttle, Paul Colton, Gerry Kelly.

1977 – v Dungannon ACL 16/10/77
Eamon McQuaide, Frank Owens, Paddy Grimes, Jim Franey, Kevin Maguire, Tommy
McGarvey, Brian McGarvey, Malachy Donnelly, Colm McAleer, Brian Owens, Paddy Rodgers,
Liam Deazley, Pat Donnelly, Dessie Donnelly, Gerry Maguire. Sub – Timothy Grimes.

1978 – v Edendork ACL Division Three Play-off 26/11/78
Eamon McQuaid, Gerry Kelly, Pete Owens, Jim Franey, Finbarr Grimes, Colm McAleer, Pat
Donnelly, Malachy Donnelly, Hugh McNamee, Gerry Maguire, Vincent McMackin, Paddy
Grimes, Gerry Ward, Tommy McGarvey, Mickey Rodgers. Subs – Barney Cunningham and
Louis McNamee, Frank McQuaide, Liam Deazley, Francie Grimes, Colm Ward, Brian Owens,
Dessie Donnelly, Kevin Maguire, Eamon McQuaide, Pat McCartan.

1979 – v Stewartstown Intermediate Championship 13/5/79
Eamon McQuaide, Gerry Kelly, Pete Owens, Jim Franey, Pat Donnelly, Colm McAleer,
Finbarr Grimes, Malachy Donnelly, Hugh McNamee, Liam Deazley, Vincetn McMackin,
Brian McGarvey, Gerry Maguire, Tommy McGarvey, Mickey Rodgers. Others – Gerry Ward,
Finbar Grimes, Louis McNamee, Colm Ward, Brian Owens, Hugh Franey.

1980 – v Killyman Intermediate Championship 11/5/80
Joe Franey, Martin Grimes, Pete Owens, Jim Franey, Gerry Maguire, Colm McAleer, Paddy
Rodgers, Pat Donnelly, Louis McNamee, Brian McGarvey, Hugh McNamee, Liam Deazley,
Finbar Grimes, Frank Owens, Tommy McGarvey. Subs – Mickey Rodgers, Gerry Ward.

1981 – v Brocagh Junior Championship Final 10/8/81
Panel - Gerry Maguire, Martin Grimes, Martin Grimes, Mickey Slane, Tommy McGarvey,
Paddy Grimes, Finbar Grimes, Pat Donnelly, Pete Owens, Colm McAleer, Louis McNamee,
Aidan McMullan, Brian McGarvey, Louis McNamee, Hugh McNamee, Seamus Collins,
Frank Owens, Gerry Ward, Mickey McNally, Barney Cunningham, Martin Kerr, Brian
Owens.

1982 – v Coalisland Intermediate Championship 9/5/82
Gerry Maguire, Paul McGlinn, Martin Grimes, Mickey McNally, Finbar Grimes, Tommy McGarvey, Pat Donnelly, Colm McAleer, Pete Owens, Frank Owens, Gerry Ward, Louis McNamee, Malachy Owens, Hugh McNamee, Liam Deazley. Subs – Martin Kerr for McNally, Colm Ward for M Owens.

1983 – v Clonoe Intermediate Championship Semi-Final 29/5/82
Colm Ward, Martin Grimes, Pete Owens, Paul McGlinn, Pat Donnelly, Mickey Slane, Tommy McGarvey, Colm McAleer, Hugh McNamee, Barry Donnelly, Gerry Ward, Seamus Collins, Finbar Grimes, Brian McGarvey, Mickey McNally. Others – Brian McGarvey, Paddy Grimes, Martin Kerr, Patsy Farley, Barry Donnelly, Frank Owens.

1984 - v Aughabrack Intermediate Championship 20/5/84
Brian Owens, Paul McGlinn, Martin Grimes, Seamus Boyle, Mickey Slane, Martin Kerr, Tommy McGarvey, Malachy Donnelly, Pete Owens, Finbar Grimes, Seamus Collins, Gerry Ward, Declan Grimes, Mickey McNally, Louis McNamee.

1985 – v Aughabrack 29/9/85 –
Brian McGarvey, Paul McGlinn, Pete Owens, Martin Grimes, Eamon Hackett, Mickey Slane, Tommy McGarvey, Malachy Donnelly, Hugh McNamee, Patsy Farley, Seamus Collins, Gerry Boyle, Declan Grimes, Mickey McNally, Niall Grimes. Others – Sean Grimes, Malachy Owens, Fergal Grimes, Mark McCann, Seamus Boyle, Frank Owens, Gerry Ward, Louis McNamee.

1986 – Joe Franey, Brian Owens, Brian McGarvey, Aidan Grimes, Paddy Rodgers, Fergal Grimes, Eamon Hackett, Malachy Donnelly, Hugh McNamee, Seamus Boyle, Gerry Ward, Declan Grimes, Adrian Nixon, Pete Owens, Gerry Ward.
Others – Enda McClean, Mickey Rodgers, Mark McCann, Anthony Owens, Gerry Boyle, Anthony Lyttle, Niall Grimes.

1987 – v Greencastle Junior Championship 2/8/87
Joe Franey, Stephen Farley, Brian McGarvey, Seamus Boyle, Aidan Grimes, Fergal Grimes, Paul Donnelly, Sean Donnelly, Malachy Donnelly, Eamon Rodgers, Hugh McNamee, Barry Donnelly, Patsy Farley, Gerry Ward, Mickey McCann. Subs – Barry McCartan, Gerry Boyle, Sean McCartan.

1988 – v Strabane Junior Championship 11/9/88
Pete Owens, Stephen Farley, Brian McGarvey, Aidan Grimes, Sean Donnelly, Malachy
Donnelly, Paul Donnelly, Patsy Farley, Sean Grimes, Eamon Rodgers, Hugh McNamee (capt),
Mickey McCann, Adrian Donnelly, Tommy McGarvey, Gerry Ward. Subs – Joe Franey,
Eamon Hackett, Gerry Boyle, Gerry Owens, Sean McCartan, Brian Owens, Malachy Owens.

1989 – v Gortin Intermediate Final
Beragh – Pete Owens, Stephen Farley, Brian McGarvey, Aidan Grimes, Shane Fox, Sean
Donnelly, Patsy Farley, Malachy Donnelly, Hugh McNamee, Gerry Boyle, Barry McCartan,
Adrian Donnelly, Gerry Ward, Seamus Collins, Mickey McCann.
Subs – Eamon Rodgers for G Boyle.

1990 – v Ardboe Intermediate Semi-Final 1/7/90
Leo Donaghy, Aidan Grimes, Pete Owens, Shane McCarney, Fergal Grimes, Stephen Farley,
Sean Donnelly, Hugh McNamee, Patsy Farley, Cathal Grimes, Mickey McCann, Adrian
Donnelly, Sean McCartan, Brian McGarvey, Barry Grimes.

1991 – v Intermediate Championship Second Replay v Galbally 9/6/91
Cathal Grimes, Stephen Farley, Martin Grimes, Pete Owens, Fergal Grimes, Shane McCarney,
Sean Donnelly, Aidan Grimes, Hugh McNamee, Eamon Rodgers, Paul Donnelly, Barry
McCartan, Patsy Farley, Adrian Donnelly, Barry Grimes.
Subs – Sean Grimes for A Grimes, Aidan Grimes for B Grimes. Others – Mickey McCann, Sean
Owens, Gerry Ward, Niall Farley, Brendan Barrett, Stephen Donnelly.

1992 – v Eglish Intermediate Final
Cathal Grimes, Stephen Farley, Aidan Grimes, Terry McKenna, Fergal Grimes, Shane
McCarney, Patsy Farley, Sean Grimes, Sean Donnelly, Barry McCartan, Adrian Donnelly,
Barry Grimes, Sean Owens, Hugh McNamee, Mickey McCann.
Subs - Paul Donnelly for P Farley, Paul McGlinn for S Grimes.

1993 – v Gortin Intermediate Final
Paddy Grimes, Stephen Farley, Aidan Grimes, Niall Farley, Patsy Farley (captain), Sean
Donnelly, Sean Owens, Terry McKenna, Paul Donnelly, Eamon Rodgers, Hugh McNamee,
Cathal Grimes, Mickey McCann, Barry McCartan, Barry Grimes.
Subs - None used. Other panel members - Seamus Grimes, Gerry Ward, Aidan Grimes,
Michael Montague, Stephen Hall, Kevin Connolly, Stephen Mullan, Martin Grimes, Gary
Donnelly, Stephen Donnelly, Fergal Grimes, Paul McGlinn.

1994 – v Errigal Ciaran Senior Championship First Round 20/5/94
Paddy Grimes, Stephen Farley, Aidan Grimes, Michael Montague, Patsy Farley, Sean Owens, Sean Donnelly, Terry McKenna, Paddy Grimes, Eamon Rodgers, Cathal Grimes, Barry Grimes, Adrian Donnelly, Barry McCartan, Hugh McNamee. Others – Dominic Donnelly, Gary Donnelly, Damien Kelly, Mickey McCann, Paul McGlinn, Shane McCarney, Seamus Grimes, Stephen Mullan, Fergal Grimes, Ciaran Cox, Brendan McNamee.

1995 – v Carrickmore Senior League Semi-Final 14/1/96
Paddy Grimes, Stephen Farley, Gary Donnelly, Stephen Donnelly, Patsy Farley, Paul Donnelly, Sean Owens, Terry McKenna, Seamus Grimes, Ciaran Cox, Niall Farley, Barry Grimes, Mickey McCann, Eamon Rodgers, Barry McCartan.
Subs – Aidan Grimes for Gary Donnelly, Cathal Grimes for Mickey McCann, Mickey McCann for Barry Grimes.

1996 – v Errigal Ciaran Senior Championship Semi-Final 13/9/96
Paddy Grimes, Stephen Farley, Sean Owens, Shane McCarney, Gary Donnelly, Paul Donnelly, Niall Farley, Terry McKenna, Adrian Donnelly, Ciaran Cox, Sean Donnelly, Stephen Donnelly, Eamon Rodgers, Barry Grimes, Cathal Grimes.
Other panelists – Barry McCartan, Hugh McNamee, Mickey McCann, Patsy Farley, Barry McMahon, Martin McMahon, Aidan Grimes, Peter McNamee, Barry McNamee, Ciaran Donnelly, Michael Montague, Paul Meenagh, Barry Conroy, Dominic Donnelly, Seamus Grimes.

1997 – v Carrickmore Senior Championship
Paddy Grimes, Stephen Farley, Sean Owens, Dominic Donnelly, Ciaran Cox, Michael Montague, Patsy Farley, Niall Farley, Terry McKenna, Martin McMahon, Paul Donnelly, Barry Grimes, Barry McCartan, Shane McCarney, Cathal Grimes.
Subs - Adrian Donnelly for M McMahon.

1998 – v Newtownstewart Intermediate Championship
Paddy Grimes, Stephen Farley, Sean Owens, Adrian Donnelly, Dominic Donnelly, Barry McCartan, Michael Montague, Seamus Grimes, Terry McKenna, Eamon Rodgers, Niall Farley, Barry Grimes, Niall Owens, Patsy Farley, Ciaran Cox. Sub – Cathal Grimes for P Farley.

1999 - Beragh Team v Brackaville (6-6-1999)
Paddy Grimes, Stephen Farley, Gary Donnelly, Stephen Nixon, Dominic Donnelly, Barry McMahon, Barry Conroy, Terry McKenna, Paul Meenagh, Niall Farley, Martin McMahon, Paddy Kelly, Patsy Farley, Ciaran Cox, Barry Grimes. Sub Used: Shane Donnelly.

2000 – v Gortin Intermediate Final 10/9/00
Cathal Grimes, Stephen Farley, Paddy Kelly, Barry McMahon, Martin McMahon, Dominic Donnelly, Niall Farley, Sean Owens, Terry McKenna, Stephen Donnelly, Gerard Loughran, Niall Owens, Paul Donnelly, Ciaran Cox, Patsy Farley.
Subs - Barry Grimes for N Farley. Other panelists –Sean Munroe, Ciaran Donnelly, Shane Donnelly, Stephen Franey, Brian McCartan, Brendan Montague, Mickey McCann, Michael Montague, Barry McMahon, Barry Conroy,

2001 – v Clonoe Senior Championship 6/5/01
Cathal Grimes, Stephen Farley, Paddy Kelly, Barry Conroy, Michael Montague, Dominic Donnelly, Stephen Donnelly, Terry McKenna, Seamus Grimes, Mickey Franey, Sean Owens, Niall Owens, Gerard Loughran, Patsy Farley, Barry Grimes. Sub – Paul Donnelly for M Franey.

2002 - v Gortin Intermediate Championship
Sean Munroe, Barry Conroy, Paddy Kelly, Niall Meenagh, Gerard Loughran, Barry McMahon, Dominic Donnelly, Niall Farley, Sean Owens, Sean McMahon, Michael Franey, Barry Grimes, Niall Owens, Cathal Grimes, Michael Ward. Others- Seamus Grimes, Mickey McCann, Stephen Nixon, Stephen Donnelly.

2003 – v Fintona Junior Semi-Final Replay 10/7/02
Paddy Grimes, Stephen Farley, Paddy Kelly, Niall Meenagh, Gerard Loughran, Barry McMahon, Martin Nixon, Enda Donnelly, Adrian Donnelly, Mickey Franey, Sean Owens, Niall Farley, Sean McMahon, Mickey Ward, Cathal Grimes.
Sub – Stephen Donnelly for A Donnelly.

2004 – Junior Championship v Stewartstown 8/8/04
Ciaran Donnelly, Damien Meenagh, Barry Conroy, Martin Nixon, Damien Meenagh, Mark Daffey, Barry McMahon, Enda Donnelly, Niall Farley, Sean McMahon, Stephen Nixon, Daniel Boyle, Mickey Franey, Sean Owens, Mickey Ward. Subs – Paddy Kelly for M Nixon, Mark Franey for N Farley, Niall Meenagh for D Boyle.

2005 – v Brocagh Junior Championship 3/7/05
Colm Grimes, Conor Boyle, Gerard Loughran, Barry Conroy, Michael Owens, Barry McMahon, Dominic Donnelly, Terry McKenna, Enda Donnelly, Christopher Donnelly, Mickey Franey, Martin McMahon, Michael Ward, Damien Meenagh, Sean McMahon.
Subs – Niall Boyle for C Boyle, Niall Meenagh for M Owens, Mark Daffy for Mickey Franey

2006 – v Newtownstewart Junior Championship
Cathal Grimes, Niall Boyle, Paddy Kelly, Damien Meenagh, Barry Conroy, Niall Meenagh, Dominic Donnelly, Barry McMahon, Terry McKenna, Niall Owens, Michael Ward, Sean McMahon, Conor Donnelly, Daniel Boyle, Martin McMahon.
Subs - Gerard Owens for B Conroy, Michael Franey for C Donnelly.

Senior Team Managers 1966-2006

1966 - Ollie Slane
1967 - Frank Rodgers/Liam McGrath
1968-1974 - Frank Rodgers
1975-1976 - Mick Kerr
1977-1978 - Kevin Grimes
1979-1980- Kevin Maguire
1981-1982- Kevin Maguire and Mickey Heaney
1983 - Kevin Maguire, Mickey Heaney and Fr Peter McParland
1984 - Mick Kerr
1985 - Fr Peter McParland
1986-1987 - Brian Donnelly, Gerry Owens and Frank Owens
1988-Tommy McGarvey
1989 - Tommy McGarvey and Gerry Ward
1990 - Tommy McGarvey
1991-1992 - Kevin Maguire and Mickey Heaney
1993-1994 - Sean O'Kane
1995 - Gerry Owens
1996-1997-Liam Donnelly
1998-1999-Gerry Ward
2000-2001-Palor McNulty
2002-Sean McCrory
2003-2005-Terry McCann
2006 - Sean Owens and Niall Farley

Beragh Red Knights
History at a Glance

1901 – Formation of Beragh Parochial Branch of
the United Irish League.

1906 – Formation of Sixmilecross Wolfe Tones GAA Club.
During that year they competed in the Mid-Tyrone
Gaelic Football League.

1907 – SMX Wolfe Tones in Mid-Tyrone League
and McAnespy Cup.

1908 – Co Final played in Sixmilecross. Wolfe Tones played
regular games.

1909 – Activity throughout the year, but died out in autumn.

1910-1912 – No organised GAA in Tyrone or Sixmilecross.

1913 – Sixmilecross Wolfe Tones to forefront of GAA
revival. HK McAleer President of Tyrone
County Board.

1914 – Sixmilecross in West Tyrone
League/Championship games.

1920 – GAA Sports held at Cooley Park.

1921 – Formation of Beragh Red Knights. One of few teams
active in Tyrone GAA.

1922 – Teams named Brackey Young Ireland and Beragh
Erin's Hope meet.

1923 – Beragh Erin's Hope played at start of year. Known as
Red Knights later in year. Also youth team named
'Junior Knights.'

1924 – Red Knights reached Co Semi-Final.

1926 – Beragh Shamrocks compete in West Tyrone
Championship.

1928 – Sixmilecross competing in Mid-Tyrone SFL. Beragh
taking part in 'Junior' underage League.

1929 – Sixmilecross team to play Dungannon in Senior Championship. Beragh to play in West Tyrone Championship. Beragh Juniors win Junior League.

1930 – Beragh dropped out of Medal Tournament. Some players with Ballygawley.

1931 – Beragh United in West Tyrone League. Referred later to just Beragh and as 'Sons of the Gael' Clogherney team meet Altamuskin on two occasions.

1932 – Beragh in West Tyrone League. Team from Sixmilecross played Mullaslin. Beragh Juvenile team played and Committee formed. Beragh Juniors in West Tyrone Football League.

1933 – Beragh in West Tyrone League. Team from SMX taking part in West Tyrone Junior League. Beragh Schoolboys team.
Sixmilecross St Brigid's Camogie team formed, later described as Beragh St Brigid's.
Beragh winners of Mid-Week League

1934 – Beragh in West Tyrone SFL, Sixmilecross in West Tyrone JFL.
• Hurling Team formed

1935 – Beragh reach Co Semi-Final (West Tyrone Final). No mention of SMX team.
• Camogie teams representing Beragh and Ramackin.

1936 – Beragh in SFL, Brackey in Junior Football League.

1937 – Brackey in Junior Football League. No record of Beragh team playing.

1938 – Brackey in JFL, winners of Herald Cup.

1939 – Brackey won Junior title (1938 competition) but later disqualified. Won Herald Cup.

1939 – Brackey reach Junior Final, won Herald Cup.

1940 – Brackey compete in early part of year. Down to play 1939 JF Final in June. From then on Beragh in Senior Football League. Paddy McCrumlish representing Beragh.

1941/1942 – Beragh competing in Senior Football League.

1943 – No mention of teams from parish in SFL or JFL.

1944 – Sports held.

1945 – No teams competed in SFL, but St Mary's Club formed in autumn.

1946 – Sixmilecross team in South Tyrone Junior League. Football held as part of Beragh Sports.

1947 – Brackey compete in South Tyrone League. In October Beragh signalled intention to enter West Tyrone Senior Football League.
  • Won Junior title.

1948 – Beragh in SFL. Juvenile and Schoolboys Leagues played.

1949 – South Tyrone Juvenile League Finalists.

1950 – Winners of Davis Cup. West Tyrone Minor Champions and Co Minor Finalists.

1951 – McElduff Cup Finalists.

1952 – Co Minor Finalists.

1953 – Feis Cup winners.

1954 - New grounds purchased and opened. Fourth club in Tyrone to have grounds vested in the GAA.

1955 – Co Senior Semi-Finalists. July – Tournament first held.

1956 – Mick Kerr on first Tyrone team to win Ulster Senior title.

1958 – St Enda Cup Champions. Formation of Brackey Handball Club.

1960 – Further development of grounds includes erection of new posts, pitch paled and marked out. Beragh in Tournament Final.

1961 – Co Convention held in St Mary's Hall, U-14 League begins, Juveniles win South Tyrone League.

1963 – South Tyrone Juvenile League Finalists.

1964 – Beragh relegated to the newly introduced Intermediate grade after finishing bottom of SFL and losing to Clogher in play-off.

1965 – West Tyrone Juvenile, reach West Tyrone Minor League Final.

1966 – Reached Intermediate Semi-Final, West Tyrone Minor League Champions.

1968 – Beragh players taking part in hurling coaching, Camogie team re-formed.

1972 – Renamed Red Knights to mark Jubilee of original Red Knights. Won West Tyrone Intermediate League and McElduff Cup, reached Championship semi-final, promoted Senior.

1974 – Back in Intermediate, completion and official opening of redeveloped St Mary's Park.

1975 – Signing of 35 year Lease with Omagh District Council.

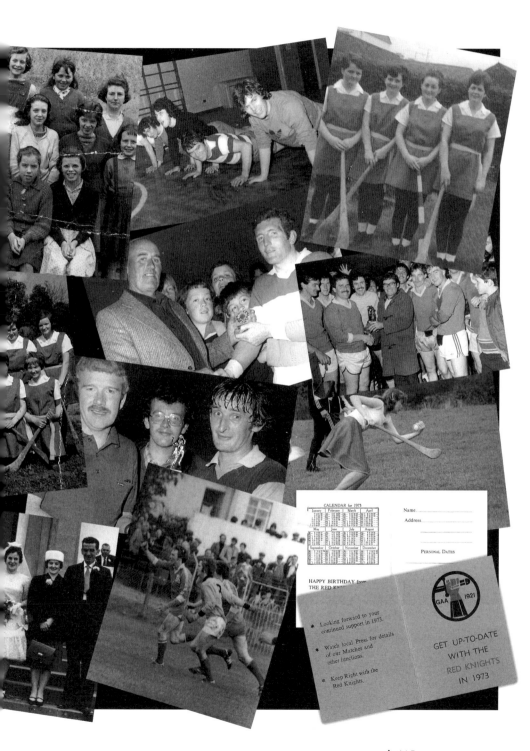

1977 – Parish Magazine, Link, launched.

1979 – Club Secretary, Frank Rodgers, wins McNamee Award for 'Best Secretary Report'.

1980 – Relegated to Junior.

1981 – Won Division Three League and reached Junior Final. Won Division 3 Reserve League. Handball Alley built.

1982 – Reached Intermediate Semi-Final.

1983 – Lost Jim Devlin Cup Final. Hurling team established.

1984 – Won Reserve Championship and Club of the Year award.

1985 – Won U-16 Grade 1 Championship, Reserve Championship, lost U-16 League Final, relegated to Division 3.

1986 – Club structure and training programme re-organised.

1987 – Won Reserve Championship.

1988 – Won Junior and Reserve Championship and Division 3 League. Promoted to Intermediate. Lost to Castlederg in Minor League Final.

1989 – Lost Intermediate Final to Gortin, runners-up in Intermediate League. Lost to Moy in Division One Promotion Play-off. Won West Tyrone U-16 League, lost to Dungannon in U-16 League Final

1990 – Lost to Trillick in McGarrity Cup Final.

1992 – Lost Intermediate Final to Eglish.

1993 – Won Intermediate Final, defeating Edendork. Runners-up in Reserve Championship and League. Ladies football team formed.

1994 – Beat Killyclogher in relegation play-off to stay in Division One.

1995 – Reached Senior League Semi-Final, lost to Carrickmore. Intermediate Ladies Champions.

1996 – Reached Senior Championship Semi-Final, lost to Errigal Ciaran. Reached Senior League Semi-Final, lost to Errigal Ciaran. Lost to Dromore in McGarrity Cup Final.

1997 – Relegated to Division 2

1998 – Lost to Aghaloo in Division 2 play-off. Lost to Loughmacrory in Frank O'Neill Cup Final.

1999 – Won McElduff and McGarrity Cups, defeating Fintona and Brackaville in the finals.

2000 – Intermediate League and Championship double winners. Promoted to Senior.

2001 – Relegated from Senior, Intermediate Ladies Champions.

2002 – Relegated to Junior.

2004 – Ladies U-16s win Championship and League double. Reserves win Division Three title.

2005 - U-14 Ladies complete C'ship and League Double.

2006 – Centenary Year, Opening of New clubrooms by President of GAA, U-14s win Grade Two C'ship title, Ladies capture Junior C'ship title. Hurling re-started. Ruairi Kelly and Shane O'Neill crowned World Handball Champions

1 - The double winning Ladies Juveniles

2 - A first Ladies success as the team of 1995 wins in the Intermediate title

3 - More youth glory for the girls in the 2000s

4 - Aishling Hagan receives the Intermediate Cup

5 - Time to celebrate for the Ladies team of 2001

1 - Sean Owens holds aloft the Paddy Cullen Cup following Beragh's second Intermediate success

2 - The 2000 Intermediate Champions celebrate a great triumph

3 - Nicola Nugent and Helen Ward with more Ladies silverware

4 - The Beragh dug-out during the 2000 Intermediate Championship campaign

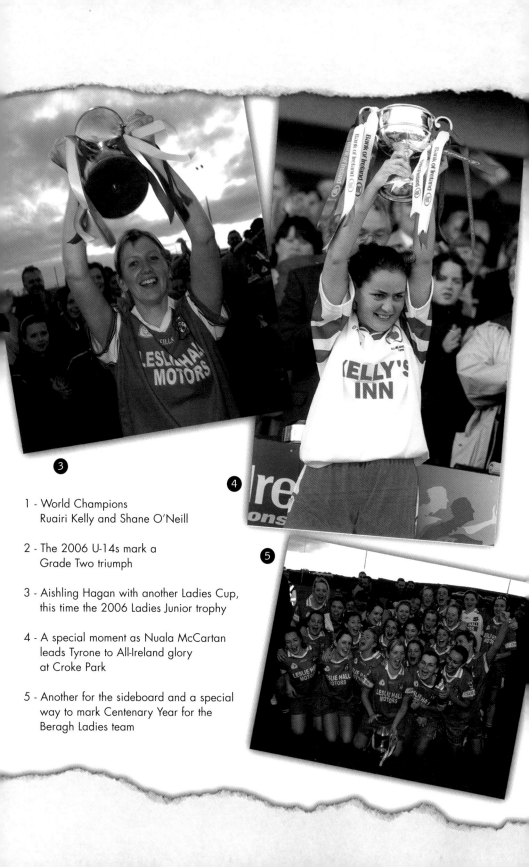

3

4

5

1 - World Champions
    Ruairi Kelly and Shane O'Neill

2 - The 2006 U-14s mark a
    Grade Two triumph

3 - Aishling Hagan with another Ladies Cup,
    this time the 2006 Ladies Junior trophy

4 - A special moment as Nuala McCartan
    leads Tyrone to All-Ireland glory
    at Croke Park

5 - Another for the sideboard and a special
    way to mark Centenary Year for the
    Beragh Ladies team

1 - A panoramic view of St Mary's Park before re-development

2 - Martin Rodgers with the 2004 All-Ireland Skills Award

3 - Looking back through decades of sterling GAA involvement are brothers Frankie, Barney and Hughie Owens pictured with Mick Kerr in the summer of 2006

4 - A presentation for the President from Beragh officials Mickey McCann (Chairman), Barry Conroy (Secretary), Frank Rodgers (Trustee) and Gerard Treacy (Development Chairman) during the President's historic visit to the village in January 2006

UACHTARÁN NA hÉIREANN
PRESIDENT OF IRELAND

MESSAGE FROM PRESIDENT McALEESE

I am delighted to send my very best wishes and congratulations to everyone associated with Beragh Red Knights Gaelic Athletic Club on the occasion of the 2006 centenary celebrations.

Since the foundation of the Club in 1906, you have gone from strength to strength, providing sport, leisure and social activities for all members of the community. The official opening of the new sports pavilion at St. Mary's Park in July is a milestone in the history of the Club and one in which you can all take a just pride.

All those involved in Beragh Red Knights Gaelic Athletic Club down through the years, deserve enormous credit for their tremendous dedication and hard work in building up the Club to where it is today. Sport has always served us well and has been instrumental in helping to forge bonds of close and lasting friendship between players, officials and fans alike. The Club is now an integral part of community life in Beragh and has played an important role in creating a sense of local identity.

I have fond memories of my recent visit to Beragh and I would like to take this opportunity to wish everybody associated with the Beragh Red Knights Gaelic Athletic Club every success for the next hundred years and very best wishes on your centenary celebrations during 2006.

Mary McAleese

MARY McALEESE
PRESIDENT OF IRELAND

4

From Duff's Holm in 1906, through Deroar Park and McGirr's Holm, to the ultra-modern facilities at St Mary's Park in the 21st Century providing the focus as the next generation carriers the torch of GAA involvement forward to the future